WASHINGTON SCHOOL OF PSYCHIATRY
1610 NEW HAMPSHIRE AVE., N. W.
WASHINGTON 9, D. C.

REFERENCE ONLY
DO NOT REMOVE
FROM LIBRARY

EVOLUTION OF PSYCHOSOMATIC CONCEPTS

ANOREXIA NERVOSA: A PARADIGM

EVOLUTION OF PSYCHOSOMATIC CONCEPTS

ANOREXIA NERVOSA: A PARADIGM

M. RALPH KAUFMAN, M.D., *Editor*

MARCEL HEIMAN, M.D., *Co-Editor*

INTERNATIONAL UNIVERSITIES PRESS, INC.
New York   New York

Copyright 1964, by International Universities Press, Inc.

Library of Congress Catalog Card Number: 64:16017

Manufactured in the United States of America

The Mount Sinai Seminar Group
The Institute of Psychiatry
The Mount Sinai Hospital
New York, New York

M. RALPH KAUFMAN, M.D., *Chairman*

Collaborators

ABRAM BLAU, M.D.	EDWARD JOSEPH, M.D.
FRED BROWN, Ph.D.	LOUIS LINN, M.D.
CHARLES FISHER, M.D.	SYDNEY MARGOLIN, M.D.
PAUL GOOLKER, M.D.	LAWRENCE ROOSE, M.D.
MARCEL HEIMAN, M.D.	VICTOR ROSEN, M.D.

CONTENTS

Acknowledgments ix

Introduction 1
   THE MOUNT SINAI SEMINAR GROUP

Psychosomatic Medicine in the Nineteenth Century 6
   EDWARD STAINBROOK

Pathologic Anatomy in Modern Medicine 36
   PAUL KLEMPERER

Psychoanalysis and Internal Medicine 47
   FELIX DEUTSCH

Psychological Aspects of Medicine 56
   FRANZ ALEXANDER

Psychogenicity 78
   THE MOUNT SINAI SEMINAR GROUP

The Address on Medicine 104
   WILLIAM W. GULL

Why Anorexia Nervosa 128
   THE MOUNT SINAI SEMINAR GROUP

Anorexia Nervosa (Apepsia Hysterica, Anorexia Hysterica) ... 132
   WILLIAM W. GULL

Anorexia Nervosa 139
   WILLIAM W. GULL

On Hysterical Anorexia 141
   E. C. LASÈGUE

Excerpts from *The Major Symptoms of Hysteria* 156
   PIERRE JANET

Some Excerpts 160
    DUBOIS—CHARCOT—RYLE

German Papers 165

Medical and Psychotherapeutic Treatment of Endogenic
    Magersucht (Anorexia) 167
    L. R. GROTE—H. MENG

Dreams in So-called Endogenic *Magersucht* (Anorexia) 181
    VICTOR V. WEIZSÄCKER

Discussion and Summary of "On Pituitary Anterior Lobe
    Insufficiency" by M. Schur and C. V. Medvei 198
    M. RALPH KAUFMAN—MARCEL HEIMAN

Anorexia Nervosa: A Metabolic Disorder of Psychologic
    Origin 202
    R. F. FARQUHARSON—H. H. HYLAND

Prepsychotic Anorexia 227
    GRACE NICOLLE

Anorexia Nervosa: A Psychosomatic Entity 245
    JOHN V. WALLER—M. RALPH KAUFMAN—
    FELIX DEUTSCH

A Psychosomatic Study of Anorexia Nervosa including the
    Use of Vaginal Smears 274
    RUTH MOULTON

Anorexia Nervosa: Report of a Case 298
    SANDOR LORAND

Psychodynamisms in Anorexia Nervosa and Neurotic
    Vomiting 320
    JULES H. MASSERMAN

Conclusions 352
    THE MOUNT SINAI SEMINAR GROUP

Bibliography 355

Index 377

ACKNOWLEDGMENTS

The editors wish to thank Mrs. Irene Azarian for her constructive editorial assistance. Her devotion and scholarship have made the publication of this volume possible.

We wish to thank the editors of the various journals and the authors for permission to reprint the papers.

INTRODUCTION

THE MOUNT SINAI SEMINAR GROUP

In view of the profusion of books both popular and technical in the field of psychiatry and psychosomatic medicine, it becomes necessary for the editors of this book to attempt to convey to the readers their justification for adding another volume. The most recent trend toward systematized studies in the so-called psychosomatic area is barely twenty-five years old and might be related in a general way to the publication of Dunbar's *Emotions and Bodily Changes* in 1935. One historical landmark was the founding of the *Journal of Psychosomatic Medicine* in 1939. The first article on "Psychological Aspects of Medicine" by Franz Alexander is reprinted in this volume because of this historical significance. Of course, it is common knowledge that workers like Felix Deutsch, Ferenczi, Groddeck, Jelliffe, and Freud himself, were preoccupied with the basic problems inherent in the field for many years. Since it is not the intention of this introduction to survey the total field, the names of many workers will of necessity not appear. It should be emphasized that the practicing physician working with the family has always recognized in one way or another that there is an interrelationship between soma and psyche. In spite of the tremendous volume of reports and work that has been done, or perhaps because of it, there exists a state of confusion which is related to many factors.

The purpose of this volume is to attempt clarification of present concepts. A series of key papers on a syndrome, anorexia nervosa, are reprinted and discussed in terms of the basic concepts available to the authors at the time when their papers were written. It is, of course, not possible to reprint all the important papers relating to any syndrome.

Nevertheless, it is the hope of the editors that they have been able to select examples of key papers. These papers are reprinted in toto so that the reader may refresh his knowledge in a new context and have the opportunity to draw his own conclusions which may differ from possible editorial distortion or bias.

The aim is also to review historically the background against which the scientific observations were made. It is clear that the absence or presence of certain speculations, hypotheses, theories, or methods influence both the observations and the conclusions that are drawn from the material. In order to accomplish this task, pertinent papers are selected which deal with the clinical syndrome, in an effort to demonstrate the evolution of scientific concepts and methodology. There can be no arbitrary time span set. The first papers in the volume are those in which psychic factors are noted by the authors. Later papers have been selected on the basis of their contribution to the historical development of the psychosomatic concepts. This involves a tremendous task which the editors approach most humbly, since it requires a knowledge of history, sociology, economics, cultural anthropology, and many other factors in which the editors are aware of their own limitations. Nevertheless, if the basic premise is a valid one, the attempt may prove of some value to other workers in this field.

Methodologically, it becomes necessary to set up a frame of reference within which all of the papers here reprinted can be evaluated relatively uniformly. Points of reference have to take into consideration a number of factors: (1) Knowledge of the observer set against the basic concepts of the medicine of his time. This involves a knowledge of what was considered the nature of disease and what role the person played in relation to his illness and the presence or absence of ecological theories of illness. (2) The techniques and diagnostic devices available to the observer for the recognition of physiological and pathological manifestations within the individual. (3) The methodology actually employed, both diagnostically and therapeutically.

It has been stated that confusion exists. One of the factors may be the particular orientation of the worker in the field. For instance, the editors of this volume are a group of physicians trained in psychoanalytic psychiatry, and therefore their point of view is of necessity influenced by this experience and training. For purposes of this monograph, we utilize that aspect of psychoanalysis which in our opinion is a method of observation permitting the accumulation of data not otherwise obtainable. One could compare it to the microscope which opened a whole new world of data. It is of paramount importance as to whether one's concept of the unconscious is limited to a system which involves a mere lack of awareness, such as was implied by Janet, for example, or in this country by Morton Prince and Adolf Meyer, or whether the concept includes a dynamic organization of the psyche as was developed by Freud and his school of psychoanalysis, with certain laws of mental functioning, such as primary process, timelessness, energy economics, and a relationship of the unconscious to the other components of the mind. The observer with the former concept would necessarily be limited by his own theoretical frame of reference and method to one kind of data; whereas the observer utilizing the second concept would have a far wider range of observation, and therefore a different kind of raw data. Even though both observers subscribe to a holistic approach, the totality of their observations would differ depending upon their basic theoretical concepts. This matter is of the greatest importance in present-day medicine, since without any attempt at this time to justify one or the other theory, it is quite clear that the point of departure will necessarily be different.

In view of the multiform points of view in the field, it is essential that the editors state what constitutes, for them, the area of psychosomatic medicine. It is an operational approach to the theory and practice of medicine in which the structure and function of the psychic apparatus are also indicated as variables in health and disease. It is apparent that this definition requires that the psychological factor be homogenized into every aspect of the evaluation of the patient and the disease process. It specifically denies the type of thinking in which the psychological factor is considered as a separate layer or as an afterthought in the evaluation of the patient.

To further implement this psychosomatic formulation of the theory and practice of medicine, an illness may be divided into the following phases with respect to the psychological factor:

1. The premorbid personality in terms such as the social, economic,

somatic, and psychosexual adaptation of the patient, including the presence or absence of frank neurotic or psychotic symptoms.
2. The latent period of the disease, i.e., the interval between the beginning of the disease process and the manifest symptoms or signs.
3. The recognition of symptoms by the patient.
4. The course of the disease.
5. The reaction of the patient to the disease.
6. The reaction of the patient to the therapist and to therapy.
7. The role of the reaction of the therapist to the patient and to the illness.
8. Convalescence and recovery or invalidism.

An essential point of these considerations is the elimination of the need to see the psychological factor as exclusively etiological or as a concomitant or a consequence of an illness in any specific sense. The psychological factor is always present, but it may vary in its dominance and significance in the same disease, in the same individual, at every stage of the disease process.

With the full recognition of the overwhelming task involved in a documentation of the historical aspects of the concepts involving body-mind relationships, nevertheless an attempt is made to bring into focus the highlights of the problem. As is well known, even before the time of Hippocrates, the psychic factor was already involved in various systems of medicine. The nineteenth century may be utilized as a time period during which the earlier conceptual frameworks were still present, either unchanged or in derivative form. Gradual changes in theory and practice began to take place, to be climaxed by the dramatic and revolutionary work of Sigmund Freud at the very end of the century.

In this volume, anorexia nervosa will be the paradigm syndrome used. Before the presentation of the material on anorexia nervosa, a historical perspective centering around the nineteenth century will be attempted. Since the illustrative theme centers on anorexia nervosa, and since Gull's name is so intimately associated with this syndrome, and since Gull was also an outstanding example of the advanced thinking in medicine in the nineteenth century, his "Address on Medicine" is included in the presentation.

The problem of etiology is involved in the study of any syndrome, and in our area the questions centering around the concept of psychogenicity are of paramount importance. Therefore, a discussion of the general concept of psychogenicity is introduced.

PSYCHOSOMATIC MEDICINE IN THE NINETEENTH CENTURY

EDWARD STAINBROOK, PH.D., M.D.
(1952)

It is better to live unknown than to die of dyspepsia.
—Bayard Taylor
(1825-1878)

This paper is of such relevance to our major thesis that it is presented in toto rather than summarized, since it sets the nineteenth-century stage so well. The importance of "climate" cannot be underestimated. For example, Rosen's[1] description of the reaction to Beaumont's original work in Europe emphasizes the fact that, whereas its reception in Europe was sympathetic, only in England and France was there a recognition and emphasis on the importance of the psychological factors noted briefly by Beaumont, and the German literature made no reference to this aspect of Beaumont's findings.

General Theoretical Survey

The history of medicine has always been intimately involved with the philosophic destiny of the ideas about the interrelations of mind and body. The interactions between the conceptual worlds of the medi-

---

Reprinted from *Psychosomatic Medicine*, 14:211-227, 1952.
[1] Rosen, G.: *The Reception of William Beaumont's Discovery in Europe*. New York: Schuman's, 1942.

cine of the body and of the medicine of the mind are largely determined by the prevailing cultural preferences for the resolution of the mind-body complex.

Thus, at the beginning of the nineteenth century, the organization and use of medical knowledge were significantly conditioned by the existing conceptions of mind-body relationships as well as by the general cultural atmosphere in which the medical theory and practice were being developed. Moreover, although the medicine of the body had appreciably liberated itself from theological and moral restrictions in its freedom of investigation and speculation, the medicine of the mind was still considerably handicapped by being largely bound to religion and to philosophy.

From philosophy, psychological medicine of the early nineteenth century inherited a long-standing conception of the mind as an organization of faculties with a content of ideas related to each other by associations based on similarity, contiguity, or contrast.

The mind-body problem, which is a projection of psychosomatic relations to the metaphysical plane, was formulated largely in terms of two philosophical premises, one of which had been clearly stated by Descartes. This philosophic solution, popularized as Cartesian interactionism, conceived mind and body as substantially distinct but as reacting upon each other.

Spinoza had emphasized an opposing description of mind and matter as the co-existent and infinite attributes of one absolute substance and denied that there was any relationship between mind and body. This was the parallelistic position.

An epiphenomenal conception of mind became increasingly popular during the shift in nineteenth-century medical psychology from a study of the mind and soul to a progressively increasing scrutiny of the brain and nervous system. This denied that mental processes could cause or affect brain processes, and insisted that mind was a product or function of the body. It found perhaps its most extreme and succinct expression in the dictum, *"Kein Gedanke ohne Phosphor!"* uttered later in the century by the physiologist Moleschott.

As a balance and antithesis to the latter position of "modern materialism," as it was then designated, the influence of Anton Mesmer and his disciples was transforming miraculous healing and exorcism into the suggestion therapy of nineteenth-century medicine. Perhaps one of the most important meanings of Mesmerism and its many ramifications throughout the century was that it provided a continual reminder of the influence of the mind on the body.

Nevertheless, if one had to indicate with a word the general attitude of nineteenth-century medicine to the relationship of mind and body in disease, the term "somato-psychic medicine[2]," a phrase actually popularized by the German psychiatrist Jacobi, would be the most apt.

Of course, there was much anecdotal and empirical evidence before 1800 of the importance of the individual's thinking, feeling, and doing in relation to his disease. Sydenham, for example, had made many such observations, one of the most interesting in terms of today's psychosomatic awareness being the insistence that about two thirds of the diseases in his day were fevers, and of the other third, he felt that at least one half of these were cases of the "hysteric passion." Sydenham, it will be remembered, also observed that he could always bring on an attack of gout by thinking for half an hour of his great toe.

Almost at the turn of the century, in 1796, William Falconer published in London a book entitled *The Influence of the Passions upon Disorders of the Body* (23) in which he stressed the relationship of disease and emotion. This work, based on a thesis written two years earlier, made one of the first distinctions between the idiopathic influence of the nervous system itself and the influence of the various emotions, or "states of mind," in affecting or inducing bodily disease.

---

[2] Margetts (41) has recently described some of the early history of the word, "psychosomatic," which occasionally occurs in the German psychiatric literature of the early nineteenth century. He points out particularly Heinroth's use of this term by 1818 in referring, among other matters, to the psychosomatic determinants of insomnia. Zilboorg (64) has alluded briefly to Jacobi, Nasse, and the early nineteenth-century German somatogenic school as giving formulations to psychosomatic medicine. Actually, Jacobi, who was the chief of the Sieburg Asylum and the spirit of the German somatic or physiologic school, stressed in his polemic against Heinroth's dictum, "All alienation reposes on sin," that insanity was the result of disorders of the organs of respiration and circulation and especially (as also stressed by Schröder van der Kolk) of the colon. It is true, however, that Jacobi, along with Reil, J. Frank, Georget, Neumann, Auenbrugger, Esquirol, Nasse, Hill, Cox, Guislain, and others in this period, "counted the pulse, listened to the heart, watched the ebb and flow of the blood in the skin, and felt the temperature of the body." They were thus seeing the physiology of psychopathology but they recognized only the physiopathology as the cause of the psychopathology.

Four years later, a fellow countryman, Dr. John Haygarth, undertook to refute the doctrine of Perkinism, which had originated with the Connecticut physician, Dr. Elisha Perkins. By substituting pieces of wood for the brass, iron, and zinc tractors developed by Perkins to cure disease by galvanism, Haygarth came to a positive conclusion as to the effect "of the imagination as a cause and as a cure for diseases of the body." His opinions were published in 1800 (26).

One hundred and twenty-six years after Nicholas de Blegny founded the Zodiacus Medico-Gallicus, the first regular medical periodical in the western world, the first medicopsychological journal was established by Reil and Hoffbauer in Germany in 1806. Although short-lived, it was an attempt to unite psychology and medical science. That this unification was a persistent interest of nineteenth-century medicine is evidenced by the appearance of a long article by Cerise (15) on psychological and physical interrelations in the first volume of the *Annales médico-psychologiques,* which appeared initially in 1843.

At about this same time, Baron Ernst von Feuchtersleben was giving succinct and specific utterance to psychosomatic assertions. "Fear," he wrote in 1838, "causes especially enuresis, diarrhea, seminal discharges, erysipelas, and eruptions about the lips; facilitates the reception of contagion and miasma; disturbs crises and aggravates every disorder. Fear and horror act, moreover, variously either exciting or paralyzing according to the greatness of the danger and according to the individuality of the persons affected by them" (24).

Actually, however, for contemporary psychosomatic medicine, one of the most significant developments in nineteenth-century medical science was the theoretical and experimental growth in general physiology.

At the beginning of the century, Haller's textbook on physiology was still influential in most medical schools. The concepts of irritability and irritation, which displaced the earlier vital force or vital principle conceptions of van Helmont, Barthez, Chaussier, and others, were therefore widespread. In France, where nineteenth-century medicine found its earliest and best expression, Xavier Bichat (7), who introduced into medical science the subjects of histology and cell biology, postulated sensibility and contractility as fundamental physiological phenomena. Bichat also elaborated the conception of two divisions of the nervous system, the brain and the visceral ganglionic system, which set the stage for the subsequent development throughout the rest of the nineteenth century of the theories of the vasomotor, reflex, and trophic neuroses.

Bichat also considered that there existed a purely organic sensibility which was ordinarily beyond conscious perception but which could occasionally intensify into conscious sensation. Hence, in the earliest days of the nineteenth century we can pick up the thread of the various theories of unconscious behavior which culminate at the end of the century in the logical construct of the unconscious created by Freud in the psychoanalytic theory of behavior.

The description of pre-Freudian concepts of unconscious behavior is a subject in itself, but from the point of view of the history of the theory of psychophysiological interrelations, one of the most significant ideas in nineteenth-century psychosomatic medicine was elaborated by Marshall Hall in 1833. Hall described reflex action and "excitomotor acts" which, when nerves were irritated, could result in movements in the muscular system independently of sensation or volition. The conception of "unconscious" excitomotor acts thus became plausible and possible for nineteenth-century medicine.

Daniel Hack Tuke, for example, whose book, *The Influence of the Mind on the Body*, published in 1872, deals with psychosomatic medicine in a surprisingly modern manner, accepted the possibility of excitomotor acts without conscious ideation as an explanation of somnambulism and other automatic behavior (60).

Another significant derivation from the concept of reflex action found expression in the writings of Charles Creighton, an epidemiologist and medical historian, who published his *Unconscious Memory in Disease* in 1886 (20). Creighton's main thesis was that memory is a generalized function of organic matter and that many forms of recurrent diseases may be determined by the unconscious organic memories of the body. More pertinent to psychosomatic theory, however, were his observations on "reflex actions continuing after the cause is gone." Here he writes that as a result of "the unexpressed emotion of anxiety, worry, and paralyzing misfortunes, the grief unrelieved by tears, the load of care borne without help, the mind, turned forever inwards upon itself and checked in its active outgoings . . . with all such repressions or want of expression by the usual channels—is apt to take a peculiar revenge or to find a peculiar outlet by discharging itself unconsciously upon the glandular system."

Aided by the expanding neuroanatomical and neurophysiological knowledge of the nineteenth century, clearer formulations were being developed in medicine by which the mechanism of emotional discharge upon the glandular system, in Creighton's description, might be explained. The concept of vasomotor neurosis was one of the most important of these clarifications.

Before 1800 Raymond Vieussens, among others, had attempted an explanation of the influence of the mind on the vascular system. This was done in the face of an earlier refutation by Haller of the doctrine of a nervous influence on arteries, although Haller nevertheless felt that depressing emotions, such as grief and fear, directly slowed the circulation while anger, love, joy, and terror augmented blood flow. It is interesting also that for a time Bichat, after observing a relationship between the French Revolution's creation of extreme anxiety in Parisians and a high frequency of disorders of the heart, lungs, and stomach, discarded the influence of the nervous system entirely and postulated a direct effect of the anxiety upon the vital functions. Lucae (40), in an essay published in Frankfurt in 1810, convincingly and significantly re-established the hypothesis of the influence of the nerves on blood vessels.

By the end of the first half of the century the research of Claude Bernard, Brown-Séquard, Donders, Kussmaul, and others had shown that vasodilatation and vasoconstriction were reactions to nervous stimulation induced in various sensory modalities. Brown-Séquard, who was the first to galvanize sympathetic nerves, was particularly responsible for establishing the effects of the excitation of vasomotor nerves as being essentially the constriction of blood vessels with diminution in the blood flow, associated with temperature change and alteration in the activity of nutrition.

At about the same time Kronecker, in Leipzig, attempted to localize on the floor of the fourth ventricle the vasomotor centers through which such reflexes were mediated, while Luys and Jewell presumed a continuous column of such centers for the whole body in the medulla and spinal cord. In addition, Brown-Séquard was writing that the vasomotor centers existed in the cerebrum and cerebellum.

The Haller conception of nervous irritability, the neuro-anatomical descriptions, popularized by Bichat, of what Langley at the end of the century was to call the autonomic nervous system, the hypotheses concerning excitomotor reflex action culminating in the descriptions of Marshall Hall, and the observations deriving from the neurophysiological research of Claude Bernard and Brown-Séquard became, therefore, the basic physiological concepts of mid-nineteenth-century psychosomatic medicine.

A psychophysiology of mind-body functioning was easily added to these fundamental first principles by the implicit or explicit assumption that the description of behavior required no world of discourse, no theoretical system of its own, but that all the phenomena of "mind" could be described with the concepts available for the description of "brain." In his book on mind-body relationships, Daniel Hack Tuke, for example, expressed this very well. "Mind or brain influences— excites, perverts, or depresses," he wrote, "the sensory, motor, vasomotor, and trophic nerves and causes changes in sensations, muscular contraction, nutrition, and secretion" (60).

Nervousness and neurosis were understood by nineteenth-century medicine, therefore, largely in the physiopathological sense which coincides with the etymological meaning of such designations. Certainly such a theory of neurosis can be divorced with facility from any demonstrable connection with concomitant psychological behavior and can be considered solely in terms of an intrinsic physiopathology. This was essentially the thinking of Cullen, for example, when in modifying the classifications of disease created by Linnaeus and by Sauvages, he described so much of disease as neurosis.

The popularity throughout most of the century of the idea of reflex irritation as a cause of disease is another illustration of such thought. Early in the century reflex irritation had been proposed as a cause of neurosis. Actually this was occasioned by pouring the old wine of disease by sympathy into the newer casks of the developing theories of reflex action. The prominence even to the end of the century of the concept of reflex neurosis was due in significant measure to Brown-Séquard and particularly to his lectures on the *Physiology and Pathology of the Nervous Centers* which he delivered in London in 1858.

As a treatment of reflex neurosis, a great wave of surgical aggression directed against the cervix, vagina, clitoris, and ovaries by Sayre, Emmet, Baker-Brown, Tait, Battey, and others marked the last three decades of nineteenth-century somatopsychic medicine.

Indeed, it was not until 1894 when Morton Prince, in this country, supported by the work of Charcot and the French school of psychiatrists, could say with acceptable authority to the Boston Society for Medical Improvement that "... it is evident that we must look for the origin of hysteria in the brain or mind itself and not in irritation from distant parts." He went on to insist that the causes, particularly of hysteria, might be found "in certain fixed ideas or in fixed morbid nervous processes which do not rise perhaps as high as ideas" (45).

The study of hysteria, it must be remembered, had been vigorously pursued throughout the nineteenth century. However, until the last quarter of the century, when hysteria became the great proving ground for the theories of Janet, Charcot, Breuer, Freud, Prince, Putnam, and many others, it was generally the internists and surgeons who had been concerned with the psychosomatic meaning of what were then called the hysterical reactions.

As early as 1830, Sir Benjamin Brodie in his lectures on surgery was saying, "I do not hesitate to declare that among the higher class of society, at least four fifths of the female patients who are commonly supposed to labor under diseases of the joints, labor under hysteria and nothing else" (11). In England and Scotland "Brodie's knee" quickly became a widely used description of a hysterial reaction.

Such observations were characteristic of most of the great medical practitioners and teachers of the century. Indeed, some of the psychosomatic relationships indicated by nineteenth-century physicians were much more radical than we would be willing to accept today. Sir Astley Cooper, for example, remarked on how frequently carcinoma of the rectum ensued on mental distress. In one of his lectures, he went on to say, "I should have observed that one of the most frequent causes of breast cancer is grief or anxiety of mind. . . . It arrests the progress of secretion, produces irritative fever, and becomes the forerunner of scirrhous tubercle. . . . The mind acts on the body, the secretions are arrested, and the result is the formation of scirrhus. Look then in this complaint," he continued, "not only at altering the state of the constitution, but relieve the mind, and remove if possible the anxiety under which the patient labors" (19). In a similar vein Bichat wrote about "the keen impression felt at the pylorus in violent emotions, the indelible trace of them which this organ sometimes retains, and whence originate the scirrhous tumors of which it is the seat" (7).

Almost throughout the century the etiology of hysteria was ascribed to a constitutionally and hence hereditarily determined over-irritability of the nervous system, which decompensated in the presence of mental or emotional stress or which was pathologically increased by reflex irritability arising from some other body organ. The concept of dissociation which had been popularized by Janet as a descriptive explanation of the altered states of consciousness characteristic of many hysterical reactions did not fundamentally alter these long-held underlying etiological considerations. At the end of the century, even Freud still largely held to the conceptions of hereditary predisposition and of emotional "shock" as basic notions in hysteria, although he was bringing the nineteenth century to a close with his significant advances in establishing the theory of purposeful repression, of the unconscious existence of psychologically unelaborated excitation, and of the partial escape of the repressed excitation in conversion and displacement symptoms.

At least three other developments in the nineteenth-century history of ideas are relevant to our discussion. Hughlings Jackson was the most influential example in medicine of one aspect of this ideological history. His application, in the Croonian lectures (30), of the principles of Darwin and of Herbert Spencer (both of whom, incidentally, were ardent psychophysiologists) to his own thinking on the evolution and dissolution of the nervous system exerted a profound influence on the psychophysiological theories of the nineteenth century as well as on the theories of psychopathology and neuropathology. Jackson had also been strongly influenced by Thomas Laycock and Henry Munro. Munro, for example, had earlier enunciated positive and negative symptoms in terms of the partial paralysis and of the irritable excess of nervous action. Laycock,[3] as early as 1840, had extended the conception of reflex action to cerebral activity (39).

Jackson's theories were the culmination of the nineteenth century's achievement in describing and interpreting the anatomical and functional organization of the nervous system. The first adequate description of neurological integration in terms of dynamic and homeostatic equilibrium had been made. As Hack Tuke wrote, "The conclusion is being forced on us that there may be (psychopathological) cases in which no change takes place in the brain which the ablest microscopist is likely to detect, but a dynamic change—one more or less temporary, in the relative functional power of different cerebral centers, involving loss or excess of inhibition" (58).

Another significant theoretical advance affecting the psychosomatic medicine of the century was the elaboration of thermodynamic principles in physics.[4] By 1870, medical science had related human fatigue and exhaustion to the reduction of the storage of energy in the neurons. Beard had popularized by this time the concept of neurasthenia to describe most of the symptoms which we now group together under the designation of psychosomatic diseases. He believed these symptoms were the manifestation of an irritable neuronal weakness occasioned by an excess of waste over repair in the nerve cells.

The next phase in the history of neurasthenia occurred a little later, in 1896, when Freud described an anxiety neurosis, selected from the earlier, more inclusive syndrome of neurasthenia, which included most psychosomatic disorders and certain phobias. As is well known, Freud assumed that these symptoms were the reflection of a biochemically conditioned pathology due to an accumulation of sexual excitation without adequate outlet.

This concept of the underlying pathology of psychosomatic disease was not unlike that of the general theory of autointoxication preva-

---

[3] Thomas Laycock, Professor of the Practice of Medicine and of Clinical Medicine in the University of Edinburgh, was greatly influenced by Sir William Hamilton and by phrenology. He is a significant figure in the nineteenth-century phase of the history of the concept of unconscious behavior.

[4] It is interesting to keep in mind, here also, the extent to which thermodynamics influenced Freud's elaboration of psychoanalytic instinct theory.

lent in the last thirty years of the century.[5] It was certainly very close to the ideas of Kraepelin, who felt that autointoxication, particularly that arising from metabolic disturbances associated with sexual functions, might be a significant etiology of mental disease.

Finally, the great experimental activity in psychophysiology which reached its climax in Germany provided a broad factual basis for psychosomatic hypotheses in late nineteenth-century medicine. Wilhelm Wundt and his pupils, Gent, Mosso, Kiesow, Binet, and Ernst Weber, experimentally described the relations between emotion and blood pressure and pulse volume. Mosso, particularly, who was the founder of a school of psychophysiologists and who had constructed a plethysmograph for estimating the quantity of blood in the forearms and hands, experimented on the relations of the circulation to psychological behavior. Vasoconstriction in response to sounds and other stimuli during sleep and in hypnosis was described by him and his coworkers. Tanzi, a member of Mosso's laboratory, correlated temperature changes of the skin with variations in thought and feeling.

As historical forerunner to a widely used contemporary method of psychosomatic investigation, Féré, in a report to the Société de Biologie in 1888, noted that there was a lessening in bodily resistance to electricity when reactions to various stimuli occurred and that emotions also caused the same decrease. In 1890, Tarchanoff published his studies on the psychogalvanic reflex, which were corroborated by Sticker in 1897.

It is of more than incidental interest to note that by this time experimental psychology had been joined to psychiatry. About 1885 Buccola began to study in Italy the reaction time of psychopathologic persons. In Russia, a little later, a few psychiatrists influenced by Wundt attempted psychological experiments, and Kraepelin, returning from Wundt's laboratory, introduced the methods of experimental psychology into German psychiatry.

Meanwhile, at the close of the century, Morton Prince, without being aware, apparently, of Freud's work on anxiety neurosis, described a fear neurosis as consisting of the physiological manifestation of fear without any conscious and specific ideas of fear (46). Janet, it will be

---

[5] J. H. Denny, in 1867, thought of a "toxic agency of mind acting through the cerebrospinal system as a mental irritant poison," and spoke of "desire as an acute mental neurotic poison" (21).

remembered, had already described hysterical patients who exhibited anxiety with its physiological expression without knowing why they were anxious.

At the end of the century, therefore, both in the laboratory and in the clinic, psychosomatic medicine was a discipline with an experimental as well as an empirical body of knowledge.

Specific Psychosomatic Diseases

The Gastrointestinal System

The extraordinary influence of François Broussais during the first few decades of the century made gastritis a central, and indeed, almost exclusive concern of early nineteenth-century medicine. Broussais developed somatopsychic medicine with a vengeance by publishing in 1828, *De l'Irritation et de la Folie* (13), in which he insisted that neuroses and insanity were due to gastric irritation arising from inflammatory or subinflammatory processes in the stomach or intestines. John Hunter, too, had much earlier expressed the idea of the stomach as the controlling organ of the body.

But just as Pierre Louis was soon to displace the speculation of the school of Broussais and to establish medicine as an inductive science by continuous and meticulous clinical observation, so William Beaumont (6), by 1833, was able to demonstrate in the exposed gastric mucosa of Alexis St. Martin the effect of emotion and other stimuli on the healthy gut. From his observations extending over eleven years, Beaumont concluded that "In febrile diathesis or predisposition, from whatever cause—obstructed perspiration, undue excitement by stimulating liquors . . . fear, anger or whatever depresses or disturbs the nervous system—the villous coat becomes sometimes red and dry, at other times pale and moist, and loses its smooth and healthy appearance . . . fright or any sudden affection of the passions causes material alterations in its appearance . . . fear and anger check its secretion also; the latter causes an influx of bile into the stomach, which impairs its solvent properties."

So, too, about twenty years before Beaumont's observations, Le Gallois had discussed the influence of nervous excitation on stomach secretions.

Amariah Brigham, an early American psychiatrist who was a contemporary of Beaumont's and who published in 1833 his *Remarks on the Influence of Mental Cultivation and Mental Excitement upon Health* (9), felt that dyspepsia was often the result of a disturbed and irritated brain. He remarked that "the most careful diet will fail unless existing pressure and irritation can be removed from the mind."

Similarly, in 1855, James Jackson in his *Letters to a Young Physician Just Entering upon Practice* (31) advised that "In many instances instead of prescribing a medicine, I have found it necessary to give my dyspeptic patient a moral lecture; and that even though he wore a black coat . . . not infrequently I have had to descant upon the evils and the impropriety, if not the sin, of over-conscientiousness; of too great an anxiety to do right, and of distressing regrets from the fear of having erred. . . ."

By 1872 Tuke was able to say that "In dyspepsia, a change in character or amount of gastric secretion may or may not be the principal cause, but that morbid feelings acting directly on the stomach through the organic nerves do form one important element in the psychical genesis of the dismal symptoms comprised under this term cannot admit of doubt" (58).

At about the same time that Beaumont was studying the physiologic functions of the stomach, Cruveilhier and other French pathologists were adequately describing the postmortem pathology of peptic ulcer. Langston Parker (44), writing shortly after this in 1839 on a simple ulceration of the stomach, quoted the history of a case of recurrent ulcer with vomiting of blood as a major symptom. In a footnote, he observed that "This part of the history confirms a remark in another part of the paper and which I feel substantiated by the experiences of M. Cruveilhier, that is to say that the ulceration of the stomach, after having by care and judicious treatment been brought to a state of cicatrization, is exceedingly prone to recur from slight dietetic errors or even from strong mental impressions." Parker felt that peptic ulcer occurring in males was generally the result of inflammatory indigestion, but he admitted more psychosomatic determination of the disease in females by observing the frequency of its occurrence in women of "hysteric or debilitated types already exhausted by uterine irritation." Because he believed the gastric stroma to be thick in males and thin in females, Parker thought that perforation of an ulcer was more frequent in the female than in the male. He believed, however, that simple ulceration, itself, occurred more frequently in men than in women.

The question of frequency of ulcer, both in absolute terms and relative to its sexual occurrence, was debated throughout the century. Johann Oppolzer observed in 1855 its frequent general occurrence in Vienna. He recorded that cicatricial evidence was found with especial frequency in the stomachs of old women. J. B. S. Jackson, in a letter written in 1869 to the editor of the *Boston Medical and Surgical Journal* insisted that the number of ulcer cases seen in this country was small compared to the number of diagnoses made in Europe. Dr. Wood, of Philadelphia, is quoted as not having seen a single case during twenty-five years of hospital practice.

However, William Brinton (10), who in 1857 published a book on the subject of peptic ulcer, stated that the frequency of occurrence in persons autopsied in St. Thomas' Hospital ranged annually from 2 to 13 per cent, including both open and healed lesions. He found ulcer more frequent in the female by a ratio of 2 to 1. The incidence was highest in middle and later life, but the female exhibited a significant tendency to perforation between the ages of 15 and 30. Brinton found the absolute frequency of perforation to be 13 to 15 per cent of all ulcers. In 80 per cent of all the ulcer cases the lesion occupied a parapylor position on the posterior surface and the lesser curvature of the stomach. Interestingly, Brinton also noted a greater frequency of association of amenorrhea and ulcer in young females than in older women.

At the end of the century, Greenough (25) reviewed the ten-year interval, 1888-1898, for cases of gastric ulcer admitted to the Massachusetts General Hospital. Out of 13,097 patients entering the hospital, 187 cases of ulcer were diagnosed. This incidence of 1.4 per cent is somewhat higher than reported elsewhere in this country and in England at that time. Diagnosis was based chiefly on the triad of symptoms of vomiting, pain, and hematemesis. The sexual ratio of Greenough's cases was 157 females to 30 males, or 5 to 1. Of the females, 113 were under 30 years, and servant girls and cooks made up 75 per cent of the total number of women. Autopsy reports from Germany and England at the same time gave sexual ratios in incidence of gastric ulcer as high as 14 females to 1 male. The opinion of Ballantyne (4), in Edinburgh, who had a particular interest in stomach ulceration, was that gastric ulcer generally occurred in young women between the ages of 15 and 30, while duodenal ulcer was seen generally in men between ages of 30 and 50 years.

In general, no psychosomatic hypotheses were entertained in the direct etiology of peptic ulcer throughout the century, nor did the treatment, largely determined by Oppolzer as rest and liquid diet, give any evidence of consideration of psychosomatic factors.

By 1886, the common existing etiological theories of gastric ulcer were Kleb's conception of arterial anemia, Key's postulation of a venous hyperemia of the gastric mucosa, Gunsberg's idea of a venous stasis in the hepatic vessels, Leube's insistence on a diminished alkalinity of the blood, and Virchow's theory of circumscribed hemorrhages.

William Stokes, writing in 1834 on the pathology and treatment of chronic gastritis (56), came as close as any one in his time to a psychosomatic etiology when he wrote that "In consequence of long-continued functional injury, what was at first but a mere nervous derangement may afterwards become complicated with organic disease."

Some years later Rokitansky put forth his well-known neurogenic hypothesis of the origin of peptic ulcer.

However, it was in the study of ulcers of the stomach that hyperacidity came under closer medical scrutiny, and hyperacidity, at least, was almost universally considered to be a neurosis, in the nineteenth-century meaning of that term, and had long been observed as a frequent concomitant of hysteria and neurasthenia. This was particularly true after Kussmaul, Leube, and Ewald had progressively perfected the stomach tube, thus making the stomach contents accessible for analysis as well as establishing size, position, and motility of the stomach as definable concepts. A little later, in 1879, von Velden contributed a color reaction for hydrochloric acid, after which chemical and clinical study of the stomach was facilitated. By 1898, Cannon, following the suggestion of Bowditch, was studying gastric motility by fluoroscope and bismuth subnitrate.

Elliott Joslin (32), in this country, believed that the hyperacidity associated with ulceration was the result of exposure of nerves at the base of the ulcer or was excited by the pressure exerted on gastric nerves by the scar if the ulcer had healed. However, he also related some hyperacidity to psychological stress and observed a frequent association with migraine, the migraine being described as usually disappearing when the stomach was washed out. In Germany, Rossbach (52), too, described "acid vomiting" which affected the upper classes and persons exposed to great mental strain and which was usually set off by anger, trouble, and excitement.

By 1885, the German school of Magenärzte, particularly Stiller, Oser and Glaz, classified the neuroses of the stomach according to vasomotor, secretory, sensory, and motor functions. In their system, anorexia nervosa, for example, became a sensory neurosis, characterized by a deficiency in hunger sensation, while nervous vomiting was described as a hyperkinetic motor neurosis. The etiological concept of irritability still underlay much of this description.

The intimate association of nausea, disgust, and vomiting was occasionally mentioned in nineteenth-century medicine without being etiologically or therapeutically applied. However, Kaltenbach (33), by 1890, was insisting that some of the uncontrollable vomiting of pregnancy might be due to hysteria and that it was sometimes cured by suggestion.

Anxiety as a cause of *mal de mer* was considered by Gueprat in 1840 largely because he observed the appearance of symptoms of seasickness in mariners of long standing after they had been subjected to danger. The colonopathies were not so minutely classified as were the stomach neuroses. But even folklore had long recognized the psychosomatic implications of diarrhea and constipation. Nineteenth-century medicine did not hesitate to suggest a psychological causation for these disturbances. Birch, for example, whose book on *Constipated Bowels* (8) had gone through three editions by 1868, regarded "pure nervousness and excessive anxiety regarding the frequency and regularity of the . . . evacuations as one of the important causes of costiveness." He incidentally felt that obstinate constipation was infinitely more common among his fellow Britishers than among the French or Germans. Similarly, the American physician, Ware (62), felt that women were more liable than men to develop constipation and that city dwellers suffered more from this disorder than did inhabitants of the country.

Cardiovascular System

The sympathetic participation of the heart in the emotions was a commonplace observation, of course, long before the nineteenth century. The nineteenth century, however, supplied much of the modern anatomical and physiologic knowledge of the interaction of mind and heart. This added information, particularly about the neurophysiology and pathology of the heart, particularly influenced the thinking about angina pectoris.

Angina had been first correctly described in 1768 almost simultaneously by Rougnon and by Heberden, and for a while thereafter it was called Heberden's disease, although Heberden himself had named it angina pectoris.

At that time the theory was that angina was either a primary or symptomatic neurosis of the cardiac plexus. Laennec, for example, wrote of the disease as a primary affection occurring sometimes in the pneumogastric nerve and sometimes in the cardiac portion of the sympathetic nerves. He felt that the brachial plexus frequently became implicated. Bouillaud had described angina as a neuralgia of the phrenic nerve.

The conception of angina as a result of reflex irritation was being advanced in 1870 by Eulenburg and Guttman, who thought that organic disease of the heart might irritate the cardiac plexus or the ganglia in the heart itself.

However, as early as 1799, Dr. Parry was insisting that true angina never occurred without organic disease of the heart or of the arteries in its vicinity. By 1851, in a paper read before the Royal Medical Society in Edinburgh, Francis Campbell (14) was able to establish a psychosomatic hypothesis for angina. He insisted that the fact that the heart is diseased and that there is ossification of the cardiac vessels would have to be accepted. He added, "Hence, when unusual exertion is required, the power of the heart may fail under the new demand and accordingly we find that angina is readily excited by those passions, the tendency of which is to stimulate the heart to excessive contraction. Thus we find that many of the recorded cases proved fatal while the patient was in a violent transport of anger." Campbell also remarked that death during sleep might be produced by the sudden "starting" of the patients due to dream emotion. Additionally, he stated that "females enjoy an almost complete immunity" from angina and that the disease nearly always occurred in men above the age of fifty years and "of a leucophlegmatic habit of body." At the end of the century, Huchard (29), in his textbook on diseases of the heart and vessels, considered that lesions of the coronary arteries, coronary spasm sometimes emotionally induced, and ischemia of the myocardium were the essential components of the anginal reaction.

It is worth remarking that the pharmacodynamics of nitrite amyl, suggested by Lauder Brunton in London in 1867, as a treatment for angina, was worked out in 1871 by the American, H. C. Wood, at the Massachusetts General Hospital. Later, in 1876, Brunton studied the physiological action of nitroglycerine and this drug was introduced into the clinical management of coronary vasoconstriction by Dr. Murrell in the same year.

An awareness of the psychosomatic implications of hypertension occurred sporadically in nineteenth-century medicine. Perhaps no clearer statement on this subject was made than that by Huchard in his classic text. After indicating the possible relations of psychological tension and vascular tension, he wrote, "Let us suppose that the emotions are repeated, are perpetuated, as is the case with many politicians, financiers, or others involved in business schemes, who lead restless, anxious, worried lives, and then you will understand why it is that their arterial systems, in a state of permanent hypertension, must in the long run be doomed to the lesions of arteriosclerosis" (29).

In 1862 Maurice Raynaud (51) had described a "symmetrical gangrene of the extremities" and had collected twenty-eight cases from the hospitals of Paris. He defined the disease as a "neurosis characterized by an exaggeration of the excitomotor power of the spinal cord presiding over the vasomotor nerves and called attention to the spasm of the peripheral vessels and proposed the designation, "local asphyxia." By 1890 the existing theories of the nature of the disease were Raynaud's original conception of an angioneurosis, with competing descriptions of a trophoneurosis, an endarteritis obliterans, and a local neuritis. By this time, too, the disorder was found to be most prevalent in young females.

Reports also existed in the accumulating literature which stressed an emotional determinant in the precipitation or exacerbations of the disease. Levi, in 1895, described a form of Raynaud's disease and erythromelalgia, arising from intense emotional disturbance, which began quite acutely and, in some cases, proceeded to gangrene. A little later, Minor reported the case of a woman telegraph operator, frightened during a thunderstorm, who developed swelling, cyanosis, and finally gangrene of the fingers of the right hand with a weaker pulse in that hand.

The recent interest among ophthalmologists in the possible psychological factors in central angiospastic retinopathy makes it worthwhile to note that in 1894 Henry (27) reported dimness of vision and contraction of the central retinal artery and its branches in association with cases of Raynaud's disease.

At the end of the century it was well accepted that, in the language of the time, a "functional disturbance" of spinal vasomotor centers was the initiating pathology leading to vascular spasm, thrombosis, and gangrene. The basic vasomotor disturbance could sometimes be an intrinsic irritability, but abnormally irritable vasomotor nervous centers bombarded by abnormal sensory irritations was the favorite hypothesis. In terms of the psycho-physiology of the time, this was essentially a psychosomatic attitude.

Somewhat similarly, the acute circumscribed edema of the skin described by Quincke in the last decades of the century was observed to occur sometimes after psychological stress. Quincke ascribed its etiology to heredity, neuropathic predisposition, local chilling of the skin, and to emotion.

Disorders of Women

Writings about the disorders of menstruation occupy a large volume of nineteenth-century medical literature. For some time early in the century, suppression of the menses was considered to be a cause of insanity, and indeed, even later, Krafft-Ebing proposed the term, "menstrual insanity" and advocated menstruation as an extenuating circumstance in forensic psychiatry. By 1843, however, Voisin had pointed out that amenorrhea may be the result rather than the cause of a behavior disorder. In the same year, Samuel Ashwell wrote that "the two great causes of acute [menstrual] suppression are mental emotion, especially of a depressing and anxious character, and the application of cold" (3). In London, at the same time, Dr. Churchill was relating that almost all of the women who were sent up to the Richmond Penitentiary, after having been tried in court, "labour under suppression in consequence of the mental agitation and distress they have undergone" (18).

There was a rather common acceptance throughout the nineteenth century of the hypothesis that strong emotional reactions might be accompanied by menstrual disturbances. Dr. Fazio, for example, who was an eye-witness of the severe earthquake at Ischia in 1884, described many cases of the sudden arrest of menstruation in the female inhabitants of the town.

By the last decades of the century Krieger (38) and others had established that the menstrual fluid was venous blood mixed with vaginal and uterine mucus and epithelial cells and so disproved the earlier idea that the issue of the menses was analogous to the secretion of toxins. A theory of dysmenorrhea as a vasomotor neurosis, in terms of vascular dynamics, thus became possible. This was elaborated by Palmer (43), among others, who insisted that dysmenorrhea was not due to abnormalities of the uterus but was essentially a "purely neurotic or spasmodic" disease many times related to "too much ovarian excitement . . . especially in young widows in good health before." Champneys (16), in the Harveian Lectures for 1890, devoted one lecture to this conception of spasmodic dysmenorrhea.

Galvanism, with the cathode over the hypogastric region and the anode applied to the perineum or to the uterine cervix, became a favorite method of treatment.

Perhaps the most startling psychosomatic formulations about amenorrhea were those offered in Paris by Raciborski in 1865. "Excessive dread of pregnancy," he wrote, "or immoderate desire of bearing children . . . may induce more or less delay in appearance of catamenia and even a protracted state of amenorrhea" (50). The too-ardent wish for children was considered to act in a reflex manner on the vasomotor nerves of the ovaries and so to produce the amenorrhea. The treatment adopted by Raciborski consisted in "arguments" calculated to remove the fears of pregnancy, and in the exhibition of harmless drugs. Raciborski, incidentally, also spoke of "mental frigidity" as a cause of impotence in men.

In relation to obstetrical medicine, at least one instance of psychosomatic thinking may be quoted from Tyler Smith's *Manual of Obstetrics* published in London in 1858. Here Smith insisted that "a very powerful influence may be exerted on the uterus by emotion. A fright or any violent mental disturbance may bring on labor prematurely, or produce abortion. During labor, any sudden emotion of the mind may increase or arrest uterine action.... Emotion often plays the part of Tantalus to the accoucheur. His entrance into the lying-in room may arrest the pains of labor for a time, through the influence of emotion; but if he should leave the house, they as often return with increased vigor and terminate the labor abruptly in his absence.... Emotional, like voluntary action, is psychical in nature and originates in the cerebrum, but it acts upon the uterus and other parts through the spinal marrow." de La Motte, in his *Traité des Accouchements,* written in 1726, records an instance of a parturient woman dying of fright consequent upon his attendance.

It is of incidental interest that the first recorded instance of the use of chloroform as a method of differential diagnosis of pregnancy or hysteria was published by Keiller in 1855 (34). Dr. Simpson of Edinburgh administered his anesthetic to a long-standing case of pseudocyesis and "much to his astonishment and to the amazement of all present, the abdomen became quite flat, the tympanic protuberance of the belly entirely disappearing.... As soon as the effect of the chloroform wore off, the abdominal parietes assumed their former condition and the belly again became (as it had so long and so very puzzlingly been) tympanitic as a drum."

Diseases of the Skin

In the last half of the nineteenth century considerable attention was paid to the psychosomatic aspects of skin diseases. Tuke, in what we might call his textbook of psychosomatic medicine, writes that "as without actual disease, we see the influence of moral causes upon the function of the skin, fear checking perspiration and other emotions causing congestion, it is not surprising that definite eruptions should reasonably have a similar origin. The transition to eczema, impetigo, etc., is not difficult to understand" (60).

In 1883, Schwimmer (54), who was a pupil of Hebra, published a text on the neuropathic dermatoses, which paid particular attention to the "sympathetic nervous system and its related vasomotor and trophic nerves in connection with the skin."

Some thirty years earlier, Wood, in an article "On the nervous element in inflammation and its influences on treatment," published in the *Edinburgh Medical Journal* in 1856, described among other occurrences of psychosomatic skin disease a case of an elderly lady with chronic eczema of the ankle and leg. "Circumstances existed at the time which kept her mind in a state of perpetual harassment," he continued, "and it soon became obvious that every fresh mental excitement was followed by an aggravation of the eruption. She was only relieved by . . . treatment calculated to allay nervous irritability, and by the cessation of the cause of that anxiety which seemed to produce the disease" (63).

The psychological aspects of pruritus were frequently recognized by nineteenth-century physicians. Bronson (12), in 1890 for example, stated this very clearly by remarking that "scratching relieves itching by directing the excitation into freer channels of sensation . . . substituting for the pruritus either painful or voluptuous sensations."

The well-known interest in suggestion-produced cutaneous lesions led to a large literature on this subject in the last two decades of the century. All varieties of cutaneous lesions—erythema, vesicles, bullae, papules, lesions resembling burns, ecchymoses, and bloody exudates from initial dermographia, were reported as produced by hypnotic suggestion.

Even the psychosomatic implications of dentistry received attention in the nineteenth century, as evidenced by an article appearing in 1886 in the *British Journal of Dental Science* written by Gallippe, in which he insisted that mental strain creates increased decay of teeth and increased sensitivity of the dentine.

Other Disorders

The subject of headache, and of migraine particularly, received a great deal of attention in nineteenth-century medicine. The etiology of migraine, for example, was very early in the century established on the basis of a "vasomotor neurosis." Dubois-Reymond described hemicrania as caused by an abnormal excitation of the sympathetic nerve on the affected side. He observed a retraction of the temporal artery, pallor of the countenance, and dilation of the pupil, all of which he attributed to a tonic contraction of vascular and oculopupillary muscles. Moellendor: (42) proposed the opposite view that migraine was initiated by a unilateral relaxation of the vessels of the head because of lack of energy of the vasomotor nerves. Later, Eulenburg stated that there existed two types of migraine, a sympatheticotonic or angiopastic hemicrania and an angioparalytic or neuroparalytic form. As a resolution of this dialectic, Jaccoud then insisted that Eulenburg's two types were actually only phases in the continuum of the process. The initiatory phase was an abnormal excitation of the sympathetic innervation followed by a paralysis of exhaustion which terminated the migraine paroxysm.

"Mental excitement" and "emotional causes" were commonly accepted as determinants of migraine. Moellendorff also felt it to be more a common disorder in females and in the middle and upper classes.

Migraine played an important part in the development of the interesting theory of the alternation of neurosis, which received transitory but widespread attention, particularly in England in the last few years of the century. Based largely on his observations on the destiny of migraine in subjects who developed psychiatric disorders, Savage was interested to perceive that individuals suffering from migraine lost their headaches if they became psychotic. "I have frequently met with cases of severe migraine," he wrote, "and I have found, as a rule, that patients who suffer from this disorder, if they became insane, lose their headaches, and I have seen one man who appeared to improve but relapsed when he had not developed migraine; but when he began again to improve and had a recurrence of headaches his sanity was assured" (53).

Similar observations were also recorded about asthma. Kelp (35), for example, spoke of the "vicarious relation" between psychosis and asthma and wrote down the aphorism, "So long as asthma obtains a recurrence of psychosis is not to be feared."

In more general relation to the subject of hay fever and asthma, Abramson (1), in a recent article, has sketched some of the broad outlines of the psychosomatic history before the twentieth century. It is interesting to note that even in the first half of the century, psychosomatic implications in asthma were openly accepted. Allen (2), writing in 1839 in America, was particularly struck by the frequency of asthma "among those who earn their living by thinking," and that "paroxysms of asthma from mental causes happen, perhaps, more often in physicians than in any other class of people."

In 1858 Trousseau, the great French medical teacher and himself a sufferer from asthma, in his lectures in the Hotel Dieu, recited the circumstances of one of his own attacks which occurred one day while he was in his coach barn. "Under the influence," he wrote, "of the moral emotion [his detection of his coachman's thievery] . . . my nervous system was excited, and under these conditions a cause [barn dust] which under ordinary circumstances would not have had any such effect . . . acted in this particular case." "Asthma has, then," he added, "its personality" (57).[6]

After the middle of the century, asthma was almost universally accepted as being either a reflex excitomotor reaction, idiopathically or symptomatically engendered, or as being produced by the tumefaction of the bronchial membranes as a result of the dilation of blood vessels under vasomotor influences. In either case this conception of "nervous irritability" as a predisposing cause involved the consideration of the parent's psychological state as a factor in the disease.

By the end of the century Frederick Knight, one of whose interesting patients was a Boston banker who could stop an asthmatic attack by entering a card game and playing for high stakes, summed up the three factors which were rather generally believed to be the necessary determinants of asthma. He described these as (1) "the neurotic habit"; (2) "a morbid condition somewhere in the respiratory tract . . . whose irritation shows itself by a reflex exhibition in the bronchial tubes"; and (3) "the exciting factor, which may be atmospheric, digestive, mental or other remote irritatives, which act reflectively on bronchial tubes" (37).

In addition, at the end of the century a considerable number of re-

---

[6] This experience of Trousseau calls to mind an instance recorded by Laennec of a nobleman whose asthma invariably came on when any person inadvertently shut his bedroom door or when his nightlamp happened to go out.

ports of the cure or the amelioration of asthma by hypnosis appeared in the medical literature.

In the medical journals at this same time, there was considerable disagreement about the nature and treatment of exophthalmic goiter. By 1895, the principal theories about the causes of Graves' disease were: (1) that the disorder was due to localized lesions in the medulla; (2) that it was toxic in origin, related in some way to disease of the thyroid gland; and (3) that it was a neurosis. In this country, James J. Putnam was a proponent of the latter view. Putnam (47) described the disease as a "caricature of fear" and believed that the first outbreak was usually emotionally caused. In substantiation he cited many such instances, one particularly being a woman in whom the onset of exophthalmos and other symptoms dated from her experience in being subjected to an attempted sexual assault.

The last decade of the century was also marked by the considerable interest manifested by surgeons in postoperative delirium. Many studies in France, Germany, and America seemed to prove the frequency with which postoperative psychoses followed gynecologic operations. Fear and anxiety before the surgical experience was instanced by Sears (55), Kiernan (36), and others as determining factors, and psychological preparation of the patient before operation was advocated by a number of surgeons.

Closer to contemporary concerns about the problems of neurosis was the late nineteenth-century interest in the chronic invalid. As early as 1860, Walter Channing had described the "bed case, or an imaginary affection which confines the patient in bed, and is preceded or not by disease" (17). He found this to be rare in males but common in married and unmarried women. Channing decried the abandonment of such cases and insisted that treatment should be "patient listening" and getting the confidence of the patient.

Robert Edes' well-known Shattuck Lecture on the *New England Invalid* (22) was given in 1895, thirty-five years after Channing's article, and is noteworthy not only for his nine-point classification[7] of New

---

[7] (1) The malingerer, (2) the exaggerator, (3) the constitutionally neurotic, (4) the hysterically excitable, (5) the neuromimetic, (6) the confirmed neuromimetic, (7) the tense neurasthenic, (8) the limp neurasthenic, and (9) the melancholic.

England's neurotic women, but also for his reference to and acceptance of Breuer and Freud's hypothesis about hysteria.

The diagnosis of neurasthenia was the common designation for chronic invalidism, particularly after the popularization of this concept by Van Deusen and Beard. Beard accepted the etiology as an asthenia and exhaustion of nerve cells and divided the symptoms into those referable to spinal neurasthenia and those arising from cerebral neurasthenia. Later Hecker introduced the idea of a neurasthenia of the sympathetic nervous system manifest as anxiety and so bridged the transition which Freud effected in the conception of the anxiety neurosis.

Similarly, a change was being made in the nineteenth century's considerations about traumatic neurosis. "Spinal concussion" and "railway spine" were long in use to designate symptoms, following injury. The belief in the actuality of spinal concussion was progressively abandoned and replaced by Charcot's conceptions of hysterical elaboration of the local injury. So, too, in cases of cranial trauma, the last years of the century were marked by the Oppenheim-Strümpell controversy over how much the enduring posttraumatic symptoms might be due to structural changes in the central nervous system as against Strümpell's contention that an "incongruous fright reaction" to the accident created a "traumatic hysteria."

The whole problem of psychotherapy in the nineteenth century must be developed elsewhere. Here it must suffice to say that in the last decades of the century there was an increasing concern with the meaning of the personality in disease and with efforts to deal with and to understand the person who was ill. In a speech at a dedication of a new building in the Harvard Medical School in 1883, Oliver Wendell Holmes (28) gave voice to some of this concern by saying, "I have often wished that disease could be hunted by its professional antagonists in couples—a doctor and a doctor's quick-witted wife.... Many a suicide would have been prevented if the doctor's wife had visited the victim the day before it happened. She would have seen in the merchant's face his impending bankruptcy, while her stupid husband was prescribing for his dyspepsia and endorsing his note. She would recognize the love-lorn maiden by an ill-adjusted ribbon—a line in the features—a droop in the attitude—a tone in the voice—which mean nothing to him."

At the turn of the century, when Lewellys Barker returned from his continental visit, he was very much impressed by what he saw on the Pinel ward of the Salpêtrière where Déjerine was treating hysteria and neurasthenia by isolation and psychotherapy. "Hypnosis was not used; yet," he wrote, "paralyses, anorexias, gastropathies, etc. were cured in days to a few months" (5). Barker's insistence was that psychotherapy should be mastered by general practitioners.

From this brief survey it is thus evident that nineteenth-century medicine had an extraordinary body of psychosomatic hypotheses about disease. What was conspicuously lacking was an adequate system of behavioral concepts by which a genetic and dynamic explanation of the meaning of the various emotional states which were described could be elaborated for understanding and for psychotherapeutic treatment. The psychological system and the psychotherapeutic skills waited on the developments of the twentieth century.

At the change of the century James Putnam was already pointing out the way comprehensive medical education should go. In the Shattuck Lecture in 1899, he said, "I should rate a thorough preliminary course in psychology . . . far above a knowledge of botany or zoology, and as following closely on chemistry and physics as a preparation for the work of a general practitioner" (49).

REFERENCES

1. Abramson, H. A.: Psychosomatic aspects of hay fever and asthma prior to 1900. *Ann. Allergy*, 6:110-121, 1948.
2. Allen, N. H.: The effects of mental emotions in producing asthma and dyspnoea in general. *Boston Med. Surg. J.*, 21:42-46, 1839-1840.
3. Ashwell, S.: *A Practical Treatise on the Diseases Peculiar to Women.* Boston: Press of T. R. Marvin, 1843.
4. Ballantyne, H.: Remarks on duodenal ulcer, with notes of a case. *Edinburgh Med. J.*, 14:532-535, 1903.
5. Barker, L.: Some experience with the simpler methods of psychotherapy and re-education. *Am. J. Med. Sci.*, 132:499, 1906.
6. Beaumont, W.: *Experiments and Observations on the Gastric Juice and the Physiology of Digestion.* Plattsburg: F. P. Allen, 1833.

7. Bichat, M. F. X.: *Anatomie Générale, Appliquée à la Physiologie et à la Médicine.* Paris: Brossow, Gabon, 1802.
8. Birch, S. B.: *Constipated Bowels, the Various Causes and Different Means of Cure.* Philadelphia: Lindsay & Blakiston, 1868.
9. Brigham, A.: *Remarks on the Influence of Mental Cultivation and Mental Excitement upon Health.* Boston: March, Copen & Lyon, 1833.
10. Brinton, W.: *On the Pathology, Symptoms and Treatment of Ulcer of the Stomach; with an Appendix of Cases.* London, 1857.
11. Brodie, B. C.: *Pathological and Surgical Observations on the Diseases of the Joints.* London: Longman, 1836.
12. Bronson, E. B.: A study on pruritus. *Boston Med. Surg. J.,* 123:253, 1890.
13. Broussais, F. J. V.: *De l'Irritation et de la Folie, Ouvrage dans lequel les Rapports du Physique et du Moral Sont Etablis sur les Bases de la Médecine Physiologique.* Paris: Fils Casimir Broussais, 1839.
14. Campbell, F. W. Angina pectoris. *Boston Med. Surg. J.,* 67:390, 1862.
15. Cerise, L.: Influence du moral sur le physique, influence du physique sur le moral. *Ann. méd.-psychol.,* 1:1, 1843.
16. Champneys, F. H.: *On Painful Menstruation.* The Harveian Lectures, 1890. London: H. K. Lewis, 1891.
17. Channing, W.: The bed cases, or an imaginary affection which confines the patient in bed, and is preceded or not by disease. *Boston Med. Surg. J.,* 63:72-80, 1860-1861.
18. Churchill, F.: *The Diseases of Females, Including Those of Pregnancy and Childbed.* Philadelphia: Lea & Blanchard, 1843.
19. Cooper, A. P.: *The Lectures of Sir Astley Cooper on the Principles and Practice of Surgery.* Frederick Tyrrel, Ed. Philadelphia: A. Sherman, 1826.
20. Creighton, C.: *Illustrations of Unconscious Memory in Disease, Including a Theory of Alternatives.* London: H. K. Lewis, 1886.
21. Denny, J. H.: Mental toxicology. *Boston Med. Surg. J.,* 76:243, 1867.
22. Edes, R. T.: The New England invalid. Shattuck Lectures for 1895. *Boston Med. Surg. J.,* 133:53-57, 1895.
23. Falconer, W.: *A Dissertation on the Influence of the Passions upon Disorders of the Body.* London: C. Dilly, 1796.
24. Feuchtersleben, E. von: *Medical Psychology.* Trans. by The Sydenham Society. London, 1847.
25. Greenough, R. B.: Gastric ulcer at the Massachusetts General Hospital, 1888-1898. *Boston Med. Surg. J.,* 141:389, 1899.
26. Haygarth, J.: *Of the Imagination, as a Cause and as a Cure of the Disorders of the Body.* Bath: R. Cruttwell, 1800.
27. Henry, F. P.: A clinical report of two cases of Raynaud's disease. *Boston Med. Surg. J.,* 130:621, 1894.

28. Holmes, O. W.: The new century and the new building of the medical school of Harvard University. *Boston Med. Surg. J.*, 109:361-368, 1883.
29. Huchard, H.: *Maladies du Coeur et des Vaisseaux*. Paris: O. Doin, 1889.
30. Jackson, H.: *Remarks on Evolution and Dissolution of the Nervous System*. London: J. Bale & Sons, 1888.
31. Jackson, J.: *Letters to a Young Physician Just Entering upon Practice*. Boston: Phillips, Sampson, 1855.
32. Joslin, E.: Hyperacidity of the stomach and its treatment. *Boston Med. Surg. J.*, 138:389-392, 1898.
33. Kaltenbach, R.: Ueber Hülfsmittel des gynäkologischen Unterrichtes. *Z. f. Geburtshülf. u. Gynäk.* 21:288, 1891.
34. Keiller, A.: On spurious pregnancy and hysteria. *Edinburgh Med. Surg. J.*, 82:19-23, 1855.
35. Kelp, L.: Asthma und Psychosis. *Allg. Ztg. f. psychol. u. psychisch-gerichtliche Med.*, 29:446, 1873.
36. Kiernan, F.: Medical history after the operation and certain special features of the case. *Am. J. Med. Sci.*, 102:660, 1891.
37. Knight, F. I.: The rational treatment of bronchial asthma. *Boston Med. Surg. J.*, 122:80-82, 1890.
38. Krieger, F. J.: *Die Menstruation*. Berlin, 1869.
39. Laycock, T.: *Mind and Brain: or, The Correlations of Consciousness and Organization*. Edinburgh: Sutherland & Knox, 1860.
40. Lucae, S. C.: *Observationes anatomicae circa Nervos arterios Adeuntes et Comitantes*. Frankfurt, 1810.
41. Margetts, E. L.: The early history of the word "psychosomatic." *Canad. Med. Assn. J.*, 63:402, 1950.
42. Moellendorff, W.: Ueber Hemikranie. *Virchows Arch. f. path. Anat.*, 41:385, 1867.
43. Palmer, C. D.: Some points connected with the subject of dysmenorrhea. *Boston Med. Surg. J.*, 109:303, 1883.
44. Parker, L.: On simple ulceration of the stomach. *Eclectic J. Med.*, 3:193-201, 1839.
45. Prince, M.: Discussion of Putnam's paper on neurasthenia. *Boston Med. Surg. J.*, 132:517, 1895.
46. ———: The educational treatment of neurasthenia and certain hysterical states. *Boston Med. Surg. J.*, 139:332, 1898.
47. Putnam, J. J.: Recent observations on the function of the thyroid gland, etc. *Boston Med. Surg. J.*, 130:153-159, 1844.
48. ———: Modern views of the nature and treatment of exophthalmic goiter. *Boston Med. Surg. J.*, 133:131-137, 1895.
49. ———: Not the disease only, but also the man. *Boston Med. Surg. J.*, 141:53-57, 1899.

50. Raciborski, A.: De l'aménorrhée par causes psychiques. *Arch. de méd.*, 1:529, 1865.
51. Raynaud, M.: *De l'Asphyxie Locale et de la Gangrène Symétrique des Extrémités*, 1862.
52. Rossbach, M. J.: Nervöse Gastroxynis, als eine eigene, genau charakterisierbare Form der nervösen Dyspepsie. *Dtsch. Arch. f. klin. Med.*, 35:383, 1884.
53. Savage, G. H.: Alternation of neurosis. *J. Ment. Sci.*, 32:485-491, 1886-1887.
54. Schwimmer, E.: *Die neuropathischen Dermatosen*. Vienna: Urban & Schwartzenberg, 1883.
55. Sears, G. D.: Insanity following surgical operations. *Boston Med. Surg. J.*, 128:642-644, 1893.
56. Stokes, W.: Pathology and treatment of chronic gastules. *Boston Med. Surg. J.*, 10:245, 1834.
57. Trousseau, A.: *Lectures on Clinical Medicine* (Delivered at the Hotel-Dieu, Paris). London: R. Hardwicke, 1867.
58. Tuke, D. H.: Illustrations of the influence of the mind upon the body in health and disease, with especial reference to the imagination. *J. Ment. Sci.*, 17:153, 1871; 18:8, 1872.
59. ———: *Sleep-Walking and Hypnotism*. London: J. & A. Churchill, 1884.
60. ———: *Illustrations of the Influence of the Mind upon the Body in Health and Disease, Designed to Elucidate the Action of the Imagination*. London: J. & A. Churchill, 1872.
61. Villeneuve: Du mal de mer ou de la gastroenterologie des navigateurs. *Acad. Roy. Med.*, October, 1844; *Ann. méd. psychol.*, 3-4:128, 1844.
62. Ware, J.: Lectures on general therapeutics. *Boston Med. Surg. J.*, 65:149, 1861.
63. Wood, A.: On the nervous element in inflammation and its influence on treatment. *Edinburgh Med. J.*, 1:586-605, 1856.
64. Zilboorg, G.: Psychosomatic medicine; a historical perspective. *Psychosom. Med.*, 6:3, 1944.

PATHOLOGIC ANATOMY IN MODERN MEDICINE

PAUL KLEMPERER, M.D.
(1953)

In the literature one most frequently encounters the statement that dynamic medicine was handicapped by Virchow's emphasis on cellular pathology, and so it seems to the editors that the statement by Dr. Paul Klemperer places the role of Virchow in its proper historical perspective as a dynamic thinker. Most probably what had happened was that the overemphasis of the role of psychological factors in health and disease served in part as a screen for ignorance. The general thesis had a correlative validity but seemed to be utilized for the purpose of diagnosis by exclusion[1] in the sense that in those diseases in which at that time there was no demonstrable anatomic or pathologic basis, a psychic etiology became the rule.

It was perhaps due to a misinterpretation of Virchow's fundamental thesis that only his emphasis on the cellular pathology came to the forefront, and therefore medicine became tied to a point of view which, roughly stated, is that where there is no cellular pathology, there is no disease. In actuality, as is brought out in Klemperer's paper, Virchow, the first histopathologist, was not limited to a descriptive characterization of cell changes. While he believed that the site of the disease was in the cells, his aim was the comprehension of the process which underlies the alteration of form and function in disease. This included

---

[1] See Dubois, *This Volume*, p. 160.

physiological and chemical principles. To him disease was the "progress of vital phenomena under altered conditions ... life handicapped by various external and internal factors." To Virchow disclosure of the cause is not the sole objective: "Parasitic beings, including of course bacteria, are never more than causes; the nature of the disease depends upon the behavior of the organs or tissues with which the bacteria or their metabolic products meet."

It would seem that Klemperer makes the significant point that Virchow really represented an organismic point of view rather than the limited one which is usually ascribed to him. Nevertheless, dealing essentially with the problem from a somatically oriented point of view, consideration of the psyche did not enter into his thinking. The dynamic conceptual framework was of such a nature that psychic influences might very readily have fitted into it. Since, apparently, Virchow's essentially dynamic approach was either missed or misinterpreted, the emphasis on the cell as such was given undue prominence and became firmly attached to the name of Virchow to the extent that it resulted in a perversion of his basic formulations.

The justification for the publication of Klemperer's paper in this volume is the attempt to undo this historical distortion and to illustrate a dynamic approach at the somatic level.

In his famous farewell address Rokitanski could justly assert that he had pursued pathologic anatomy as a scientific vocation aimed at fertilizing clinical medicine; and his eulogist, Heschl, epitomized Rokitanski's contribution to medicine by stating that "through him alteration of structure became the focal point of the problem of disease." But forty years later, one reads that pathologic anatomy is only dead-house pathology that can contribute nothing to the understanding of disease, which is a problem of disturbed function and must, therefore, be investigated with the methods of physiology. Though in subsequent years the contributions of pathologic anatomy were again more appreciated, there is no question that the esteem it enjoyed in the nineteenth century has never been reached again. The pathologic

---

Eighteenth Harrison S. Martland Lecture delivered before Essex County Pathol. and Anat. Soc., December 10, 1953.

anatomist who has been raised in the traditions of the classical era must question the reasons for this decline. He must try to understand whether the lessened appreciation is due to deficiencies inherent in the method or due to lack of leadership which, in turn, might have been the result of the great attraction exercised by the more dynamic approach of physiology, supported by the rapidly advancing methodology of biochemistry and biophysics. The critical investigation demands a clarification of the essential aims of the anatomical concept in pathology, and necessarily must trace them back to their origin. It must pursue its object in a detached manner and with due consideration of the values of different approaches to pathology in its broadest sense: the comprehension of disease.

Anatomical observations of morbid states of the human body were recorded after anatomy had come into its own through the influence of Vesalius and his school. Among the first is the report of William Harvey of the postmortem findings of Thomas Pratt, and Baglivi's description of the necropsy of Malpighi. A collection of autopsy records of Bonetus has been assembled in his *Sepulcretum,* published in 1705, and Morgagni drew freely from these and other sources. However, they were not only rare, but also merely individual descriptions without theoretical abstraction. The immortal contribution of Morgagni lies not so much in his admirable records of clinical and anatomical observations, but far more in his conceptual generalization expressed in the title of his work, "On the Seat and Cause of Diseases as Investigated by the Anatomist."

The advance of Morgagni's theory can only be appreciated if one considers it in relation to the epistemologic state of contemporary medicine. The knowledge of disease was still dominated by Hippocratic tradition and purely descriptive. Ideas of pathogenesis were still under the influence of the Platonic, mystical, four humors embellished by vague, mechanistic and chemical speculations. By correlating the fleeting manifestations of disease, as seen in the living, with the tangible organ alterations in the dead body, Morgagni established the first scientific system in medicine. This anatomical concept has become so ingrained in our thinking that we are hardly aware of its application in our present-day medical operations. But it is no exaggeration to assert that our deliberations and methods in the diagnosis of disease are, even today, largely directed toward a visualization of the underlying anatomic alteration. Morgagni's principles became the foundation of diagnostic medicine as it developed in the nineteenth century. The great clinician-pathologists of France and England, Laennec, Bretteneau, and Bright, the famous Vienna School of Medicine led by the clinician, Skoda, and guided by Rokitanski, were among the first who helped to complete the work. Even Semmelweis' great discovery rests upon Morgagni's inspiration. Yet in the light of subsequent developments, it is evident that Morgagni's anatomic concept could not accomplish what he had promised. The ultimate cause of disease could not be revealed by anatomic investigation only. By correlating clinical symptoms with structural alterations, pathologic anatomy could better circumscribe morbid entities which were ill-defined by mere clinical manifestations. But this descriptive characterization can neither account for the *why* nor explain the *how* of the alteration of form and function characteristic of disease, which is the ultimate goal of pathology. This inadequacy was brought to attention by the anatomist Henle who asserted that medicine, under the influence of pathologic anatomy, has only exchanged the old clinical terms for new ones which stand for the anatomical alteration. How appropriate were Henle's words of caution as one reads, in Soemmering's preface to the translation of Baillie's *Morbid Anatomy,* the following smug sentence: "Frequent experience has taught me that one easily acquires a precise and real concept of a disease by careful investigation of the morbid alteration." Soemmering was one of the leading German physicians of the early nineteenth century and one can assume that his point of view was shared by a majority of his colleagues, the more so since Rokitanski's influence dominated the development of medicine in Austria. This attitude of appreciating pathologic anatomy merely because of its usefulness for clinical diagnosis would have aborted the future development of medicine. But, fortunately, natural science was already firmly established, and the inquiry into cause was the dominant force in its explorations.

Mere static observation was no more sufficient. Life as a process came under scrutiny; anatomy was linked with physiology, and pathologic anatomy was forced into a dynamic direction. It is possible that this development would have gradually taken place. Actually, however, it was the genius of one man who gave the new orientation to pathologic anatomy and who expanded the system of Morgagni. Rudolf Virchow is often regarded as the first histopathologist, and his cellular pathology as a mere revival of Morgagni's organic pathology (*Rindfleisch*). According to this idea, pathologic histology shows how the coarse alterations of organs revealed by pathologic anatomy are founded upon certain changes of tissue constituents. But Virchow's vision was not bounded by the descriptive characterization of cell changes. While he believed that the seat of disease was in the cells, the elementary constituents of the living body, his aim was the comprehension of the process which underlies their alteration of form and function in disease. This is the fundamental idea which animates his entire life work and which he precisely expressed in the enthusiastic articles of his youth and the judicious statements of his advanced age: "To understand the volution of morbid states—that is the contribution of science and the objective of thinking man." This was the principle which guided him as pathologic anatomist and inspired his immediate disciples and those who followed him. Today, in a period of expansion and specialization, we are hardly aware that medical investigation is still under the influence of this "regulative principle," as Royce expresses it.

As the modern pathologic anatomist tries to reproduce structural alteration characteristics of human disease by animal experiment, he should not only recall Virchow's experiments on thrombosis and embolism, but especially his introductory remarks that the experiment is only the control for the pathologic anatomic conclusion reached by unbiased anatomic perception. As anatomic pathology of today tries to penetrate the mysteries of cellular abnormality by the application of histochemistry, or utilizes ultracentrifugation for the identification of elementary constituents of the cell, one is reminded of the words of Virchow: "By calling attention to the cell, I desired to force the investigators to determine the process within the cells, and it was quite evident that this exploration was to aim the discovery of the physical and chemical foundation upon which manifestation of life and vital activity rest."

While the influence of the great physiologists and bacteriologists of the nineteenth century, such as Claude Bernard, Karl Ludwig, Pasteur and Koch, upon the development of clinical medicine cannot be evaluated too highly, Rudolph Virchow's concise definition of disease as the course of vital phenomena under altered conditions remains even today an epitome of the highest precision. It has already been asserted that Virchow must not be regarded merely as a profound pathologic anatomist and histologist. His own words refute such an estimate when he maintains that "chemical and physical investigation is of a higher order than anatomy and morphology." But he affirms the fundamental value of anatomy for the progress of medical science with the statement "that at all times, permanent advances were determined by anatomic disclosures, and that each greater epoch was initiated by a series of important discoveries of the structure and equipment of the body." Accordingly, Schwann's discovery of the cellular constitution of the animal body became the cornerstone upon which Virchow could build the morphologic-physiologic system of his cellular pathology.

The evolution of science in general, and that of medicine in particular, can only be understood if one correlates it with the philosophical climate of the contemporary period. As Burghart says: "there are men who are by nature mirrors of what surrounds them." Morgagni's association of ill-defined symptoms of disease with tangible organ changes as perceived by anatomic observation, seems to me to rest upon the prevailing epistemology of the eighteenth century, upon Francis Bacon's empiricism, and John Locke's theory of cognition by sense perception. In fact, Morgagni's conclusions were foreseen by Bacon who, pleading for the performance of necropsies, maintained that "in the difference of the internal parts are also found the immediate causes of many diseases." The influence of Bacon upon Morgagni is quite obvious in the two indexes appended to the last volume. There are the catalogues of morbid manifestations, clinical as well as anatomical, according to Bacon's precept to "prepare as a foundation for the old [interpretation of nature] a complete and accurate natural history." But in the years subsequent to the publication of Morgagni's work, the foundation of Locke's philosophy, which had related sense perceptions to Newton's unobservable particles, had been undermined by Berkeley and by Hume's criticism which accepted reality for the sense data only. Thus, the congruence of abstract philosophical cognition and common-sense observation became illusory again. Kant's postulate of the a priori principle of causality, and the discoveries of physics and chemistry, changed the philosophical concept of the early nineteenth century. The disclosures of these sciences, such as the atom theory, the laws of motion and of dynamics, with the corollary theory of cause and effect, could not fail to influence the philosophical conceptions of the time, and, in turn, biological investigations which so far had been limited to mere description of facts and their vitalistic interpretation. How deeply Kant's idea of the a priori principle of causality influenced biology may be exemplified by a quotation of Claude Bernard: "The mind of man cannot conceive an effect without a cause, so that the sight of a phenomenon always awakens an idea of causation."

Some historical considerations let one understand the amazing phenomenon of the twenty-five-year-old Virchow, just after completion of his medical studies, publishing his conceptual articles in which he set medicine's goal, pathologic physiology through synthesis of dynamic investigation of form and function. In repeated variations he has expressed his belief that disease is life handicapped by various external and internal factors. It is obvious that he realized that exploration of these factors must be one of the important objectives of medical investigation; but the disclosure of cause is not the sole objective. Virchow has also been accused of not appreciating the significance of bacteria in pathogenesis and that his authority blocked the advance of bacteriology. His point of view is well illustrated by his own words, "Parasitic beings, including of course bacteria, are never more than causes; the nature of the disease depends upon the behavior of the organs or tissues with which the bacteria or their metabolic products meet. From my point of view, this distinction is of cardinal importance." I believe that modern microbiology can accept this statement of Virchow as evidence that he was well aware of the importance of bacteria for the study of infectious diseases. But the exploration of etiologic factors is not the ultimate aim of scientific medicine; it is only a means to an end. The ultimate aim is the comprehension of morbid life, and this goal can only be achieved by co-ordinated investigation of the manifestations of disease in the living and the dead, aided by the methods of the exact sciences. In this ideal sense "medicine becomes the science of man, anthropology in its broadest meaning, the highest form of natural science." Medicine of the nineteenth century had been built upon this principle and it still inspires the medical science of the present. It is impossible to apportion the shares which the individual sciences have had in the advances of medicine in the past, although it is evident that today all opinion gives most credit to the contributions of biochemistry. It would be equally unfair to answer that Virchow was the sole or foremost architect of the imposing empire of modern medicine, but it may well be said that he was its most articulate prophet.

But pathologic anatomy can and must look up to him as the creator of a new science of pathology who led this important branch of medicine from the impasse of mere description to a dynamic interpretation of the dead. The validity of this new concept to interpret structural manifestations of disease in terms of vital process is best illustrated if one compares textbooks of Pathologic Anatomy of the early nineteenth century with the compendia of our time. The vague term "cellular degeneration" has been replaced by "disturbance of cellular metabolism because it has been recognized that the morphological alteration is the result of abnormal chemical and physiochemical processes within the cell. It must be conceded that the nature of these processes is still obscure and it might be questioned whether we do not simply substitute one term for another one, or in other words, if we do not interpret the ill-defined phenomenon of structural alteration in terms of unknown chemical or physical processes. This criticism seems reasonable, but it can be met, in part at least. When Virchow first observed cell stenosis, he explained the accumulation of fat as the result of a transformation of the cytoplasmic proteins. This was in line with his dynamic approach to morphology, although the answer was wrong. Today we know that the accumulation of lipid substances can be the result of interference with enzymatic processes which result from anorexia, or other factors. While we have to agree to the limitation of our knowledge, we know the problem, and as Virchow said: "The posing of the problem is the first step in scientific investigation."

The problems of scientific medicine are the phenomena of disease, be they functional or structural. Pathologic anatomy, since the days of Morgagni, has supplied a vast number of such problems. It could be asked, and indeed it is being asked, whether pathologic anatomy as observational discipline has not been exhausted and can no more provide investigative medicine with new problems. It seems accepted by some that the morphological manifestations of disease have been fully perceived (Letterer) and that scientific morphology should now devote all its energy to the investigation of the physical and chemical factors responsible for alteration of structure. Parenthetically, it might be said that a similar point of view seems to prevail in the field of clinical investigation, where the pursuit of descriptive phenomenology of disease, the diagnostic art of old-fashioned medicine, has been eclipsed by the introduction of exact physiologic research. In pathologic anatomy this trend of modern times has expressed itself in emphasis upon experimental research.

There cannot be a question that alterations of structure characteristic of disease must be investigated with the precise methods of controlled experimentation in order to evaluate the factors responsible for their evolution. But the old-fashioned pathologic anatomist, whose interest still centers in the correct perception of the anatomic lesion in disease, might well be disturbed by certain tendencies in our academic institutions which reveal a disregard for the anatomic foundation of pathology, and a misconception of its role in medicine. He who believes that the advance of medicine can be assured only if it retains its connection with the past, must show that the basic observational principle of pathologic anatomy can still contribute to the advance of medicine and, that even in recent years, observations made at the autopsy table have thrown the first light upon hitherto unknown maladies, or provided basic information which was focused upon the pathogenetic problem of an obscure disease. I am embarrassed by the abundance, rather than by the scarcity, of material in support of this thesis and would like to present only a few examples.

Dorothy Anderson's classical studies of fibrocystic disease of the pancreas demonstrate that, even as late as 1939, a new morbid entity could be discovered by exact pathologic anatomic investigation. The recognition of causal relations between environmental factors and the morphology of disease, which Virchow regarded as one of the most significant objectives of pathologic anatomy, cannot be better illustrated than by reference to the work of the man to whom we pay homage. Simple, unbiased anatomic observation led Dr. Martland to the far-reaching discovery of the effects of radioactive substances upon the human body, especially the development of bone sarcoma. This disclosure, to paraphrase the words of Aschoff, posed a problem which has engaged biologic and fundamental sciences for years to come. Now the almost stubborn insistence that pathologic anatomic investigation can reveal facts of strategic importance for the comprehension of disease might be illustrated by reference to the anatomic studies of systemic lupus erythematosus which have occupied us at Mount Sinai for so many years. The unequivocal diagnosis of this puzzling disease has been made possible by the studies of exclusively morphologic character, and the observations have posed questions regarding the intercellular substances of the connective tissue which transcend the inquiry of this particular malady into a yet uncharted area of human disease. As a primarily observational discipline, pathologic anatomy has always endeavored to improve upon the methods of perceiving structural alteration in disease. Great advances were made by the steady progress of histopathology, and the heuristic value of a refined technique of microanatomy is well illustrated by recent investigations of renal disease. The pioneer work of Jean Oliver with microdissection has clarified a field in which speculation had been rampant because of the ambiguity of clinical and physiologic data and the inadequacy of morphologic comprehension. Most recent investigations of glomerulonephritis (Jones) and other nephropathies (Churg and Orishman) with extremely thin tissue sections have revealed glomerular alterations which throw new light on the morbid process and necessitate a reinvestigation of the problem of glomerular structure and function. As so often in the history of medicine, pathology points the way to an understanding of the normal.

These illustrations may suffice to indicate that observational pathologic anatomy is still a powerful tool in the advance of scientific medicine. But our question as to the role of pathologic anatomy in modern medicine must not be limited to its value for the advancement of research. Medicine in the service of humanity must concern itself with the problem of education of the coming generations. I believe it is Utopian to expect that the practice of medicine will soon mature into an exact systematic scientific activity, and I think medicine in its universal scope is not only applied natural science. Is it not evident that the future physician cannot acquire, within the short period of his schooling, all the factual knowledge which is required for professional competence or for productive scientific achievement? What he must receive is training in unbiased observation and in the ways of scientific thinking. Dr. Griswold's words about college apply equally well to medical school education: "It is not a quantitative body of memorized knowledge salted away in a card file. It is a taste for knowledge, a taste for philosophy if you will, a capacity to explore, to question, to perceive relationships between fields of knowledge and experience." It is this equipment which the young physician must acquire in medical school, and it will serve him well in the interpretation of the puzzling manifestations of disease with which he will be confronted in his future practice. This attitude of mind cannot be taught by mere verbalization of facts, but only by the demonstration of intrinsic relationships. To make the chaotic diversity of disease manifestations correspond to a logical system of thought—that is the ultimate aim of medicine. Pathologic anatomy, for nearly two centuries, has developed along these lines. Under the leadership of Morgagni, it has brought order into the perplexity of clinical phenomena by fastening them to the anchor of tangible organic alteration. Under the inspiration of Virchow, it has begun to interpret the structural changes as physical or chemical processes accessible to the laws of fundamental science. If ontogenesis is abridged phylogenesis, it may be well that the future physician should develop under the guidance of pathologic anatomy.

PSYCHOANALYSIS AND INTERNAL MEDICINE

FELIX DEUTSCH, M.D.
(1927)

It is rather curious that in this country the credit for the conceptual framework which we now call psychosomatic medicine is given to writers in the mid-thirties, when actually, in a paper entitled, "Psychoanalysis and Internal Medicine," published in April 1927, Felix Deutsch not only used the term, "psychosomatic" but essentially formulated the basic concept as we understand it today.

He has continued to do pioneer work in this field and has established a conceptual frame of reference based on a holistic point of view within classical analysis. His concept of the psychosomatic unit is in that tradition.

His essential point of view may best be expressed in the following quotation from "Three Score and Ten"[1]*:*

"His consistent emphasis on the intimate, fused relationship of all psychobiological phenomena from the earliest time is again emphasized in his statement that even though events may be of a primary organic nature or a primary psychic nature, the one will always draw the other into its realm, and that at an early level of development when sensory perceptions 'have no other objectifications than those related to the own body, purely organic disturbances, i.e., diseases or injuries, or

---

Deceased January 2, 1964.

[1] M. Ralph Kaufman in: "Two Annotations on the Occasion of the 70th Birthday of Helene Deutsch and Felix Deutsch."

operations, will be of great importance for an unharmonious, uneven psychosomatic development.' The feeding stimulus becomes the most important factor for the foundation of the ego structure 'because it leads to the acquisition of an extraneous reality which can be reached, accepted, rejected, unified with or separated from the body reality. . . . This psychosomatic process begins on a primary narcissistic level, passes through the oral and anal up to the genital stage, forever retaining elements of each throughout life.' Thus the structural organization of the body ego may be disarranged at any level of development. 'It can be transitorily distorted, interrupted, arrested, or fixed.' "

It is an empirical fact that during the analytic treatment organic symptoms occur which precede or accompany specific psychic complexes of which correlations the patient is unaware. Moreover, he tries at this point to direct the attention of the physician as much as possible to the organic origin of his sensations. However, the experienced physician recognizes these bodily sensations as the well-known forerunners of a memory emerging from the unconscious. It is almost the rule that, when the patient relives certain developmental phases of his childhood during analysis, there appear some specific bodily manifestations representing the organic correlate of the repressed unconscious. As the analysis proceeds, more specific correlations between certain psychic stages of development and their corresponding physical processes will crystallize. This results in an individual psychosomatic body schema which—after a sufficiently deep analysis—becomes so transparent that even the patient recognizes a certain bodily symptom—be it a headache, a coughing spell, some borborygmus, sweating somewhere on his body, etc.,—as the familiar signal of the reappearance of a repressed and correlated psychic content. The thousandfold subtle connections which become evident to the alert observer are too numerous to describe.

It is possible, however, to determine within these close "psychosomatic" interrelations those of a more loose as well as those of a more firm fusion. I say fusion, avoiding purposely the customary term of

---

Translated from: *Bericht über den II. Allgem. ärztl. Kongr. f. Psychotherapie*, Bad Nauheim, April, 1927.

"psychophysic parallelism." To speak of parallel processes seems to me completely inappropriate; the paradox lies already in the word "parallel," since parallels will never meet. We are dealing here with firm entanglements and interlacings, reciprocal causations, thus causal successions. If I say that we are dealing here with both looser and firmer ties, I mean that the looser ties are those connected with instinctual drives, while the more fixed ones are those which have a stronger relationship to the character.

I wish to point briefly to the fact that, speaking in analytic terms of an anal or oral character, we can with certainty conclude that with these character types correspond certain specific functional gastrointestinal behaviors. It is also a known fact that certain skin manifestations, due to greater irritability of the capillaries or even bigger blood vessels, are organic determinants of a narcissistic personality. All these well-known facts are prompting us to the conclusion that the developmental stages of the instinctual human life always have their complementary physical correlate, and that during disturbances of the psychic development the corresponding organic function is somehow affected as well.

Thus, if fixations or regressions occur in the instinctual life, the corresponding organic function must likewise lead to changes which deviate from the norm and which will recur throughout life. At this point we will refrain from elaborating as to how far—conversely—psychic fixation may become necessary; in other words, how far certain developmental disturbances in the instinctual life must occur due to the presence of functional organic alterations which are constitutionally conditioned. I am not speaking of "organic inferiority," because that is a too superficial—or rather too narrow—viewpoint, because it describes the psychosomatic fusion only as ego behavior, and even then only from a fraction of it.

This reference that those psychosomatic correlations belong to the normal life, seems necessary for an explanation that they are always present and normal components of the emotional life. Thus fear, guilt feelings, needs for punishment, etc., must necessarily have their predetermined specific expressions in the organism. That implies that certain organic behaviors belong to certain emotional factors. This means, that we may feel justified—with certain reservations—to infer merely from the kind of functional organic responses to an emotional experience which apparently mobilizes anxiety or guilt or need for punishment, the type of personality of the individual.

It is only fair to assert that analysis has provided us with a deep understanding of the psychosoma, both topically and dynamically. If we are then able to draw some conclusions from a functional bodily behavior to the instinctual and character structure of an individual, without depending on informations supplied by the patient, and vice versa, it needs no further emphasis how important it is for the internist to familiarize himself with analytic principles not only from a theoretical point of view, but also in the interest of his better understanding of disease.

However, the presupposition for the ability to observe a patient from both angles—so to speak—is more than a superficial knowledge of psychoanalysis. This does not infer that a patient who appears to suffer from a disease which is accompanied by psychic symptoms should be analyzed—by no means. I only wish to emphasize that we should be on our guard not to overlook the emotional components which are at play when organic dysfunctional behavior outlasts excessively the etiologic factors of the disease. We will thereby be in a position to adjust our therapeutic intervention accordingly when we do not remain ignorant of the fact that the organic symptoms are not merely due to the original causative factors. It fits into this concept that we should not be surprised when, for instance, several members of a family become the victims of the same intestinal infection and the symptomatology, the course and duration of the sickness are quite different; one showing only transitorily frequent bowel movements, another profuse diarrhea, and still another the same symptoms but also vomitus and long-lasting tenesmus. We may infer from this different picture a different psychic constellation which is determined by the premorbid personality make-up as well as by more recent emotional factors.

It goes without saying that it is of equal importance whether and how often gastrointestinal disorders have occurred previously. Adequate history taking will guard us here against too far-reaching conclusions. If identical conditions have existed which caused the illness, and no other organic factors for the persistent symptoms can be found, then our attention should turn to the patient's emotional life. This immediately brings up the question of what kind of psychologic examination should be chosen for such cases. It is safe to say that it should be one which can help determine the decision as to whether psychotherapy or even analysis should be taken into consideration. In any case, a psychoanalytic orientation will determine the content of information which will be obtained. That does not mean that the anamnesis should be centered only around sexual problems and how far sexual conflicts and traumatic psychic experiences have contributed to the development of the organic symptoms. Particularly with regard to the latter, one can easily be misled if the patient is trying to construct a connection from a traumatic emotional situation to his organic symptoms. It is true that the knowledge of an existing psychic trauma will help us to comprehend the importance of the time factor for the appearance of the organic symptoms, since it is necessary that a certain emotional event weaken the ego sufficiently so that the organic sickness can become conscious. The role of psychic factors which make the organic illness conscious will unquestionably be of lesser importance when external etiologic factors can sufficiently explain the sickness. Psychoanalysis, however, maintains that a traumatic experience in the present can only provoke manifest pathologic symptoms if during the psychic development a scar remained which sensitized the patient to the traumatic effect of the later emotional shock.

Therefore, from the analytic point of view, all pathologic manifestations of this kind have their roots in the past. This concept leads to a far different evaluation of the actual emotional condition of which the patient is conscious, as it would from the phenomenologic viewpoint. Thus the interview of the patient will not overlook the weight of the present stress and strain, but it will pay special attention to details of deviations in the psychic development of the patient. This kind of investigation into the patient's psychic life has its drawbacks. These lie in the fact that a person suffering physically will not understand why the physician should be interested in the emotional past, for he is unwilling to grasp how it could possibly relieve his physical discomfort if he talks about his feelings as a child. Consequently, his resistance may lead to distrusting the physician. We know that this defensive attitude is partly the expression of the patient's unconscious anxiety about being deprived of the secondary gain from his illness. It is indeed a common human phenomenon that as the organic need for being sick increases the more it serves to relieve unconscious conflicts of which the individual would not like to be reminded. By and large, the human being insists on the privilege of an escape into sickness.

The afore-mentioned difficulties can, however, be circumvented with sufficient tact and experience. We sometimes see the opposite, namely, that the relief which the patient feels after having spoken out of the abundance of his heart, is followed by a devaluation of his organic discomfort. This is often expressed in a patient's claim that he feels already much improved, at a time when the objective examination cannot find any change in the physical conditions. These improvements are, of course, most of the time only transitory. Occasionally, however, they have also an effect on the physical condition which takes a turn for the better, and even leads to a permanent cure. Those "miracle healings" are mostly due to the so-called "positive transference," i.e., the patient sees in the doctor an image for whose sake he gives up his sickness. Knowing that, one will see a successful treatment in the proper light. Unfortunately, many well-publicized psychotherapeutic methods owe their wide promulgation to the fact that their authors erroneously ascribed their successes to the methods they used and were unacquainted with the process of transference.

In case the psychiatric interview has revealed that psychic factors play an important role in the symptomatology of the sickness, or else, that the organic process which seems to be the core of the illness is only the partial expression of a neurosis, then one has to decide whether a deep-digging psychotherapeutic method like psychoanalysis should be recommended. There one has to be aware that, since it is necessary to explain to the patient that his organic symptoms are conditioned emotionally, one might often encounter insurmountable difficulties to convince the patient that this is true. The reason is partly that he is only conscious of his bodily sensations which—because of his neurosis —he resists to give up, since they serve partly in the solution of his unconscious neurotic conflicts. Also, we should not forget that his organic illness has been confirmed by his physician and he thus hides himself behind the authoritative diagnosis.

The second difficulty lies in the fact that upon starting the analysis, the intake of drugs should be given up gradually. Furthermore, it belongs to the framework of analysis that the analyst does not treat symptoms but the whole person on all levels, without regard to the presenting symptom. This is all the more important since these patients express their unconscious conflicts in physical symptoms to which they draw the physician's attention, and for which they ask sympathy. However, the impartial attitude and seemingly disinterested behavior of the doctor very often let the patient feel frustrated, and he stops coming for treatment. A similar stumbling block appears when after the initial improvement, or perhaps disappearance, of the organic symptoms they recur again. This is particularly the case when highly charged material is stirred up together with the former physical symptoms.

Nevertheless, these incidents can be mastered. Unquestionably the latter is to be regarded as the hardest blow, since the patient's capacity to endure any suffering is limited, even if the analysis has progressed sufficiently so that the patient can understand the relation between the present psychologic situation and the relapse. It should be emphasized how important it is that the internist be acquainted with the possibility of such incidents, because it is he alone who must decide whether the patient who has entrusted himself to his care should be analyzed. It has to be kept in mind that the task and the goal of analytic therapy by far exceed the general aim of therapy, since its purpose is to change the whole personality. As pointed out at the beginning, analysis looks upon bodily processes as always correlated with the total emotional setting and with the entire instinctual life. This is being reshuffled during the therapeutic process. Since in analysis all strata of the instinctual life are examined at different times, including those which are not so intimately connected with the present organic illness, the analyst can only turn his attention to the meaning behind the symptoms—like a physician examining the abdomen cannot at the same time listen to the heart.

For these reasons, the recurrence of organic symptoms during analysis is not surprising to the analyst, as he does not regard them as a turn for the worse, knowing that the analytic treatment must finally render the organic expression of the conflicts superfluous. *What is really essential is to loosen psychosomatic ties, to purify the organs from their psychic cathexis, so to speak, and to assure their organic function unaffected by too strong libidinal forces.*

It is difficult to give exact devices for ascertaining when cases with organic symptoms require analysis, and at what moment. In principle, it will be advisable when the organic disease is used as a secondary gain and thereby remains unchanged by treatment. Likewise, it can be—with certain reservations—the method of choice if the disorder is only the expression of a neurosis, i.e., what is termed an "organic neurosis." However, it should be pointed out that organic symptoms often may cease as soon as certain provoking factors are eliminated. But sometimes they disappear also by merely being with the patient, without any active intervention; sometimes only suggestions in one form or another may suffice.

However, that situation is different in organoneurotic disorders where the symptoms are those of a hysteria, a compulsive neurosis, or of a hypochondria. It is true that also in these cases suggestive therapy, beginning with the simplest suggestion up to hypnosis, can be successful insofar as the organic symptom disappears temporarily. But that does not change the neurotic condition nor the need to express it in organic symptoms. If, therefore, neither the patient nor the physician is to be satisfied with a temporary relief from a symptom, but wants the underlying neurosis to be treated—a course which has to be followed anyway if the organic symptoms recur—then psychoanalysis is indicated. In these cases no other therapy can bring about a more satisfactory effect.

A number of diseases have hitherto been considered as belonging entirely to the field of internal medicine because the patient's physical complaints appear sufficiently explained by the objective findings, although they were often accompanied by emotional feelings, especially pain and anxiety, and although the therapeutic results were far from being encouraging. To these disorders belong certain vascular diseases as well as some form of pseudo angina pectoris or of claudicatio intermittens which, despite their known organic bases, still bear some vestige of the inexplicable and the mysterious. Further included here are allergies such as asthma bronchilis and various skin diseases of similar etiology. Finally, a series of spastic disorders such as intestinal colics, gallbladder and bladder colics, etc.

The encouraging therapeutic successes in some cases of these disorders following analytic therapy indicate the necessity for further investigations to obtain more extensive data.

It remains to be determined where the line should be drawn between the task of the internist and that of the analyst as far as those cases are concerned. This will be self-evident if one is aware that purely theoretical psychoanalytic knowledge does not suffice for the evaluation of psychosomatic conditions, but that only the insight into one's own unconscious through being analyzed oneself can give an adequate understanding of the correlation between instinctual drives and bodily behavior. For this reason it is recommended that before applying psychoanalysis to internal medicine, one should be analyzed in order to be protected against his own resistances. In brief, analysis has to be learned like any other technique. And, although intuition and empathy are often of great value in psychotherapy, they are still only presuppositions or supplements for a systematic therapeutic procedure which has often enough been discredited through dilettantism and ignorance to the disadvantage of the patient.

PSYCHOLOGICAL ASPECTS OF MEDICINE

FRANZ ALEXANDER, M.D.
(1939)

When Psychosomatic Medicine first made its appearance in January 1939 Franz Alexander was honored by being asked to write the lead article, "Psychological Aspects of Medicine."

Almost a quarter of a century later, in reading Alexander's paper, we are impressed by the clarity with which he introduced what are now accepted concepts of psychosomatic medicine. We can subscribe to every one of his ideas with one exception, i.e., Alexander's expectation that emotional conflicts like pathological microorganisms differ from each other and in accordance with their specificity affect different internal organs. Is it possible that because of Alexander's medical background, in which there was a specific microorganism for every disease, he used this concept as his model?

In tracing the history of medicine, Alexander pays tribute to Virchow to whom we owe the view that there are "no general diseases, only diseases of the organs and the cells." His "dogma of cellular pathology" was at one and the same time "the greatest accomplishment" only to become later "the greatest obstacle against further development." It took some time to discover that local anatomical changes might be "the result of more general disturbances which develop as the effect of overstress or even emotional factors."

The search for a resolution of the problem "dichotomy of mind and body left us by Descartes" (Alan Gregg) remained on the whole unsuccessful. Psychiatry—the Johnny-come-lately among medical specialties—was able to "introduce a new synthetic aspect into medicine."

However, psychiatry before Freud was in no position to accomplish this. On the contrary, pre-Freudian psychiatry endeavored with the help of the laboratory to discover the cellular pathology of brain tissue responsible for mental illness. When this turned out to be a signal failure, the neurotic and psychotic patients were abandoned altogether: they were sacrificed in the way a limb is amputated to save the rest of the organism.

At this point, Freud entered the stage of medicine. Regardless of what will remain of psychoanalysis as a form of therapy, no historian will fail to see the influence of psychoanalysis on medical thought in general. "Historically viewed, the development of psychosomatic medicine can be considered as one of the first signs of a reaction against the neglect of the fundamental biological fact that the organism is one unit and the function of its parts can only be understood from the point of view of the whole system."

Alexander defines personality "as the expression of the unity of the organism," psychiatry as the study of morbid personality became of necessity "the gateway for the introduction of the synthetic point of view into medicine." Only after psychiatry had discovered that "personality was its main topic," could it accomplish this synthetic function, and this was due primarily to Sigmund Freud.

A similar advance toward synthesis can be seen in the field of non-medical psychology. There, too, as a reaction against the fractionating laboratory methods of the experimental school (Fechner and Weber), Alexander specifically singles out the accomplishments of gestalt psychology (Kohler, Wertheimer, Koffka) in its "clear formulation of the thesis that the whole is not the sum total of its parts...." The unity of the organism is most clearly expressed in the functions of the central nervous system. What we call "personality" is "this integration of all the external and internal affairs of the organism" as the function of "a central government represented by the highest centers of the nervous system." It soon became obvious that "the physiological study of the highest centers of the central nervous system and the psychological study of personality deal with one and the same thing from different points of view." The "psychological" are "the subjective reflections of physiological processes."

Another powerful stimulus for the synthetic point of view came from the discovery and gradual better understanding of the endocrine systems which are governed also from a central regulating system similar to that of the nervous system. There is increasing evidence that "the ductless glands ultimately are also subject to the function of the highest centers of the brain, that is to say, to the psychic life."

Finally, the basic fact that the mind rules over the body could not be overlooked any more. Our whole life consists in the body "aiming at the realization of ideas, wishes, and the satisfaction of subjective feelings." All our emotions are expressed by physiological processes—sorrow by weeping, shame by blushing, etc. All emotions are accompanied by physiological changes, e.g., fear by heart palpitation, despair by deep inspirations and expirations called sighing. These physiological phenomena are the result of complex muscular interactions under the influence of nervous impulses carried to the various muscles and glands. All these nervous impulses arise in certain emotional situations of life in our interaction with other people. "The originating psychological situations can only be understood in terms of psychology, as total responses of the organism to its environment."

The application of these considerations to certain morbid processes of the body led to a new chapter of medicine, so-called psychosomatic medicine. An apparent dichotomy disappears if we understand psychic phenomena as being the subjective aspect of certain bodily (brain) processes.

While under normal conditions the physical changes accompanying emotional situations are of a transient nature, psychoanalytic study of neurotic patients revealed that under the influence of permanent emotional disturbances, chronic disturbances of the body may develop; these changes were first observed in "conversion hysteria" (Freud) in the muscles controlled by will and in the field of sense perception. Whenever emotions become repressed, i.e., excluded from consciousness and thus from overt expressions, a chronic tension results which causes hysterical symptoms.

Emotionally conditioned disturbances of vegetative organs were called "organ neuroses" such as "gastric" or "cardiac neurosis." Another term for these conditions was "functional disturbance," since no morphological change was discernible, yet. The function of the organ was disturbed. Since these disturbances are caused by emotional factors, psychotherapy gained a legitimate entrance into medicine proper, and the patient as a personality became an object of therapy: In these cases of organ neuroses the emotional influence of the physician upon the patient became a main therapeutic factor.

The functional disorders were considered milder as compared to the permanent tissue changes of organic disorders. Gradually, this distinction lost its importance, and the clinician realized that functional disorders of long duration may lead to serious anatomical changes and to the clinical picture of severe organic illness; for example, emotional conflicts may lead first to a "stomach neurosis" and eventually result in an ulcer. These observations have been crystallized in the concept of psychogenic organic disorder: its first phase is the functional disturbance of a vegetative organ, its second phase an organ disease due to irreversible tissue changes. This view of the causation of certain organic disorders meant a remarkable change of traditional concepts.

Up to this time, the symptoms of the disease are explained as the result of pathological tissue changes. The significance of the new concept of psychogenic organic disorders consists in the demonstration of a fundamentally different causation of disease. While formerly every pathological function was explained as the result of pathological structure, now another causal sequence had been clearly recognized, i.e., pathological function as the cause of pathological structure.

At that time, Alexander stated that it was difficult to be certain as to what types of organic diseases followed this etiological pattern. He thought that in addition to peptic ulcer and essential hypertension, some endocrine disturbances might be the result of chronic emotional disturbances, such as toxic goiter and diabetes.

He conjectured that there was much evidence that, like the pathological microorganisms, emotional conflicts are different from each other and are liable, in accordance with these differences, to afflict different internal organs.

To Alexander belongs the credit of being one of the pathfinders in this field. Whereas it is true that subsequent travelers may not utilize the same paths, yet the direction has been indicated.

Reprinted from *Psychosomatic Medicine*, 1:7-18, 1939.

I. Historical Perspective

Once again, the patient as a human being, with his worries, fears, hopes and despairs, as an indivisible whole and not only as the bearer of organs—of a diseased liver or stomach—is becoming the legitimate object of medical interest. In the last two decades increasing attention has been paid to the causative role of emotional factors in disease and a growing psychological orientation manifests itself among physicians. Some sound and conservative clinicians deem this a threat to the so arduously acquired scientific foundations of medicine, and authoritative voices warn the profession against this new "psychologism" as incompatible with medicine as a natural science. They would prefer that medical psychology should remain restricted to the field of medical art, to tact and intuition in handling the patient, as distinct from the scientific procedure of therapy proper, that is based on physics, chemistry, anatomy and physiology.

From a historical perspective, however, this psychological orientation is nothing but a revival of old prescientific views in a new and scientific form. It was not always that the care of the suffering man was divided between the priest and the physician. Once the healing functions, whether mental or physical, were united in one hand. Whatever the explanation of the healing power of the medicine man or of the evangelist or of the holy water of Lourdes might be, there is little doubt that they often had a spectacular curative effect upon the sick, in certain respects even a more fundamental effect than many of our drugs, which we can analyze chemically, and the pharmacological effects of which we know with great precision. This psychological portion of medicine survived only in a rudimentary form as medical art and bedside manner, carefully separated from the scientific aspects of therapy, and is considered mainly as the suggestive, reassuring influence of the physician upon his patient.

Modern scientific medical psychology is but an attempt to place medical art, the psychological effect of the physician upon the patient, on a scientific basis and to make it an integral part of therapy. There is little doubt that much of the therapeutic success of the healing profession, of the medicine man and of the priest as well as of the modern practitioner, has been due to the undefined emotional rapport between physician and patient. This psychological function of the physician, however, was perhaps never more disregarded than in the last century in which medicine became a genuine natural science based on the application of the principles of physics and chemistry to the living organism. The fundamental philosophical postulate of modern medicine is that the body and its function can be understood in terms of physical chemistry, that living organisms are physicochemical machines and the ideal of the physician is to become an engineer of the body. The recognition of psychological forces, a psychological approach to the problems of life and disease, appears as a relapse back to the ignorance of the dark ages in which disease was considered as the work of the evil spirit and therapy was exorcism, the expelling of the demon from the diseased body. It is only natural that the new medicine based on laboratory experiments jealously defended its newly acquired scientific halo against such antiquated mystical concepts as those of psychology. Medicine, this newcomer of the natural sciences, in many respects assumed the typical attitude of the newcomer who wants to make one forget one's low origin by becoming more intolerant, exclusive, and conservative than the genuine aristocrat. Medicine became most intolerant toward everything which might have reminded it of its spiritual and mystical past, at a time when the aristocrat of the natural sciences, its older brother, physics, was undergoing the most profound revolution of its fundamental concepts, questioning even the shibboleth of science, the general validity of determinism.

These remarks, however, are not intended to minimize the accomplishments of the laboratory period in medicine which represents the most brilliant phase of its history. The physicochemical orientation characterized by the precise study of fine details is no doubt responsible for the great progress as displayed by modern bacteriology, surgery, and chemotherapy and pharmacology. It belongs to the paradoxes of historical development that the greater the scientific merits of a method, or scientific principle, the greater will be their retarding influence in a later, more advanced period of development. The inertia of the human mind makes it stick to the ideas and methods which have been proven of great value in the past even though their usefulness has already served its term. The development of the most exact of sciences, physics, is full of such examples. Progress in every field requires a reorientation and the introduction of new principles. These new principles, although actually not always contradictory to the old ones, nevertheless are often rejected and must struggle for their recognition. The scientist in this respect is just as narrow-minded as the man on the street. The same physicochemical orientation of the laboratory era to which medicine owes its greatest accomplishments has become on account of its one-sidedness an obstacle to further development. This new scientific laboratory era of medicine is characterized by its analytic attitude.

Typical of this period was a specialized interest in detailed mechanisms, in the understanding of partial processes. The discovery of finer methods of observation, especially the microscope, disclosed a new microcosm in giving an unprecedented insight into the minute parts of the body. Accordingly, in etiology, in the study of the causes of the diseases, the principal aim became the localization of the disease. Ancient medicine was governed by the humoral theory according to which the fluids of the body were claimed as the carriers of the diseases. The gradual development of the methods of autopsy during the Renaissance made posible a precise study of the details of the human organism and thus led to more realistic but at the same time more localistic etiological concepts. Morgagni, at the end of the eighteenth century, claimed that particular organs such as the heart, the kidney, or the liver, were the seat of the diseases. With the introduction of the microscope, the localization of the disease became even more narrowed down: the cell became the seat of disease.

No one was more responsible for this particularistic concept in medicine than Virchow to whom pathology owes more than to anyone else. He declared that there are no general diseases, only diseases of the organs and of the cells. His great achievements in the field of pathology and his great authority made of cellular pathology a dogma, which has influenced medical thinking up to the present day. Virchow's influence upon etiological thought is the most classical example of the above-mentioned paradox of history. The greatest accomplishments of the past become later the greatest obstacles against further development. The discovery of histological changes in diseased organs by the help of the microscope became the universal pattern for etiology. The search for the causes of diseases long remained limited to attempts to discover local pathological changes in the tissues. The concept that such local anatomical changes are but the immediate cause and themselves might be results of more general disturbances which develop as the effect of faulty functioning, overstress or even emotional factors, had to be discovered later. The less particularistic humoral theory which became discredited when Virchow successfully defeated its last representative, Rokitansky, had to wait for its revival in the form of modern endocrinology.

Few have understood the essence of this phase of medical development better than Stefan Zweig (5), a layman. In his book, *Mental Healers,* he says: "Disease meant now no longer what happens to the whole man but what happens to his organs.... And so the natural and original mission of the physician, the approach to disease as a whole, changes into the smaller task of localizing the ailment and identifying it and ascribing it to an already specific group of diseases.... This unavoidable objectification and technicalization of therapy in the nineteenth century came to an extreme excess because between the physician and the patient became interpolated a third entirely mechanical thing, the apparatus. The penetrating, creative synthesizing grasp of the born physician became less and less necessary for diagnosis."

Not less impressive is the statement of Dr. Alan Gregg (3), a man who views the past and future of medicine from a broad perspective. "The totality that is a human being has been divided for study into parts and systems; one cannot decry the method but one is not obliged to remain satisfied with its results alone. What brings and keeps our several organs and numerous functions in harmony and federation? And what has medicine to say of the facile separation of 'mind' from 'body'? What makes an individual what the word implies—not divided? The need for more knowledge here is of an excruciating obviousness. But more than mere need there is a foreshadowing of changes to come. Psychiatry is astir, neurophysiology is crescent, neurosurgery flourishes, and a star still hangs over the cradle of endocrinology.... Contributions from other fields are to seek from psychology, cultural anthropology, sociology and philosophy as well as from chemistry and physics and internal medicine to resolve the dichotomy of mind and body left us by Descartes."

II. THE ROLE OF MODERN PSYCHIATRY IN THE DEVELOPMENT OF MEDICINE

It was reserved to the most neglected and least developed portion of medicine, to psychiatry, to introduce a new synthetic aspect into medicine. For a long time during the laboratory period, psychiatry remained a rather isolated domain which had little contact with the rest of medicine. It was concerned with the mentally diseased, a field in which the usually accepted methods of medicine proved to be much less productive than in all other fields. The symptomatology of the mental disturbances unpleasantly differed from the disturbances of the body. Psychiatry had to deal with delusions, hallucinations, and the disturbances of the emotional life. These symptoms did not permit even a description in the usual terms of medicine. Inflammation can be described in physical terms: swelling, increased temperature, and definite changes in the cells observable under the microscope. Tuberculosis is diagnosed by definite changes in the afflicted tissues and the presence of well defined micro-organisms. The pathological mental functions, however, had to be described in psychological terms. Since the functions of the mind roughly could be connected with brain functions, the interest turned toward the histological study of the brain tissue of deceased psychotics, and histopathology became the scientific basis of psychiatry. Unfortunately—or perhaps from the point of view of progress, fortunately—in most cases of even severe mental disturbances no constant pathological changes could be discovered in the brain. It was only natural that one hoped for light to come from a further advancement of the knowledge of the cellular physiology of the brain. Even though one could not find gross pathological changes in the brain, one expected that with the progressive refinement of investigative methods one would be able to find that basis of psychological disturbances in the disturbed function of the brain cells. Theoretically, of course, the validity of this expectation is undebatable. A powerful re-enforcement of these hopes came from the discovery of the infectious nature of general paresis. Although there was still a big gap to be bridged between the tissue changes and the psychological symptoms of general paresis, a new hope arose from the understanding of mental disturbances on the basis of pathological anatomy of the brain. However, the next step toward the solution of the mysteries of the diseased mind came from another source, from the psychoanalysis of Sigmund Freud.

We have seen that clinical psychiatry tried to approach the problems of mental disturbances by the help of the microscope, and in this effort became disinterested in the very essence of its own field, in psychological phenomena. The solution of these problems required another type of microscope, a psychological microscope. When medicine, this newest of all natural sciences, developed a definite distaste for the psychological aspect of the living organisms, it naturally transferred this attitude toward psychiatry which out of necessity had to deal with mental phenomena. Physicians felt instinctively that this was the weak spot where the old medieval demonology threatened to creep in again into medicine. Psychiatry with its psychological problems became the stepchild of medicine and was not considered as equal to the other fields but rather a foreign body threatening the purity of scientific medicine which has fully adopted the methods of physics and chemistry. Psychiatrists, in self-defense, made strenuous efforts to make the rest of their colleagues accept them as equals and overemphasized their non-psychological attitude. They did not want to be considered as mental healers but as physicians like the other specialists, engineers of the body. They refused even to take cognizance of the existence of psychic problems. Psychological symptoms were only considered insofar as they served for the classification of certain diseases as in the system of Kraepelin, but no attempt was made to study their meaning.

Life, however, is stronger than theories. There was the large number of mental sufferers who did not profit from the laboratory studies of the scientists and wanted help. The severe cases, the psychotics, were considered generally beyond help. Being often apathetic and deeply submerged in their ailment, they did not rebel against this disregard of their needs. But the even vaster group of milder cases, the psychoneurotics, who constitute probably the majority of all human sufferers, wanted help. One of the saddest anomalies of medical history developed. The physician whom these patients forced to listen to their psychological complaints, who was unable to understand and to handle these symptoms with his one-sided laboratory equipment, began to dislike this type of neurotic patient. In order to hide his ignorance he refused to consider them as really sick and accused them of malingering. In order to defend their scientific aura, physicians had developed a distaste for psychological facts and now they turned this distaste against their psychoneurotic patients. The psychoneurotic patient was regarded as a nuisance, and felt as a living accusation against the inadequacy of prevailing methods and dogmas.

The hysterical patient played a cruel joke on his physician, indeed. He developed nervous symptoms which seemingly did not follow the laws of anatomy and physiology. He developed bodily symptoms of the kind which did not correspond to the distribution of the nerves but to morbid ideas, thus demonstrating the superiority of the "mind" over the "body." In response, the physician became impatient with the nervous sufferer and stubbornly refused to deal with his symptoms on a psychological level.

This was the situation in which the young Freud, influenced by Charcot's hypnosis experiments, decided to earn his living by giving real help to the psychoneurotic. For this purpose he felt he must understand the nature of the neuroses. The end results of this endeavour were known as the psychoanalytic therapy, together with a new contribution to the knowledge of man.

III. The Contributions of Psychoanalysis, Neurology, and Endocrinology

I am not concerned here with the details of the psychoanalytic theory or with the technique of psychoanalytic therapy. There exists a vast scientific and popular literature of this field both defending and attacking this new approach to the problem of life and disease. How much of the original concepts will survive, be modified or abandoned, must be left for the future. Psychoanalysis as a theory of personality reaches beyond the realm of medicine into all fields which are concerned with human behavior—the field of anthropology, social sciences, and the problem of education. As a therapy of nervous disorders, it has its definite limitations as all forms of therapy do. Its influence on medical thought in general, however, can be well defined already.

Historically viewed, the development of psychoanalysis can be considered as one of the first signs of a reaction against the one-sided analytical development of medicine in the second half of the nineteenth century, against the specialized interest in detailed mechanisms, against the neglect of the fundamental biological fact that the organism is one unit and the function of its parts can only be understood from the point of view of the whole system. The laboratory approach to the living organism disclosed an incredible collection of more or less disconnected details, and this inevitably led to a loss of perspective. The fact that the organism is a most ingenious mechanism in which every part co-operates for definite purposes was not only neglected, but defamed as an unsound teleological point of view. It was claimed that the organism develops through certain natural causes but not for a certain purpose. A man-made machine, of course, can be understood on a teleological basis; the human mind creates it for a certain definite purpose. But man was not created by a supreme intelligence—this was just the mythological concept from which modern biology fled, insisting that the animal body should not be understood on a teleological but on a causal and mechanistic basis. As soon, however, as medicine, *nolens volens*, turned toward the problem of the diseased mind, this particularistic attitude—at least in this field—had to be abandoned. In what we call personality, the fact that the organism is an intelligibly co-ordinated unit comes to such striking expression that it cannot be overlooked. William White (4) expressed this fact in simple terms: "The answer to the question, What is the function of the stomach? is digestion, which is but a small part of the activity of the total organism and only indirectly, though of course importantly, related to many of its other functions. But if we undertake to answer the question, What is the man doing? we reply in terms of the total organism by saying, for example, that he is walking down the street or running a foot race or going to the theater or studying medicine or what not.... If mind is the expression of a total reaction in distinction from a partial reaction, then every living organism must be credited with mental, that is, total types of response.... What we know as mind in all its present infinite complexity is the culmination of a type of response to the living organism that is historically as old as the bodily types of response with which we are more familiar." Personality thus can be defined as the expression of the unity of the organism. As a machine can be only understood from its function and purpose, the understanding of the synthetic unit which we call body can be only fully understood from the point of view of the personality, to the aims and purposes of which, in the last analysis, all parts of the body are subjected in an intelligible co-ordination.

Psychiatry as the study of morbid personality therefore necessarily was to become the gateway for the introduction of the synthetic point of view into medicine. But psychiatry could only accomplish this function after it had discovered the personality as its main topic, and this was the accomplishment of Sigmund Freud. Psychoanalysis consists in the precise detailed study of the development and functions of the personality. Although somewhat paradoxically the expression, "psychoanalysis" contains the word, "analysis" yet its historical significance consists in its synthetic influence.

Psychoanalysis, however, was not the only scientific movement toward synthesis. The development of scientific methods in all fields during the last century resulted in an eager collection of data. Discovery of new facts became the highest goal; their interpretation and correlation in the form of synthetic concepts was looked upon with suspicion as unsound speculation or philosophy in contrast to science. As a reaction to this excessively analytic orientation, a strong desire for synthesis appeared as a general trend of the last decade.

Thus, for example, this new synthetic trend can also be clearly observed in nonmedical psychology. Here too the tradition of the nineteenth century was the analytic approach. After the introduction into psychology of the experimental method by Fechner and Weber, psychological laboratories sprung up in which now the human mind was dissected into its parts. There developed a psychology of vision, of hearing, of the tactile sense, of memory, of volition. But the experimental psychologist never even tried to understand the interrelationships of all these different mental faculties and their integration which we call the human personality. Kohler's, Wertheimer's and Koffka's gestalt psychology can be regarded as a reaction against this particularistic analytic orientation. Probably the most important accomplishment of these gestalt psychologists has been the clear formulation of the thesis that the whole is not the sum total of its parts but something different from them and that from the study of the parts alone, the whole system never can be understood. Just the opposite is true; the parts can be thoroughly understood only after the meaning of the whole has been discovered.

In medicine, a similar development took place. The advances in the field of neurology paved the way for a more comprehensive understanding of the relationships between the parts of the body. It became more and more evident that in the last analysis all parts of the body directly or indirectly are connected with a central governing system and are under the control of this central organ. Not only the voluntary muscles, but all the vegetative organs, via the so-called autonomic or vegetative nervous system, are connected with the highest centers of the nervous system. The unity of the organism is most clearly expressed in the functions of the central nervous system. The central nervous system has both the function of the regulation of the internal vegetative processes of the organism and also the regulation of its external affairs, its relations to the environment. The integration of all the external and internal affairs of the organism is the function of a central government represented by the highest centers of the nervous system which in human beings we call the personality. In fact it became obvious that the physiological study of the highest centers of the central nervous system and the psychological study of personality deal with one and the same thing from different points of view. Whereas physiology approaches the functions of the central nervous system in terms of space and time, psychology approaches it in the terms of those subjective phenomena which we call psychological and they are the subjective reflections of physiological processes.

Another stimulus for the synthetic point of view came from the discovery of the ductless glands, a further step toward the understanding of the extremely complicated interrelationships between the different vegetative functions of the organism. The system of the ductless glands can be considered also as a central regulating system similar to that of the nervous system: whereas the governing influence of the central nervous system takes place through the conduction of regulating nervous impulses via the peripheral nerve trunks to the different parts of the body, the chemical control of the ductless glands takes place through the conduction by the blood stream of certain chemical substances.

Recently more and more evidence is emerging that probably the functions of the ductless glands ultimately are also subject to the function of the highest centers of the brain, that is to say, to the psychic life.

These physiological discoveries gave us an insight into the detailed mechanism of the fundamental details of how the mind rules the body. The fact that the mind rules over the body, no matter how much it was neglected by biology and medicine, is the most fundamental fact which we know about the process of life. It is the fact which we observe continuously during all of our life. From the moment when we awaken every morning on, our whole life consists in carrying out voluntary movements aimed at the realization of certain ideas, wishes, the satisfaction of subjective feelings such as thirst and hunger. Our body, this complicated machine, carries out most complex and refined motor activity under the influence of such psychological phenomena as ideas and wishes. The most human of all bodily functions, speech, is nothing but the expression of ideas through a refined musical instrument, our vocal apparatus. All our emotions we express by physiological processes: sorrows, by weeping; amusement, by laughter; and shame, by blushing. All emotions are accompanied by physiological changes: fear by heart palpitation; anger by increased heart activity, elevation of blood pressure, and a change in carbohydrate metabolism; despair, by a deep inspiration and expiration called sighing. All these physiological phenomena are the results of complex muscular interaction under the influence of nervous impulses carried to the expressive muscles of the face and to the diaphragm in laughter, to the lacrimal glands in weeping, to the heart in fear, and to the adrenal glands and to the vascular system in rage. All these nervous impulses arise in certain emotional situations during our life in our interaction with other people. The originating psychological situations can only be understood in terms of psychology, as total responses of the organism to its environment.

IV. THE CONCEPT OF PSYCHOSOMATIC MEDICINE: CONVERSION HYSTERIA, ORGAN NEUROSIS, AND PSYCHOGENIC ORGANIC DISTURBANCE

The application of these considerations to certain morbid processes of the body led gradually to a new chapter of medicine, to "Psychosomatic Medicine." This expression maybe is not most fortunate because it may imply a dichotomy between psyche and body (soma). If however we understand psychic phenomena as nothing but the subjective aspect of certain bodily (brain) processes this dichotomy disappears.

These psychosomatic studies in combination with psychoanalytic investigations meant an entirely new approach to the study of the causes of diseases. As has been already mentioned, the fact that acute emotions have an influence on body functions belongs to the most common everyday experience. To every emotional situation there corresponds a specific syndrome of physical changes, psychosomatic responses, such as laughter, weeping, blushing, changes in the heart rate, respiration, etc. Because, however, these psychomotor processes belong to our normal life and have no ill effects, medicine, until recently, paid little attention to their finer investigation. These changes in the body as reactions to acute emotions are of a passing nature. After the emotion disappears the corresponding physiological processes, weeping or laughing or heart palpitation, or elevation of blood pressure, also disappear and the body again returns to its equilibrium.

The psychoanalytic study of neurotic patients revealed, however, that under the influence of permanent emotional disturbances, chronic disturbances of the body may develop. At first such chronic bodily changes under the influence of emotion were observed in hysterical patients. Freud introduced the concept of "conversion hysteria" in which bodily symptoms develop from chronic emotional conflicts. These changes were first observed in the muscles controlled by the will and in the field of sense perceptions. One of the most important discoveries of Freud was that whenever emotions cannot be expressed and relieved through normal channels through voluntary activity they may become the source of chronic psychic or physical disorders. Whenever emotions on account of psychic conflicts become repressed, that is to say, become excluded from consciousness and thus from normal expression, they sustain a chronic tension which is the cause of the hysterical symptoms of the body.

Also, emotionally conditioned disturbances of the internal vegetative organs which are not controlled by conscious voluntary impulses, such as the stomach or the heart, have been observed. Such observations came not from psychiatrists, but from specialists in the field of internal diseases, and led to the concept of "organ neurosis." These are disturbances of the internal vegetative organs caused by nerve impulses, the ultimate origin of which are emotional processes most probably localized in the cortical and subcortical centers of the brain. At first the neurotic or functional disturbances of the stomach, the bowels, and of the cardiovascular system became well known under the name of gastric, intestinal, or cardiac neuroses. Another term often used for this type of disorder is "functional disturbance," referring to the fact that in such cases, even the finest study of the tissues does not reveal any morphological changes discernible by the microscope. In such cases the anatomical structure of the organ is not changed, only the co-ordination and the intensity of the organ functions are disturbed. Such disturbances are considered as less serious because they are reversible, in contrast to those diseases in which the tissues show definite pathological alterations often constituting irreversible damages. Since these functional disturbances are caused by emotional factors, psychotherapy thus gained a legitimate entrance into medicine proper and could not be restricted any longer exclusively to the field of psychiatry. The chronic emotional conflicts of the patient, the cause of the trouble, had to be eliminated by psychological treatment. Since these emotional conflicts arose during the life of the patient in his relationship with other human beings, the patient as a personality became an object of therapy. This is the avenue in which the emotional influence of the doctor upon the patient, medical art, gained entrance into scientific medicine and could not any longer be considered an appendage of therapy, so to speak a last artistic touch in the therapeutic activity of the physician, which in its essence was considered an entirely different, thoroughly scientific procedure. In these cases of organ neuroses the emotional influence of the physician upon the patient became the main therapeutic factor.

The significance of the psychotherapeutic function of the physician, however, at this phase of development remained restricted to these functional cases considered generally as milder disturbances in contrast to the more serious genuine organic disorders based on permanent tissue changes. Of course in such organic cases the emotional state of the patient had for a long time been recognized as an important issue, yet a real causal connection between psychic factors and genuine organic disturbances had not been generally recognized. Gradually, however, it became more and more evident that nature does not know such strict distinctions as "functional" versus "organic." More and more clinicians began to suspect that functional disorders of long duration gradually may lead to serious genuine organic disorders based on visible anatomical changes. A few instances of this kind of disorders have been known for a long time, for example that the hyperactivity of the heart may lead to hypertrophy of the heart muscles or that the hysterical paralysis of a limb may lead, due to inactivity, to certain degenerative changes in the muscles. One had to reckon therefore with the possibility that a functional disturbance of long duration of any organ may lead finally to definite anatomical changes and to the clinical picture of severe organic illness. Intensive psychological and somatic studies of cases of peptic ulcers brought weighty evidence for the assumption that emotional conflicts of long duration may lead as a first step to a stomach neurosis which in time may result in an ulcer. There are also indications that emotional conflicts of another kind may cause continued fluctuations of the blood pressure which constitutes an overtaxation of the vascular system. This functional phase of fluctuating blood pressure in time may cause organic vascular changes and, as an effect of these changes, a continued irreversible malignant form of hypertension.

These observations have been crystallized in the concept of "psychogenic organic disorder." These disorders, according to this view, develop in two phases. The first phase consists of a functional disturbance of a vegetative organ, caused by a chronic emotional disturbance called psychoneurosis. In the second phase, the chronic functional disturbance leads in time, gradually, to irreversible tissue changes, to an organic disease.

V. Progress in Etiological Thought

This view of the causation of certain organic disorders means a remarkable change of traditional concepts. The traditional etiological view, as has been described before, was a localistic one essentially based on Virchow's cellular pathology. The symptoms of the disease are explained by morphological changes in the organs. As to the origin of these morphological changes, different factors have been generally accepted. For a long period after Pasteur's and Koch's discovery of pathogenic micro-organisms, the infectious origin of the pathological tissue changes was in the center of research. It was found that the specific diseases are caused by specific micro-organisms according to the point of their attack in the different parts of the body. In these cases the causal chain is: entrance of a specific micro-organism in the body, the dissemination of these organisms within the body through the blood and lymph circulation and further development of the micro-organism in different parts of the body, destroying the normal structure and hence the normal functioning of the cells. This etiological theory could be validated through the experimental introduction of micro-organisms into animals reproducing tissue changes similar to those observed in human beings. This one well-defined mechanism soon became the model for all etiological research.

Apart from micro-organisms, other external factors have been discovered as responsible for certain tissue changes—factors such as mechanical, thermic, or chemical influences, the action of which followed similar principles. For example, the inhalation of certain small dust particles by industrial workers and miners became another well-established etiological process. Another generally accepted pathogenic factor is the natural aging process of the organism, explaining such widespread disturbances as the sclerosis of the arteries in later life.

In all these cases the symptoms of the disease are explained as the result of pathological tissue changes which can be traced back to certain external, mechanical, chemical or infectious factors, or to the natural aging process. The significance of the new concepts of psychogenic organic disorders consists in the demonstration of a fundamentally different causation of disease. In these cases the pathological anatomical changes are the secondary results of disturbed function and the disturbed function itself is the result of chronic emotional conflicts. If formerly every pathological function was explained as the result of pathological structure, now another causal sequence has been clearly recognized: pathological function as the cause of pathological structure. Although this etiological view is not entirely novel—yet also explicitly formulated—many clinicians who are raised in the tradition of

Virchow's principle and are still under the impressive influence of the simple and experimentally validated etiological discoveries of bacteriology, are not inclined to accept it without reservations. Usually, whenever a functional disorder is described, it is accepted with some doubt and the hope is expressed that further, more precise histological studies will finally disclose tissue changes. The modern clinician is inclined to fall back upon the well-proven classical concept that disturbed function is the result of a changed morphological substratum.

So, for example, von Bergmann (1), who in 1913 still claimed that peptic ulcers are probably the results of a chronic gastric neurosis caused by emotional factors, fourteen years later felt the necessity to revise his views, return to a more conservative attitude and to recommend great reservation toward the diagnosis of an "organ neurosis" (2). He expressed his belief that in most such cases further research will disclose organic causes. Only slowly can this new concept overcome the traditional views, although it is not in the least contradictory to them. It only shows a different causal sequence in the development of certain diseases, changed function leading to tissue changes in contrast to the opposite sequence, when disturbed function is the result of structural changes.

Previously, the scientific credo in medicine was that further finer histological studies will reveal an anatomical basis of all so-called functional disturbances; today we feel without questioning the soundness of this principle that in many cases a thorough investigation of a life history might reveal the functional beginnings of truly organic disturbances. In these early phases the disturbance of function has not produced as yet necessarily histologically discernible organic changes. The resistance against this concept is based on the erroneous dogma that disturbed function is always the result of disturbed structure and on the disregard of the opposite causal sequence.

At present it is difficult to foresee what types of organic disease follow this etiological scheme. It is most probable that in the great chapter of medicine which might be called "disorders of unknown origin," many will fall under this category. Some types of peptic ulcers and of essential hypertension probably belong to this group. Since the functions of the ductless glands are partially under psychic control—for example, the adrenal system is influenced by rage—it is probable that many endocrine disturbances in the last analysis will turn out to be the results of chronic emotional disturbances. This is clearly indicated in cases of toxic goiter, the beginning of which often can be traced back to emotional traumata. Furthermore, the influence of emotions on carbohydrate metabolism makes it possible that in the development of diabetes emotional factors may play an important causative role.

Essentially this functional theory of organic disorders is nothing but the recognition, apart from external causative factors, of internal causes of diseases. In other words, many chronic disturbances are not caused by external, mechanical, chemical factors or by micro-organisms, but by the continuous functional stress arising during the everyday life of the organism in its struggle for existence. All those emotional conflicts which psychoanalysis has recognized as the basis of psychoneuroses, and recently also as the ultimate cause of certain functional and organic disorders, arise during our daily life in the social contact with the environment. Continuous fears, aggressions, wishes, if repressed, result in permanent chronic emotional tensions which disturb the functions of the vegetative organs. Many emotions due to the complications of our social life cannot be freely expressed and relieved, through voluntary activities, but remain repressed and then are diverted into wrong channels: Instead of being expressed in voluntary innervations, they influence the internal vegetative functions such as digestion, respiration, or circulation. As countries thwarted in their external political ambitions often show as a result internal social upheavals, also the human organism, if its normal relation to the external environment is disturbed, shows a disturbance of its internal politics, of its vegetative functions.

There is much evidence to show that just as the pathological microorganisms are specific and have a specific affinity to certain organs, so also the emotional conflicts are different from each other and are liable in accordance with these differences to afflict different internal organs. Inhibited rage seems to have a specific relationship to the cardiovascular system; dependent help-seeking tendencies, as recent psychoanalytic studies show, seem to have a specific relationship to the functions of nutrition. Again a different and specific conflict between sexual wishes and dependent tendencies seems to have a specific influence upon respiratory disturbances. The increasing knowledge of the relations of emotions to normal and disturbed body functions requires that for the modern physician emotional conflicts should become just as real and tangible issues as visible micro-organisms. The main contribution of psychoanalysis to medicine was to add to the optical microscope a psychological microscope, a psychological technique by which the emotional life of the patients can be subjected to a detailed scrutiny.

This psychological approach to the problems of life and disease brings the internal body processes into a synthetic unit with the individual's external relations to his social environment. It gives a scientific basis to such empirical everyday observations as that a patient often shows marvelous recovery if he is removed from his family environment or if he interrupts his everyday occupation, and thus is relieved from those emotional conflicts which arise from family life or professional activity. The detailed knowledge of the relation of emotional life and body processes extends the function of the physician: the physical and mental care of the patient can again be united in one hand. The division of the healing profession between religion and medicine (the "lay analyst" is the last residue of this division) has been an artificial division based on insufficient knowledge of the functions of the body and personality in their mutual interrelation.

REFERENCES

1. Bergmann, G. von: Ulcus duodeni und vegetatives Nervensystem. *Berliner Klin. Wschr.,* Vol. 50, 1913.
2. Bergmann, G. von: Zum Abbau der Organ Neurosen als Folge interner Diagnostik. *Deut. med. Wschr.,* Leipzig, Vol. 53, No. 49, 1927.
3. Gregg, A.: The Future of Medicine. *Harvard Medical Alumni Bulletin,* Cambridge, October, 1936.
4. White, W. A.: The Meaning of Disease. Baltimore: Williams & Wilkins, 1926, pp. 38-40.
5. Zweig, S.: *Die Heilung durch den Geist.* (*Mental Healers.*) Leipzig: Inselverlag, 1931.

PSYCHOGENICITY

THE MOUNT SINAI SEMINAR GROUP

The problem of psychogenicity and the related problem of etiology still remain in an unclear state. It would be of value, therefore, to discuss the historical evolution of the concept of psychogenicity. In the last century, there was at least partial acceptance of the belief that some mental disturbances are essentially nonorganic in etiology. This referred largely to the psychoses. The etiological factors in the neuroses were only superficially studied prior to Freud.

In common usage, "psychogenic" implies etiology of disease. However, the idea of psychogenicity should not really be limited to disease. As stated in Klemperer's paper,[1] in another connection referring to Virchow, "In repeated variations he has expressed his belief that disease is life handicapped by various external and internal factors." Furthermore, the difference between diseased and normal may only be a quantitative one.

Psychogenic should refer to the psychic aspect of function, i.e., that component which is mediated through the mind. Ideation, in its broadest sense, once experienced, is never lost. It maintains its psychic reality and is thus a potential factor of influence. The psychic component is present as part of function, whether normal or abnormal. The psychic factor as a stimulus in itself is of the same order as any other stimulus and can come into play in a stimulus-response situation. The psychic factor includes any component of function, conscious, preconscious, or unconscious, which is mediated through the mind.

---

[1] *This Volume*, p. 42.

This would include perceptions; apperceptions; ideation, verbal and nonverbal; feelings, etc. Each psychic component has its own genetic history, but nevertheless it may act at any given moment as a stimulus in a stimulus-response situation. The psychoanalytic hypothesis maintains that all mental phenomena are based on an organic substrate and that the instinctual or innate forces supply the motor power to mental activity. Hartmann, E. Kris, and Loewenstein have attempted to clarify this hypothesis by differentiating some of the energy used for autonomous ego functions as desexualized and deaggressivized.

The term, "psychoneurosis," for instance, is deeply imbedded in present-day psychiatry, and it is of interest to note that Dubois, only at the beginning of this century, was credited with its introduction and emphasis on psychogenicity, although Freud, in 1898, had already used the term psychoneurosis.

In short, when pathological anatomy discovers a lesion, a focus of inflammation, a hemorrhage, a thrombosis, and when chemical analysis discloses a condition of intoxication, we no longer speak of neuroses, even though the symptoms might have been essentially "nervous." We thus recognize the first cause of the clinical syndrome in the various somatic affections, syphilis, tuberculosis, arteriosclerosis, alcoholic intoxication, uremia, etc. These conditions do not exist in the affections which we *always* call neuroses, or, as I propose to do, *psychoneuroses*, even when we succeed in revealing the cellular changes which have produced the nervous or mental trouble. Just here we find ourselves face to face with a fundamental factor: *the influence of the mind and of mental representations*. The affections of psychic life are no longer simply secondary and determined by a primary change of cerebral tissue, as in general paralysis and other diseases of the brain. The source of the trouble is, on the contrary, often psychic; it is the *ideation* which causes or harbors functional disorders. One could boldly classify such neuroses along with the insanities and designate them under the name of *psychoses*. Theoretically I do not hesitate to say that nervousness in all its forms is a psychosis. But practically this appellation would have great drawbacks. First of all, it hurts the feelings of the neuropaths. We accept the term *nervous disease* without any sense of shame, but we do not like to be characterized as psychopaths. It is good, however, to separate from the confirmed psychoses those mild psychoses which, as we shall see later, differ but very slightly from the normal state. The former, the vesanias or insanities, call forth a much more unfavorable prognosis, and their treatment more often demands a sojourn in the institutions of the insane [2].

In addition to the above, Dubois also emphasized that *"Nervousness is a disease preeminently psychic, and a psychic disease needs psychic treatment."* This is a statement that might by some be considered trite, and by others a matter of great controversy.

It is important to emphasize that the problem of psychosomatic interrelationships was in the forefront of Freud's thinking from the very beginning. Both he and Ferenczi formulated aspects of this problem in many ways. Early in the twentieth century, both made fundamental contributions in this area which, with but little reformulation and paraphrasing, may very well represent the most modern approach.

Hinsie and Shatzky (13) define the psyche or mind as one of the organs of the individual "with its own form and function, its embryology, gross and microscopic anatomy, physiology and pathology.... Like the cardiovascular system it reaches all parts of the body; it also serves to adjust the total organism to the needs and demands of the environment." Mental functions are visualized in terms of the central nervous system. The mind as an organ implies a development above the simple reflex arc stage, i.e., mechanisms which oppose and regulate the response to the stimulus. This interaction and counteraction of forces forms a dynamic system with a genetic background.

Freud tried to chart the psyche by a concept of levels, i.e., topographically. He distinguished three levels functioning as systems: conscious, preconscious, and unconscious. This was a dynamic approach visualizing interacting systems. We believe that psychosomatic phenomena in their totality can be studied comprehensively only if one accepts a dynamic unconscious in this sense. Later Freud added a metapsychological schema (structural classification) of the mind centering around sources of energy and regulation of related spheres of function: the id (source of energy), the ego (implementing mechanism), and the superego (critical function). Both of these schematizations are used as guideposts in the investigation of psychic phenomena.

Freud offered or developed the libido theory to explain psychic life, normal and abnormal. The conception was analogous to and modeled after electrodynamics or hydrodynamics. Freud (7) thought originally that sexual energy when repressed can flow from its normal outlet into other organs which become the foci of symptoms. "We can apply this hypothesis... in the same sense as the physicist employs the conception of a fluid electric current [p. 75]." It is in this fashion that blocked energy was transformed into bodily expression, both in conversion hysteria and in the actual neurosis. In contrast, in nonsomatic illness (e.g., obsessions or phobias) energy was transformed from intolerable ideas to lesser or insignificant ones. Energy not bound to a symptom was converted into anxiety.

It has been restated recently that basically Freud's psychoanalytic thinking is biologically based and body-bound. Freud traced the motor force of psychic life to its biological source, i.e., instincts. However, as Ferenczi has stated, he had to conclude that psychic life ultimately was accessible only through introspective methods and to insist that facts obtained by subjective methods have psychic reality. Interpretation of observed behavior as a response to psychic stimuli can ultimately be validated only by the communications of the subject. Psychoanalytic as well as physiological knowledge had not reached a point of development to make it possible to relate psychiatric phenomena within a framework of neurophysiology. Still, psychoanalysis could be used as a research instrument to elucidate biological problems.

In the formation of a conversion symptom like blindness, Freud conceived of the latter as being the result of an autosuggested idea in the unconscious not to see which excludes the ability to see from consciousness. The autosuggestion creates the condition (8). This is quite different from Janet's theory of dissociation which assumes an incapacity for synthesis as the basis for the loss of a specific function. In Janet's (14) own words he states the following.

We then arrive at another group of definitions in which I range mine. They are definitions, in my opinion, more profound, into which enter the phenomena of *dissociation of consciousness,* such as is observed in all hysterical disturbances. Suggestion itself is but a case of this dissociation of consciousness. There are many others beside the one in somnambulisms, in automatic words, in emotional attacks, in all the functional paralyses. Many authors, Gurney, Myers, Laurent, Breuer and Freud, Benedict, Oppenheim, Jolly, Pick, Morton Prince, have thought like me that a place should be made for the disposition of somnambulism. Was not the somnambulic attack for us the type of hysterical accidents in 1889? 'The disposition to this dissociation and, at the same time, the formation of states of consciousness, which we propose to collect under the name of hypnoid states, constitute the fundamental phenomenon of this neurosis,' said MM. Breuer and Freud of Vienna in 1893.

The point which seems to me to be the most delicate in this definition is to indicate to what depth this dissociation reaches. In reality we might say that dementias themselves are dissociations of thought and of the motor functions. We must remember that, in hysteria, the functions do not dissolve entirely, that they continue to subsist emancipated with their systematization. What is dissolved is personality, the system of grouping of the different functions around the same personality. I maintain to this day that, if hysteria is a mental malady, it is not a mental malady like any other, impairing the social sentiments or destroying the constitution of ideas. It is a malady of the *personal synthesis,* and I will take up again, very slightly modified, the formula I have already presented. *Hysteria is a form of mental depression characterized by the retraction of the field of personal consciousness and a tendency to the dissociation and emancipation of the systems of ideas and functions that constitute personality* [pp. 331-332].

Freud's dynamic hypothesis postulates that the loss of the conscious function of vision is brought about in the service of repression of opposed instinctual drives and thus formulates one of the basic psychoanalytic concepts, namely that of conflict. But the loss of vision is not limited to the repressed. It includes all vision as though the eye had become the instrument of the repressed impulse. The total loss of function also involves the idea of talion and punishment. "When an organ which serves two purposes overplays its erotogenic part, it is in general to be expected that this will not occur without alterations in its response to stimulation and in innervation, which will be manifested as disturbances of the organ in its function as servant of the ego." Freud suspected an actual change in the organ involved or misused. "An organ which ordinarily serves the purpose of sensorial perception presenting as a result of the exaggeration of its erotogenic role precisely the behavior of a genital, we shall even suspect that there are toxic modifications as well in that organ." Freud thus early tried to visualize speculatively what took place in the part of the soma affected by psychic stimulus.

In his paper on "Psychogenic Visual Disturbances," Freud (8) includes in "somatic compliance" the idea that some particular constitutional conditions predispose the organs "to overdo their erotogenic part and thus provoke repression of the impulse."

From psychoanalysis there branches out another line of thought conducting to organic research. We may ask ourselves whether the suppression of the sexual component-instincts induced by environmental influences suffices in itself to set up functional disturbances of the organs, or whether there must not be some particular constitutional conditions which predispose the organs to overdo their erotogenic part, and thus provoke repression of the impulse. These conditions we should necessarily regard as the part played by the constitution in the tendency to disease when considering psychogenic and neurotic disturbances. This would represent that factor which, in hysteria, I have already designated as the "somatic compliance" of the organs.

In his paper on "Types of Neurotic Nosogenesis," Freud (9) concludes that the cause of an outbreak of a neurosis should be traced to a definite mental situation, which can be brought into being in different ways by external and internal factors.

There still remains a few words to be said about the relation of these "types" to clinical experience. When I review the number of patients with whose analysis I am at this moment occupied, I must admit that none of them represents any of the four types in its pure form. Instead, I find in each an element of frustration operating along with a certain degree of incapacity for adaptation to reality; the standpoint of inhibition in development, which of course coincides with a tenacity of fixations, is to be reckoned with in all of them; and the significance of the quantity of libido we can never, as was set forth above, afford to overlook. Indeed, it is my experience that in several of these patients the illness has been manifested in accesses, between which there were intervals of health, and that every one of these accesses was to be traced to a different type of exciting cause. The formulation of these four types has therefore no great theoretical value; they are merely different paths by which a definite pathogenic constellation in the mental economy may be achieved—I refer to a damming-up of the libido which the ego is not able to master with the means at its disposal without some damage. The situation itself, however, becomes pathogenic only as a result of a quantitative factor; it is in no way a novelty in the mental economy, nor is it created by the advent of a so-called "cause of illness."

A certain practical importance may readily be granted to these types of falling ill. Indeed, in individual cases they may be observed in pure form; we should not have been made aware of the third and fourth types if they did not comprise the sole exciting causes of onset in some persons. The first type reveals to us the extraordinarily powerful influence of the outer world; the second that, no less significant, of the peculiarities of the individual who opposes himself to that influence. Pathology could never master the problem of the outbreak of illness in the neurotic so long as it was occupied merely with deciding whether these affections were of an endogenous or an exogenous nature. To all the experience which points to the significance of abstinence (in the broadest sense) as an exciting cause, pathology then necessarily objected that other persons suffered a similar fate without falling ill. But if it elected to lay emphasis upon individual peculiarities as essential in sickness or health, it was obliged to bow to the objection that persons with such peculiarities could permanently retain their health provided only that they could preserve their peculiarity. Psychoanalysis warns us to abandon the unfruitful antithesis of external and internal factors, of fate and constitution, and has taught us regularly to discover the cause of an outbreak of neurosis in a definite mental situation, which can be brought into being in different ways.

The parallelism between Meyer and Freud in this instance is striking.

Sandor Ferenczi (3) investigated those neuroses that supervene upon organic illness or injury, and pinpointed the importance of the antecedent history of the locality involved. He found that in "very many cases the libido that is withdrawn from the outer world is directed, not toward the whole ego, but chiefly to the diseased or injured organ, and evokes symptoms at the injured or diseased area that must be referred to as a local increase of libido." For example, dental disturbances may lead to oral-erotic and cannibalistic fantasies with secondary influence on the psychosexual attitude in that area. Clinically, whooping cough may be followed by nervous coughing which persists in spite of recovery from the infective process. Ferenczi called these conditions pathoneuroses to distinguish them from sexual neuroses, where the disturbance of libido is the primary factor, and the organic disturbance, the secondary factor (hysterical blindness). He stressed that injury or disease to erotogenic zones is more likely to be accompanied by far-reaching disturbances of libido.

Ferenczi also believed that in the genitalization of a part of the body, a periodically heightened hyperemia, edema and turgescence accompanied by corresponding nervous excitation take place. To differentiate further, he states, "But if the ego defends itself against this localized increase of libido by means of a repression, then an hysterical, or if there is complete identification, a narcissistic patho-neurosis, or possibly a simple disease-narcissism, may be the result of the injury or illness" (3, p. 88). This demonstrates a difficulty in the separation of the patho-neuroses from the more purely hysterical conditions.

In 1919, in a paper on "The Phenomena of Hysterical Materializations" (4), Ferenczi again attempts to bridge the "mysterious leap from mental to bodily" manifestations (Freud, 10). Conversion hysteria genitalizes those parts of the body in which the symptoms are manifested. There is also a regression to the stage of development where adaptation is achieved not by a modification of the external world, but of one's own body.

The Unconscious will of the hysteric brings about motor manifestations, changes in the circulation of the blood and glandular function, in the nourishment of tissues, such as the conscious will of the non-hysteric cannot achieve. The smooth musculature of the alimentary canal, of the bronchi, the tear and sweat glands, the nasal erectile tissue, etc., are at the disposition of the hysteric. He can bring about individual innervations, for instance, of the musculature of the eyes and Adam's apple, that are impossible for healthy persons. His capacity for manifesting local hemorrhages, blisters, and cutaneous and mucous swellings, though certainly rarer, is also well known. The primitive vital processes which hysteria seems to fall back upon consists of body changes which are quite natural and habitual, although when they are psychogenic they impress one as supernormal. The movement of the smooth muscle fibres, of the vascular walls, the functioning of the glands, the entire process of tissue nourishment are regulated infrapsychically. In hysteria all these physiological mechanisms are at the disposal of unconscious wish-impulses so that by a complete reversal of the normal path of excitation a purely psychic process can come to expression in a physiological body change [4].

Ferenczi believes that in globus hystericus "the corresponding contractions of the circular and longitudinal musculature of the esophagus produce not only the parasthesia of a foreign body, but that a kind of foreign body, a lump, really is brought about." The hysteric thus creates a physical alteration to which he gives an illusory misinterpretation. This constitutes the *materialization phenomenon*. In essence it consists of the realization of a wish out of the material in the body. It is a more complicated phenomenon than dream hallucination. In materialization, "the unconscious wish, incapable of becoming conscious, does not content itself with a sensory excitation of the psychic organ of perception, but leaps across to unconscious motility." Ferenczi considers materialization a prototype physiological reflex brought about by unconscious wish-impulses. The extraordinary power is supplied by their being associated with libido at the phallic level.

Ferenczi thus does not limit conversion phenomena to sensory motor systems. He also described disordered function of the lower part of the bowel in symbolic terms and called it organ neurosis.

In this connection attention should be drawn to the work of Georg Groddeck whose writings in the second decade of this century centered about the relationship between psyche and soma. Ferenczi (6) in a review translated into English in *Final Contributions to the Problems and Methods of Psychoanalysis,* discussed Groddeck's work and demonstrated its relevance to our theme in the following words:

It will certainly not have escaped the attentive reader of psychoanalytic literature that we consider the unconscious as the layer of the mind nearest to the physical; a layer that commands instinctual forces which are not at all, or only to a much lesser extent, accessible to the conscious. Psychoanalytic case histories tell of intestinal disturbances, catarrhs of the throat, anomalies of menstruation, etc., which have developed as reactions to repressed wishes, or which represent such wishes disguised and unrecognizable to the conscious mind. Although the paths linking these phenomena to normal and pathological physiology have always been left open (here I refer, for instance, to the repeatedly stated identity of the mechanism used in hysteria and when expressing emotion), psychoanalysis has confined itself mainly to the study of the physical changes in hysteria conditioned by mental processes.

Dr. Groddeck, in this pamphlet, is the first to make the courageous attempt to apply the results of Freud's discoveries to organic medicine, and this first step has already led him to such surprising results, new points of view and fresh perspectives, that at least the heuristic value of the step appears beyond any doubt. He has even succeeded through psychoanalytical work, that is through making such tendencies conscious, in improving, even curing, very severe organic illnesses such as goiter, scleroderma, and cases of gout and tuberculosis. Groddeck is far from assuming the role of a magician, and he states modestly that his aim was merely to create, through psychoanalysis, more favorable conditions "for the *it* by which one is lived." He identifies this "*it*" with Freud's unconscious [pp. 342-343].

Groddeck is generally considerel as somewhat of an extremist in his point of view. His flair for a well-turned phrase and dramatization perhaps distracted attention from his main thesis. No discussion in the field of psychosomatic medicine, however, can be complete without reference to his work.

The psychobiology of Adolf Meyer emphasized the interaction of body and mind. He stressed the importance of pluralistic factors—physical, sexual, social and environmental. The total personality had to be considered in its environmental setting. In an early paper, Meyer (17, p. 584) points out the difficulties encountered in accepting psychogenicity.

Why the dissatisfaction with explanations of a psychogenic character?
(1) Because the facts are difficult to get at and difficult to control, critical, and often used for stupid inferences, for instance, a notion that a psychogenic origin, i.e., a development out of natural mental activities which need not harm you and me, could not explain occasional lasting and frequently progressive disorders (in the face of the fact that nothing is more difficult to change than a political or religious or other deeply rooted conviction or tendency and nothing more difficult to stem than an unbalanced tendency to mysticism, lying, etc.].
(2) Because there prevail misleading dogmatic ideas about mind.

It is unfortunate that science still adheres to an effete and impossible contrast between mental and physical. More and more we realize that what figures to our mind as *matter* is much better expressed in terms of combinations of electrons, if not simply of energies, which throw off many of the forbidding and restrictive features of those masses which form the starting point of our concept of inert matter, which is practically sufficient for most demands of ordinary physics, but a hindrance to a better conception of the more complex happenings of biochemistry. Mind, on the other hand, is a *sufficiently organized living being in action;* and not a peculiar form of mind-stuff. A sufficiently organized brain is the main central link, but mental activity is really best understood in its full meaning as the adaptation and adjustment of the individual as a whole, in contrast to the simple activity of single organs such as those of circulation, respiration, digestion, elimination, or simple reflex activity.

We know, of course, that in these reactions which we know as mental, the brain forms the central link at work, although we know but little of the detail working. Sensorimotor adjustments form an essential part and as soon as we pass from the simple representative reactions such as sensations and thoughts, to the affective reactions, emotions and actions, we get a distinct participation of the work of glands, of circulation, of respiration and muscular adjustments, so that organs serving *as such* more limited 'infrapsychic' purposes enter as intrinsic parts into emotions, appetites, instincts and actions, so as to form the concrete *conduct and behavior,* which is the main thing deranged in our patients.

Meyer also called attention to the difficulty of reversing processes and resultant changes even though they were brought about by psychic factors (17, p. 585). "Every mental adjustment must be in keeping with the laws of anabolism and catabolism; it has its somatic components. It is, therefore, intelligible that it *may* be easier to precipitate harm than to correct it, and that some disorders or conflicts may permanently damage the processes of anabolism."

Meyer's concept of the total reaction is summarized by him as follows (17, p. 586):

But there *are* cases in which the apparent disorder of individual organs is merely an incident in a development which we could not understand correctly except by comparing it with the normal and efficient reaction of the individual as a whole, and for that we must use terms of psychology—not of mysterious events, but *actions* and *reactions* of which we know that they *do* things, a truly dynamic psychology. There we find the irrepressible instincts and habits at work, and finally the characteristic mental reaction type constituting the obviously pathological aberrations, and while it may be too late in many cases to stem the stream of destructive action—action beyond correction and in conflict with the laws of balance of anabolism and catabolism—seeing the facts in the right way will help us set aright what *can* be set aright, prevent what *can* be prevented and do what *can* be done to secure gymnastics and orthopaedics of mind—i.e., of the conduct and efficiency of the person as a whole.

In another paper, Meyer (16) is very critical of the emphasis on "disease" and of neurologizing mental concepts.

With these supposedly *specific* products of "disease" the psychopathologist proceeded to apply the venerable formula *ubi est morbus,* and it utilized the systematized inferences of neurology, until finally the dogma arose that what we call mental in daily life could not be scientific unless it was translated into a form of metaneurology—a systematization of neurological inferences, usually least supported by *those* who *have* a first-hand knowledge of the brain and its lesions [p. 595]. Most of what is offered as neurological explanations of mental processes and especially abnormal mental processes is a tendential precipitation of a mixture of truisms and assumptions into the terminology of a field in which there is today no possibility of bringing the conclusions to a test. It is neurologizing tautology of what had better be expressed as we experience it: biological reactions of the mental type [p. 596].... if we see what certain mental experiences aggravate conditions and precipitate new attacks or determine an improvement, we might well derive from this some courage at least to consider the possibility that the mental factors or reactions *may* really constitute the essential element in certain disease conditions and that it is only distracting to speak of a "physical disease," wholly unknown in "merely physical" terms, where the facts are so plain and so easily understood—or slighted [p. 602].

One might speculate as to what the impact on American psychiatry would have been had Adolf Meyer included Freud's concept of the unconscious in his own system instead of his idea of a "more or less conscious." The whole context of American psychiatry would have been enriched at a much earlier date, and the whole relationship of psychoanalysis to medicine would have been more firmly integrated.

The study of character traits in relating them to specific erotogenic zones as initiated by Freud, Abraham, and later Jones, was another instance of early attention to biophysical relationships. Here repetitive patterns of behavior and attitudes are related to a physiological substrate.

Paul Federn, and later Felix Deutsch and Phyllis Greenacre, called further attention to the importance of a somatic trauma (e.g., infections, surgical interventions) during the plastic libidinal stages of infancy in the choice of organ dysfunction. In a somewhat different sense, Alfred Adler, by stressing the concept of organ inferiority, has contributed to the problem of organ choice and of psychobiologic relationships.

Melanie Klein, in stressing early aggressive drives, has been able to postulate superego conflict at the level of oral and anal stages. Furthermore, by using introjection from the point of view of aggression, she thought she could delineate a pregenital conversion which could occur in the form of an organ neurosis and would be associated with meaningful significance. In this connection it is of interest that Fenichel also talked of pregenital conversion.

Felix Deutsch's contribution (1) was the introduction of a basic concept: the psychosomatic unit.

An organ neurosis is the necessary expression of a neurotic conflict in terms of an organic disorder which has a specific character. The organ involved is determined by the fact that it was originally affected at a time antedating the full evolution of instinctual life. The instinctual response at that time to the organic dysfunction created a psychosomatic unit, i.e., an active or latent coordination of, and interaction between, a given organ and a psychic conflict. This psychosomatic interrelation will be used under certain somatic or emotional conditions as the pathological solution of a psychic conflict and will lead to a certain symptom complex. Thus when the old psychic conflict becomes active, the organ originally associated with the conflict is called upon to produce those symptoms. In the case of certain specific conflicts, we shall witness manifestations of both components whenever one is stimulated, reproducing the other component of the original situation. More specifically, a certain phase of an emotional complex becomes causally and by necessity related to a certain organic dysfunction [p. 1].

Thus, the somatic components in a given situation which occurred when a certain type of conflict was present made for the psychosomatic unit. In later life when one component of this complex was touched upon it triggered off the whole complex. He utilized actual somatic manifestation, as in posturing, to demonstrate the symbolic acting out and the defensive use of the soma in the total picture.

Deutsch further stated (1, p. 2) that "This concept of organ neuroses stresses three facts: (1) the specificity of the personality organization; (2) the specificity of the organic symptom complex; and (3) the interaction between these two factors."

Flanders Dunbar and Franz Alexander have reviewed the psychosomatic field and attempted to work out specificity factors. Dunbar delineated a personality profile for many psychosomatic syndromes. She did not use the psychoanalytic technique in constructing the profiles and has therefore been criticized for evaluating only the superficial aspects of the personality.

Alexander pointed out that the symbolic channel of expression could not be used to explain the organ neuroses. In the latter, the autonomic nervous system was a focus of emotional tensions; suppressed drives prolonged vegetative innervation. This resulted in disturbed function which in turn could lead to morphological changes in the tissues. Alexander utilized the psychoanalytic techniques to delineate specific character structures for various diseases. For example, in peptic ulcer the basic disturbance was related to a character structure oriented toward dependency. However, the wish to receive was found intolerable and therefore repressed or blocked by external forces. The basic ungratified wish continued to excite and overact the autonomic nervous system.

One of the more recent formulations of psychosomatic phenomena with emphasis on the multiplicity of factors involved has been made by Grinker (11) who stresses that the "actual functioning of the organism cannot be understood except by a study of its transactional processes as occurring in a total field" at a given time. Such a field includes physical, physiological, and psychological factors and embraces reactions to both internal and external conditions. Somatic and psychic systems are in a constant state of transaction with each other. By a study of the total field with its multiple cross-sections one avoids linear causal chains or mere correlations between two functions. In addition, the study of successive fields from birth to maturity provides the maturational or developmental history of the organism.

The question can be asked, when can a hysterical conversion symptom begin? It would seem that we would come closest if we would say that hysterical conversion symptoms occur in relation to a conflict at: (a) a level of psychosexual development comparable to the phallic stage; (b) a temporal level, the oedipal situation; and (c) the symbolic representation.[2] Conversion, insofar as it is a symbolic process, can only occur in an individual who is mature enough *to* equate, consciously and unconsciously. The achievement of symbolization in the development of the individual gives him another technique for the unconscious resolution of a conflict. One cannot have a conversion phenomenon without the possibility of displacement from one thing to another. Even a pregenital symbolic conversion is only possible if the symptoms can represent a symbolic displacement from one phenomenon to another or one function to another. The arrival at the oedipal phase of the development results in a definite type of conflict, namely, the utilization of the phallus in the specific setting of the oedipal situation with resultant genital castration anxiety.

The utilization of various factors in the resolution of a conflict situation depends upon the presence of those factors as variables in the situation. Thus, hypothetically, the individual who has achieved genitality, is in a certain phase of his oedipal development, and has achieved a level of symbolic thinking will then be able to resolve a conflict arising from his oedipal relationship in terms of the various factors that are present at the time of the conflict. Therefore, he will be able to utilize symbolic equivalents as part of the resolution of the conflict.

When these three elements—phallic, oedipal stage, and symbolic processes—are present, and the resolution of the conflict takes place at that level, a conversion hysteria results rather than a hypochondriasis which necessitates a deeper regressive defense. The most important factors nosologically are the phallic and the oedipal level of the development, since the symbolic part can also be true of hypochondriasis.

[2] It should be taken for granted in this aspect of the discussion that since the editors are a group of psychoanalytically trained psychiatrists, their frame of reference is psychoanalytic psychology and all of the discussion is set against this context. In addition to the hereditary and constitutional aspects of the individual, the structural, topographic, dynamic, genetic, and economic aspects of the total psychobiological development of the individual are implicitly involved. Certain aspects of the problem have been selected for discussion because of their relevance to the particular area under review.

Therefore, the somatic area involved has to have significance in relation to these three aspects. In addition, there is also a historical element in that the conversion symptom represents a fragment of some somatic action appropriate at the time as a response to the stimulus. Historically, the particular somatic expression was a suitable one.

The somatic manifestation or the utilization of the soma in relation to the resolution of a conflict situation is not limited to any specific period. At any level, the soma can become implicated and can become one factor in the conversion or symptom formation. We ought not to talk in terms of pregenital or genital conversion as if each represented a different process. *Hysterical* conversion, however, needs time, place, and symbolic process, since, for example, at the anal-sadistic level, conversion phenomena are also possible. From the very beginning the infant is a psychobiological and a psychosomatic organism. Therefore, the soma can be utilized as one discharge area at any level as one part of the total homeostatic adaptive mechanism. It has different meanings at different levels. To the extent that the soma participates in the psychobiological total function at any given level, the soma can be utilized in the resolution of any conflict situation at that level or as a result of regression.

The above involves the utilization of the libido theory as it has been elaborated. Libido cannot be invested into an object, only in the representation of an object. Once there is a hypothesis which says that the psychic representation of an organ can be invested with libido and then as a result of that certain changes can take place in the organ itself, the change in the libidinal cathexis in the organ representative can lead to various physiological phenomena. The process leads to changes in the organ. There are many physiological examples of this—the phenomenon of erection is one.

What we are really looking for is what is the integrative pattern and the various steps which are established psychically so that the physiological phenomena will allow for the symbolic equation. There are two ways in which this can take place: (1) A nongenital organ may become genitalized, i.e., a bloodshot eye may be equated with a tumescent genital; (2) the function of a nongenital organ becomes sexualized and the organ genitalized. In most instances this combination is probably present. The function of the eye would represent the function of the genital to make this symbolic equation a physiological equation. It is not only that the eye is genitalized—the function of the eye is sexualized. The blindness is not the genital equivalent but has to do with the function of the eye; namely, if visual stimuli excite one sexually, vision has to be blocked out. The function of the eye has thus become erotized. But in the first example, there is another equation—the eye itself becomes the equivalent of a penis. In the erect penis there are certain physiological concomitants, such as tumescence. Therefore, the eye as an erect penis has to become tumescent also. At that point certain physical mechanisms which would allow for the eye to become engorged would have to be triggered off.[3]

For simplification of presentation we have to separate psychic disturbances which are based largely on the inhibition of a function because the function is prohibited, and psychic disturbances which come about because of a certain organ having become identified with a genital or with another organ. In such a case there may be a tendency to repeat in the secondarily identified organ some of the phenomena which usually take place in the original organ.

Is there a difference between somatization and libidinization? Freud talks about libidinization of an organ in hypochondriasis. If an organ is libidinized, is it somatized? Is an organ that becomes the focus of symptomatology in hysteria somatized? Is the paralyzed hand of the hysteric somatized? Is the gut of the ulcerative colitis a somatization?

How basic and valid is the concept of libidinization? The basic hypothesis of Freud is that libidinal energy flows back into an organ and that the physiological function of the organ is thereby altered in some way. From our point of view the basic concept is of an energy cathexis or energy flow. The concept of an energy flow (which is an energy that arises in the borderline between the organic and the psychic) relating itself to an organ, organ system, and/or fantasy of function of an organ system, results in certain consequences, for instance, change in perception. This is a possible position from which to evaluate further or investigate the relationship between the psyche and soma.

The difference between somatization and libidinization is that in somatization the organ or organ system involved becomes manifest in

---

[3] See Freud (8).

symptoms or signs. The original awareness of the body is brought about through a narcissistic libidinization of the organ and organ systems. This primary narcissistic libidinization through perception of stimuli, conscious and unconscious, that flow up through the psychic apparatus results in a psychic representation of the body or the organs. In the process of growth and maturation the outside world or objects in it are also cathected. This actually means that it is the psychic representation of the world or objects which is cathected. In a conflict situation where there is a withdrawal of libido from the outside world, it is reflected back onto the organ representation which is recathected. This is secondary libidinization. This secondary libidinization then reflects itself in two ways: (1) increased perception, or increased awareness of the organ or organ system or (2) obversely by decreased perception as a result of anticathexis which leads to the repression not only of the original conflictual fantasy but also of the newly recathected organ representation, i.e., the anesthesia of the hysteric. Secondary libidinization of the organ serves two functions: (1) repression of the conflict, and (2) discharge.

Somatization phenomena would be an involvement of an organ or an organ system, or the fantasy of function of an organ system, through regressed narcissistic libidinization in a symptom complex. To put it in another way, the regressed libidinization of an organ or organ system or fantasy of function of an organ system which becomes manifest in symptoms or signs is somatization. A point of differentiation between libidinization and somatization might be that libidinization would be the cathexis or energizing of an organ *representant*. Somatization would be the actual changes within the organ or organ system which may come into the field of awareness. The problem still remains as to how the libidinization of an organ representation is mediated to the physiological manifestations of somatization. This brings us back to Gull's nerve force.

We may approach the problem by examining the status of those areas or functions of the ego which are in a state of primary or secondary autonomy (Hartmann). These functions belong to the conflict-free ego sphere. They include the preformed tools of adaptation, the human equivalents of those mechanisms which guarantee "fitting-in" in animals. The preformed tools include endowment, special talents, and general apparatuses, such as memory and perception. Primary autonomy refers to inherent capacities. Secondary autonomy designates behavior which was originally brought about as a defense of a drive but which in the course of time became an independently working structure (Hartmann, 12).

Many of the functions regulated by the autonomic nervous system are by definition automatic in nature. The question remains whether these functions have psychic representations in relation to the unconscious portion of the ego. An answer in the affirmative would allow visualizing psychopathological phenomena as taking place in the psychic representation of the autonomic functions which have entered the sphere of conflict.

We are, of course, confronted by an age-old problem which has been dealt with at many levels during the evolution of our concepts. In many ways it is not too far removed from the theological and philosophical question of "does only man have a soul?" In other words, is man the only organism whose psyche functions in a psychophysiological interrelationship? The crudest kind of observation will indicate that animals, too, possess systems which have modalities and processes not unlike that which we ascribe to the human psychic system. The problem, therefore, is at what point in the evolution of the organism does a psychic component appear. Before that point physiology is only a vital biochemical phenomenon; beyond that point does this phenomenon continue as a basic property of protoplasm? How do these functions relate to the gradual evolution of the psychic system?

Evidence denotes that in the phylogenic scale a system which might be denoted as psychic becomes part of the total organism relatively far down the scale.

Among the more regularly occurring of the higher developments in active animals is the elaboration of the coordinating system and the inclusion within it of mechanisms for modifying its operations in adjustment with the individual's experiences. The basic feature in this process, which from the objective standpoint is called *conditioning* and from the subjective standpoint *learning* or *association,* is the formation of connections among different groups of neuronic (nerve cell) reactions that have been aroused at or nearly at the same time, so that subsequently the arousal of either tends to invoke the other as well. These connections form an ever more intricate web, since if reaction group A becomes connected with B at one time and B becomes connected with C at another time, it follows that A thereby becomes connected with C, in the arrangement of ABC [Muller, 18].

In the human the evolution of this system takes place in utero in the fetus.

The recent writings of Grinker, Engel, and Karl Menninger in one way or another attempt formulations of the organismic function in terms of the homeostatic or steady state involving the psychic system as an integrating component of the organism. Menninger's (15) recent formulations perhaps state in the most specific way what the role of the ego consists of. "Effecting this reconciliation, maintaining this physiopsychosociological balance, is *the chief function of the ego.* . . . It is under pressure from instinctual urges, from somatic needs, and from environmental offers, demands, and threats . . . the achievement of optimum tension through the arrangement of the least expensive compromises."

In earlier publications Alexander introduced the vector concepts. This attempted to describe simple biopsychological units which participate in function. They were "elemental tendencies" such as the wish to receive, wish to retain, and the wish to eliminate. They related to fundamental directions of biological acts and processes or vegetative functions which could be expressed in meaningful terms like "intake," "retain," or "eliminate." This was helpful in studying the influence of psychological factors upon vegetative function. The vectors stressed by Alexander are found in unicellular organisms: to move toward, to move away, to take in, to eliminate, to retain and digest. The vectors can relate to both physical and psychological stimuli. It is probable that every system of the body can participate in such reactions—gastrointestinal, cardiovascular, musculoskeletal, endocrine, and reticuloendothelial system.

In a certain sense the problem of modern medicine in regard to the organismic point of view is whether or not the psychic system is acceptable as a system in the sense of the cardiovascular, central nervous, or enzyme systems. There is no difficulty in conceptualizing and experimentally demonstrating the interrelationship of all somatic systems to each other. As a matter of fact, it is difficult to conceive of any point of view in modern medicine which would run contrary to such an acceptance of interaction. When the psychic system is involved, the old dichotomies seem to enter into the picture. Perhaps one of the problems is the relative difficulty in obtaining observational data which fit into the so-called "objective" scientific approach. In relation to the sensory modalities no difficulties exist. It is when one deals with thought processes, fantasies, and especially unconscious mentation that this begins to act as a stumbling block toward the acceptance of the psychic system at the same level as the others. Once this system is viewed from the same frame of reference, the difficulties should disappear. The following quotation should illustrate that point:

The precise mechanism through which an emotional response is evoked by a particular stimulus and then comes to involve some autonomic function in its final expression cannot be defined at present. Some of the theories proposed by psychiatrists do not inspire confidence in the mind of a physiologist. However that may be, once a stimulus has found its way from one of the peripheral sense organs to one of the viscera by way of the central mechanism for emotional expression, a second stimulus will tend to take the same path [Thomas, 20].

There are a number of factors which lead to the nonrecognition of the psychic system as one of the biological systems. There is no question that variations in metabolism affect the psychic apparatus which responds in its fashion. There is a tendency to look upon this as a unidirectional phenomenon from the metabolic to the psychic rather than to see the total picture as including a possible feedback from the psychic to the metabolic. Thus, lack of oxygen may lead in the psychic sphere to attempts to obtain it and/or to various types of manifestations such as annoyance, anger, or euphoria. However, psychic defenses such as displacement, isolation, or conversion may obscure the picture by their respective somatic manifestations.

The psychic system like all systems has a phylogenetic and ontogenetic species specificity. The unique development of the psychic system in an individual is dependent not only upon the phylogenesis, ontogenesis, somatogenesis, and experiences of that individual but is related also to maturational processes. For example, accidental somatic events may lead to defects in its development which then would make for specific modification reflected in its function, for instance, ego modifications in the postencephalitic child.

The main lines of our conceptual frame of reference would lie in the above direction. The organismic reaction at any given moment in time and space is the resultant of phylogenetic, ontogenetic, somatogenetic, and experiential factors relating at all times in an ecological interreaction. With the concept of the psychic system as one of the organism's systems with perhaps a somewhat different valence than the cardiovascular system, we are able to incorporate the findings of psychoanalysis into the total psychobiology of the individual.

A methodological problem in the presentation of our point of view arises here. One may present a summary of psychoanalytic psychology or one may take for granted that the reader is already familiar with the evolution of the basic hypotheses and theories which make for Freudian psychoanalysis today. We accept this second assumption and will discuss various aspects of psychoanalytic psychology in relation to the specific papers published in this volume.

The problem of adaptation, though not always explicitly defined, assumes an ecological point of view. Charles Darwin in his work on natural selection focused attention on the problems of adaptation as a fundamental factor in biology. In his book *Expression of the Emotions in Man and Animals* (1872) he studied the emotions in terms of their adaptive functions. He thus traced the expressions of fear and anger to preparation for fight or struggle. He also identified other forms of expression as part of nonverbal communication. It was thus early recognized that man in adaptation to his environment had to master stresses that arose from within or without.

From the medical standpoint, Claude Bernard was the first to enunciate clearly the dictum that health and disease represent phases of life processes. Psychoanalysis added to the study of adaptation a more detailed investigation of processes going on within the organism both consciously and unconsciously. Psychoanalysis stresses a hypothetical energy of a biological nature in terms of instincts or drives and their vicissitudes. This becomes an important dynamic factor in adaptation.

In recent years the problem of adaptation has attracted additional attention because of the work of Selye (19) who stated that: "1. Any systemic stress (viz., one affecting large portions of the body) elicits an essentially similar syndrome with general manifestations. 2. This syndrome helps adaptation. 3. Adaptation can cause disease [p. 4]." He stressed the hypothesis that certain diseases are in the nature of an adaptation sparing and protecting the total organism from some stressful situation. This point of view was also taken up by Grinker who considered the idea of sacrifice of one organ to establish a steady state. This is reminiscent of Ferenczi (5) who in his paper on the "Acceptance of Unpleasant Ideas" states, "at the next stage, the organism is able to thrust off parts of its self that cause pain, and in this way save its life (autotomy). I once called these sequestra a physiological prototype of the process of repression."

Regression as an adaptational phenomenon is the return from a higher level of function to a previously lower level of function which involves a partial reversal of phenomenological and dynamic function to an earlier state. When one talks of regression one usually is describing phenomena of a functional nature in the sense that there is a return to an earlier pattern of behavior. However, one must be clearly aware of which components were present in the original pattern of behavior. To use the diarrhea in ulcerative colitis as an example, we have a diarrhea which superficially resembles the frequent stools of the infant in the precontrol stage. However, in ulcerative colitis we have an additional factor of an irritated bowel which was not present in the infant. In other words, both in psychological and physiological regression it may very well be that the pattern is reminiscent of rather than carrying a one-to-one correlation with the original state.

The concept of physiological regression is one that has been previously stated by various authors (J. J. Michaels, I. Hendrick), and relates to the work of Hughlings Jackson. This involves the reappearance of earlier patterns of structure-function under situations of organismic stress.

In psychoanalysis the concept of regression involves a return to earlier libidinal positions with behavior recurring that was appropriate at the time that position had been reached. The libido theory involves a hypothesis of fixation at various levels. The strength of a fixation at any particular level will be related to subsequent regressions to that level. The stronger the fixation point, the more likely the regression to it in the face of conflict situations that are not resolvable at the more advanced level of development. Insofar as organ and organ system function become of significance and enter into the fixation unit during the course of development, the more likelihood there is that when regression occurs these organs or organ systems will be involved in the organismic functioning at the regressed level.

When we talk of regression in the psychosomatic field, we are referring to the giving up of an advanced psychosomatic unit and the return to an earlier psychosomatic unit. When the term psychosomatic is used, it is used in the same sense as one utilizes the terms cardiorenal, cardiovascular, neurocirculatory. In the latter sense, however, the term expresses an emphasis on the direct relationship but does not imply that the cardiovascular and renal systems function in any isolated way. The term psychosomatic is a generic term rather than a delimiting term.

A psychosomatic unit is any psychophysiological response. It can be at a simple level or at a highly complex hierarchal level involving any number of systems in the total interrelated reaction. A skill is a psychosomatic unit. At the risk of oversimplification, one might utilize the work of Benedek and Rubenstein to indicate the relationship between the hormonal systems and the ovulatory cycle to the psychic system. There appears to be a definite relationship in the content and affects of the woman to specific phases of the ovulatory cycle.

The most important conclusions to be drawn from the above review of the concept of psychogenicity is its complex character. This is really the essence of the transactional point of view which is receiving more and more emphasis in recent psychosomatic literature. The choice of a psychosomatic illness, in the limited sense, like the choice of a neurosis or psychosis, is dependent on multiple factors. Some of them are:

1. Genetic factor.
2. Occurrence of the trauma at an early age—at the undifferentiated core of oral phase and subsequent precipitating factors.
3. The failure to promote a solution of the disturbing situation, by behavior or symbolic representation or even psychosis, at the ideational level leads to direct physiological expressions via autonomic pathways.

4. Regression to an early level with corresponding methods of reaction. This includes character traits which are genetically associated with respective levels of erotization.
5. Adaptation principles which promote shifting and limiting of stress to certain organs and systems. This is essentially an energy distribution problem.
6. The point at which the symbolic process enters the reaction or situation (a) as stimulus, (b) as giving secondary meaning.
7. The abnormal distribution and utilization of sexual and aggressive drives.
8. The accumulation of nondischarged affect.
9. The position in and relation to family unit.
10. The reaction to the socioeconomic situation.
11. Quantitative factor of pathogenic elements.

All of the above add up to the apparently trite truism that all psychosomatic reactions are organismic in character, that multiple factors always play a role, and that there never can be a simple one-to-one relationship between any two factors that would explain any given reaction. At the present time it would seem indicated that a point of view which lies within the area of transactionalism as emphasized by Grinker based essentially on the concepts of Von Bertalanffy offers the best hypothetical basis for the understanding of these complicated patterns. It also seems clear that the system of psychology which comes closest pragmatically to being of most value in terms of its utility is the psychoanalytic psychology of Freud, since without the basic concepts of analysis, such as the system unconscious and the primary process, psychological factors would lack dimension. It would seem that at this time the findings of psychoanalysis lend perspective to the transactional point of view.

REFERENCES

1. Deutsch, F.: The choice of organ in organ neuroses. *Int. J. Psychoanal.,* 20:252-262, 1939.
2. Dubois, P.: *The Psychic Treatment of Nervous Disorders.* New York: Funk & Wagnalls, 6th ed., 1909, pp. 25-26.
3. Ferenczi, S.: Disease- or pathoneuroses. In: *Further Contributions to*

the Theory and Technique of Psychoanalysis. New York: Basic Books, 1952, p. 78.
4. ———: The phenomena of hysterical materialization. In: *Further Contributions to the Theory and Technique of Psychoanalysis.* New York: Basic Books, 1952, pp. 89-104.
5. ———: The problem of the acceptance of unpleasant ideas: advances in knowledge of the sense of reality. *Int. J. Psychoanal.,* 7:313-323, 1926.
6. ———: *Final Contributions to the Problems and Methods of Psychoanalysis.* New York: Basic Books, 1955.
7. Freud, S.: The defence neuro-psychoses. *Collected Papers,* I. London: Hogarth Press, 1924, pp. 59-75.
8. ———: Psychogenic visual disturbances according to psycho-analytical conceptions. *Collected Papers,* II. London: Hogarth Press, 1924, pp. 105-112.
9. ———: Types of neurotic nosogenesis. *Collected Papers,* II. London: Hogarth Press, 1924, pp. 113-121.
10. ———: *A General Introduction to Psychoanalysis.* New York: Boni & Liveright, 1920, p. 229.
11. Grinker, R. R.: *Psychosomatic Research.* New York: Norton, 1953.
12. Hartmann, H.: Ego psychology and the problem of adaptation. In: *Organization and Pathology of Thought,* ed. D. Rapaport. New York: Columbia University Press, 1951.
13. Hinsie, L. E. & Shatzky, J.: *Psychiatric Dictionary.* New York: Oxford University Press, 1940, p. 437.
14. Janet, P.: *The Major Symptoms of Hysteria.* New York: Macmillan, 1929.
15. Menninger, K. A.: Psychological aspects of the organism under stress. Part I: The homeostatic regulatory function of the ego. *J. Am. Psychoanal Assn.,* 2:67-106, 1954.
16. Meyer, A.: The problems of mental reaction-types, mental causes, and diseases. *Collected Papers of Adolf Meyer,* II. Baltimore: Johns Hopkins Press, 1951.
17. ———: The role of the mental factors in psychiatry. *Collected Papers of Adolf Meyer,* II. Baltimore: Johns Hopkins Press, 1951.
18. Muller, H. J.: Life. *Science,* 121:6, 1955.
19. Selye, H.: Adaptive reactions to stress. In: *Life Stress and Bodily Diseases,* Association for Research of Nervous and Mental Diseases, 29: 4, 1950.
20. Thomas, E. J.: The autonomic nervous system in gastrointestinal diseases. *J. Am. Med. Assn.,* 157:211, 1955.

THE ADDRESS ON MEDICINE

WILLIAM W. GULL, M.D.
(1868)

Emphasis has been placed on the climate at a given time and its influence on the observer, both as to data emphasized and formulations reached. Some comments on Gull's "Address on Medicine," may serve to focus these aspects.

Gull starts with diffidence because his "subject lies on the confines of human knowledge, and that too often the highest effort of the clinical student is to arrive at some feeble probability, in the presence of uncertain, or even delusive, evidence." He, however, is ready to defend the scientific status of clinical medicine. "It is elucidated by the light of physics, chemistry and physiology, yet is not comprehended by them as they now stand. In ages gone by Hippocrates had to vindicate the study of disease from the inroads of superstition; at the present day we have to guard it against assaults on the side of science, and need to watch lest we betray it by accepting a too chemical or physical limit to our thoughts." In other words, the clinician must make his own observations, strengthened and abetted by collateral aid from the basic sciences.

Gull takes a comprehensive view in the study of the patient. "The stock whence he may have sprung, the circumstances of his birth, the time he may have lived, the diseases he may have undergone, the habits he may have acquired—are all subjects to be brought into the focus of thought at the bedside, and made to clear up the problem of disease." He takes the same point of view in regard to organs and tissues. "These have each their own life . . . their own tendency to disease and their specific power and mode of repair." As an example, he cites the almost complete immunity to disease of certain parts of the body, such as the jejunum, in spite of its length.

Gull pays special attention to the neural element. "Whatever is living has nerve quality in it. The highest expression of this quality is conscious intelligence; the lowest it is, from the nature of the case, at present impossible to mark. This much, however, it appears important to recognize clinically, that morbid brain force may give rise to a variety of disorders, apparently distinct from their original cause. There is a neuropathology from the brain to the tissues, as there is a reverse order from disturbance from the tissues to the brain. If we trace the history of morbid brain force through the various members of a family, we shall often recognize a great variety of related phenomena, which, in nosological classification, are separated and considered as distinct. The intellectual disturbance in one, may appear as epilepsy in a second, as mere dyspepsia and so-called acidity in a third; in a fourth, as some peculiar neuralgia; in a fifth, if a female, in many varieties of capillary disturbance, as amenorrhea, vicarious menstruation, haematemesis, or even haemoptysis; in a sixth, some part of the intestinal tract, the colon chiefly, may appear to be the recipient of the morbid nerve process, and the patient be tortured with fears of a tumor."

He calls attention to the variability of response in different individuals: "As if in different individuals, different portions of the grey matter were the seat of the same kind of morbid action, the equivalent of mental disorder in one, occurring as colon disorder in another, and so on." He enlarges on the point by discussing illness in relation to age and the varying "aging" of tissues. "Senile changes may thus occur in childhood, as the ephemera is born but for the day."

He follows the same point of view in discussing the basis of locomotor ataxia and considers it as being "plainly one of decay, like baldness, or greyness, or the occurrence of the arcus senilis." He supports his theses by the fact that pathological changes were not limited to the posterior columns of the cord but involved even the brain. Here we have an example of the erroneous explanation and correlation of facts due to deficient knowledge of the etiological factor; in this case it was lues. Interestingly he accuses his opponents "that they arrived at this opinion against clinical evidence, and partly biased, though uncon-

sciously, by the way we were first taught to dissect and think about the nervous system." The basic sciences without clinical observation are a series of discontinued data. With clinical medicine they become a continuum. One shall depend on the other so that the specificity of the basic sciences related to the psyche will be integrated through the medium of the clinician.[1]

Similar limited knowledge led him to an erroneous concept about the relationship between cancer, tubercle, and inflammation. "Although, for practical purposes, it is convenient to intensify the differences between cancer, tubercle, and the inflammatory process, we have abundant evidence of intimate relations between them. Thus, the children of parents dying of cancer are not rarely tubercular, and those of the third generation are liable to various forms of chronic inflammation; whilst in the same families are healthy individuals, in whom we can discover no evidence of any special morbid tendency. It is not improbable that that which seems most special to us in cancer and tubercle may depend more upon gradation than change of diathesis, and that both are allied to more common degenerations.... The tubercular peritonitis of childhood corresponds with great strictness to the cancerous peritonitis of age. It is probable that cancer is nearer to the simple degradation of tissues than tubercle."

He argues against the concept—abetted by the study of pathology—that disease is an entity which must be combatted and cast out. He looks at the disease process as a reaction in which nervous tissue is especially involved and where the aim of therapy is to limit the violence of the attendant symptom.

Epilepsy is looked upon as a condition of nerve force, in which may occur not only the common phenomenon of epilepsy, but coma without convulsions, paralysis following convulsions, sudden and transient mania, and even some strange forms of neuralgia.

Gull stresses the absolute need of experience and knowledge of possibilities in diagnosis. It is in this connection that he uses "hysteric apepsia" as an example of diagnosis made by knowledge of its occurrence and supported by the absence of tubercular disease elsewhere—

---

[1] See Klemperer, *This Volume*, pp. 36-46.

a diagnosis which is made on positive evidence related to the absence of other pathology.

He is quite modern in saying: "The strength of modern therapeutics lies in the clearer perception than formerly of the great truth that diseases are but perverted life processes, and have for their natural history not only a beginning, but especially a period of culmination and decline. . . . The effects of disease may be for a third generation, but the laws of health are for a thousand." He deplores our deficiency in estimating the reparative powers as compared with our ability to discover the presence of disease.

Mr. President and Gentlemen, I deeply feel the honor and responsibility which you have put upon me, by placing me here today as your exponent of the present position of Clinical Medicine. My task is difficult from the distinguished character of my audience, and from the imperfections of our knowledge in the subject of which I have to speak. I feel, indeed, as one about to undergo the ordeal by fire, the difficulty and delicacy of my task being so great that I dare not hope to escape adverse criticism.

You have been listening to learned discourses on the physics and physiology of living things, wherein the learned lecturers have been able to instruct and satisfy the mind with details more or less capable of demonstration; whilst I have to admit that my subject lies on the confines of human knowledge, and that too often the highest effort of the clinical student is to arrive at some feeble probability, in the presence of uncertain or even delusive, evidence.

Clinical Medicine, though a special department of knowledge, is so intimately connected with other sciences, that, when the claims of these are satisfied, it might seem that nothing would remain to it. This appears to me the present error of our schools. It would not, however, be too much to assert that, were it possible to conjoin in one human intelligence all that is now known of other sciences, such knowledge would be compatible with entire ignorance of the department of clinical medicine. As the physiologist must yet assert, that the phe-

---

Reprinted from Lancet, 2:171, 1868.

nomena of living tissues are not explained by their chemical composition, or, as the chemist himself has equally to admit, that mere isomerism may be no clue to chemical qualities, so the clinical physician knows that the phenomena of disease are not explained by the knowledge of healthy textures, nor by the action of healthy organs. Clinical work is a work by itself, and yet, if I may use the comparison, only so far by itself as one form of organic life may be considered separate from another. It stands apart, but has the most intimate relations to all that surrounds it. It is elucidated by the light of physics, chemistry, and physiology, yet is not comprehended by them as they now stand. In ages gone by Hippocrates had to vindicate the study of disease from the inroads of superstition; at the present day we have to guard it against assaults on the side of science, and need to watch lest we betray it by accepting a too chemical or physical limit to our thoughts.

We should all contemplate with great satisfaction such inroads of collateral sciences upon medicine, as that at length medicine might have no separate existence; but this consummation appears to be, as yet, far distant, and must be so acknowledged. Happily, such is the extension of the human mind into Nature, that almost daily new regions are discovered; and the boundaries of the old are so extended as to require fresh subdivisions in order to bring them within the domain of thought. Formerly, the physician might have been able to comprehend all that then constituted the allied sciences of medicine; but that can never again be possible. His duty lies, therefore, in giving an exact and scientific character to the department which remains to him—to investigate its phenomena with that concentration which is necessary in every physical inquiry and with all those aids which are afforded in increasing perfection by modern science.

It is not, however, to be overlooked, that even science herself is apt to have her moments of dogmatism, and, by throwing the light of some particular inquiry full in our eyes, to blind us for the time to that which lies beyond. How often has medicine been thus diverted from her difficult path. A discovery in physics has made us for the moment no more than galvanic batteries, or a discovery in chemistry at another, mere oxidizing machines. Today, however, we go to bedside work untrammeled by any exclusive theories of this kind, ready to investigate disease in every way that investigation is yet possible, and forming our judgment in no narrow spirit of a foregone conclusion. We have no system to satisfy, no dogmatic opinions to enforce. We have no ignorance to cloak, for we confess it: but we have to bring into the court of inquiry all possible evidence, and to decide upon it by the light of science and experience. They whose work lies more open to experiment and demonstration are apt to forget the difficulties we have to encounter, and the mental labor required in dealing with them with any measure of success. They would have us postpone these difficulties to a more convenient season, until, by the advancement of other branches of science, they could be undertaken with less risk of failure.

However gratifying and proper this might be, were the end of our knowledge contemplation only, and were there no motives to present action, yet, as we are in the midst of human suffering and have some knowledge for its relief, it is plainly the duty of some, and worthy of the highest intellects, to apply themselves to this work, even though by so doing they may forego the immediate rewards which pure science so liberally affords.

Whilst thus asking for the unstinted recognition of clinical medicine as a scientific department, I am not forgetful of the obligations imposed upon us, nor that in it there lie problems, as yet, far beyond a scientific solution. No one can hope, even as the sciences now stand, and much less as they shall further advance, to obtain a foremost knowledge of them and of medicine at the same time. Yet such knowledge is to us of daily necessity. We must, therefore, refer our physiological difficulties to the physiologist, and our chemical questions to the chemist, and still admit that there remains an unlimited area of study for us, in tracing the causes and relations, and in recognizing the presence of disease. I would not be understood to say that the physician should neglect the sciences of chemistry and biology and devote himself to the limited study of morbid phenomena. If any should desire to do so, the attempt would prove its impossibility. The interchangeable relations of things are such as to make necessary the most discursive operation of the mind, if it would successfully inquire into that which is most special. I desire only that that which is our proper work should have our entire energies, strengthened and directed by every collateral aid.

Whilst the biologist traces downwards the relations of the various forms of living things, and, breaking away, one by one, the barriers of separation between them, at length views them all as springing from a common germ, the student of clinical medicine, working in another direction, seeks opposite results. To him, one form of life absorbs and centralizes all other forms. His object is to see the facts of human organization in their most special relations. The very perfection of his work lies in this. It is not even man in general; it is in the individual man upon whom his attention has to concentrate. The stock whence he may have sprung, the circumstances of his birth, the time he may have lived, the diseases he may have undergone, the habits he may have acquired—are all subjects to be brought into the focus of thought at the bedside, and made to clear up the problem of disease.

Medicine is a specialism, but of no narrow kind. We have to dissect nature, which, for practice, is better than to abstract it.[2] Every form of life has to us a value, but in an order the reverse of the generalizations of natural history. We desire to know what limits, specializes, and perverts. We study in order to distinguish, and not to classify.

Yet it is not the individual only that we have to isolate for the purposes of clinical study; we have further to inquire into the life of his several organs and tissues. These have each their own life, and, correlative with it, their own tendency to disease, and their specific power and mode of repair. To clinical medicine, therefore, the body becomes a pathological museum. In every part we recognize certain proclivities to morbid action; and the purpose of our study is to trace these tendencies to their source on the one hand, and to their effects on the other. Histology and anatomy are daily widening this fundamental department of medicine; and we may be sanguine that an acquaintance with the morbid changes to which the same parts are liable, where present in the lower animals (comparative pathology), will afford further valuable aid, as by it we shall have in some degree a dynamic test of the general tendency to these morbid states, in addition to that furnished by human pathology. A knowledge of these intrinsic tendencies to pathological change in the several organs prepares us beforehand to recognize their occurrence where, without such knowledge, the signs and symptoms which are present would convey no information.

---

[2] *Melius autem est naturam secare quam abstrahere.*—Bacon: "Novum Organum."

To know, for instance, that the brain from the early period of adult age, in persons otherwise healthy, is prone, without obvious exciting cause, to the formation of tumor in its substance—to be aware of the probability of insidious ramollissement of the central commissures in younger subjects—often enables us to suspect these conditions, and to give weight to what might otherwise seem some unimportant ailment. As I name these two instances, I feel sure your clinical reminiscences will supply the proof of what I state, and read a sad page of suffering, death, and error.

There would appear to be some textures of the body endowed with an almost complete immunity from disease, whilst others are equally liable to it—a difference of which at present we cannot give a sufficient account. Both stand as glaring instances to warn us against the adoption of some of our current theories. There is, perhaps, no part of the body organized for more rapid cell-life, or that is more extensive or more vascular, than the mucous membrane of the jejunum; yet, with the exception of the choleraic and diphtheritic processes, it is almost exempt from primary organic changes—so much so that at the bedside, in considering the probabilities of disease in the abdomen, we have, on the one hand, to exclude this part from our consideration (except in mechanical obstruction), and as necessarily to direct special attention to certain seats of lesion whence the trouble is likely to have sprung. Contrast the limited area presented by the lesser curvature and pyloric region of the stomach, the duodenum, caecum, and rectum with the enormous extent of the valvulae conniventes, and compare the frequency and character of the lesions in the one with those of the others, taken together, and it is obvious how much our diagnosis of abdominal disease depends upon our acquaintance with the tendency of certain textures in the abdomen to morbid changes.

The investigations of morbid anatomy have thrown a flood of light upon the so-called acute idiopathic diseases. Formerly they were supposed to be of common occurrence, and the treatment of the day was adapted to their apparent violence. But how rarely now do we meet with a case of acute inflammation of the membranes of the brain, or of the peritoneum, or, indeed, of any other texture, which we cannot refer to some chronic lesion, or to some distinct cachexia; the only idiopathic part of the case being that which was formerly overlooked or unrecognized—some chronic tissue change, unnoticed in the storm of acute disease to which it may have given rise.

Oken has said that all the tissues are nervous, and bone is hardened nerve. I shall not discuss this assertion on the present occasion; but, no doubt, modern physiology and pathology are advancing the evidence that whatever is living has nerve quality in it. The highest expression of this quality is conscious intelligence; the lowest it is, from the nature of the case, at present impossible to mark. This much, however, it appears important to recognize clinically: that morbid brain force may give rise to a variety of disorders apparently distinct from their original cause. There is a neuropathology from the brain to the tissues, as there is a reverse order of disturbance from the tissues to the brain. If we trace the history of morbid brain force through the various members of a family, we shall often recognize a great variety of related phenomena, which, in nosological classification, are separated and considered as distinct. The intellectual disturbance in one, may appear as epilepsy in a second; as mere dyspepsia and so-called acidity in a third; in a fourth, as some peculiar neuralgia; in a fifth, if a female, in many varieties of capillary disturbance, as amenorrhea, vicarious menstruation, haematemesis, or even haemoptysis; in a sixth, some part of the intestinal tract, the colon chiefly, may appear to be the recipient of the morbid nerve process, and the patient be tortured with fears of a tumor. And a tumor indeed there may be—though a mere phantom, yet calculated to mislead the unwary. Nor does this list exhaust the catalogue of these strange vagaries. It would seem as if sometimes this morbid brain action expended itself upon the voluntary muscles, which, if of the abdomen, may be shaped into forms that defy diagnosis and bewilder the most cautious.

It might be thought unnecessary for me to point to this strange field of pathology, which has long been recognized as in part connected with hysteria, but I have reason to think our views on the subject are still wanting in distinctness, and that the term hysteria, as now understood, does not include all I here intend. These morbid conditions occur as essentially, if not so frequently, in the male as in the female, though the form of them may be determined by the sex. As if, in different individuals, different portions of grey matter were the seat of the same kind of morbid action; the equivalent of mental disorder in one occurring as colon disorder in another, and so on. And, besides these mere functional disturbances, the history of medicine and my own individual experience supply instances of actual tissue changes which admit of no explanation until thus looked at; and, I need not add, such cases are entirely distinct from feigned and fictitious disorders.

The flatulent dyspepsia of the student, the tears of the distressed, the dry mouth of the anxious, and the jaundice of fright, daily remind us how far the cerebral influence extends, and physiology will hereafter teach us to trace the steps whereby these effects are produced. As there is no explanation of laughter when the axillary nerves are tickled, so there seems to be none of the morbid fears which oppress those who are the subjects of some affections of the colon, and who weary our patience with their doleful complaints. Yet surely we have no more ground to deny the reality of the one than of the other, though we must at present refer both to some ultimate fact of our natural history. "As face answereth to face" by mysterious sympathy, so do these and other peripheral impressions excite or depress, in an equally mysterious way, the subjects of them.

I cannot turn from this hasty glance at the idiopathic pathology of the tissues without mentioning how much clinical medicine has gained by recognizing the relations of the tissues to time. The wise man says, "There is a time to be born, and a time to die." What the physiological limit of the latter may be has not been determined, but at the bedside its presence has often to be recognized and distinguished from that of removable or remediable disease.

Abercrombie was among the first to point out that the paralytic affections of age were due to senile changes in the tissues; and more recently, the convulsive affections of otherwise healthy, but aged people, have been included in the same category. The epileptic attack of the old man is an evidence of failing power, as his paralytic seizure is an evidence of failing tissue. Though the actively growing organs of the child contrast in a striking manner with the same in decay in the old, there is yet, in some respects, a similarity between the disease of the two periods of life, like the tints of the rising and the setting sun. In the first period, the organism has not acquired its forces; in the latter period, it is losing them. Infantile convulsions, and senile convulsions; infantile diarrhea, and senile diarrhea; infantile eczema, and senile eczema; uric acid deposits in childhood, and uric acid deposits in age, may afford illustration of the truth of my statement.

Time, moreover, acting differently upon different parts of our organism, often performs a kind of pathological dissection, exposing the inherent weakness of entire organs, or parts of them, and giving rise to diseases, for which at present we have often no name but that which designates some prominent symptom. This process of decay, due to time only, occurs at almost every period of life, according to the constitution of the individual. The fatty degeneration of muscular fibre, occurring in the children of certain families, affords such an illustration, and we have yet more striking ones in the progressive muscular atrophy, which occasionally exhibits itself from primary changes in the nervous system, in equally young subjects. Senile changes may thus occur in childhood, as the ephemera is born but for the day. My thoughts have been specially directed to this subject of late, whilst passing in review the facts of locomotor ataxy. The condition of the nervous system which most commonly gives rise to this form of unsteadiness of gait is plainly one of decay, like baldness or greyness, or the occurrence of the arcus senilis. It occurs to individuals of particular families, in which other forms of nerve degeneration are prevalent. It happens to be limited almost entirely to males, at the middle or after the middle period of life; and, if we may venture to draw general conclusions from the few observations that have been made post mortem, is connected with fatty degeneration of the posterior columns of the cord, not, however, limited to these, but associated with changes of the like kind in other parts of the cord, and in the brain itself.

My friends, Mr. Lockhart Clarke and Dr. Hughlings Jackson, endorse the opinion first put forward by Duchenne, and subsequently maintained by Trousseau, that this locomotor ataxy is due to disease of the spinal marrow only; but I am disposed to think that they arrived at this opinion against clinical evidence, and partly biased, though unconsciously, by the way we were first taught to dissect and think about the nervous system.

It is only fair to English pathologists here to state, that this form of disease has long been known to them. Matthew Baillie regarded it as the most common form of paraplegia, and had an anatomical explanation of its peculiarities, which, though certainly not applicable, proves that, with his usual acumen, he had investigated its post-mortem anatomy. His theory was that the malady arose from a morbid effusion of cerebrospinal fluid, which, when the patient was erect, gravitated into the lower part of the theca vertebralis, and, by pressing upon the cord, rendered the patient unable to steady his movements; whilst, from the same cause, these became free again when he was placed in a recumbent position. I quoted these observations of Baillie in the year 1849, and took occasion then to call the malady encephalic paraplegia. It is probable that this was too restricted a term, as is that of locomotor ataxy, and that in our consideration of the special disease, we must recognize a general diminution of nervous power from failing nutrition, as well as special lines of more unequivocal decay, most marked in the posterior columns of the cord. In support of this opinion I may state that ataxy alone occurred but three times in fifty cases referred to by Trousseau. Notwithstanding this, he draws the characters of the disease which he would typify from three cases, and not from the forty-seven others in which there was evidently disease of parts of the brain, as of the cord. If, however, all that has yet been done still leaves the question of the lesion occasioning this form of paralysis in dispute, one suggestive fact remains—namely, the singular isolation of the posterior columns of the cord by the degenerative process. This fact appears to indicate that the affected structures have their own vitality, and probably, therefore, a separate function from that of adjacent parts. Todd maintained this separate function on other grounds, and concluded that the posterior columns were merely commissures. This theory seems the more probable from the facts now alluded to, inasmuch as textures having such a function may have a lower vitality than others which are more essential. This supposition is strengthened by what is observed under extreme inanition, it having been proved by the well-known experiments of Chossat that the nervous centers resist atrophy more than other tissues. Related to these intrinsic morbid changes, whether local or general, are the cancerous and tubercular affections, and the universal liability of the tissues to that perverted process of nutrition which we call inflammation. Although, for practical purposes, it is convenient to intensify the differences between cancer, tubercle, and the inflammatory process, we have abundant evidence of intimate relations between them. Thus, the children of parents dying of cancer are not rarely tubercular, and those of the third generation are liable to various forms of chronic inflammation; whilst in the same families are healthy individuals, in whom we can discover no evidence of any special morbid tendency. It is not improbable that that which seems most special to us in cancer and tubercle may depend more upon gradation than change of diathesis, and that both are allied to more common degenerations.

In tubercular phthisis this has long been felt and acknowledged. Those who have given most attention to the subject (and I could name no one whose experience would have more weight than that of the late Dr. Addison) have had to confess that the larger their observation, the greater became their difficulty in drawing a line of demarcation, limiting tuberculous from simple inflammatory productions. No doubt many of the errors of prognosis, in phthisis, some willful, some unwitting, arose from assuming a distinction which does not exist, except in extreme cases where, as the logicians would say, the quantum passes into the quale. Although it has been observed that the scrofulous diathesis of early life may show its special characters in age, still we have, on the other side, frequent proof of a change of diathesis to that which is malignant; and your experience will, I am sure, confirm my statement that the tubercular peritonitis of childhood corresponds with great strictness to the cancerous peritonitis of age. It is probable that cancer is nearer to the simple degradation of tissues than tubercle. It appears to be more independent of an external exciting cause; and although in its structure there is an appearance of vital activity, it had no correlation with healthy organic processes, but is a mere eddying off and separation from the organic cycle. A closer inquiry into the local origin of cancer, and of the mode whereby the system becomes infected by it, are yet desiderata. The tendency to infect the body generally may, after all, not be dependent upon a more marked cancerous diathesis, but upon local circumstances only. Something analogous appears to exist in the infecting and noninfecting chancre, for though, according to some authorities, one is essentially local, and one is essentially infecting, yet it appears certain that even the infecting kind has not always the same infecting power.

In passing from these idiopathic or intrinsic morbid conditions to such as arise from accident or *ab extra,* the fevers chiefly claim our notice. In the elucidation of these, smallpox stands for first consideration, since, through vaccination, we have it clearly demonstrated, at least for this one form of fever—and it seems but fair to infer the same of others—that recovery and subsequent immunity are produced by a process of impregnation and assimilation, and not, as was early believed, and is still by some maintained, of elimination. The old theory of depuration, though true of gross chemical poisons, as lead, or mercury, or arsenic, appears to have no application to those operations which take place in the body, in contagious diseases, as the effect of organic poisons. After any one of these, the organism is not restored to its former condition, as if any poison had simply been cast out, but there is notoriously a residual and permanent effect, which has been induced under the superficial disorder, this effect being shown by permanent indisposition to a repetition of the same morbid process. Unfortunately for science, the phenomena of fermentation have been assumed in explanation of what takes place under these circumstances; and by the theory of zymosis we are carried back to the days of ignorance, when concoction and maturation were made to explain whatever was obscure. We discover, however, at the bedside, nothing in the phenomena of febrile disease proper to zymosis. As well might we call the evolution of the germ after impregnation by such a name. The physiological disturbances induced by any one of the fever poisons—namely, the excess of heat, the rapid waste, the quick action of the heart, the altered functions of secretion and excretion, etc., the so-called symptoms of the disease—are but the outward effects common to the class, and only so far peculiar to each as they may vary in time and intensity. That which really constitutes the specific character of each is the attendant tissue change, which when completed according to the special poison, is followed by convalescence.

If this be in any degree an approach to a true conception of these diseases, it follows that the object of medicine must be rather to limit the violence of attendant symptoms, than, with our present knowledge of therapeutics, to aim at arresting or neutralizing their specific processes. Had anyone formerly been asked the remedy for smallpox, he would hardly have seriously supposed the answer to be the poison of smallpox itself. Yet so it has proved; and from this experience we have learned that help may come precisely in the opposite direction to that looked for in our theories, and we obtain a striking proof of the truth of Bacon's aphorism, *"Natura non nisi parendo vincitur."*

Yet, notwithstanding this teaching, pathology still persists in looking in another direction; and therapeutics are governed by the idea that disease is an entity which must be combatted and cast out. I fancy that the habit of calling these and similar affections blood diseases insensibly fosters the idea of depuration. Now, though I am not disposed to stir up a discussion between *solidism* and *humoralism,* I cannot but express my conviction that the susceptibility to the various contagious fevers no way lies in the blood, except so far as this may be a channel through which the poisons reach the tissues, and that it is in these, and especially in the nervous tissues, that the true fever processes begin and end. The facts of habit, such as that of taking opium or using tobacco, the facts of acclimatization, and of the commoner experience of our life, whereby the nervous system becomes accustomed and indifferent to continued sources of irritation, render such an opinion the more probable; a confirmation of it is gained by that enduring effect which ensures against a repetition of morbid actions.

Were I to give liberty to my imagination, I might perhaps trace here a much more extensive law of our nervous organization, whereby that which is new excites, and that which is old becomes indifferent. For my own part, the views which have been put forth as to syphilization have, on these grounds, seemed to deserve the fullest consideration; and, though I have not experience to set against the adverse conclusions of some who have made the subject a matter of experimental inquiry, I feel that we cannot set aside the more extensive experience of those who have asserted its success.

I cannot conclude these general remarks on some difficulties which now occupy our minds in respect to pathology without alluding to the vexed question of rheumatic fever. Is this state due, or is it not, to a *materies morbi*? Further, have we any grounds for assuming that such *materies morbi* is lactic or acetic acid? I put these questions thus explicitly, because it seems to have been settled, upon mere authority, that they may both be answered in the affirmative. I say authority alone, not forgetting the experiments which have been made on animals in proof of this theory, since such experiments appear to me to prove only this, that the acids named, entering the blood, may cause endocarditis and some other pathological changes simulating those of rheumatism; but I cannot recognize in them the rheumatic state, as I am acquainted with it at the bedside. There are, so far as I know, no analyses of the blood in rheumatism which show that it differs from normal blood in respect of its acidity. The theory of an acid *materies morbi* appears to be supported chiefly upon the excessively acid secretion of the skin in this disease, and the increased acidity of the urine. But neither of these can be considered in any degree characteristic; for not only in the worst forms of the rheumatic process is the secretion of the skin not acid, but alkaline, but in conditions of the system totally dissimilar from rheumatism—as, for instance, in phlebitis, and especially in that form following injuries to the head, as well as in arterial embolism—we often meet with excessive acid sweating, misleading to a false diagnosis those who believe this to be characteristic of rheumatism. Notoriously, a proper function of the skin is to secrete and, probably, to form in itself lactic and acetic acid. Under different kinds of irritation this becomes excessive; but I know of no facts to show that this excess indicates a special pathology, or may be regarded as a salutary process, whereby the system is relieved of a *materies morbi*. In so supposing it, we seem to be misled by the same fallacies as, before the time of Sydenham, misled practitioners in the treatment of eruptive diseases. I confess to a strong sympathy with those errors, and, though my reason is convinced that they were errors of the most dangerous kind, I cannot but excuse them and admire the genius and courage of Sydenham, which enabled him to detect and correct them.

If, failing the evidence of the cutaneous secretion, the rheumatologist adduces proof of an acid diathesis from the character of the urine, must not the force of his argument be abated by the admission that urates replace urea in a large number of other morbid conditions, so that we cannot attach any specific value to this fact, the general significance of which will be better appreciated by the physiologist, who will see in the presence of uric acid and the urates a debased condition of organic waste, common to the life of inferior organisms?

To pass, however, from these desultory observations, which the present position of pathology has suggested, the subject of diagnosis claims a few words. We must all admit the diagnosis ultimately rests upon an exhaustive pathology. Without a knowledge of what is possible in disease, diagnosis must be defective, and is, therefore, in that degree defective at the present day, since it is plain that we are unacquainted with many pathological states, if, indeed, we be fully acquainted with any. Moreover, a knowledge which might seem exhaustive today, might, by the changing circumstances of the world, be defective tomorrow. Without raising the question, whether disease has within historical periods changed its type, it may be maintained, as was long ago pointed out, that the pathological tendencies of the body do vary with the *genius anni,* as witness the changes in epidemic disease. Within our present experience, cholera has afforded us new pathological questions, which are not yet solved, and strangely, side by side with it—to make the contrast more impressive—diphtheria has revived, laying before us, as if to teach us how feeble our pathological science is, two opposite conditions: two diseased mucous surfaces—one digestive, one respiratory—from the former of which, by mysterious inversion of its normal forces, the salines and water of the blood may be fatally diffused, and from the latter, as by a kind of morbid polarity, the fibrine only is poured out. Although the perfection of diagnosis cannot be reached till we have a perfect pathology, we have to confess that it falls behind the pathological knowledge we at present possess, as the revelations of the post mortem tables abundantly confirm.

And this brings me to the second principle of diagnosis, a knowledge of the probable in disease. Of this, experience alone can inform us, and experience of the most varied kind. But when so varied, and supported by a large knowledge of pathology, it often enables us, as by prophetic insight, to diagnosticate conditions, which neither direct physical examination, nor the most systematic arrangement of symptoms, could explain. These suggestions are amongst the best fruits of experience— of that experience which is able to anticipate causes, and from causes their effect. The advancement of diagnosis depends upon the capacity of medicine to make these anticipations with increasing certainty, which, though *anticipationes mentis,* are truly *interpretationes naturor.* To illustrate these remarks, what could I better quote than the clinical history of thrombosis and embolism? What mysterious obscurity, until recently, involved the phenomena of which embolism was the cause; but, thanks to Kirkes and Virchow, when once the pregnant fact of embolism in vein or artery is recognized, not only present facts arrange themselves in order, but we are able to anticipate the possible occurrence of others, and, by anticipation, often to prevent them. Symptoms and physical signs may supply us with abundance of clinical facts; but, until the one great fact be recognized in such cases, we can make no step in diagnosis.

Nor does this instance by any means stand alone, for wherever, from the nature of the case, we are unable to make a complete physical examination, as must occur in diseases of the brain, and as often occurs in diseases of the abdomen, pathological inference, or pathological anticipation, has to supply a meaning to other portions of the evidence. In brain diseases, this method of interpretation comes largely into play, and the neglect of it has much to do with the obscurity in which, at the bedside, these diseases are still involved. It is often impossible to form any opinion whatever of the malady under which a patient with brain disease may be laboring, from an inquiry however acute, and however complete, into the mere statical facts, as they at the moment present themselves. The attempt to do so is perhaps more likely to lead to error than to truth; a fact which, if I be right in the statement of it, shows of how little value mere symptoms are in the diagnosis of such diseases.

Abercrombie felt this to its full extent, and one of the objects of his treatise on cerebral disease was to make it clear, and to warn us against future attempts in that direction. A perusal of his writings will leave upon the mind the impression that the most diverse affections of the brain may, at the bedside, present the same symptoms; that in the most extensive lesions there may be none at all; or that the whole catalogue of symptoms may appear without any lesion. But the feeling of despair which such a perusal formerly induced is now in great part dissipated by the success with which the inquiry can be made in the direction pointed out. Admitting that we shall never diagnosticate cerebral lesions by their symptoms—partly, because different lesions may produce the same symptoms if the seat be the same, partly because there appear to be surplusage portions of brain tissue, as in the hemispheres, where lesions cannot make their presence known, and partly because in that monster disturbance epilepsy, we may have a variety of states simulating organic lesion—we betake ourselves again with renewed energy to the study of morbid anatomy and pathology, which first caused the confusion by disturbing our ignorance, feeling assured they will at last afford us a full clue to the difficulty. To a large extent they have already afforded this clue. To begin with the last fallacy I have named, I may remark that we are better acquainted than formerly with the various forms of the epileptic state. A better pathology has prepared us to recognize in this condition a great variety of effects. Todd drew attention to epileptic hemiplegia. In the same subjects there occurs also a remarkable form of coma, which has often led to the supposition of effused blood, or tumor, or abscess, suppositions which have been falsified by the recovery of the patient. Whilst our notion of epilepsy included nothing more than a convulsive state with unconsciousness, numerous errors in diagnosis must have occurred from this source alone. It now represents to us a condition of nerve force, in which may occur not only the common phenomena of epilepsy, but coma without convulsion; paralysis following convulsion; sudden and transient mania, or an approach to it; as well as, according to Trousseau, some strange forms of neuralgia. A knowledge, therefore, that a patient is liable to epilepsy, or comes of a family in which such a state has directly or indirectly occurred, must make us pause in our diagnosis, and thus save us from a precipitate or erroneous conclusion. The proneness of the aged to epilepsy is a fact probably not sufficiently borne in mind in the diagnosis of these cerebral disorders. As to the second fallacy, when disease is situated in what may perhaps be called, without misuse of the term, the surplusage portion of the cerebrum or cerebellum, we are often led to suspect its presence, and as often correctly to infer its nature (and avoid the third fallacy), from a knowledge of the fact of surplusage, and of what is probable under collateral circumstances, though the symptoms of organic disease may be apparently of an insignificant kind. For instance, headache with occasional bilious vomiting in a young and healthy adult—tumor; the same symptoms, with chronic suppuration about the ear, or in some distant part—abscess; nearly the same symptoms, with syphilitic cachexia—syphilitic affection of the brain. This is the merest outline, but the drawing is true to nature. May I say, once for all, that any peculiar shape of head, large or small, has, like the epileptic brain, long been admitted to defy diagnosis. Further, how much have we not gained in the diagnosis of cerebral disease by the known tendency of renal cachexia to induce chronic or subacute cerebritis, and of embolism to cause plugging of the vessels?

In turning from the diseases of the brain to affections of the chest, we find that we are here able to combine our knowledge of the possible and the probable with direct physical signs; consequently the diagnosis of chest affections has very steadily advanced. Old errors, however, still linger even here, and a true dynamic estimate of lung lesions is yet a desideratum. This must be supplied by improved interpretation of physical signs through attendant physiological conditions. The word phthisis, which has now too often a specific value, will dilate so as to include a whole genus of chronic affections, which, when duly recognized and classified, will afford more secure grounds of prognosis, and spare us the perusal of worthless records of so-called consumption cured.

In the diagnosis of abdominal diseases, we want an increase in the number of our more cardinal facts, such facts, for instance, as that the enlarged gall bladder changes its shape under contraction, or that of the two characteristic notches in an enlarged spleen, or that of the peculiar position of the colon in enlarged kidney, etc. At present our diagnosis is mostly one of inference, from our knowledge of the liability of the several organs to particular lesions. Thus we avoid the error of supposing the presence of mesenteric disease in young women emaciated to the last degree through hysteric apepsia by our knowledge of the latter affection, and by the absence of tubercular disease elsewhere. We infer alcoholic changes in the liver from the aspect of the face, mottled by venous stigmata and the yellowish conjunctiva, even without any direct knowledge of the state of the liver, or the habits of the patient. We suspect a cancerous disease of the peritoneum in the aged from the pain with effusion. It is obviously from the perfection of physical diagnosis, aided by pathology, that we must look for the advancement of medicine. The feelings of the patient, so-called symptoms, are of little value taken by themselves; often, in fact, their mere number and variety are a proof of the absence of disease, and it is admitted that they always need interpretation through physical inquiry.

The eye, the ear, the touch—and chemistry replacing the other two senses—are impressed into our daily service, and we may hope that what the ophthalmoscope has effected for the eye, these other means may do for other parts. To chemistry we owe much, but there are two wants we ought to express. We want analyses of the residuum of the urine, especially in disease, in which we may hope to discover new elements for diagnosis; and we further want ready clinical means for recognizing what has been discovered by more elaborate processes. Our hope in the direction of chemistry ought to be unlimited, seeing that changes in the urine must correspond to intimate changes in the organs and texture.

To return, however, to physical diagnosis, the fidelity with which the characters of a disease are often marked in its tissue changes must excite equally our wonder and attention. It may be no more than the tint of the morbidly vascular part—a condition apparently the most trivial and accidental—and yet it returns with unerring certainty under the like conditions, as our guide to diagnosis. The multiplied generations of the vaccine vesicle from one lymph, maintaining to this day, in all respects, the characteristics of that which first arose under the hand of its immortal discoverer, is one of the strongest evidences that I could adduce of such fidelity, and may well encourage us to the investigation of physical signs as an evidence of the pathological causes to which they are due.

But our diagnosis is not always of a single morbid state. There may be grafted upon some special diathesis, as of tubercle or of gout, the effects of alcohol, syphilis, mercury or miasm. No doubt even more complicated instances could be given, but this will suffice to show the character our diagnosis must take before we can proceed to treatment.

As health is our object, or as near an approach to it as circumstances admit, *hygiene* and *therapeutics* claim the last and highest place in our thoughts. Happily, at length, hygiene has gained strength enough to maintain an independent vitality as a science. To know and counteract the causes of disease before they become effective is evidently the triumph of our art; but it will be long before mankind will be wise enough to accept the aid we could give them in this direction. Ignorance of the laws of health and intemperance of all kinds are too powerful for us. Still we shall continue to wage against them an undying crusade; and truly we may today congratulate ourselves that no crusade ever called forth more able and devoted warriors than are engaged in this.

The diseases of the young are in large part preventable diseases. Epidemics carry off in great proportion the healthy members of a community. It is futile, if not worse, to speak as some do of leaving diseases to work out their own ends, as agents of a moral police. Medicine allows no such prerogative to our judgment. It is enough for us that diseases prevail, to stimulate our best efforts for their prevention, without our asking a question beyond.

Nothing can stimulate science more to the investigation of therapeutics than the feeling that the diseases calling for treatment prevail in spite of our best efforts to prevent them. Where hygiene fails, properly commences the work of therapeutics; but it is painful to find ourselves occupied in making feeble and often useless efforts to combat the effects of a poison which might perhaps have been stamped out in its beginnings.

The strength of modern therapeutics lies in the clearer perception than formerly of the great truth that diseases are but perverted life processes, and have for their natural history not only a beginning, but equally a period of culmination and decline. In *common* inflammatory affections, this is now admitted to be the all but universal law. By time and rest, that innate *vis medicatrix,* "Which hath an operation more divine than breath or pen can give expression to," reduces the perversions back again to the physiological limits, and health is restored. To this beneficent law we owe the maintenance of the form and beauty of our race in the presence of all that tends to spoil and degrade it. We cannot pass through the crowded streets and alleys of our cities without recognizing proofs of this in the children's faces, in spite of all their squalor and misery; and, when we remember what this illustration in all its details reveals, we may well take heart, even when our work seems most hopeless. The effects of disease may be for a third or fourth generation, but the laws of health are for a thousand. Bearing this in mind, I have often had occasion to remark in practice how little we can estimate the reparative powers, however able we may be to discover diseases. This is, perhaps, never more striking than in some chronic affections, which, having resisted all our efforts at cure, may have been abandoned in despair, or at length placed under some indifferent treatment. Under these circumstances, with what interest have most of us day by day watched the lessening deviations of disease, until the balance of health has been again all but restored, unstable though the equilibrium thus gained may, from the nature of the case, have been.

Therapeutics were at one time directed only by two ideas—of *strength* and of *weakness*. Sthenic and asthenic expressed in general terms the morbid conditions requiring treatment. Of the same import, but of older date, were the thoughts derived from the then current theory of phlogiston; and the terms phlogistic and anti-phlogistic still linger in medical treatises. From a better physiology, however, we have learned that perverted functions in disease, however exaggerated, are due to failure, and not to excess of the vital powers.

Organic strength lies nowhere but in the vital circle of nutrition and function.

A rapid pulse and active delirium, like the increase of the animal heat, are signs of deficient *balance power*—a power which we have been so slow to recognize in living organisms, that we have not yet an accepted expression for it. How different seems to us at the present day the value of the symptoms which were formerly considered indicative of strength.

In an increase of temperature we see but increased waste. Every degree of rise in the thermometer indicates to us a corresponding decline in that nervous control which regulates the functions in health; and this decline is the more important, if it be true in complex organisms, as it is in simple machines, that this combination which limits the mere working forces is the highest and most characteristic. The terms, "strength" and "weakness," are valueless as expressive of conditions so complicated as those of disease. They are deduced for the most part from the feelings of the patient, and a few superficial phenomena. They are empty idols, impressive only by the extent of their emptiness. Surgical treatment was greatly advanced by the imaginary discovery of the *sympathetic powder,* which being placed upon the instrument inflicting the wound, the injured part, by time and rest, was allowed to recover under the simplest means. We need now to import into medicine a large part of the best surgical principles so deduced. The surgeon is contented to place a wounded part under the conditions of physical and physiological rest, and after attention to hygienic conditions, the *res non naturales* of our forefathers, to abide the result. This, no doubt, expresses the largest part of our treatment of common acute disease. We now know that we cannot directly control the morbid processes in pneumonia, pleurisy, or pericarditis; we know further that the means formerly considered essential to the cure of these diseases, tested by better clinical observations, were either useless or pernicious; that instead of favoring the plastic processes in inflammation, whereby the normal decline of the disease was promoted, the effused material was often more or less degraded and spoiled by the treatment employed, and remained in the affected parts, either as a foreign body, or in different degrees approaching thereto.

And this must always have been so, had we continued to regard these effusions as simply foreign products. But as soon as we perceived their physiological relations, and that they had a life like the tissues from which they sprang, they took a different aspect, and it became our duty, often without much interference, to stand by and watch this course to the end. With an audience like the present, so capable of supplying the proper safeguards to these expressions, I am not likely to be misunderstood, as if the duties of the physician were of a negative kind. There is a sufficient sphere for our activity, in ways too numerous for me to mention: in the relief of symptoms where the lesion may be left to its natural course, in the treatment of the lesion itself where we have means adapted to it—and of these we have many—and in maintaining the health when the degeneration or lesion is incurable. Time would fail me, if it were otherwise proper in this place, to enumerate and enlarge upon the valuable applications of medicine. The discovery of disease, the alleviation of its symptoms, the obviating its inroads, the placing our patient under favorable conditions to bear it, the guarding him against what would be injurious, and the administration of remedies often in themselves effectual for its removal, are surely services of no unimportant kind.

There is probably no human work which daily confers greater good upon society than does ours; and when we consider that from the ranks of our profession the chief cultivators of modern sciences have sprung, whether we speak of botany, comparative anatomy, chemistry, physiology, biology, hygiene, or social science, we may feel some justifiable pride and be encouraged in spite of all failures to go on, assured that our future must be one of ever-increasing usefulness and honor.

WHY ANOREXIA NERVOSA

THE MOUNT SINAI SEMINAR GROUP

We have selected the sydrome of Anorexia Nervosa since it has remained the same at the descriptive level for the past century. Psychological factors were recognized to be of primary and paramount importance by the original authors. The unitary nature of the syndrome allows for a series of papers which offer an opportunity to trace the development of the basic medical concepts in this field over a period of approximately one hundred years.

It is of interest that Stanley Cobb in his paper, "Anorexia Nervosa as a Psychosomatic Problem," has used Anorexia Nervosa as a paradigm of the psychosomatic syndrome.[1]

A tentative psychological explanation has been worked out in the course of time. Gull, who is usually credited with describing the syndrome, recognized the primacy of a psychic constellation. He chose the term Anorexia Nervosa because it emphasized the mental aspect. He seemed to adopt a purely psychological point of view in which the somatic manifestations of the syndrome were purely secondary. Gull appreciated psychological influences on the function of eating. The result of not eating led to starvation with its attendant somatic results. Gull recognized the phenomena of the syndrome including the interdependence of the total clinical picture and the relationship to the environment. He observed the variability of the underlying psychiatric picture. He also noted the periods of bulimia, the overactivity of the patients who did not get tired, and the absence of organic lesions. It was also recognized that there may be a fatal termination.

[1] *Emotions and Clinical Medicine.* New York: Norton, 1950, pp. 140-182.

Gull visualized the psychological factors as acting via a nerve force, a nonspecific kind of energy which relates itself to the other organs. This is a psychophysiological concept. The lack of appetite was the result of the failure of the gastric branches of the pneumogastric nerve, which was in turn due to disturbed nerve force. Nosologically, Gull thought of hysteria but felt that the symptoms were not like those of hysteria. He said, "the want of appetite is due to morbid mental state. The treatment is like that of patients with unsound mind."

The state of neuropsychiatric thinking in the period preceding Gull has been recently reviewed by Stainbrook. He calls attention to the following. Marshall Hall (1833) extended the concept of reflex action and of excitomotor acts. He pointed out that when nerves are irritated, muscular movements can result independently of volition. Thus an excitomotor act could be unconscious. Thomas Laycock (1840) extended the theory of reflex action to the brain. Daniel Hack Tuke (1872) used the principle of reflex action to explain somnambulism and other dissociative behavior. Later Claude Bernard and Brown-Séquard demonstrated vasodynamic reactions to sensory nervous stimulation. All the above were utilized in the nineteenth century to explain the neuroses in terms of reflex irritability, intrinsic or sympathetic, localized in the cerebrum, the "spinal soul," or the ganglionic system.

The intrinsic intensity of irritability was determined by inherited predisposition. This could be increased by direct disease of the nervous system or reflexly by uterine or other organ irritation or disease. In addition, psychological excitement, tension, or emotion could cause nervous hyperirritability.

Gull went one step further and stated in his "Address on Medicine" that as a result of psychic influences tissue changes can take place.[2] He ascribes the pathology to morbid brain force. This he correlates with his main thesis that the total organism is nerve tissue, that whatever is living has nerve quality, and therefore whatever arises in the brain can be transmuted into pathology in other organs. In the morbid state there is apparently a direct neural energy which induces the pathological changes.

[2] *This Volume*, pp. 104-127.

This raises a number of pertinent problems. It is difficult at times to be certain as to whether or not a writer in that era, when talking about psychic forces, utilized the term in the same way as one does currently. It is difficult to determine in what way psychic stimuli were related to somatic functions or to morbid brain force, the term used by Gull. Traces of phrenological influences seem to be present in some of Gull's formulations. The statement that "I believe it to be essentially a failure of the powers of the gastric branches of the pneumogastric nerves" focuses this problem sharply. From some points of view it might be argued that the nineteenth-century physician emphasized psychic influences as etiologic in relation to disease over a much wider area than present-day observers. Stainbrook states that "by 1830 nosologically the neuroses were considered to include nutritional diseases, some of the currently designated psychosomatic disorders, some metabolic and infectious diseases, and that protein behavior hysteria." The apparent similarities with current concepts found in Gull may be more imaginary than real. This is one of the fundamental problems in the attempt to evaluate the historical evolution of basic concepts. Does a knowledge of the unconscious, first formulated by Freud, in principle negate the value of the earlier observations of the importance of psychic influences, or does the knowledge of the unconscious only aid in the mapping of the previously discovered territory? It is obvious that initial observations of psychophysiological phenomena are of the utmost significance. The understanding of the intrinsic mechanisms involved will only be possible when additional observations, hypotheses, and theories are added, since they should be based on increased knowledge which would allow for elaboration of earlier principles. Gull did not ascribe psychodynamics and symbolic significance to Anorexia because he did not have the necessary psychological knowledge. He was also handicapped by the then meager knowledge about menstruation, and hence could only attribute it to the cachexia. Gull did not go far enough to be able to analyze the various elements involved in the psychic influences nor the specific changes which take place in the morbid brain state and the secondary tissue changes.

With the evolution of the psychoanalytic point of view, loss of appetite is not only something which is physiologically and psychologically determined but has a meaning in itself. It relates to the meaning of eating or not eating and concerns in one aspect the fantasy of oral impregnation. Since eating symbolizes pregnancy—oral impregnation—one can understand the periodic breakthrough on an unconscious level of the need to gratify this impulse and relate it to the periods of bulemia. In relation to the cessation of menses, it can be a secondary phenomenon due to the cachexia or it can be a primary phenomenon signifying pregnancy. Waller, Kaufman and Deutsch were among the first to integrate the psychodynamics of Anorexia, to see it in terms of a totality, the various symptoms stemming from a basic fantasy. With psychoanalytic orientation the somatic symptoms assume a different weighting than they did with Gull.

An example of the difficulties which one may be led into by emphasizing one or the other symptoms of a syndrome may be illustrated by the emphasis on the cachexia. The former stress on the cachexia as the pivotal point contributed to the tendency to confuse Simmonds' disease with anorexia nervosa because if anorexia nervosa were a matter of cachexia and starvation, then Simmonds' disease was the same with a pathological basis.

Although credit must be given to Gull for having recognized this syndrome as being psychologically determined, nevertheless, the somatic symptoms in the syndrome were related by him to the single factor of not eating. It brought about a change in body nutrition and resulted in the chain of symptoms which are an integral part of the syndrome. This, as referred to above, is essentially a nonpsychodynamic point of view.

ANOREXIA NERVOSA (APEPSIA HYSTERICA, ANOREXIA HYSTERICA)

WILLIAM W. GULL, M.D.
(1873)

In an address on medicine, delivered at Oxford in the autumn of 1868,[1] I referred to a peculiar form of disease occurring mostly in young women, and characterized by extreme emaciation, and often referred to latent tubercle and mesenteric disease. I remarked that at present our diagnosis of this affection is negative, so far as determining any positive cause from which it springs; that it is mostly one of inference from our clinical knowledge of the liability of the pulmonary or abdominal organs to particular lesions, and by proving the absence of these lesions in the cases in question. The subjects of this affection are mostly of the female sex, and chiefly between the ages of 16 and 23. I have occasionally seen it in males at the same age.

To illustrate the disease I may give the details of two cases, as fair examples of the whole.

Miss A., aet. 17, under the care of Mr. Kelson Wright, of the Clapham Road, was brought to me on Jan. 17, 1866. Her emaciation was very great. It was stated that she had lost 33 lbs. in weight. She was then 5 st. 12 lbs. Height, 5 ft. 5 in. Amenorrhea for nearly a year. No cough. Respirations

---

Reprinted from *Trans. Clin. Soc. London,* 7:22, 1874. Read October 24, 1873.
Editor's note: Owing to difficulties in reproduction, the woodcuts replicating photographs of the patients which originally illustrated this paper have been omitted.
[1] See *This Volume,* pp. 104-127.

throughout chest everywhere normal. Heart sounds normal. Resp. 12; pulse, 56. No vomiting nor diarrhea. Slight constipation. Complete anorexia for animal food, and almost complete anorexia for everything else. Abdomen shrunk and flat, collapsed. No abnormal pulsations of aorta. Tongue clean. Urine normal. Slight deposit of phosphates on boiling. The condition was one of simple starvation. There was but slight variation in her condition, though observed at intervals of three or four months. The pulse was noted on these several occasions as 56 and 60. Resp. 12 to 15. The urine was always normal, but varied in sp. gr., and was sometimes as low as 1005. The case was regarded as one of simple anorexia.

Various remedies were prescribed—the preparations of cinchona, the bichloride of mercury, syrup of the iodide of iron, syrup of the phosphate of iron, citrate of quinine and iron, etc., but no perceptible effect followed their administration. The diet also was varied, but without any effect upon the appetite. Occasionally for a day or two the appetite was voracious, but this was very rare and exceptional. The patient complained of no pain, but was restless and active. This was in fact a striking expression of the nervous state, for it seemed hardly possible that a body so wasted could undergo the exercise which seemed agreeable. There was some peevishness of temper, and a feeling of jealousy. No account could be given of the exciting cause.

Miss A. remained under my observation from Jan. 1866 to March 1868, when she had much improved, and gained in weight from 82 to 128 lbs. The improvement from this time continued, and I saw no more of her medically. The Woodcut, Miss A., No. 2, from photograph taken in 1870, shows her condition at that time.[2] It will be noticeable that as she recovered she had a much younger look, corresponding indeed to her age, 21; whilst the photographs, taken when she was 17, give her the appearance of being near 30. Her health has continued good, and I add a fourth photograph taken in 1872.

It will be observed that all the conditions in this case were negative, and may be explained by the anorexia which led to starvation, and a depression of all the vital functions; viz., amenorrhea, slow pulse, slow breathing. In the stage of greatest emaciation one might have been pardoned for assuming that there was some organic lesion, but from the point of view indicated such an assumption would have been un-

---

[2] See Editor's Note, p. 132, fn.

necessary. This view is supported by the satisfactory course of the case to entire recovery, and by the continuance of good health.

Miss B., aet. 18, was brought to me Oct. 8, 1868, as a case of latent tubercle. Her friends had been advised accordingly to take her for the coming winter to the south of Europe.

The extremely emaciated look, much greater indeed than occurs for the most part in tubercular cases where patients are still going about, impressed me at once with the probability that I should find no visceral disease. Pulse 50, Resp. 16. Physical examination of the chest and abdomen discovered nothing abnormal. All the viscera were apparently healthy. Notwithstanding the great emaciation and apparent weakness, here was a peculiar restlessness, difficult, I was informed, to control. The mother added, "She is never tired." Amenorrhoea since Christmas 1866.

The clinical details of this case were in fact almost identical with the preceding one, even to the number of the pulse and respirations. I find the following memoranda frequently entered in my notebook:— "pulse 56, resp. 12; January 1868, pulse 54, resp. 12; March 1869, pulse 54, resp. 12; March 1870, pulse 50, resp. 12." But little change occurred in the case until 1872, when the respirations became 18 to 20, pulse 60. After that date the recovery was progressive, and at length complete.

The medical treatment probably need not be considered as contributing much to the recovery. It consisted, as in the former case, of various so-called tonics, and a nourishing diet.

Although the two cases I have given have ended in recovery, my experience supplies one instance at least of a fatal termination to this malady. When the emaciation is at the extremest, edema may supervene in the lower extremities, the patient may become sleepless—the pulse become quick, and death be approached by symptoms of feeble febrile reaction. In one such case the post mortem revealed no more than thrombosis of the femoral veins, which appeared to be coincident with the edema of the lower limbs. Death apparently followed from the starvation alone. This is the clinical point to be borne in mind, and is, I believe, the proper guide to treatment. I have observed that in the extreme emaciation, when the pulse and respiration are slow, the temperature is slightly below the normal standard. This fact, together with the observations made by Chossat on the effect of starvation on animals, and their inability to digest food in the state of inanition, without the aid of external heat, has direct clinical bearings, it being necessary to supply external heat as well as food to patients. The best means of applying heat is to place an india rubber tube, having a diameter of 2 inches and a length of 3 or 4 feet, filled with hot water along the spine of the patient, as suggested by Dr. Newington, of Ticehurst.

Food should be administered at intervals varying inversely with the exhaustion and emaciation. The inclination of the patient must be in no way consulted. In the earlier and less severe stages, it is not unusual for the medical attendant to say, in reply to the anxious solicitude of the parents, "Let her do as she likes. Don't force food." Formerly, I thought such advice admissible and proper, but larger experience has shown plainly the danger of allowing the starvation process to go on.

As regards prognosis, none of these cases, however exhausted, are really hopeless whilst life exists; and, for the most part, the prognosis may be considered favorable. The restless activity referred to is also to be controlled, but this is often difficult.

It is sometimes quite shocking to see the extreme exhaustion and emaciation of these patients brought for advice; yet, by warmth and steady supplies of food and stimulants, the strength may be gradually resuscitated, and recovery completed.

After these remarks were penned, Dr. Francis Webb directed my attention to the Paper of Dr. Lasègue (Professor of Clinical Medicine in the Faculty of Medicine of Paris, and Physician to La Pitié Hospital), which was published in the *Archives Générales de Médecine*, April 1873, and translated into pages of the *Medical Times*, September 6 and 27, 1873.

It is plain that Dr. Lasègue and I have the same malady in mind, though the forms of our illustrations are different. Dr. Lasègue does not refer to my address at Oxford, and it is most likely he knew nothing of it. There is, therefore, the more value in his paper, as our observations have been made independently. We have both selected the same expression to characterize the malady.

In the address at Oxford I used the term, apepsia hysterica, but before seeing Dr. Lasègue's paper, it had equally occurred to me that anorexia would be more correct.

The want of appetite is, I believe, due to a morbid mental state. I have not observed in these cases any gastric disorder to which the want of appetite could be referred. I believe, therefore, that its origin is central and not peripheral. That mental states may destroy appetite is notorious, and it will be admitted that young women at the ages named are specially obnoxious to mental perversity. We might call the state hysterical without committing ourselves to the etymological value of the word, or maintaining that the subjects of it have the common symptoms of hysteria. I prefer, however, the more general term, "nervosa," since the disease occurs in males as well as females, and is probably rather central than peripheral. The importance of discriminating such cases in practice is obvious; otherwise prognosis will be erroneous, and treatment misdirected.

In one of the cases I have named the patient had been sent abroad for one or two winters, under the idea that there was a tubercular tendency. I have remarked above that these willful patients are often allowed to drift their own way into a state of extreme exhaustion, when it might have been prevented by placing them under different moral conditions.

The treatment required is obviously that which is fitted for persons of unsound mind. The patients should be fed at regular intervals and surrounded by persons who would have moral control over them, relations and friends being generally the worst attendants.

Addendum

As a further illustration, I may add the following correspondence on one of these cases with Dr. Anderson, of Richmond.

Miss C., aet. 15 years 8 months, was sent to me in April 1873. The clinical history was that she had been ailing for a year, and had become extremely emaciated. The catamenia had never appeared. Pulse 64, resp. 16. Very sleepless for six months past. All the viscera healthy. Urine normal. Lower extremities edematous. Mind weakened. Temper obstinate. Great restlessness. No family history of disease beyond the fact that the maternal grandmother had had peculiar nervous symptoms. I wrote the following letter to Dr. Anderson:—

Dear Dr. Anderson,

I saw Miss C. today. The case appears to be an extreme instance of what I have proposed to call "apepsia hysterica," or "anorexia nervosa." (See "Address on Medicine at Oxford," 1868.) I believe it to be essentially a failure of the powers of the gastric branches of the pneumogastric nerve. It differs from tuberculosis, though that state may subsequently arise, by the pulse, which I found to be 64, by the breathing, 16, the cleanness of the tongue, etc. In fact, the disease will be most correctly interpreted if it is remembered that no symptom more positive than emaciation is presented in and throughout its course.

I would advise warm clothing, and some form of nourishing food every two hours, as milk, cream, soup, eggs, fish, chicken. I must only urge the necessity of nourishment in some form, otherwise the venous obstruction, which has already begun to show itself by oedema of the legs, will go on to plugging the vessels. With the nourishment I would conjoin a dessert-spoonful of brandy every two or three hours. Whilst the present state of weakness continues, fatigue must be limited, and if the exhaustion increases beyond its present degree the patient should for a time be kept in a warm bed. I do not at present prescribe medicines, because the nursing and the food are more important than anything else. Such cases not infrequently come before me; but as the morbid state is not yet generally recognised, I should be glad if you would second my wish of having a photograph taken of Miss C. in her present state, that we may compare it with some later one, if, as I hope, our plan of treatment is successful, as in my experience it generally is. I would, as I say, enclose a prescription, but I feel it most necessary to insist on food and stimulants, at least for a time.

Yours truly,

April 30, 1873.

On May 24 I received the following note from Dr. Anderson:

Dear Sir William,

I enclose photograph of Miss C. . . . There is rather an improvement in one respect, viz. there is less aversion to food. Want of sleep and swelling of the feet are the two great troubles. You have given us all new hope, however, and I trust I may one day send you a *plump* photograph, like what she was two years ago. With renewed thanks, I am, dear Sir William,

Yours very truly,

On Oct. 23, 1873, I received a further report.

Dear Sir William,

Miss C. is now at Shanklin, but returns very soon. I hear she is much better. She had a bad slough on the leg near the ankle, from persisting in wearing a tight boot.

The great difficulty was to keep her quiet, and to make her eat and drink. Every step had to be fought. She was most loquacious and obstinate, anxious to overdo herself bodily and mentally. I will give you particulars when they return, but I am told she is much improved. Rest, and food, and stimulants as prescribed, undoubtedly did her a great deal of good. She used to be a nice, plump, good-natured little girl. Believe me. . . .

The last report I received was on April 15, 1874.

Dear Sir W.,

I am sure you will be delighted to hear that Miss C., in whose case you were so kindly interested, . . . has now made a complete recovery, and is getting plump and rosy as of yore. . . .

ANOREXIA NERVOSA

WILLIAM W. GULL, M.D.
(1888)

It may interest the readers of *The Lancet* to look at the accompanying wood engravings, which were made from photographs of a case of extreme starvation (anorexia nervosa) which was brought to me on April 20th of last year by Dr. Leachman, of Petersfield. Dr. Leachman was good enough subsequently to send me the following notes, and afterwards, at my request, the two photographs, taken by Mr. C. S. Ticehurst, of Petersfield. The case was so extreme that, had it not been photographed and accurately engraved, some assurance would have been necessary that the appearances were not exaggerated, or even caricatured, which they were not.

Miss K. R., aged fourteen, the third child in a family of six, one of whom died in infancy, Father died, aged sixty-eight, of pneumonic phthisis. Mother living, and in good health. Has a sister the subject of various nervous symptoms, and a nephew epileptic. With these exceptions, there have been no other neurotic cases on either side in the family, which is a large one. The patient, who was a plump, healthy girl until the beginning of last year (1887), began, early in February, without apparent cause, to evince a repugnance to food; and soon afterwards declined to take any whatever, except half a cup of tea or coffee. On March 13th she travelled from the north of England, and visited me on April 20th. She was then extremely emaciated, and persisted in walking through the streets to my house, though an object of remark to the passersby. Extremities blue and cold. Examina-

---

Reprinted from *Lancet*, 1:516, 1888.

tion showed no organic disease. Respiration 12 to 14; pulse 46; temperature 97 deg. Urine normal. Weight 4 st. 7 lb.; height 5 ft. 4 in. Patient expressed herself as quite well. A nurse was obtained from Guy's, and light food ordered every few hours. In six weeks Dr. Leachman reported her condition to be fairly good; and on July 27th the mother wrote: "K is nearly well. I have no trouble now about her eating. Nurse has been away three weeks."

This story, in fine, is an illustration of most of these cases, perversions of the "ego" being the cause and determining the course of the malady. As part of the pathological history, it is curious to note, as I did in my first paper, the persistent wish to be on the move, though the emaciation was so great and the nutritive functions at an extreme ebb.

ON HYSTERICAL ANOREXIA

E. C. LASÈGUE, M.D.
(1873)

The great value of Lasègue's paper lies in the brilliant clinical description in which the phenomena of the syndrome are related in a perspective which involves motivation and the reaction of the patient to the symptoms. In fact, he utilizes the "state of quietude—I might almost say a condition of contentment truly pathological" as part of a differential diagnosis. Historically, it is of significance that Lasègue, who apparently made his observations and published his series of cases on hysterical anorexia independently of Gull, selected the title, "Anorexia," as commented on by Gull. Lasègue's paper, both on a descriptive and dynamic level, is more psychologically oriented and richer in its descriptive and phenomenological level. There is sufficient historical justification for renaming this syndrome the Gull-Lasègue Syndrome:

"After these remarks were penned, Dr. Francis Webb directed my attention to the paper of Dr. Lasègue. . . . It is plain that Dr. Lasègue and I have the same malady in mind, though the forms of our illustrations are different. Dr. Lasègue does not refer to my address at Oxford, and it is most likely he knew nothing of it. There is, therefore, the more value in his paper, as our observations have been made independently. We have both selected the same expression to characterize the malady. In the address at Oxford, I used the term "apepsia hysterica," but before seeing Dr. Lasègue's paper, it had equally occurred to me that anorexia would be more correct."[1]

[1] Trans. Clin. Soc. London, 7:25, 1874.

In contrast to Gull who tries to explain the disturbance on the basis of a disturbed nerve force, Lasègue postulates an active reaction on the part of the patient to food leading to disgust as the beginning of the illness. The anorexia is thus psychogenically motivated. However, even though Gull stressed morbid nerve force, the latter was effected by a psychic influence. Lasègue was so impressed with psychological factors in control of appetite that he tried to explain even the voraciousness of the diabetic as being of psychological origin. This is an interesting commentary that has present-day pertinence since psychoanalytic psychiatry refers to the "orality" present in diabetes, even though it is known that the physiological action of insulin leads to an increase in appetite. Here we have a beginning attempt to relate specific symptoms of hysteria to an individual patient. He goes so far as to state, "In my opinion we shall never succeed in composing the history of hysterical affections but by the separate study of each symptomatic group. After this preliminary analytical labor, we may collect the fragments, and from them reproduce the whole disease. Regarded in its entirety, hysteria has too many individual phenomena and hazardous incidents to allow of the particular being found in the general. This procedure, very questionable when applied to disease limited as to time, as to space and localizations, and as to the modality of phenomena, here finds its legitimate employment. I have already endeavored to characterize cough and temporary catalepsy of a hysterical nature; and others have devoted valuable monographs to hemiplegia, transitory or permanent contractions, anesthesia, etc. On the present occasion I wish to treat of a symptomatic complexus too often observed to be a mere exceptional occurrence, and which possesses the further advantage of enabling us to penetrate into the intimacy of the mental dispositions of hysterical subjects."

His justification for using the term anorexia rather than hysterical inanition is that anorexia "refers to a phenomenology which is less superficial, more delicate and also more medical," by which he means that it is more etiological. The treatment of the individual has to be related to that individual. He is advocating an analysis of the etiology and the course of the symptomatology. He is trying to find out why although we have all been familiar with gastric sensations related to anxiety, and we have no hesitancy in relating them to the psychic cause, when an individual is suddenly seized with this epigastric condition, without any obvious cause, the natural impulse is to search for some organic cause. If the gastric disturbance is not too great, then it may lead to looking around for other causes which may then lead to the delusion of persecution.

How does Lasègue differ from Gull and what is the position of Lasègue in terms of the more modern concept? Lasègue is trying to prove that it is a psychogenically motivated disease. Even though both Gull and Lasègue emphasize to various degrees the psychic component, there isn't the slightest trace of the genetic component. Neither one felt the need for a history of the patient. It can be a persistent motivation but not necessarily a motivation that arises out of the personality of the individual or the history. Even Gull, when he talked of disturbed nerve force, had in mind that the nerve force was disturbed by a psychic factor. He paid special attention to the intrafamily relationship—the effect of the family on the patient and the reverse.

In my opinion we shall never succeed in composing the history of hysterical affections, but by the separate study of each symptomatic group. After this preliminary analytical labor, we may collect the fragments, and from them reproduce the whole disease. Regarded in its entirety, hysteria has too many individual phenomena and hazardous incidents to allow the particular being found in the general.

This procedure, very questionable when applied to diseases limited as to time, as to space and localizations, and as to the modality of phenomena here finds its legitimate employment. I have already endeavored to characterize cough and temporary catalepsy of a hysterical nature; and others have devoted valuable monographs to hemiplegia, transitory or permanent contractions, anesthesia, etc. On the present occasion I wish to treat a symptomatic complexus too often observed to be a mere exceptional occurrence, and which possesses the further advantage of enabling us to penetrate into the intimacy of the mental dispositions of hysterical subjects.

The disturbances of the digestive organs which supervene during the course of hysteria are numerous. They consist in repeated and sometimes almost incoercible vomiting, in gastric pains, haematemeses,

---

Translated from *Archives Générales de Médecine*, April, 1873.

in constipations, or diarrheas, which are singular, whether by their evolution or by some of their characters. Among the more serious symptoms, vomiting of blood has chiefly attracted the attention of physicians. Gastralgias—purely subjective phenomena—are ill-understood, and disturbances of the intestinal canal give rise to much uncertainty.

Attention has been paid in preference to the curious perversions of appetite, examples of which superabound in almost innumerable varieties. While relating singular cases of strange appetite, the true condition of the patients has not been investigated; and the whole is reduced to the profitless notion that hysterical patients are liable to the most out-of-the-way disorders of the digestive functions. Nevertheless, it would not be impossible to attempt a classification of this description of anomalies; but although I have had the opportunity of observing a great number of these, I do not intend to speak of them here, even incidentally.

The object of this memoir is to make known one of the forms of hysteria of the gastric center which is of sufficient frequency for its description not to be, as too readily happens, the artificial generalization of a particular case, and constant enough in its symptoms to allow of physicians who have met with it controlling the accuracy of the description, and to prevent those who have yet to meet with it in their practice being taken unawares. The term "anorexia" might have been replaced by "hysterical inanition," which would better represent the most characteristic of the accidents; but I have preferred the former term without otherwise defending it, precisely because it refers to a phenomenology which is less superficial, more delicate, and also more medical.

Of the different stages of which digestion consists, the best analyzed by patients, and the least easily investigated by the physician, is the appetite for food. If the term "anorexia" is generally adopted to represent a pathological condition, it has no physiological correspondent, and the word "orexia" does not exist in our language. The consequence is that we are defective in expressions for the degrees or varieties of inappetence—the poverty of our vocabulary corresponding to the insufficiency of our knowledge.

In certain cases there is suppression of appetite, without the patient exhibiting aught else than regret at the absence of a stimulus for taking food. Repugnance is not present, and frequently the proverb, *"l'ap-*

pétit vient en mangeant," receives its justification. Under other conditions, the patient has a more or less decided repugnance for certain aliments, while in other cases any alimentary substance whatever excites disgust. However general the inappetence may be, it always has its graduated scale, so that aliments are not indiscriminately rejected with the same insistence.

On the other hand there are affections, whether of the stomach or of the central nervous system, whether localized or diathetic, which are accompanied by an illusory sense of appetite, occurring at unequal or quasi-regular intervals. In certain hysterical and in certain diabetic patients these false appetites become exacting and imperious. Almost always such patients, in obedience to a theoretical hypothesis, entertain the idea that their uneasiness is due to inanition, and that it may be overcome by the aid of nutriment, however reduced in quantity this may be. Experience shows us that two drops of laudanum succeed better in appeasing this imaginary hunger than does the ingestion of aliments.

Exactly opposed to this exaggeration is the diminished appetite and the conviction that food will prove injurious, the patient here, as in the former case, acting in conformity to an instinctive hypothesis. When she is docile, and desirous of being delivered from her fears, she makes the effort, and acquires the conviction either that her health is improved under the employment of alimentation, even though it does cause suffering, or that her apprehensions have been ill-founded. When indocile, and anxious before all things to avoid pain, which, although hypothetical, is dreaded in advance, she persists in her abstinence from food. This is the case with the hysterical patients, whose history I shall now endeavour to depict. Cases which persist for years are not suitable for narration, and I believe that it will be better, in place of particular facts, that I should present a somewhat diagramatic sketch of the disease.

A young girl, between fifteen and twenty years of age, suffers from some emotion which she avows or conceals. Generally it relates to some real or imaginary marriage project, to a violence done to some sympathy, or to some more or less conscient desire. At other times, only conjectures can be offered concerning the occasional cause, whether that the girl has an interest in adopting the mutism so common in the hysterical, or that the primary cause really escapes her.

At first, she feels uneasiness after food, vague sensations of fullness, suffering, and astralgia post-prandium, or rather coming on from the commencement of the repast. Neither she nor those about her attach any importance to this. The same sensations are repeated during several days, but if they are slight they are tenacious. The patient thinks to herself that the best remedy for this indefinite and painful uneasiness will be to diminish her food. Up to this point there is nothing remarkable in her case, for almost every sufferer from gastralgia has submitted to this temptation, until he has become assured that such relative inanition is not only profitless but aggravates his suffering. With the hysterical things take another course. Gradually she reduces her food, furnishing pretexts, sometimes in a headache, sometimes in temporary distaste, and sometimes in the fear of a recurrence of pain after eating. At the end of some weeks there is no longer a supposed temporary repugnance, but a refusal of food that may be indefinitely prolonged. The disease is now declared, and so surely will it pursue its course that it becomes easy to prognosticate the future. Woe to the physician who, misunderstanding the peril, treats as a fancy without object or duration an obstinacy which he hopes to vanquish by medicines, friendly advice, or by the still more defective resource, intimidation. With hysterical subjects a first medical fault is never reparable. Ever on the watch for the judgments concerning themselves, especially such as are approved by the family, they never pardon; and considering that hostilities have been commenced against them, they attribute to themselves the right of employing these with implacable tenacity. At this initial period, the only prudent course to pursue is to observe, to keep silent, and to remember that when voluntary inanition dates from several weeks it has become a pathological condition, having a long course to run.

It is necessary, in order to appreciate at their value the various elements which concur in the development of the disease, to submit each of these to a minute analysis. The gastric pain, which is, or appears to be, the point of departure of the accidents, requires especially that we should dwell upon a kind of stomachal cramp, accompanied by fainting, pallor, sweats, or even shivering. There is neither vomiting nor any real desire to vomit even in extreme cases, the patient only asserting that a degree beyond would induce this. In mere appearance these painful paroxysms in nowise differ from those which are so frequently met with in all affections of the digestive organs. Food induces them, and they do not occur except after meals. If this were really so, we should want any distinctive signs, and should be reduced to adding gastralgia to the already too long list of localized hysterical neuroses.

But the painful sensation persists more or less during the intervals of the repasts, being sometimes insignificant, sometimes more considerable, and now and then so attenuated in degree that the patient complains of a general uneasiness without being able to indicate a fixed point. Whatever may be its form, seat, or degree, is this painful sensation due to a stomachal lesion, or is it not only the reflex impression of a perversion of the central nervous system? I cannot believe that the solution can rest doubtful from the moment that the question is put. At the commencement of a great number of cerebrospinal diseases we meet with precordial suffering, a sense of epigastric pressure, or contractions, which also attend even transitory emotions. All of us have felt this kind of uneasiness while referring it to the definite moral cause that has given rise to it. But supposing an individual were suddenly seized with this epigastric constriction, without any obvious cause; the uneasiness becomes such as to give rise to anxiety. The patient seeks from whence so strange an impression can arise, and it is often in such a search that the *délire des persécutés* commences. Supposing that the cephalic affection does not lead to such consequences, the first and most natural hypothesis that occurs to the patient is that he is suffering from disease of the stomach. All precordial anxiety, with apprehension and the semivertigo it entails, becomes exaggerated by food, which forms an additional reason for attributing it to gastric irritation.

The characteristics of this gastralgia from reflex causes are not impossible of discernment, the circumstances under which they may exist being by no means of rare occurrence. It is distinguished from painful irritation of the stomach because it is not exactly localized, and is accompanied by an entirely special inquietude; it is sudden, the way not having been prepared for it by gradually increasing indigestions; it is not followed by dyspeptic accidents; the intestinal functions remain unimpaired save by habitual constipation, which is easily overcome; the nature of the food taken exercises no influence on the paroxysms; and the character of the pain, when it really exists, bears no analogy to the gastric suffering determined by a lesion, however superficial.

From the moment that the nature of this malaise has been ascertained important progress has been made in the establishment of the diagnosis. I cannot too strongly insist on these splanchnic neuroses, and on their relations to certain cerebral conditions.

The hysterical subject, after some indecision of but short duration, does not hesitate to affirm that her only chance of relief lies in an abstinence from food; and, in fact, the remedies appropriate to other gastralgias are here absolutely inefficacious, however zealously both physician and patient may employ them. The repugnance for food continues slowly progressive. Meal after meal is discontinued, one of these, whether breakfast or dinner, alone being alimentary; and almost always some article of diet is successively suppressed, whether this be bread, meat, or certain vegetables—sometimes one alimentary substance being replaced by another, for which an exclusive predilection may be manifested for weeks together. Things may be thus prolonged during weeks or months without the general health seeming to be unfavorably influenced, the tongue being clean and moist and thirst entirely absent. The persevering constipation readily yields to mild laxatives, the abdomen is not retracted, and sleep continues more or less regular. There is no emaciation, although the amount of nutriment scarcely amounts to a tenth of that habitually required by the patient. The power of resistance of the general health in the hysterical is too well known for astonishment being excited at seeing them support without injury a systematic inanition to which robust women could not be exposed with impunity. Moreover, this diminution of aliment is made not suddenly, but by degrees, so that the economy more easily habituates itself to the decrease. Another ascertained fact is, that so far from muscular power being diminished, this abstinence tends to increase the aptitude for movement. The patient feels more light and active, rides on horseback, receives and pays visits, and is able to pursue a fatiguing life in the world without perceiving the lassitude she would at other times have complained of. There are no visible signs of chlorosis or anemia, or, at least, inanition cannot be accused of having induced them, for most of the patients were already in a chloro-anemic condition.

If the situation has undergone no change as regards the anorexia and refusal of food, the mental condition of the patient is brought out more prominently, while the dispositions of those surrounding her undergo modification as the disease becomes prolonged. If the physician had promised rapid amendment, or if he has suspected a bad disposition on the part of his patient, he has long since lost all moral authority. Nevertheless, the patient only exceptionally resists the administration of medicines. Just as she is invincible in regard to food, she shows herself docile even for the least attractive remedies. I have seen one chewing morsels of rhubarb whom no consideration would have induced to taste a cutlet. The most active gastric stimuli, purgatives whether mild or drastic, mineral waters, produce no effect, good or bad. The same may be said of diffusible stimuli, fetid gums, valerian, hydrotherapeutics, douches at different temperatures, as also of tonics, preparations of iron, cutaneous derivatives, etc. Laxatives alone are of use by removing constipation, none of the other agents even producing a diminution of the anorexia. When after several months the family, the doctor, and the friends perceive the persistent inutility of all these attempts, anxiety and with it moral treatment commences; and it is now that is developed that mental perversion, which by itself is almost characteristic, and which justifies the name which I have proposed for want of a better—hysterical anorexia.

The family has but two methods at its service which it always exhausts—entreaties and menaces—and which both serve as a touchstone. The delicacies of the table are multiplied in the hope of stimulating the appetite; but the more the solicitude increases, the more the appetite diminishes. The patient disdainfully tastes the new viands, and after having thus shown her willingness, holds herself absolved from any obligation to do more. She is besought, as a favour, and as a sovereign proof of affection, to consent to add even an additional mouthful to what she has taken; but this excess of insistence begets an excess of resistance. For it is a well-known law comfortable to the experience of all that the best way to double the obstinacy of the hysterical is to allow the supposition, explicitly or implicitly expressed, to transpire that if they would they could dominate their morbid impulses. A single concession would transfer them from the position of patients to that of capricious children; and to this concession, in part from instinct and in part from obstinacy, they will never consent.

The anorexia gradually becomes the sole object of preoccupation and conversation. The patient thus gets surrounded by a kind of atmosphere, from which there is no escape during the entire day. Friends join counsels with relatives, each contributing to the common stock, according to the nature of his disposition or the degree of his affection. Now, there is another most positive law that hysteria is subject to the influence of the surrounding medium, and that the disease becomes developed and condensed so much the more as the circle within which revolve the ideas and sentiments of the patient becomes more narrowed. The fault does not altogether lie in a pathological vitiation of disposition. Under the influence of sensations, which in more than one particular resemble the impressions of hypochondriacs and the delirious ideas of the insane, the hysterical constantly find themselves unable to resist this domination by a voluntary effort. At the most, distraction of attention enables them to forget at intervals, and these are the sole respites they obtain. The more their attention is intensified, the more does their idea of malaise become developed, and at the end of a variable time of this mischievous concentration the patient enters upon a new phase, and, systematizing after the manner of certain of the insane, she no longer troubles herself in search of arguments. The responses become still more uniform than the questions.

Tired of supplications, if the endeavor be made to insist, the attempt will be still more fruitless than those which preceded it. In fact, what *is* to be said? The patient, when told that she cannot live upon an amount of food that would not support a young infant, replies that it furnishes sufficient nourishment for her, adding that she is neither changed nor thinner, and has never refused encountering any task or labor. She knows better than anyone what she requires, and, moreover, it would be impossible for her to tolerate a more abundant alimentation. When told that this inanition will at last induce disease of the stomach, she says that she never was better, and suffers in no way, her state of good health contradicting all these fears. And, in fact, the pains attendant on the early stages have diminished or disappeared or only return at long intervals—an amelioration attributed by her to the regimen she has pursued. The fasting, indeed, is not absolute, and in no way resembles the refusal of food in melancholia. The anorexia has not increased, and especially it has not become transformed into the analogous disgust for food felt by some phthisical and many cancerous patients. The patient willingly joins her family at meals, on the condition that she is allowed to take only what she wishes.

What dominates in the mental condition of the hysterical patient is, above all, the state of quietude—I might almost say a condition of contentment truly pathological. Not only does she not sigh for recovery, but she is not ill-pleased with her condition, notwithstanding all the unpleasantness it is attended with. In comparing this satisfied assurance to the obstinacy of the insane, I do not think I am going too far. Compare this with all the other forms of anorexia, and observe how different they are. At the very height of his repugnance, the subject of cancer hopes for and solicits some aliment which may excite his appetite, and is ready for all kinds of trials, although incapable of triumphing over his disgust. The dyspeptic, without organic lesion, exhausts his ingenuity in varying his regimen, and complains with all the bitterness habitual to those who suffer from affections of the stomach. Here we have nothing like this, but, on the contrary, an inexhaustible optimism, against which supplications and menaces are alike of no avail: "I do not suffer, and must then be well," is the monotonous formula which has replaced the preceding, "I cannot eat because I suffer." So often have I heard this phrase repeated by patients, that now it has come to represent for me a symptom—almost a sign.

If I attach to this mental condition an importance that perhaps will appear exaggerated, it is that in fact the whole disease is summed up in this intellectual perversion. Suppress this, and you have an ordinary affection which at last yields to the classic procedures of treatment. Carry it to its extreme—and you will never go too far—and then you have a dyspepsia course, and which will not be relieved by habitual means. Moreover, I do not believe that gastric hysteria is any exceptional occurrence, for in other hysterical localizations we meet with at least an equal indifference, however inconvenient and painful their manifestations may be. The subject of hysterical convulsive cough does not demand relief from a spasm which is so irritating and sometimes so ridiculous. She joins in the chorus of those who are pitying her; but when active treatment is in question, she is more indifferent than zealous in the matter. It is the same with paraplegic patients condemned to absolute repose, and who are willing to live in this way, without ever insisting that their attendants, exhausted in useless attempts, should have recourse to heroic measures. . . .

In the end, the tolerance of the economy, marvelous as this is, becomes exhausted, and the disease enters upon its third stage. Menstruation, which up to then had been insufficient and irregular, now ceases, and thirst supervenes. An examination shows retraction of the abdomen, which has not been observed before, and palpation indicates a progressive diminution of its elasticity, a habitual symptom in prolonged inanition. The epigastric region has become tender to pressure, although the patient complains of no spontaneous pains. An obstinate constipation no longer yields to purgatives. The skin is dry, rugous, and without suppleness. The pulse is frequent. Emaciation makes rapid progress, and with it the general debility increases. Exercise becomes laborious, the patient remaining willingly lying down; and when she rises she suffers from vertigo, a tendency to sickness, or even attacks of syncope. The countenance is pale, without the lips being colourless. An anemic cardiovascular souffle is almost constant, and which, often existing in advance of the affection, rarely fails to appear at its late period. This sketch is far from representing exactly the individual diversities that are observed. Sometimes it is the emaciation, sometimes the debility, sometimes the anemia with its accompanyng local or general accidents, that is most prominent; while exceptionally nervous spasmodic disturbances, neuralgias, etc., arise, the active symptoms seeming to become effaced in proportion as the strength of vital resistance is diminished.

The appearance of these signs, the import of which can escape no one, redoubles anxieties, and the relatives and friends begin to regard the case as desperate. It must not cause surprise to find me thus always placing in parallel the morbid condition of the hysterical subject and the preoccupations of those who surround her. These two circumstances are intimately connected, and we should acquire an erroneous idea of the disease by confining ourselves to an examination of the patient. Whenever a moral element intervenes in a disease, as here it does without any doubt, the moral medium amidst which the patient lives exercises an influence which it would be equally regrettable to overlook or misunderstand. True and sincere affliction has succeeded to remonstrances. By the force of sentiments as much as by the necessities caused by new sufferings, the hysterical subject has been constituted really a sick person, no longer taking part in the free movements of a common life. It seems to me that this unconscious change in the respective positions of the patient and her friends plays here a considerable part. The young girl begins to be anxious from the sad appearance of those who surround her, and for the first time her self-satisfied indifference receives a shock. The moment has now arrived when the physician, if he has been careful in managing the case with a prevision of the future, resumes his authority. Treatment is no longer submitted to with a mere passive condescendence, but is sought for with an eagerness that the patient still tries to conceal. The struggle thus established between the past and the present is a curious one to observe, and easy of proof providing that the investigation is in nowise allowed to be suspected.

Two courses are now open to the patient. She either is so yielding as to become obedient without restriction, which is rare; or she submits with a semi-docility, with the evident hope that she will avert the peril without renouncing her ideas and perhaps the interest that her malady has inspired. This second tendency, which is by far the more common, vastly complicates the situation. It is no easy thing to reestablish the regular function of a stomach which has so long been condemned to repose. We meet with alternatives of success and failure, and frequently only obtain a very insufficient result. I know patients who ten years after the origin of the affection have not yet recovered the aptitude of eating like other people. Their health is not deeply affected, but their amendment is very far from representing a cure.

Sometimes some unexpected event comes to break through the course of the disease—a marriage, grief, or some great moral perturbation. At others it is some physical occurrence, as a pregnancy or a febrile affection; but there are causes which resist both classes of these modifying agents. As a general rule we must look forward to a change for the better only taking place slowly—by successive starts; and we should be on our guard against affirming beforehand the amount of amelioration with which we must rest content.

Well-founded as anxiety in these cases may be, I have never yet seen an anorexia terminate directly in death; but, in spite of this experimental assurance, I have passed through repeated perplexities. It is probable that the pathological sensation—the primary cause of the inanition—disappears by the fact of the increasing cachexia. It is not only of fever that we may say that it resolves spasmodic action, for the same property appertans to a great number of other morbid conditions. Delivered of her subdelirious preoccupation, the hysterical patient passes into the condition of other dyspeptic patients, and only presents the same difficulties in her cure that we are accustomed to meet with. Hysteria, whatever extreme violence it may attain, is not itself mortal, but it may become the occasional or indirect cause of fatal disease: and first among these is pulmonary tubercle. The hysterical anorexia itself is always cured more or less completely at the end of years, passing through the period of decrease with an appetite that is limited or exclusive, and occasionally fantastical. I attended with Trousseau a young woman who, having been thoroughly hysterical from the time of puberty, became, without appreciable cause, the subject of an invincible anorexia. She had reached such a state of emaciation and debility that she could no longer leave her bed. Her food consisted exclusively of some cups of tea with milk. Obstinate constipation had let to serious diarrhea, with pseudomembranous exudations. Nevertheless she became pregnant, and under the influence of that condition she set her wits to work to find out some article of food agreeable to her stomach. During six months she lived only on *café au lait,* into which she cut slices of pickled cucumbers, only adding very gradually some feculents to this singular diet. At the present time she is in a most satisfactory state of health, although always remaining excessively lean. Generally the appetite limits itself to aliments less singularly chosen, and then a free career is given to the fancy. I remember a patient twenty-six years of age, who, living in a distant province, neither would nor could eat anything but a biscuit made by a particular Paris baker. Many confine themselves to a particular kind of vegetable, refusing both meat and bread, while others will only take viands, the taste of which is disguised by spices. Although these capricious restrictions are a favourable sign, the patients continue to submit themselves without any desire to the diet they have chosen for want of a better. The anorexia persists indefinitely for long after they have returned to the ordinary regimen. I have never known the disease to relapse, and, once established, the relative or complete cure is maintaind. At the period when the hysterical affection had yielded, or had assumed other forms, I have endeavored to obtain from the patients some more precise information concerning the sensations they had experienced, and which had induced them to avoid food. None of them have been able to furnish me with anything more exact than what I have reported. The typical formula employed during the course of the disease was reproduced—"I could not; it was too strong for me, and, moreover, I was very well."

The cases which have served me as a basis for this memoir are eight in number, all women, the youngest being 18, and the eldest 32. Hysteria manifested its presence in all by various symptoms, and in one only there had not been paroxysms. She was chloro-anemic, and her mother had suffered from two attacks of hysterical hemiplegia. It was easy enough to assign the date of the commencement of the affection, but the anorexia was lost while passing through such insensible shades that the precise period of its termination could not be fixed. Speaking as nearly to the truth as possible, we may say that the affection, comprising the various phases that have been indicated, has never persisted for less time than from eighteen months to two years.

Although these cases are few in number, they so much resemble each other that the latter ones found me in no indecision in regard either to diagnosis or prognosis, and, in fact, all passed on according to rule. In describing this variety, I proposed to myself, as I said at the commencement, to detach a species or a fragment, but especially to signalize the considerable part that is played in certain forms of hysteria by the mental disposition of the patient, and to point out yet once more the intimate relation that attaches hysteria to hypochondriasis.

EXCERPTS FROM *THE MAJOR SYMPTOMS OF HYSTERIA*

PIERRE JANET, Ph.D., M.D.
(1929)

In his book The Major Symptoms of Hysteria, *Janet devotes considerable space to a discussion and evaluation of Lasègue's management of patients with anorexia nervosa. Woven through this discussion are Janet's own formulations of the explanation of the symptomatology and nosology of the syndrome.*

The patients who no longer leave their beds remain in a semidelirious, semicomatose condition. At this stage they behave in two different ways; some continue to be delirious, and, as Charcot said, have but one idea left, namely, to refuse to eat. Others, fortunately, begin to be frightened. That was what Lasègue expected; because of a singular therapeutic dignity, he judged that the physician was not justified in doing anything before. At that moment he resumed his authority, and according as the patient yielded completely or partially—which latter case was the more frequent—he cured her more or less completely. In fact, the hysterical is privileged in this respect. You know that the dog cannot be called back to life when it has lost forty per cent of its weight; the hysterical can still be saved at fifty and above. There is a limit, however. Out of his eight cases, Lasègue had not one death; the number of deaths since then cannot be numbered. I know three, for my part.

Quoted from Janet, P.: *The Major Symptoms of Hysteria*. New York: Macmillan, 1929.

It is the melancholy period when these poor girls ask to eat and it is too late. It is true that things generally take another turn, and an intercurrent disease comes on, bronchopneumonia or almost phthisis, which simplifies the situation (pp. 232-233).

Janet's Discussion of the Etiology of Anorexia Nervosa (pp. 233-235)

Lasègue, and later on Charcot, gave the pre-eminence to a delirious disturbance, to a fixed idea. The disease consists essentially in an idea of which the patient is perfectly conscious, though she often conceals it, and which has for consequences the voluntary and calculated refusal of food. Some are overanxious about their stomach, apprehend the pains provoked by digestion, or simply fear the sensation of a ball in their esophagus. Others have scruples, regrets to eat the flesh of living animals, are ashamed to eat when too many poor people have not sufficient food. I knew a girl of eighteen who died in consequence of her abhorrence of turnips, which she had contracted when at school. To the end she refused to eat anything, saying that everything smelt of turnips. Very often, they simply have the commonplace idea of suicide; for some reason or other these girls make up their minds to die because of a thwarted marriage, a reproach, for having quarreled with a friend, etc. And, in their innocence, they adopt starvation for their mode of death, judging it to be a simple, clean, not very painful process, which will arouse nobody's suspicion. The following observation of Charcot is famous: while undressing a patient of this kind, he found that she wore on her skin, fastened very tight around her waist, a rose-colored ribbon. He obtained the following confidence; the ribbon was a measure which the waist was not to exceed. "I prefer dying of hunger to becoming big as mamma." Coquetries of this kind are very frequent; one of my patients refused to eat for fear that, during her digestion, her face should grow red and appear less pleasant in the eyes of a professor whose lectures she attended after her meals.

The authors who have observed such ideas seem to me to be inclined to exaggerate their importance. This is what certainly happened to Charcot, who used to seek everywhere for his rose-colored ribbon and the idea of obesity. I believe there is on this point a diagnosis to be made, on which I have much insisted in the first volume of my work on obsessions. Refusals of food are not always a phenomenon of the hysterical neurosis; they belong at least as often to the psychoasthenic neurosis. It is in the latter neurosis that fixed ideas remain alone and play a predominant role to the end.

Janet's Attempt to Explain the Excessive Activity of Anorexic Patients (pp. 239-243)

I wish a more thorough investigation might be made, in this connection, of a phenomenon that is as yet very imperfectly elucidated, namely, the excessive fondness for physical exercise that characterizes a whole group of anorexic patients. This character was already noted by Lasègue. It is well indicated in a short and unfortunately very incomplete article of Dr. Wallet[1]. "The patient," he says, "is exceedingly fond of long walks. As she is growing thinner with enormous rapidity, they are forbidden to her. She then begins to walk, from morning to night, up and down the little garden of the house, which was likewise forbidden to her. Then she plays all day at shuttlecock. It is prescribed that she stay in her room; there she gives herself up to violent gymnastic exercises. Even in bed she goes on with her gambols and somersaults."

Another curious explanation is that which was given by H. Wallet in 1892. The patient walks in order to grow thin, in order to compensate with the exercise he takes the alimentation that is imposed upon him. With this explanation we return to the initial idea of Charcot, namely, that all these patients want to grow thin. You know that it is not true, and that if in some particular cases this exaggeration of motion can be explained by such reasoning, it would be absurd to generalize the explanation.

I believe that the phenomenon in question is much more important and serious than these authors thought. It is not the result of a little particular imposition; it is connected with a very general disturbance. This disturbance first comprises the *suppression of the feeling of fatigue,* which is here much more important, in my opinion, than the anesthesia of the stomach. It comprises, besides, something that is very

[1] Deux Cas d'Anorexie Hystérique. *Nouvelle Iconographie de la Salpêtrière*, 1892, p. 276.

little known, namely, a general excitation to physical and moral activity, a strange feeling of happiness, a euphoria, according to the medical term, which are certain but very little-studied facts. The need of food goes with the feeling of weakness and depression; persons depressed by neurasthenia are great eaters. The exaltation of the strength, the feeling of euphoria, as it is known in the ecstatic saints, for instance, does away with the need of eating. Our hysterical anorexia is to be traced to much deeper sources than was supposed.

This is how I propose to you to represent it to ourselves, without, however, pretending to explain it. The function of alimentation, if we consider it on its psychological side, is one of the most considerable systems of thoughts that exist in the brain of an animal. It comprises fundamental phenomena, such as the feeling of weakness, of depression, and the fear of death. Besides it comprises numberless secondary phenomena, such as the sensations and motions connected with all the parts of the organism that play a role in alimentation, from the hands, lips, and tongue to the rectum and anus; lastly, it also comprises phenomena of improvement, as the images of pleasant aliments, the habits of eating cleanly, and the mixture of certain social phenomena that usually complicate our alimentation. There is in the hysterical a dissociation of this system, which may totally or partially withdraw from consciousness. In complete anorexia, you will find the loss of all the elements I have just described, the loss of the sensation of weakness, replaced by a pathological euphoria, the loss of the sensations of the organs, but also, more than is generally believed, the loss of the movements. These patients can no longer cleanly convey their food to their mouths, they can no longer masticate, and above all, they can no longer swallow, nor can they go to stool. There is, besides, a phenomenon which has not been much noticed and which consists in losses of the social ideas of alimentation. Marceline[2] was very amusing when she explained to me how ridiculous she thought the act of eating, how much she wondered to see people gather for this dirty operation. Hysterical anorexia is, at bottom, a great amnesia and a great paralysis. Alimentation has become, as it were, a somnambulistic phenomenon which can only be effected in the second or somnambulistic state. This phenomenon is lost to the normal and waking consciousness.

[2] A patient.

SOME EXCERPTS

A number of authors have written on anorexia nervosa. The following excerpts are intended to give the essence of their points of view.

Dubois' (2) comments are of interest both in relation to the specific syndrome and the light they throw upon his point of view.

The name of Charcot is so intimately interwoven with the history of psychiatry, that it is of great interest to note that he was preoccupied with the various problems related to anorexia nervosa, particularly with the therapeutic management. His remarks on isolation as a form of therapy are quoted here (Charcot, 1).

A summary of Ryle's (3, 4) observations in a hospital setting elucidates his position.

DUBOIS

They have no need of eating or drinking. . . . Neither is it the fixed idea of slow suicide by inanition which prompts them.

They do not know why they do not eat; as a rule they do not even think that they are sick. All feminine coquetry has disappeared in them, and they admit, without being in any degree impressed by it, their paleness and the fact that they have wasted away to skeletons.

These are insane without any doubt. In the majority of cases this condition becomes established in consequence of emotions, such as disappointed ambitions, the loss of a friend, or family annoyances [2, p. 252].

CHARCOT

In order to render more apparent this remarkable influence which isolation has in the treatment of hysteria in young subjects, including young and marriageable girls, I might quote a number of cases where it has proved itself most efficacious. But not being able to enter here into lengthy detail I will confine myself to the following anecdote, which seems to be quite a case in point. It relates to a young girl of Angoulême, thirteen or fourteen years of age, who had grown very fat for five or six months, but who then systematically refused all kinds of nourishment, although she was not troubled with any affection of deglutition nor any disorder of the stomach.

It was indeed one of those cases bordering on hysteria, but which do not always properly belong to it, and which have been so admirably described by Lasègue in France, and by Sir William Gull in England, under the name of nervous anorexia or anorexia hysterica. The patients eat nothing, they do not wish to, they cannot eat, although they have no mechanical obstacle in the primae viae, and although there is no reason against the food remaining in the stomach when they have taken it. Sometimes they take nourishment in secret, but not always as it has been supposed; and, although the parents themselves foster this deceit by providing them with food which they prefer because they can consume it in secret, alimentation always remains insufficient. Weeks and months pass by, and it is always hoped that the desire for food will reappear. Prayers, entreaties, violence, are unable to overcome their resistance. Then emaciation soon comes on; it reaches truly extravagant proportions; and the patients, without exaggeration, become nothing but living skeletons. And what a life! Cerebral torpor has succeeded to the fictitious agitation that existed at the outset. For some while walking, and even standing upright, have become impossible. The patients are confined to bed and they are scarcely able to move. The muscles of the neck are paralyzed, the head rolls like an inert mass on the pillow. The extremities are cold and cyanozed, and one is tempted to ask how life is carried on in the midst of such decay.

The parents have been alarmed for some time, but the alarm reaches a very high degree when matters have come to this point. It is indeed quite justifiable, for a fatal termination seems to threaten, and I myself know at least four cases where it has actually occurred.

Such was very nearly the situation in the case of the little patient from Angoulême, when I received a letter from the father depicting this lamentable condition, and beseeching me to come and see his child. 'It is unnecessary for me to come,' I replied; 'I can, without seeing the patient, give you appropriate advice. Bring the child to Paris, place her in one of our hydrotherapeutic establishments, leave her there, or at least when you go away make her believe that you have quitted the capital, inform me of it, and I will do the rest.' My letter remained without reply.

Six weeks later, a medical man from Angoulême arrived at my house one morning, in great haste, and apprised me that the little girl, who was his patient, was in Paris, installed in one of the establishments that I had indicated, that she was going from bad to worse, and that very probably she had but a few days to live. I asked him why I had not been informed sooner of the arrival of the little girl. He answered that the parents had avoided doing so because they were resolved not to be separated from their child. In reply I told him that the principal element, the *sine qua non* of my prescription, had been misunderstood, and I must decline all responsibility in the unfortunate affair. However, at his request, I went to the establishment indicated, and there I saw a lamentable sight. She was a tall girl, fourteen years of age, who had reached the last stage of emaciation, in a dorsal decubitus, with weak voice, extremities cold and blue, and the head drooping, reproducing in a word the main features of the picture I have just sketched to you. There was indeed every reason to be uneasy, very uneasy.

I took the parents aside, and after having addressed to them a blunt remonstrance, I told them that there remained, in my judgment, but one chance of success. It was that they should go away, or pretend to go away, which amounted to the same thing, as quickly as possible. They could tell their child that they were obliged for a special reason to return to Angoulême. They could lay their departure to my door, a matter which was of little importance, provided that the girl was persuaded that they were gone, and that they went immediately.

Their acquiescence was difficult to obtain in spite of all my remonstrances. The father especially failed to understand how the doctor could require a father to leave his child in the moment of danger. The mother said as much, but I was animated by my conviction. Perhaps I was eloquent, for the mother yielded first, and the father followed, uttering maledictions, and having I believe but little confidence in the prospect of success.

Isolation was established; its results were rapid and marvelous. The child, left alone with the nun who acted as nurse, and the doctor of the house, wept a little at first, though an hour later she became much less desolate than one would have expected. The very same evening, in spite of her repugnance, she consented to take half a little biscuit, dipped in wine. On the following days she took a little milk, some wine, soup, and then a little meat. The nutrition became improved, progressively but slowly.

At the end of fifteen days she was relatively well. Energy returned and a general improvement in nutrition, so far that at the end of the month I saw the child seated on a sofa, and capable of lifting her head from the pillow. Then she was able to walk a little. Then hydrotherapy was brought into play and two months from the date of the commencement of the treatment she could be considered as almost completely cured. Power, nourishment, appetite, left very little more to be desired.

It was then that the girl, when questioned, made the following confession to me: 'As long as papa and mamma had not gone—in other words, as long as you had not triumphed (for I saw that you wished to shut me up), I was afraid that my illness was not serious, and as I had a horror of eating, I did not eat. *But when I saw that you were determined to be master, I was afraid,* and in spite of my repugnance I tried to eat, and I was able to, little by little.' I thanked the child for her confidence, which as you will understand is a lesson in itself [1, pp. 211-214].

It would not be possible for me to insist too much on the capital importance which attaches to isolation in the treatment of hysteria. Without doubt, the psychic element plays a very important part in most of the cases of this malady, even when it is not the predominating feature. I have held firmly to this doctrine for nearly fifteen years, and all that I have seen during that time—everything that I have observed day by day—tends only to confirm me in that opinion. Yes, it is necessary to separate both children and adults from their father and their mother, whose influence, as experience teaches, is primarily pernicious.

Experience shows repeatedly, though it is not always easy to understand the reason, that it is the mothers whose influence is so deleterious, who will hear no argument, and will only yield in general to the last extremity.

The patients are placed under the direction of competent and experienced persons. They are generally religious people who by long practice have become very expert in the management of this sort of patient. A kind but firm hand, a calm demeanor, and much patience, are here indispensable conditions. The parents are systematically excluded up to the time that a notable amelioration occurs; and then the patients are allowed, as *a sort of recompense,* to see them; at first at long intervals, and then more and more frequently in proportion as the improvement becomes more obvious. Time and hydrotherapy, without counting any internal medication, perform the rest [pp. 210-211].

RYLE

Ryle (3, 4), working at Guy's Hospital, observed 51 cases in 16 years. Forty-six were female, 5 male. In the female cases, 8 patients were over 40. The precipitating factors that he stressed were taken from the overt aspect. In the younger group they included love affairs, broken engagements, school attachments and "slimming" following criticism; while in the older women they included multiple operations, illnesses, menopausal disturbances and nosophobia. Ryle argued for the primary psychogenicity of the syndrome and against primary disturbances in the glandular system. "The occurrence of the disease in males and in women after the menopause reminds us that a primary ovarian dysfunction cannot very well be claimed as an essential cause of the disease."

REFERENCES

1. Charcot, J. M.: *Diseases of the Nervous System*, III. London: The New Sydenham Society, 1889.
2. Dubois, P.: *The Psychic Treatment of Nervous Disorders*. New York: Funk & Wagnalls, 1909.
3. Ryle, J. A.: Anorexia nervosa. *Lancet,* 2:893-899, 1936.
4. ———, et al.: Discussions on anorexia nervosa. *Proc. Roy. Soc. Med.,* 32: 735-746, 1939.

GERMAN PAPERS

The German-language literature of the 1930's (Germany, Austria, Switzerland) contains some noteworthy contributions in our area. Three outstanding papers dealing with anorexia nervosa are particularly significant. Grote and Meng's paper represents the first therapeutic approach to anorexia nervosa published by a psychoanalyst. Weizsäcker, a psychiatrist and philosopher, advanced the concept of psychosomatic thinking although he utilized mystic and allegorical ideas in place of unconscious motivations. Schur and Medvei's paper is of importance since it reassesses the controversy, organic versus psychogenic, and contributes to a separation between the syndromes of Simmonds' disease and anorexia nervosa.

Grote and Meng's paper has, as indicated, an historical significance since it was the first instance in the literature of a patient with anorexia nervosa treated by a psychoanalyst. Meng's observation on the psychophysical correlation deserves to be noted. He speaks of an "organ psychosis," making references to the "mutual relationship and reciprocal substitution of organic and psychological disturbance." Meng did not evolve any specific constellation for anorexia nervosa even though he states that "fantasies regarding parthenogenesis, the role of menstruation, and conception were worked through." It should be noted that Meng thought that he was treating a case of Simmond's disease which had remained resistant to hormonal therapy.

Schur and Medvei's paper impresses one with the degree to which clinical medicine in Germany was under the influence of the authority of von Bergmann, who had shifted his position from denying that psychological factors were significant in disease processes to an acceptance of their importance. Schur and Medvei made the point that psychological conceptualizations were hampered by the very progress in and emphasis on pathology and endocrinology. Thus the psychological fac-

tors in anorexia nervosa seem to have lost emphasis in the latter part of the nineteenth century and were only brought to the fore again in the first part of the twentieth. These papers, then, represent a step in the revivification of interest in the psychosomatic point of view.

Schur and Medvei assume that the signs and symptoms manifested by their patients were due to a functional disturbance of the anterior pituitary and make the point that such a disturbance could be caused by "neurosis." They further state that anterior pituitary disturbance may be either on a somatic or functional basis and that "neurosis" might act as a trigger mechanism which, once released, might continue in the direction of pathology to the point where it became the "sedes morbi."

Weizsäcker's paper is noteworthy since his point of view is considered to be of importance in the conceptual development of psychosomatic medicine. Utilizing the manifest content of the dreams of his patients without attempting to analyze them, he made observations and major conclusions of great significance to him. One might summarize his exceedingly complex material somewhat along these lines. He noted in his patients two alternating cycles: one, being the affirmation of life; and the other, the denial of life, as evidenced by the rhythmic alternation of abstinence from food and bulimia. He stated that one of his patients, herself, "had noticed that the days of this voracious appetite followed upon certain dreams"; their manifest content dealt with mother. On the other hand days without hunger followed upon dreams dealing with father (God), contentment. Weizsäcker finds here the "biological paradox: every time the dream experience is reversed by the instinctual life. On the path to death there follows the voracious appetite; upon blissful feelings follows denial of food."

The dreams which Weizsäcker reports are replete with pregnancy fantasies, and he gives full recognition to this aspect. "Nutrition and pregnancy belong together. . . . Pregnancy is at one and the same time sacrifice as well as addition of body substance." Just as Meng, Schur, and Medvei did, he, too, noted the depressive attitude of his patients. As a matter of fact, it is the death drive which is one of the focal points of Weizsäcker's paper.

MEDICAL AND PSYCHOTHERAPEUTIC TREATMENT OF ENDOGENIC *MAGERSUCHT* (ANOREXIA)

L. R. GROTE, M.D. AND H. MENG, M.D.
(1934)

Our quantitative method of investigation of certain syndromes has led to paradoxical and contradictory results so far. These syndromes belong to the dark chapters of the pathology of metabolism. It is about as impossible to understand how a patient with Basedow's disease continues to gain weight, despite increased basal metabolism, as it is impossible to understand how a patient with endogenic *Magersucht* (anorexia) goes on losing weight—to the extent of Simmond's cachexia—despite the decreased basal metabolism. Ignorance of the laws which govern such cases impedes really causal therapy. The endogenic *Magersucht* of concern here has been recognized as a typical syndrome. Since its first description by Falta there has been no doubt that it is predominantly a hormonal condition. Attempts have been made to subdivide the syndrome, but specificity is indicated not so much by exact tests of hormonal insufficiency, as by the clinicomorphological stigmata observed.

For instance, Tannhauser distinguishes seven such subgroups, including the lipodystrophies. Interest is directed chiefly at the pituitary

---

Translated by Marcel Heiman, M.D., from *Schweizerische Medizinische Wochenschrift*, 64:137-141, 1934.

form of *Magersucht,* usually combined with hypogenitalism. When this form assumes the proportion of Simmonds' cachexia, Tannhauser designates it as the "atrophic form of pituitary *Magersucht*" in recognition of the assumption that its pathogenesis is identical with that of simple endogenic *Magersucht*. There is no agreement among the authors regarding the identity of these two forms, or, to be more exact, as to their differences. Grafe expresses himself rather skeptically in this connection although he recently attempted to establish a schematic order of pituitary diseases from the point of view of hyper- and hypofunction and places *Magersucht* among the hypofunctions. Leschke does not acknowledge the pituitary gland as the central organ of disturbance and places the latter in the diencephalon as the center of metabolism. H. Zondek and G. Koehler take an intermediate position. They have encountered a cerebral type of endogenic *Magersucht* more often than a pituitary type, and we are confronted with the unusual concept that a lesion of the anterior pituitary lobe could be responsible for the development of disease syndromes which are as diametrically opposed as pituitary obesity and *Magersucht*. This shows the lack of clarity which exists as to the exact etiological mechanism, despite all the experimental work done to clarify this point.

The idea that the pituitary gland is deprived of its hormone persists, and one attempts to treat endogenic *Magersucht* hormonally, using such substances as prolan or praephyson. In evaluating the clinically recognizable deficiencies of other endocrine glands one would also use ovarial substances, etc. A dietary regimen to fatten the emaciated individual with endogenic *Magersucht* is rarely successful if therapy is limited to the use of hormonal substances. The only exception is Falta's insulin therapy, a procedure now so well recognized that we need not discuss it here even though it is not always successful.

The success or failure of the insulin cure cannot yet be used to differentiate an additional subdivision of endogenic Magersucht. A. Lublin introduced a new working hypothesis in this area. He believes that, without any change in the basal metabolism caused by a shift in the correlation of the hormones, either a lipogenic or an antilipogenic factor may gain the upper hand. According to Lublin, insulin, for example, exerts a lipogenic effect and enhances the change of carbohydrates into fats. Thyreiodin, adrenalin and pituitary hormones have antilipogenic effects. The glycogen content of the liver plays a central role in this mechanism. Antilipogenic hormones bring on hyperglycemia of short duration. Thus it is possible to understand fat deposit and fat loss in the organism through the shift of lipogenic and antilipogenic factors, without any change in the basal metabolism itself. Insulin therapy, which causes certain fat deposits, would be an example of this because this treatment does not actually lower the basal metabolism. We consider Lublin's concept quite noteworthy. This concept, that a specific lipogenic insulin factor is lacking, might enhance our understanding of cases of *Magersucht* which do not respond to insulin medication with the deposit of fat. At times (Steinitz and Thau) there seems to be a disturbance of carbohydrate utilization which makes one think of insular hypofunction and, of course, one would also have to think of a predominant pituitary counterregulation.

We would like, here, to compare two clinically typical cases. One was a brilliant insulin success, the other a total failure. In the course of observing this second case we found a different mode of approach—the psychotherapeutic approach. The chronological connection between psychotherapy and clinical improvement was so close that we cannot help but think of a causal connection—in the sense of psychotherapy being the trigger.

The histories in both cases are typical. In abbreviated form, they are as follows:

Case 1

Linda L., age 18. Asthenic, fragile, always thin. Migraine at the age of 13. Menstruation irregular and weak, first period at age 14. Mud baths in Pyrmont were prescribed for this, without success. Too fragile to go to school. Gradual improvement of menstruation and general strength until 17. Gradual decrease of appetite, salivated frequently, nausea. X-ray examination did not show anything except ptosis. After grippe, further loss of weight and rather severe constipation. Earlier, her bowel movements were always normal. Diagnoses of pylorospasm and tuberculosis were made at different times. On March 8, 1930, patient was admitted to our clinic in an extremely emaciated, frail condition. Height 175 centimeters, weight 37.9 kg., Rohrer index 68.7. Physical status: except typical habitus, infantile genitals (no premature senility!), nothing of note. Basal metabolism: Minus 12.4 per cent. Amounts of urine normal, good concentration. Blood picture: relative lymphozytosis, slight secondary anemia. A typical fattening cure is carried through with carbohydrate feedings hourly. Insulin doses up to 40 units during the day. In addition, ovaria siccata (Merck). Excellent weight gain: more than 10 kg. in 40 days. Somewhat depressed psychically at the outset, but she soon became accessible and had a positive attitude. After one year (without any remission) weight 60 kg., healthy and functioning well.

Case 2

Marie Y., age 17. Had not been ill before. Loss of appetite for a long time. Menarche at 14 years. Menstruation stopped completely since her sixteenth year. Menstruation was always slight and delayed. She is always cold; her hands and feet are often blue. Slight loss of hair. Loss of weight accelerated for the past year. She "eats too little," wants "only bread." Objectively one finds the typical asthenic fragile body (as in both parents and brother). Height: 171 centimeter; weight: 45.5 kg.; Rohrer index 91.6. Basal metabolism: Minus 25 per cent. No other findings of note. Very fragile, transparent skin, red hair, freckled. Amounts of urine small during the treatment. Urine concentration high and rich in pigments. Blood picture: Relative lymphozytosis (46 per cent), Hb 100, RBC 5 millions. As in Case 1, a rest cure and hourly carbohydrate-rich feedings were carried through. Insulin up to 52 units during the day. In addition, Prolan and Unden. Treatment lasted three weeks during which the patient lost an additional kilogram. Insulin was a total failure although nutrition was carried on well, often against the girl's resistance.

Zondek had already pointed out that kidney function is intact in these cases. In Case 1 we noted a very slight decrease of water excretion under the influence of increasing insulin doses. At the end of the treatment the amount of urine gradually increases while insulin decreases, without, however, influencing the gradually ascending weight curve. Perhaps this is evidence that through insulin a minute retention of water is effected. However, the main cause of the gain in weight should be correlated to the real addition of substance to the body. In the second case, during the whole period of insulin therapy, there was relative oliguria with urine highly concentrated (between 1030-1035). In this case, too, there was no retention of water because of the insulin, the weight remaining almost constant during this time. The ability of the kidneys to concentrate is good in both cases. Like Zondek we are inclined to assume a disturbance of the sodium chloride exchange in both cases. The addition of 10 grm. of sodium chloride to the food caused no noticeable increase of sodium chloride content in the urine which was ordinarily between 8 and 10 grm. Thus one may speak of a historetention.

Regarding sugar metabolism: it should be noted that despite relatively large doses of insulin there was no hypoglycemia to speak of in either case. However, there was light perspiration and some tremor. The fasting values of blood sugar were between 90 and 100 mg. per cent respectively, therefore normal. In the first case an hourly examination of blood sugar following an injection of 16 units of insulin at one o'clock showed the following: 103, 70, 64, 75, 102, 119 mg. per cent. In the second case we followed the blood sugar at two-hour intervals beginning at 8 A. M. Insulin was given at eight o'clock, at 1 P. M. and at 7 P. M., 16 units each time, thus totaling 48 units. The blood sugar determination was: 98, 89, 85, 48, 57, 148 mg. per cent. The low value of 48 mg. per cent one hour following the second injection is noteworthy, but the rise at six o'clock is more so. Because of the negativistic attitude of the patient, more detailed tests could not be made. We mention this because, in an analogous case, Steinitz and Thau saw a hyperglycemic curve following the injection of sugar. They concluded that a lack of insulin existed and based their successful insulin therapy upon this. Our observation concerns our second patient who was not helped by insulin.

Lucke recently found the very opposite in one case, namely, very low fasting blood sugar with severe hypoglycemia following small amounts of insulin, thus demonstrating decreased tolerance toward insulin. He believes that this is why his case did not respond to insulin. This hypothesis does not seem to be correct in view of our own two patients.

So far, we cannot explain why insulin was efficacious in helping one patient gain weight but was ineffectual with the other patient.

Some time ago clinical observers recognized that cases of endogenic *Magersucht* often seem rather changed psychologically. When Falta speaks of primary anorexia as the cause in quite a few of these cases, the problem of etiology is shifted, at least partially, into the psychophysical area. Without losing sight of the hormonal genesis point of view, we would like to direct attention to the psychic constellation of these patients on the basis of our experience with Case 2. Among the internists, Curschmann has emphasized the importance of psychotherapy, and our case seems to confirm his opinion to a large extent. The depressed, negativistic attitude of this young girl was readily apparent. Aside from her openly negative attitude toward food, one could not overlook her taciturn inaccessibility, a symptom that came into play upon every attempt to establish human contact between her and the physician. This attitude gave rise to the belief that a more active approach might improve the situation.

Though admittedly a rather vague idea, another attempt was made to influence the patient through a change of climate and she was taken to the mountains. It was hoped that this change of climate would influence her energy, her whole hormonal system and her psyche. The patient stayed at Engadine, 1800 meters high, for four weeks. This attempt was a lamentable failure; her weight fell rapidly to 35 kg. and general debility became so pronounced that the patient was expected to die.

After her return from the Engadine on March 19, 1931, Miss Marie Y. weighed 33.7 kg. Among other comments in his referral report of the bedridden patient, the physician at Engadine wrote: "The last weeks, increasing adynamia and anergia. Appetite is minimal. Patient is terribly emaciated, very weak; psychically—rather euphoric at times; sometimes altogether without energy. Skin is very dry, cold, acrocyanosis. Freezes constantly. Sleep is light and brief. Digestion is very difficult because of spasms which did respond to belladonna. There were no findings of note on her inner organs. Intelligence does not seem to have suffered. Extraordinarily low pulse of 46-54, and very soft; blood pressure 90/65 mm. Hg. RR, the sub temperatures 35.2-36.4 degree Cels." Blood picture and metabolism were in accordance with former findings, as they were described in the first section of this paper.

In the course of the next months the patient was given varying dosages of hormones such as Prolan. In addition, she received sulphur, silver, phosphorus. Special emphasis was placed upon a vitamin-rich diet, the energetic use of passive gymnastics, massages with oil, and treatment with heat. There was some success within the first 14 days. Primarily, the improvement was subjective. After being treated with heat for several hours—first with heating pads, later with an electric blanket—and after skin massages, the patient was not so cold and was glad her wilted skin looked fresher. Her weight increase in these two weeks, from 33.7 to 34.7 kg. was perhaps brought about through the new milieu, the new diet and the new physician. During her stay in the Engadine the patient had suffered greatly from nostalgia. In the following four and a half months, the treatment was not changed. During this time her weight fluctuated between 34.7 and 35.5 kg. and only once stabilized at 36 kg. for a few days. Her subjective status changed. All in all it was perhaps better than it had been in March. There was some euphoria, sometimes depression; occasionally there were negativistic attitudes, especially a kind of negativism to orders with an instinctual resistance *vis-à-vis* family members who, directly or indirectly, prompted her to eat more even when she had no appetite. Occasionally there were careful attempts to get her out of bed or to move her bed out into the open. Intellectual work was permitted so that the patient could keep up with her schoolwork with the help of a private tutor. Objective progress was so slight that serious objections were raised, in principle, as to whether this therapy should be continued, particularly since her weight remained around 35.5 kg. from the middle of July to the middle of August.

The decision to try psychological treatment was prompted by several observations: First, during and following puberty, psychic factors are important for both normal and abnormal physical and emotional development; second, our observation in a group of individuals with hormonal imbalance that psychological therapy could set a cure in motion; and third, our impression that Miss Y. was struggling unconsciously with something that had until now not been expressed.

I could not undertake classic psychoanalytic therapy with a patient whom I had treated medically. In their publications regarding psychoanalytic technique Freud and his pupils have shown why such combined therapy should not be undertaken. In this case it was uncertain whether psychotherapy would be found at all useful, or whether one could justify abandoning all other therapy for purely psychological treatment. Since both the parents and the patient refused to change physicians, there remained only the choice of attempting a course of therapy which would perhaps correspond with Freud's early cathartic therapy. This technique was used in that phase of the development of psychoanalysis when hypnosis was abandoned and catharsis occurred when the patient was fully conscious. Such a direct comparison is difficult because the modern psychoanalyst, who is familiar with thirty-five years of psychoanalytic development, uses the old methods with different theoretical concepts and additional practical experience. However, the patient agreed not to hold anything back consciously and to make an attempt at free association. She was assured of the physician's discretion and that he would not talk about what she had told him with anyone.

For our purposes, it is sufficient to describe the general aspect of these observations. During these interviews nothing emerged which could not be observed in any patient with a functional or somatic illness in which it was possible to precipitate the healing process through psychoanalysis or psychoanalytically oriented therapy. Genetic explanation must answer the question: which actual failure or disappointment made the individual sick and forced her to regress to an earlier developmental state? In our patient, lacunae of memory, fantasies, and dreams showed that extensive but unsuccessful processes of repression had taken place and were still going on. It was possible to clarify the amnesias sketchily. Fantasies regarding parthenogenesis, the role of menstruation, and conception were worked through; reactions of disgust and anxiety to certain aspects of the interpretations were replaced by proper understanding and a liberating absolution from anxiety. Whatever Miss Y. had learned or been told in the course of her life regarding sexual development was buried. Despite excellent general intelligence, in this area there was an almost complete intellectual and affective blocking (neurotic stupefaction). In regular sessions, from the middle of August through the fall and winter—first three to four times a week and later less frequently—a change became noticeable in the picture of the illness and the structure of her personality. Dietetic and physical treatment were continued as during the first five months, but drugs, particularly hormones, were discontinued. The patient often mentioned that she had lost her belief in the efficacy of drugs.

It is difficult to say whether it was coincidence or whether there was a causal connection, but a few hours after a certain session, the sixth, menstruation recurred. In this discussion the patient was intensely excited, working through a conflict between instinctual and religious demands which had been particularly strong at the time of her confirmation but which was, apparently, connected with conflicts in her early childhood. It is noteworthy that after the very acute psychic reaction had faded away, the patient's father made a note on her chart one day, "Feeling of joy begins." The patient's moods became more balanced; her facial expression became fresher and prettier. Her ability to learn and to study improved and, with private lessons, she quickly made up what she had missed in school. Her weight increased 1 kg. during the first eight weeks after she had begun psychotherapy.

The significant content of her problems which were discussed after six weeks of psychotherapy belonged to the oedipus and castration complex. Against strong resistance, the patient worked this through. Then a depression set in; simultaneously there was a rather light angina catarrhalis with temperatures and severe diarrhea. No fault in diet or any other external cause could be found for the latter. In the course of observation, patient had gone through two similar catarrh-like anginas, the first prior to the onset of psychotherapy, the second in August, upon commencing psychotherapy. The latter occurred when it was particularly difficult for the patient to associate despite her "good intentions." Both times chronic constipation continued without interruption, and there was no considerable fluctuation of body weight. From October 15th, her weight fell rapidly (by 2 kg.) within six days, but psychotherapy was not interrupted. From October 21st, her weight increased steadily and strikingly, 2 kg. each week, with noteworthy subjective and objective improvement. Psychotherapy continued until the middle of March. Her weight at this time was 50 kg. and continued to rise. There were continuous observations and occasional psychotherapeutic sessions up to the end of June, 1932, when her weight was 60 kg. In December, 1932, it reached 65 kg. From this point on her weight remained steady until the termination of treatment in June, 1933.

In January, 1932, the patient returned to school. She had no complaints and, without great difficulty, was able to catch up with her classwork. By Easter of 1933 she had passed the Matura examination with excellent marks, in the very same class to which she had belonged prior to her illness.

We considered it proper to publish this case although we are uncertain as to the decisive factor in the patient's cure. All the physicians who observed this patient over the past year and a half had the impression that it was the psychological approach which initiated the healing process. A few views need to be discussed:

1. The question of the nonsomatic treatment of somatic illness:

From the psychoanalytic point of view, Groddeck made the first advance in 1917 regarding psychological treatment of somatic disease. Freud was rather skeptical and hesitant since his own observations had been with neurotics and psychotics predominantly. Based, also, on our observation of psychoses, it seems quite matter-of-course to us today to consider psychoanalytically enriched therapy even for patients with somatic illnesses. After Groddeck, quite a few analysts attempted psychotherapy with such patients, notably Deutsch, Ferenczi and Simmel.[1] One might think too of recent publications by authors who were close to psychoanalysis, for instance, Alkan, Hansen, Heyer, Mohr, J. H. Schultz, Weizsäcker.

Leichtentritt raises similar questions in his observations on "Puberty Neuroses, Hunger State and Adrenal Insufficiency," published in 1932. He concludes: "This is a description of a shock during puberty to the total personality in a young girl with a healthy family background; instinctual, emotional, and intellectual life were found in a state of severe disharmony. Because of hunger, alone, or accompanied

---

[1] One of us (Meng) has now had ten years of experience in the use of psychoanalytically oriented psychotherapy with somatically ill patients who had not recovered, or had had remissions, when other therapies were used. Since some of these patients have only been discharged in the past year or two, the results of these observations will be published at another time. The later life histories of these individuals will give us some insight into the extent to which the goal of psychotherapy was reached: namely, improvement of the total personality so that the individual is adapted to the demands of his instincts as well as his environment, and remains so.

by psychic excitation, severe adrenal insufficiency developed which at first was the center of the illness. Later, more detailed analysis indicated that this should be considered the consequence of the illness. While we rarely find the malignant form (Addison's disease) in childhood, we now become acquainted with an acute to subacute form of adrenal insufficiency which improves relatively quickly but which up to now has hardly been considered as occurring in childhood. It will be necessary to be alert to the possibility that such states occur more frequently than we thought, though, of course, not in this severe form which could not be missed. Perhaps many forms of functional retardation of growth in puberty, associated with states of weakness and fainting as well as lymphozytosis in infections, could be approached to greater advantage from this point of view. This cure was instituted by a psychological approach."

Since the recent publications by Boenheim, Steinitz, Thau and others, cases of pituitary *Magersucht* have not been so rare. According to the above-mentioned authors, there had only been between 40 and 50 case histories published up to the year 1932. It might be advisable to check those therapeutic procedures which might prove efficacious following the occasional failure of hormone therapy.

2. It is general knowledge that loss of weight, poor complexion, and physical decline accompany very severe emotional suffering in individuals thus disposed. Generally speaking, neuroses are not accompanied by such physical reactions, but psychoses are. In some cases of psychogenic organic disturbances we should assume a condition which we may call *organ psychosis*. The ego of the organ-psychotic person withdraws from the environment, like the ego of the psychotic person, and regresses to earlier developmental stages than that of the neurotic person. The ego regresses to the instinctual id, out of which it grew and with which it had always remained connected. The term, organ psychosis seems paradoxical to us only because we still think in terms of body and soul. All too easily, we see problems associated with the development of the physical and psychological aspects of the individual as a dichotomy, although it is always the unit Man in whom we note the effects of psychophysical correlations. We do not want to discuss here questions of the psychological structure or therapy of the disturbed individual.

The mutual relationship and the reciprocal substitution of somatic and psychological disturbance ought to be the subject of further observation. There is much to indicate that a severe organic disturbance may be substituted for the development of a psychological disturbance and may even make the latter superfluous. What takes place is a flight into organic illness, a tying up of anxiety in the organic symptom, as a chronic, as it were materialized, anxiety equivalent (Freud).

3. Our patient's metabolism figures do not correlate with the expected average. *In a clinical sense, the patient is not in full equilibrium. Therefore, is she really healthy?* Neither the patient nor her relatives give this any thought, but I may point out two other observations. A few patients with bronchial asthma who were cured by psychotherapy, although completely free of symptoms, exhibited the typical signs of the allergy: eosinophilia, etc. In quite a few cases of *hyperemesis gravidarum* it is possible to stop the vomiting through psychotherapy although the abnormal metabolism goes on for some time.

Health then would be an adaptation to demands from without and from within, the extent of the adaptation varying in different individuals and within the same individual. The above-mentioned patients apparently learned unconsciously, in their psychotherapy, to tolerate conditions to which they were not adjusted prior to the treatment. Therapy makes it possible, too, to change mental attitudes and specific defenses against stimuli. If the response to the stimuli is different—namely, takes place consciously—although the attitude remains the same, the response does not allow the appearance of symptoms. For the patient himself, more adequate defenses against the stimulus enable him to function better. The sign of completed treatment is always the change of attitude toward the disease.

4. Psychoanalysis (every psychoanalytically oriented psychotherapy) is a specific approach. We are dealing with an unhealthy equilibrium which has been suspended in action through shock, and psychoanalysis attempts to set in motion mechanisms which were paralyzed during the illness. Thus psychoanalysis attempts to mobilize and utilize forces which press for a new balance after the effects of shock have worn off and a changed balance of forces has become established. A comparison with the *Reizkoerper Therapie* is fully justified insofar as, in proper dosages, it produces natural defensive forces of the organism.

Analytic therapy is like surgery; its success is strongly dependent upon proper indication. In our case it was the last resort, after all previous therapies proved ineffectual. The extent to which unsuccessful repressions burdened the psychic structure of the patient became apparent only during the course of treatment. Such trial psychoanalysis should be attempted in most of the refractory cases in which failure of therapy cannot be explained by the malignancy of the disease itself.

We wish to mention that after the great gain in weight, patient Marie Y. underwent another short period of clinical observation. Her weight was now 56.6 kg., height 171 centimeter, Rohrer index therefore 113.2. In two successive examinations (May 18th and 19th, 1932), we found that during a low-protein diet the basal metabolism was minus 20 per cent. The same situation was found on June 21, 1933. On the days following the low-protein diet, her basal metabolism was minus 16.8 per cent and minus 19.8 per cent respectively. Her weight was 65 kg., and Rohrer index therefore 130, which is normal. What we want to say is that despite the very satisfactory weight condition, the clinically restored health, and the patient's excellent subjective condition, functioning fully, intellectually and physically, the fundamental metabolic deviations persisted. One would have to assume, therefore, that under certain psychophysiological conditions, remission could occur. The patient lives without any hormones and without any other therapy; her menstrual periods have reappeared. In this observation we have a good example of the concept of responsivity which one of us (Grote) suggested years ago for such conditions, namely, that a considerable deviation from the statistical norm may still be compatible with a well functioning personality which gives the impression of health. Despite the pathological condition of the basal metabolism, we no longer speak of illness in this case.

Our communication regarding the successful use of insulin therapy for weight gain in pituitary *Magersucht* is nothing special. A case of Simmonds' disease which is resistant to hormonal therapy but responds to psychotherapy is a bit more noteworthy. It shows how problematic every approach is, and will perhaps lead to a broader concept of pathogenesis. We do not think that restitution took place "spontaneously" in this case. Prior to the institution of psychotherapy there had been enough time for a spontaneous remission. We do not have a clear conception of how psychotherapy sets an endocrine mechanism in motion and we are far from recommending psychotherapy as the treatment of choice for such cases. However, we believe it would be proper to try psychotherapy with those patients who do not respond to predominantly somatic therapy.

DREAMS IN SO-CALLED ENDOGENIC *MAGERSUCHT* (ANOREXIA)

VICTOR V. WEIZSACKER, M.D.
(1937)

In their paper "On Medical and Psychotherapeutic Treatment of Endogenic *Magersucht*," Grote and Meng expressed the opinion that, while it was worth trying in an individual case, psychotherapeutic treatment could not yet be recommended as the treatment of choice. They state, "We have no clear conception of how psychotherapy sets an endocrine mechanism into motion." However, despite their extreme caution, their publication of Case Y is of great importance and I can confirm that success can be achieved by following their road. Increasing such successes will certainly depend upon better insight into the "mechanism" of this illness and this form of therapy, if we do not submit to the prejudice the word "mechanism" usually introduces.

For special reasons, these authors could not publish the psychic content of their case. However, if we want to go deeper into this problem and learn what happens in the psychologic treatment of such a patient, we cannot exclude such content. Not everything we know of the patients can be told in the observations I shall communicate here. We must remain silent regarding their personal lives, but we shall use their dreams in order to illustrate the nature of the illness. Dreams are more impersonal than biography and thus follow more closely the imper-

---

Translated by Marcel Heiman from *Deutsche Medizinische Wochenschrift*, 63:253-257, and 65:294-297, 1937.

sonal nature of the physiological events in *Magersucht* (anorexia). This peculiar disease is not described adequately by the terms "metabolism" and "nutrition" but for the time being we shall grant these words the various interpretations they have in daily language, as they are employed by the layman. If one uses the word, nutrition, thus permitting anything to come to mind from one's everyday experience or knowledge, whatever it may be, one gets neither a cookbook nor a physiology of metabolism. Quite the contrary! This word, like a magnet, attracts a real "pell-mell" of shavings which arrange themselves like a garland of barbed wire. Such conglomerations of associations are different in different people and are not at all like anything our textbooks contain. On the other hand, such a conglomeration is much closer to what one sees in a clinical case of disturbed nutrition. Our uneducated psychic capacity to associate seems to work at times like the real illness, quite dissimilar to science.

Everybody knows that suspended nutrition means the loss of body weight, the wasting away of strength. We might very well reverse this and say that a weakened, emaciated person is insufficiently nourished. Such reversals are hazardous from a scientific point of view, although they are valuable as stimuli to precise and new questions. As far as patients are concerned, it is, again, exactly the reverse. Patients confound cause and effect all the time and, in addition, they place the disturbance at points completely different than the scientist does. In order to be satisfied, an obese person needs to eat more; an emaciated, melancholic person might consider himself too fat; a diabetic may express a hunger for sugar; and a patient with Basedow's disease may yearn for meat. For these patients the yardstick of proper nutrition is connected with prejudices or premonitions regarding that which might be proper and the relationship between what one eats to the expected result: satisfaction, and then a feeling of well-being. In the way the person behaves about what he eats, he gives expression to the prominent deviations of his individuality—particularly if he is palpably ill.

Physiology knows the problem contained therein under the name of "requirement" or "need"[1]. Physiology assumes this need to be constant, and then analyzes the conditions necessary for its satisfaction. In

---

Translator's note: Bedarf, in German.

the course of this analysis, it hits upon psychophysiological reflexes such as hunger and appetite, the disturbance of which is self-evident even in the healthy person. All entangled in the insoluble difficulties of the problem of appetite, physiology gladly returns to the facts of chemism. This retreat results from the point of departure: the need is not an is-value but an ought-value, a postulate which is known neither casuistically nor statistically, but which depends upon physiologically indefinite standards. These standards may be the above-mentioned prejudices, feelings, styles, or ideals of what is proper nutrition—ideals which, in patients with nutritional diseases, may seem rather peculiar. We see no possibility of circumventing this aspect of the matter; we have to study it if we wish to find out something about the meaning of need.

It is not at all simple to collect basic data about the meaning of need. Anyone who sees many patients doesn't have time to make thorough studies; and one who studies only a few patients is "stuck" on special cases. We contend that the former is the lesser evil—superficial analysis is better than none. Examination of the following two patients with *Magersucht* was not as satisfactorily thoroughgoing as might be desirable, but at least it was conducted along the necessary lines.

I

Despite her unusual height, Mrs. H. Q. weighed only 55.5 kg. at the beginning of the treatment. During the past two years the marked growth of her feet made it necessary to buy larger shoes. Aside from that there was no change which could be referred to acromegaly. The sella turcica is definitely small and of clear contours. The amount of urine is between 2 and 2.5 l. As far as medical and neurological findings are concerned, except for the extraordinary emaciation, only amenorrhea, which has been present for years, is noteworthy. Three days following admission to the clinic the patient came down with a severe angina follicularis with transitory albuminuria. Up to this point the following could be noted:

Food intake is experienced by the patient as a bothersome compulsion. Generally, the dislike is almost insurmountable. In approximately monthly cycles, the patient has embarrassing attacks of bulimia in which she gulps down her food. Each attack is followed by her feeling very out of sorts and by the formation of edemas in the legs. The patient has no doubt that these cycles take the place of her missing menstruation. In addition, abstaining from food means attaining an "elevated state." It seems to her that to live without food means to be pure and happier.

Everything in the history regarding her marriage, character formation, and other experiences, including the unnecessary diagnostic and therapeutic experiments to which the patient was submitted is here omitted. In accordance with our resolution, we shall examine only those events which focus around nutrition.

Up to this point the findings could be said to point to a case of *Magersucht,* possibly of pituitary origin, which, in addition to the physical stigmata, shows the psychic picture of an appetite perversion with reversed ideal formation. We note that the formation of an ascetic ideal is not limited to nutrition and the body per se but includes sexuality, the erotic sphere, as well as the areas of clothing and sociability. One may say that the ascetic ideal as such is not necessarily a perverted ideal, if only medicine and what medicine considers normal would not find so many defects—the amenorrhea, the edema, the attacks of bulimia, and perhaps pituitary-acromegalic symptoms. No religion exists which does not prompt its believers to realize the idea of sacrifice, be it through physical asceticism or other forms of denial. Because the saint puts a high value on this denial of the biological, he gains something, and the loss becomes a pleasure; even torture can then become pleasure. But it so happens that this path is a very difficult one and if the person fails, the results, as we can see, are not holiness but illness. There is always the possibility of retreat into health, which does not require so many sacrifices, and the physician gives his assistance in bringing about this somewhat more modest state.

As a matter of fact, from the time the patient had the angina (and not without the help of the therapy) she turned toward health. Half a year later, she weighed 67 kg. instead of 55 kg., she had her periods a few times, even if not in full strength. She was eating and her condition was excellent. There was no longer any edema and, except for the thyroid medication, there was no other therapy. Her mood is pleasant, she makes plans, and despite a very difficult external situation she is grateful and considers her change the result of the therapy.

We, however, are not equally ready to assume, definitely and exclusively, that it was the result of the therapy which was chiefly psychological. The change which took place after several years of illness is so complex that it is impossible to simplify. But it is permissible and possible to focus on the special area of nutrition. We say that the reversal in nutrition can be understood only as a revolution in the complex: metabolism by idealization. As proof, however, it is not enough that the patient simply tells about her peculiar feelings which made such a perverted impression. We wish to have a witness to the change, more unbiased and less easily influenced—a witness to the change which apparently took place in an area to which we have no access at all. What became noticeable secondarily, in the patient's conscious thoughts and in the measurable changes in her weight, etc., must have taken place in this very area. The nature of what happened was brought closer to us in three dreams immediately following the angina.

First dream—"THE WISE WOMAN"

On top of a mountain there stands a church and a school. At the bottom of the mountain I am with a woman in the kitchen and am occupied with housework. Suddenly one can hear, the church is burning and the school where my child is is in danger too. I run out but nothing happened to the school and I return. Again there is some noise. The school has gone up in flames too. I run up to save the child. There is already coming toward me a packwagon, on top—the child, safe. Now I am again in the kitchen. The woman says it would be fine if one could recognize that everything is just imagination.

Second dream—"MITHRAS DREAM"

I find myself on a brightly lit oval spot around which everything is dark. There are many people in an extremely exhausted and prostrate condition just as I am. The voice says: If the place would become brighter then it would be much worse for us. Cups were brought in and put down, with a peculiar liquid in them: blood and water, however not mixed. The people drink with contentment and thus become strong so that they can walk again; they disappear into the dark, I too. At this point the place has gotten still lighter and the darkness has become deeper.

Third dream

I am in a completely barren forest of my homeland. Suddenly the forest opens and I look at magnificent green meadows.

The theme in each of the three dreams is rescue. It is represented in three steps: first, the wise woman teaches us that one would gain much if one could grasp the illusions of this world. Apparently that is not enough, a mystic potion, in a mysterious, unreal space, saves us. Then, what had just taken place in a supernatural sphere, the miracle of the transformation, now takes effect upon the return to the natural world. The barren makes way for the new, young life.

We declare that these dreams are the best description of what takes place within the human being. And then, in the case history too, the view opens "on the magnificent green meadows," of course, only after about half a year. Step by step, it was possible to help her conquer her inner, neurotic inhibitions, to effect the return of menses and of her pleasure in food, and to enable her to acquire the strength to confront life's stresses. Only then did the patient reach the point which was predicted in her dreams. It is as if she were transposed back into her homeland.

II

Upon admission to the clinic, Mrs. V. Q. actually weighed only 32 kg., though she was of medium height. During her puberty she had been heavy, coarse, and eager to move about. As preliminary signs of disturbance came daily flimmerscotoma with vomiting and headache—in other words, a *migraine ophthalmique*. The biography of this patient, too, has to be suppressed, although it shows every desirable disclosure regarding the increasing difficulties in an individual who denied herself every satisfaction in life. At 16 she weighed 60 kg., at 19 still 54 kg., at 22 only 47 kg. At the age of 24 there came a point in her life where she was frightened because of the considerable edema of her legs, the continuous amenorrhea, and the terrible loss of weight. Up to that point she maintained that she was totally healthy and still sometimes makes such statements. An internist found retention of food in the stomach, a gynecologist found hypogenitalism, and a charlatan found a pressure of the uterus on the stomach.

Our therapeutic success with this patient was not very decisive. Here too we tried to influence the patient with pituitary and thyroid medication. In addition, the patient underwent insulin therapy. Careful clinical observations were made and extensive psychological work was done. The edema disappeared altogether, and the final gain in weight from 32 up to 35 kg. was indubitably linked with adiposity, especially in the region of the mamma. Eventually the weight fluctuated between 36 and 40 kg. These fluctuations may be ascribed to episodic retention of water which takes place following psychic conflicts and states of confusion. Menstruation did not return. The total picture was much improved physically and psychologically; nevertheless one could not speak of a cure.

If we select, from the rich sequence of psychological development, what belongs to the *Magersucht* of this patient, we again find the total absence of normal rhythm of appetite and eating, indifference toward food, especially an inability to eat butter. Again we find satisfaction in a state of abstinence from food, a feeling of discomfort during and following food intake. The personality is one of a poetic young woman, sensitive to beauty, literary, original, with esthetic tastes and capable of frankness and understanding. In the area of her illness we never were sure that she did not practice minor deceptions, speaking the untruth and being disobedient. More than once she hid food and pretended that she had eaten it. Repeated vomiting turned out to be artificially induced. Here too we find a completely developed picture of perversion of the appetite, of the quasi-esthetic ideal formation and of complete *Magersucht*. This patient also suffers from periodic attacks of compulsive, embarrassing bulimia. These attacks may appear twice a week and recently were directed at meat. After that she is glad not to have any appetite and glad that she doesn't have to eat.

She herself had noticed that the days of bulimia followed certain dreams. We shall contrast these dreams with dreams before days without appetite.

Dreams Before Days of Bulimia

1. Meerestraum (THE DREAM OF THE SEA)

She gets to the sea but is disappointed not to have the expected impression. There comes a ship. She embarks, sails across the sea. Male and female friends of hers are on it. During the voyage a message comes that the ship is going to sink and whoever wants to, can still leave. She decides to stay and so do the others.

2. *Sterbeuhr* (CLOCK OF DEATH)

She lies in bed and knows that she must die in fifteen minutes. Mother appears, whereupon tears come to her eyes. She complains: "Now only ten minutes, now only nine minutes," and so on. Mother says there is nothing special about that. Everybody has to die sooner or later and she should not consider herself so important. This is rather embarrassing to her.

3. *Saturntraum* (DREAM OF SATURN)

She sees a fireplace of an unpleasant brick-red color. A very bright, fiery-red globe appears in it which hurts her very much. Then the globe becomes hazier, paler and bluer; a disc-like ring removes itself from the globe's periphery like in Saturn. Now the globe flies at her and penetrates into her abdomen causing it to swell and hurt. But in the process the ring frees itself from the sphere and floats freely on top of it.

4. *Juenglingstraum* (DREAM OF THE YOUTH)

She sees the great bronze statue of a muscular, strong young man as it stands in front of the stadium. The figure lays itself into her own body and pushes the latter out of itself, which is very painful.

DREAMS PRIOR TO DAYS WITHOUT APPETITE

1. *Im Himmel* (IN HEAVEN)

She is in heaven, it is extraordinarily cold. Her physician is there too (on a throne?). She declares that actually he is God himself and what had helped her is God itself. She then speaks words which close with the sentence: "Now I know it piece by piece; then however, I shall know as I am known." She comprehends the meaning of these words for the first time. As she wakes up, she is surprised that she knew by heart several verses that she had never memorized and convinced herself that these verses are correct by looking them up in the Testament (1. Corinthians, 13).

2. *Schlaftraum* (DREAM OF SLEEP)

It is war; there is great confusion, hunger, and extreme cold. She cannot sleep. Her physician appears and covers her with a cape. Soon she becomes quiet and happy and falls asleep. (Her husband told her that she had said aloud, in her sleep: "Oh, sleep is so beautiful.")

The contrast between both groups of dreams is obvious. Their manifest contents are also obvious. On the one hand, the themes, mother, disembodiment, and death are connected with the days of bulimia; on the other hand, the themes, father-God, cognition, and redeemed contentment are connected with the days without appetite. Here then lies the biological paradox: Fading away and proximity to death prepare for the excessive food intake; exaltation and bliss, however, are followed by sabotage of nutrition. Each time the dream experience is reversed by her instincts. Upon the path to death follows bulimia; upon the blissful feelings there follows another life-threatening denial of food. The crosswise self-reflecting grouping of these motives cannot be solved logically. Fragments of similar formulations, while not quite clearly arranged but not yet chaotic, clearly allude to the rather peculiar images in reference to the body of the patient. The motive of painful disembodiment as is shown in the dream of the youth appeared also in other dreams which we add here to illustrate further the psychophysical situation.

Tempel der Einsamkeit (TEMPLE OF LONELINESS)

At the cemetery, there stood a circular temple, actually only a half-circle in which a sphere was on top of a square base—the world globe. On the outside, all around, there was a bench. At one end of the bench I myself was sitting. At the other end, that is, on the other side, that woman teacher on whom I had a crush and whom I later hated. Next to her a girl friend, or rather a classmate of mine. The two got up and walked around the temple. I wave to the teacher that she should take me along but she makes a rejecting gesture and so I had to stay. I become deeply saddened. Now I hear the sounds of the words: "Now the loneliness has penetrated into you forever." Thereupon my skin gets all full of holes like a sieve, and all organs, the heart, the lungs, etc., seep through the holes to the outside until

I am completely empty inside. There is only the loneliness within me and it is totally black. (Awake, crying.)

Die Eisenkugel (THE IRON GLOBE)

I lie in bent position; my head is erect and bent forward, the legs too are pulled up. In my lower belly there is a big black cavity. A large iron globe with rough surface flies up to me and lowers itself, very smoothly, into the cavity of my lower belly. There it grows powerful and becomes big so that I can't look beyond it anymore. I get very anxious that I won't be able to get rid of the globe, it presses and chokes me, my heart palpitates, my breath becomes short and I wake up full of excitement and anxiety.

Characteristically, the patient states that she feels that the meaning of the dream is going to come to her but there is something that interferes with her finding it. The motif of pregnancy was taboo for her. She repressed her aversion against conception and pregnancy, albeit with difficulty. The motif of the globe, which connects this dream with the temple dream, at the same time leads to the Saturn dream mentioned earlier. This planet, as is known, carries the name of the God who eats his own children, thus he, too, is not a friend of the next generation. The spheres of cosmology, of motherhood, and of world death are connected with each other. Pregnancy is *at one and the same time* the sacrifice as well as addition of body substance; for the mother it can bring death or a son. In any case it brings renunciation and the dreaming woman fights against it.

The dreams *and* physiology teach us that nutrition and pregnancy belong together. In the following dream the spheres of creation and possession of the body are again connected.

Die Schlange (THE SNAKE)

I stood in a beautiful wheat field. At my feet there arose a black and yellow speckled snake. It started to twist around my legs, higher and higher; actually not unpleasant, my arms are still free. Then the snake coils around them too, tighter and tighter. Finally I do become anxious and as I look down at myself, the snake has penetrated within me, altogether, and now, as it were, forms the skeleton of my own body. Only its head stands in front of my face, looks at me, and suddenly changes into the eyes of my woman teacher. Then I hear Beethoven's Funeral March and suddenly I am free of the snake. In the rhythm of the March I walk toward a door which is formed of two columns on top of which is a cross-log with beautiful decorations and sculptures. But the place where you walk through is totally black. I walked up to it to the sound of the March.

Thus there are three dreams in which the own body is expelled and something alien is substituted: either the darkness of loneliness, a youth, or a snake. Actually they are three myths of disembodiment. The imagery makes three attempts to decipher the enigma of the power directed against life which has attacked the living substance of the body. It would be worth our while to contemplate each of these myths and compare them.

Mother, pregnancy, death and salvation, murder, and suicide play undisguised roles in many other dreams of these patients. What they have in common is the quality of floating between life and death, and the painful contradiction of the patients' feelings *vis-à-vis* their closest relatives. We want to report one more dream which shows an important link between these family tensions and the perverted attitude toward food intake.

I am standing and around me are heaped provisions and food which I must eat. I am very unhappy about it because all around me there are eyes, nothing but eyes, *eyes* watching how I will eat. A pair of eyes changes into the face of my brother, how he snickers, mean and ornery.

Here then is the inner tension of narcissism common to all neuroses, anxious to guard its secrets and always believing that it is being watched, or even persecuted—a tension which fosters paranoid development and, simultaneously, is the force through which the neurotic person again and again feeds and re-enforces his symptoms. In comparison, it is rather inessential that actually the environment always did demand that the patient eat more and his own instinctual drives always ordered him to do the opposite. This battle (which has taken place often enough in reality) is nothing but a reflection of the battle which rages within the patient between his inner life and his physiological processes.

As one can now see, there can be no doubt that Magersucht *is not an isolated process.* With *Magersucht* there is a deep refusal, a refusal to surrender, to conceive, to become pregnant, of twosomeness—yes, refusal even of life itself. The refusal of all this, to the highest degree of spiritual perfection, becomes the ideal. "I will know, as I will be known." In the dream, "In Heaven," it is really the physician who should help the patient reach this stage. This patient did not eventually return to a natural, normal condition (as was true in our first case); the physician appears as the helper in the victory of a principle hostile to the body, and actually the clinical cure has been sacrificed for "knowledge." The forces which denied the life of the flesh remained unconquered.

Naturally one has the choice of considering the physiological *Magersucht* as primary, and the encroachment of its negative tendencies—the renunciation of procreation and perhaps of one's very life—as secondary, or, in reverse, of considering the longing for death as primary, and the undermining and perversion of nutrition as its consequence. As far as I am concerned, we do not need to choose between these concepts. Terms like somatogenic and psychogenic represent an unwarranted limitation to a unilateral causal principle. If one reacts to the whole, then more than a limited explanation consisting of cause and effect is offered. One can certainly say that these illnesses are inadequately, yes, even falsely, characterized by the word, *Magersucht*. The desire *(sucht)* is not to be thin *(mager)*. What really happens is quite different: Magersucht embraces (physiologically, too) the spheres of nutrition, generation, and redemption from the body, namely death. The pathology of this disease has been enriched by something which could not have been readily anticipated if one had not sought the *inner* aspects of this matter.

It can be said that this new knowledge throws greater light on clinical experience. It is known that not only *fattening patients with Magersucht,* but also *slenderizing obese people* through diet is often extraordinarily difficult if other problems such as debility, depression, circulatory disturbances and inability to work are to be avoided. On the other hand, it is easy enough for depression or melancholia to accomplish what cannot be accomplished through diet, i.e., the rapid loss of weight. But it it is true that in order to maintain normal nutritional balance it is essential that there be naturally positive attitudes toward life, a feeling of well-being, part of which is a rhythm of appetite and feeling of satiation, and, if it is part of abnormal weight loss and abnormal obesity that there is a perversion of specific subjective attitudes in regard to nutrition—if thus "nutrition" becomes *integrated* because of such subjective factors—then the impossibility of controlling the state of nutrition only by adding or subtracting calories becomes understandable. If we call that subjective sum total of judgment, ideals, feelings, wishes, and drives, euphoria, then we cannot describe this euphoria as the cause, but only as part and parcel of healthy nutrition.

If this concept is correct then it must be seen too in those material factors of what we call metabolism. If the metabolism is constant, increase and decrease of weight depend on intake; a plus of intake means adding weight, a minus means a loss of weight. Physiology, too, has found that metabolism does not depend simply upon adding something, but stubbornly and within narrow limits, represents a quantity called "need." Maintenance of this quantity against encroachment from above or below requires a special arrangement, and this is where the difficulties start.

In both cases we obtained the most important insight from the dreams of the patient. *There are no scientific laws which say that these dreams should rank lower, as far as experiential fact is concerned, than the amplitude of a scale.* Both need to be interpreted and evaluated properly. If we omit the biography of the waking life, submerge ourselves into this dream life, and follow all the possible and impossible incidents which take place, we still are not in too strange a world. Our everyday world and the dream world are fairly different, but comparable. What is comparable is felt even sooner than what belongs in a conceptual system. Here then lies a challenge. We see human beings caught in the dilemma between the demands of normal life (such as nutrition and procreation) and those drives which they experience immediately. The environment and one's own reason require satisfaction of that normal life; drives and a secretly erected ideal push away from it into the intellectual, spiritual sphere. *Over this dilemma the concept of health is torn asunder, and physiological functions become abnormal—to such a degree that life is threatened.*

It is not that a blind material force interferes with the physiological functions, enforcing or mitigating them, and, as a consequence, the biological functions become abnormal, health becomes disturbed and finally instinctual life perverted and ideals pathologic. Not at all! From the very beginning we see a revolution all along the line and in all manifestations as a result of the *altered aim* of life in reference to its *final fate*. It is not a small cause with a big effect which will make the whole thing understandable. If this is the way one considers the connection causal, then fundamentally one understands nothing. The relationship of the part to the whole becomes understandable only if one looks toward the final destination and sees the various manifestations as way stations toward that final goal. The interconnection here, therefore, is not a causal chain *within* time, but, rather, the tying up, backwards, of the end with the beginning—toward time and therefore through time. The dreams of the patients precipitated the understanding of the physiological and psychological events as directed toward such an aim or ideal. One has to admit that the waking life of these two individuals could have been used. They knew that not eating and not needing was more beautiful and purer for them; yet that was only one aspect, shrouded in numerous contradictions and compromises. It is as if they wanted to achieve something impossible. Finally, they ended up at the doctor's. The dreams, on the other hand, are radical and show things in their climactic state: unhappiness and death, as well as transubstantiation and blissful redemption. What had remained in balance biologically was brought to a spiritual decision in the dream. Thus, dream life is much further advanced than waking life. But at the same time it is much more disguised. It does say the final things but it says them only through imagery. This symbolic language may be interpreted in different ways; this symbolic writing may be translated into different languages. Perhaps it needs the disguise because what it says is not the penultimate, but rather the final thing.

At this point we have to make a correction in our explanation of the problems of nutrition. It is still true that one can understand and grasp weight increase or decrease more easily if one uses the images, judgments, feelings, and ideals which can be observed in the waking as well as in the dream experiences of the patient. It is true, too, that these conscious elements, as part of nutrition, integrate the variations of the latter and that the "euphoria" is such an integration. It would not, however, be correct to imagine this integration as permitting one interpretation and one meaning only and thus something that occurs according to laws or as having general validity. The preferential interest which pathological cases have depends somehow upon the fact that, in these instances, the individuals have a feeling of well-being and are in some way euphoric, although they undermine their nutrition with this kind of euphoria. It is exactly this *biological contradiction* which permits neither a physiologically nor a psychologically rational solution and which forced research to go from the rational into the mythical. This transition was not made by the scientist first, but by the patient himself, insofar as what the patient delineated in sketchy strokes in wakefulness, he expressed in strongly demarked strokes and powerful colors in dreams. We only followed him there. However, we do not deny our responsibility in that, by our medical attitude, we forced him to a decision. The patient dreamed those dreams in the situation of therapy and not before.

The proleptic destination of the processes, their final aim, as well as this transcending into an alien, mythical sphere, can now be recognized as peculiarities of such an investigation and therapy which we should not evade but should pursue in all their consequences. The fundamental character of these steps can no longer be overlooked. Prolepsis and transcendence point toward a special position for our research and its subject which, if we want to do justice to it, has to be found not as something causal and isolated, but as an all-embracing order.

If we resume the discussion of the dreams of our patients from this point of view, we see that they are by no means understood exhaustively by the few interpretative comments. If one looks at their parts and elements of style, one can see something rather diametrically opposed among them. Side by side with the theme of one's own body and its loss of substance, one can see allusions to matters which have a contemporary, historic, cultist, or intellectual content. These two opposing groups are tied into an artistic unity through the story which takes place in the dream and which we may call the myth of the dream. Thus it is the myth which connects the individual concern of the dreamer—in this case the loss of his body substance—with the suprapersonal powers under which he lives. It then becomes evident that for the patient and for his physician the dream plays the same role, i.e., that of an intermediary. The patients learned to understand (partly due to therapy) that the messed up state of affairs regarding their physical health was actually nothing else but the contradictorily tied-up bundle of their attitudes toward love, marriage, procreation, soul, life and death. They did not grasp the similarity through intellectual explanations; they simply recognized it. And then followed a sweeping change in the first patient and a new equilibrium, without radical changes in the second patient. The first as well as the second course become understandable because of the nature and discussion of the thoughts and feelings which have now entered consciousness.

To state it again: The dream is the mediator between bodily events and conscious life. We can anticipate that this role has not necessarily been played solely by dreams; other mediators are also possible. It is fate itself, with its concrete hammer blows and surprises, which makes the surrogate of dreams superfluous and which, if it wants to, can remove the deep cleavage between body and consciousness in a straightforward manner.

This contribution to the question of psychosomatic relations is based wholly on dream research and wishes to recommend its validity for the category of nutritional disturbances. It seems that progress in this area is possible only if we can free ourselves, not only from the narrow physiological, but also from the narrow biological approach. In the final analysis, the biological interpretation of pathological events, psychic as well as physical, amounts to adaptation, compromise, regulation—in short, to life itself. Such optimistic classifications are both confirmed and contradicted by life events. We took account of that here and focused on the contradictory and the biologically useless with all their inner contradictions. If one does not omit such things from the case histories, then it becomes evident that opposed to the biological, i.e., the regulating order, one finds a suprabiological order whose absolute character is ready to tear the biological order to pieces without any compromise. The first result is individual death, and one just cannot deny its existence. Even those who believe they can demonstrate adequately disease as a consequence of regulation would have to admit that death represents an interruption of this order.

The question of specificity presents the greatest difficulty in the apparently newly revived research into psychosomatic relations. Has a certain organ disease tangible psychic significance? Such a question is far from answered. For the present investigation one might, however, attempt a brief formulation. It is out of the question that we will be able to designate satisfactorily the psychic content of organs or their diseases, over and beyond the self-perception due to pain, weakness, dizziness, and so on. On the other hand, deeper, clinical (not experimental!) study has always proved very clearly, even in trivial and banal nonfatal illnesses, that we are dealing with the effects and results of those suprabiological orders which appear in this paper under the names, love, marriage, procreation, soul, life, death. If we compare—to mention just recent publications, for instance—the studies on heart diseases by H. Pluegge with those on "Tonsillary Angina" by R. Bilz, and my own contribution on disturbances of metabolism, then it becomes evident that those great themes are ubiquitous, and thus can certainly not be considered "specific" in any way. The deciding issue is not the seizure of any particular organ or its functions, but the kind and the manner of such an order and its potentiality. The strongest proponent of this view has been R. Bilz in the above-mentioned study, knowledge of which is indispensable for these problems.

Thus, if an organ or an important function becomes diseased, one will not be able to grasp the *most characteristic* aspect of the whole event, either from its psychological meaning or through an anatomic-physiological description. One cannot derive the meaning of organic events from psychology, nor can one fathom the causes or the elements of psychic experience from material events. What we can do, and where we can contribute at this time, is the illumination of one individual case through the juxtaposition of those supraindividual orders which are givens in the somatic as well as in the psychic sphere. The characteristics of the heart patient or of the angina patient shape themselves into a picture to which the organ contributes as much as the world of the suprapersonal order, which is similarly constructed and which unfolds its character only in its very own characteristic way. Thus one can say that, while one cannot explain the specific, it is the specific through which the more general can be explained.

DISCUSSION AND SUMMARY OF "ON PITUITARY ANTERIOR LOBE INSUFFICIENCY" BY M. SCHUR AND C. V. MEDVEI

M. RALPH KAUFMAN, M.D. AND MARCEL HEIMAN, M.D.

A major portion of this paper is devoted to a polemic between the authors and the well-known German clinician, *von Bergmann*. The issue which the authors argue about is whether or not there is adequate evidence for the nonorganic etiology of syndromes which originally were considered organic, pituitary conditions.

In mentioning the symptomatology of their cases, the authors note as did the authors before them, the similarity of symptoms, i.e., loss of weight, lack of appetite, absence of menstruation, sexual difficulties, mental attitude of apathy and indifference or depression. In reviewing the literature, the authors then arrive at a distinction between primary pituitary illness which would be exemplified by Simmonds' disease and symptoms developing in connection with an insufficiency of the pituitary because of "a correlation disturbance." Like Weizsäcker, Schur and Medvei come to the conclusion that the changes in the pituitary gland might be as much the cause as the consequence of the eating disturbance.

In discussing the complexity of the processes which are comprised under the term appetite, the authors follow much the same course as *Weizsäcker* in stating, "the desire to eat is one of the fundamental, vital

---

Ueber Hypophysenvorderlappeninsuffizienz. *Wiener Archiv für Innere Medizin*, 31, 1937.

drives. A disturbance of the desire to eat . . . therefore represents a neurotic disturbance of vitality." Further on, the authors again echo what *Weizsäcker* stated when they claim that "one can hardly assume that from the conscious wish 'to get slender hips' there could result such a disintegration of vitality which almost or actually may lead to death. *Here one must deal with a preponderance of destructive tendencies which exist in every human being.*" (The authors make clear that Weizsäcker's paper was published after they had written this paper!)

Despite the fact that there are only two kinds of therapy which are reasonable, namely therapy on the affected organ and a systematic "psychotherapy," the authors note that the most peculiar therapeutic approaches may lead to success, as they later exemplify in their cases. "Perhaps," they continue, "these successes have something to do with the fact that we find very often *one* powerful ally in our therapy: The drive for self-preservation which in most cases seems to be strong enough so that finally it wins out over the destructive tendency; otherwise all those cases would lead to death."

In their final division of anterior lobe insufficiencies, the authors arrive at the conclusion that they may (a) be the result of primary destruction of the anterior lobe, or (b) occur through disturbance of another endocrine gland influencing the anterior lobe, or through the effect of neuroses.

Schur and Medvei then present six cases, which as far as their psychological structure or dynamics are concerned, are rather superficial.

The first case, a woman described as severely neurotic and homosexual, did not respond to any kind of therapy which was available at the time of observation (in 1923). She suddenly improved when transferred to a tuberculosis sanitarium.

The second case, a woman with hysterical character and hysterical fits, did not respond to any of the organic therapies until the family called upon a "Magnetiseur."

The third case, a woman who underwent a stomach resection as a consequence of her complaints, had some unhappy experiences in her love life. Some ventilation of her conflicts took place in addition to organic therapy with hormones.

In the fourth case, the patient's acute illness was precipitated by a fatal accident to her only child. Hormonal therapy brought about an improvement.

The fifth case, described as very inhibited and blocked, made a "silly" attempt at suicide by drinking ink at the age of sixteen. An appendectomy is the somatic experience which led to the symptoms of pituitary insufficiency. Because the patient was considered "schizoid," no psychotherapy was attempted.

The sixth and last case also had stomach troubles in the foreground. Here, too, a stomach resection was performed. The patient did not respond to the therapy as given by the authors and, after they had lost track of her, she presented herself a number of years later, "completely cured and as a person willing and liking to work." This woman "had lost all confidence in orthodox medicine and had gone to a homeopathic physician. In addition to homeopathic therapy she had gotten *gynecological (vaginal) massage.*"

In their final summary the authors state that in patients who are of a certain make-up and live in a certain milieu, a trauma or a conflict brings about symptoms of an anterior lobe insufficiency. "In these patients we had some insight into the battle between two antagonistic tendencies: self-preservation drive and destructive drive in violent battle for the fate of the individual." Finally, they state that a detailed analysis of this disease picture is not only of importance for full understanding of the pathogenesis of the anterior lobe insufficiency, it shows also "the importance of the uniform approach for the understanding of the pathology of function. It shows us the functional connections of whole organ systems which are in the service of the 'vitality.' It teaches us the importance of the instinct theory for the pathology and the dependence of certain drive tendencies. Thus it shows us the way which could turn out to be fruitful in the approach to all organ neuroses."

These three papers, taken together, give an interesting view on the state of psychosomatic medicine in the German literature of the 1930's. You can see the authors wrestle with the problem, you can almost feel the granite resistance against which they have to hew out their right to consider anorexia either from a psychological point of view or as a psychologically explicable condition. We believe that Weizsäcker has made the most significant contribution to the understanding of ano-

rexia despite the fact that he passes over the significance of the unconscious. The importance of Meng's contribution to the problem of anorexia we would see in his pointing at the link between psychosis and organic disease. Schur and Medvei's paper, while it does not add to our psychological understanding of the syndrome, is helpful in emphasizing the psychological aspects in a condition which up to that time was considered by most clinicians to be purely organic.

ANOREXIA NERVOSA
A METABOLIC DISORDER OF
PSYCHOLOGIC ORIGIN

R. F. FARQUHARSON, M.B. AND H. H. HYLAND, M.D.
(1938)

Farquharson and Hyland recognized anorexia nervosa as a metabolic disorder of psychological origin based on "some prolonged emotional conflict, either avowed or concealed." No attempt is made to determine a specific conflict. Difficult home situations or ridicule for being fat are stressed. It is also noted that the patients are "usually impulsive, willful, introspective, and emotionally unstable." This temperament acts as a basis (constitution and emotional conflicts).

They stress the psychological character of anorexia nervosa and are opposed to attributing it to secondary disturbance of the anterior lobe of the hypophysis or any other endocrine gland.

In the six female patients of their series, amenorrhea was an early symptom. But this was not associated with other evidence of sexual function. If anorexia nervosa were a "functional Simmonds' disease" there should be characteristic secondary changes in gonads and other endocrine glands. "The available data [post mortem] suggest that there is no characteristic change in the endocrine glands in anorexia nervosa."

The authors emphasize the psychological aspects of the syndrome with secondary metabolic changes. Although they talk about concealed conflicts, there is no emphasis upon unconscious conflicts in the psychoanalytic sense.

It is of significance that in the 1930's, with the basic concepts of psychoanalysis or so-called psychodynamic psychiatry available, neither Ryle nor Farquharson utilized any of these concepts in evaluating the so-called psychological aspects of the syndrome.

In 1873, under the title of "Anorexia Nervosa," Sir William Gull[1] described a syndrome characterized by extreme emaciation and amenorrhea in the absence of any demonstrable structural disease. The illustration is a reproduction of the pictures of one of his early patients before and after treatment. At about the same time, Lasègue[2] described the condition as "hysterical anorexia." Numerous articles on the subject since then have added little to the clear, concise accounts of these authors.

The disorder occurs chiefly in adolescent girls, less commonly in men. Following some prolonged emotional conflict, either avowed or concealed, the appetite fails and the intake of food becomes grossly insufficient, leading to loss of weight. Commonly there are mild symptoms, such as an uneasiness after food, epigastric distress or constipation, which provide a further excuse for the anorexia. Emaciation increases and the patient's health becomes an object of great concern to her family. Yet she remains quick, alert, active and restless and denies ill health until emaciated to a degree not seen in patients with organic disease still able to get about. "These willful patients are often allowed to drift their own way into a state of extreme exhaustion, when it might have been prevented by placing them under different moral conditions[3]." When emaciation is at its greatest, weakness increases and edema of the lower extremities may supervene. Occasionally death results from starvation. Amenorrhea may appear early or only after considerable loss of weight has occurred. When the syndrome is well

---

Reprinted from *Journal of the American Medical Association*, 111:1085-1092, 1938.

[1] Gull, W. W.: Anorexia Nervosa. *This Volume*, pp. 132-138.
In 1868, Gull (The address on medicine, *This Volume*, pp. 104-127.) had used the term "hysteric apepsia" to describe the same condition.
[2] Lasègue, E. C.: On hysterical anorexia. *This Volume*, pp. 141-155.
[3] Gull, *This Volume*, p. 136.

developed the temperature is often subnormal, the pulse rate and the blood pressure low.

Ryle[4] remarks on the tendency of "physicians subject to the lure of endocrinology" to look for the cause of this syndrome in a primary deficiency or disharmony of the internal secretions. The ovaries, thyroid, adrenals and pituitary have all been blamed. In recent years attention has been directed more and more to the hypophysis, and the finding of low basal metabolic rates and altered sugar tolerance, in addition to emaciation and amenorrhea, would appear to support this idea. Recently Sheldon (7) has suggested that anorexia nervosa, which he recognizes clearly as a definite syndrome may be "a 'functional' Simmonds' disease—a pituitary 'black-out' of psychological origin." This conception has won the approval of others (Langdon-Brown, 4; Dunn, 2).

On the other hand, in the literature on Simmonds' disease one finds reports of many cases that appear to present the typical picture of anorexia nervosa. Some of these patients have responded well to the administration of various pituitary extracts and their recovery has been taken as evidence of the correctness of the diagnosis of Simmonds' pituitary cachexia. The two syndromes have a superficial similarity but, in our opinion, they are fundamentally different.

It is our purpose in this paper to report eight cases of anorexia nervosa and to point out in discussion the nature of the disorder and its various manifestations. Reasons will be presented to support the belief that this metabolic disorder is based primarily on psychologic disturbance and that its various manifestations should not be attributed to dysfunction of any endocrine gland.

Report of Cases

The following case histories are reported in brief. All the patients were carefully examined and special investigations were carried out as indicated. Negative observations, however, are mentioned only if of particular significance.

[4] Ryle, J. A.: Anorexia Nervosa. *Lancet* 2:893, 1936.

Case 1.

E. L., a Jewish girl, aged 15, was admitted to the hospital February 11, 1932. She had come to the outpatient clinic because her mother was concerned about the patient's loss of weight. Five months previously she weighed 75 pounds (34 kg.) but had gradually lost 16 pounds (7 kg.) during that time. Menstruation had commenced in 1930. The periods were fairly regular, occurring every twenty-eight days until September 1931, since which date she had not menstruated. She stated that she did not have any gastrointestinal symptoms but said that she had been eating very small meals because of abdominal discomfort that followed a large intake of food.

The patient was emaciated. She did not appear acutely ill but was apprehensive about being in the hospital. The secondary sex characteristics and distribution of hair were essentially normal. There was no anemia. The blood pressure was 83 systolic, 50 diastolic; the basal metabolic rate, -37 per cent; the pulse rate, from 60 to 95 per minute; the temperature from 96 to 99 F. The fasting blood sugar determined on six occasions varied between 69 and 77 mg. per hundred cubic centimeters. The first sugar tolerance curve (100 gm. of dextrose) showed a slow and prolonged rise; after eight days, during which time she began to eat voraciously, the test was repeated with only 50 gm. of dextrose and the curve was flat (Table 1).

At the time of admission her perceptions were a little slow and her memory defective. Emotionally she was fairly stable. On enquiry she stated that she had been worried and unhappy at home for the past six months and that this had contributed to her lessened intake of food. The only causes for worry that she would admit were the cessation of menstruation and the fact that her mother was "always fussing about her."

Under observation in the hospital, she showed considerable variability in mood. Most of the time she seemed content and cheerful, but there were days when she was depressed and uncommunicative. A hypochondriacal trend developed and she talked at great length about her digestive system. She said that she could not taste food properly and demanded an X-ray examination of her intestine because there seemed to be something wrong with the passage of food through it. She complained that she did not have the proper feeling when her bowels moved and asked that this be investigated. Under reassurance, her appetite increased greatly and she commenced to eat ravenously and complained that no matter how much she ate she was never satisfied. On discharge from the hospital, February 23, her weight was 64½ pounds (29 kg.) and her basal metabolic rate -28 per cent.

The diagnosis lay between anorexia nervosa and acquired anterior pitui-

TABLE 1
OUTLINE OF EIGHT CASES

Case	Sex	Date	Age, Yrs.	Height	Weight, Lbs.	B.M.R. %	B.P.	Fast.	½ Hr.	1 Hr.	2 Hr.	3 Hr.	Menses	Comment
Case 1 E. L.	♀	1932 Feb. 12	15	4'6"	59	−87	82/50	69	93	171	178	165	Absent 5 mos.	Mentally bright; state of marked anxiety with hypochondriacal trend
		Feb. 20						71	82	80	64	61		
		April 1933			73	−16	102/52							
		November 1934											Returned	Mentally and emotionally stable
		January 1938		4'8"	86	−5	112/76						Regular since Nov., 1933	Working steadily; feels and looks well
		February	21	4'8¼"	99½		122/84							
Case 2 D. K.	♀	1933 May	18	5'4"	91		98/70						Menstruated once in 8 mos.	Intellectual: sensitive and apprehensive
		June			88									
		1934 August			72	−25							Returned Dec. 1934; regular thereafter	
		1935 January	20		100									
Case 3 R. V.	♂	1933 December	21	5'9"	101	−25	95/58	80	97	104	67	64		Quiet and seclusive
		1934 March			131	−10	100/60	110	114	143	102	80		Interested and sociable Able to work
		July			140									

	♂	Jan. 31	13	5'4"	75	−45	108/70	76	100	103	120	91		Variability of mood; suspicious; obsessed regarding food
		Feb. 8			78	−35						
		Feb. 17			92	−27						
		March 31 1938			94	−29		75	67	108	99	89	
		April 1938	17	5'11"	159	−8							Feeling well; happy; attends school regularly
Case 5 M. A.	♀	1934 Sept. 27	16	5'5"	91	−28	95/60	68	132	181	207	220	Absent for 18 months	Intellectual, introspective and seclusive
		Oct. 6						68	131	156	130	142	
		November 1936			102½	−28							
		May 1938		5'5⅝"	150	−17							Returned early in 1936
		May	20	5'5¾"	139	−17	104/68	83	91	71	87	92	Regular since returning	Nervous and easily upset; attending university; working hard
Case 6 I. A.	♀	1935 November 25		5'1½"	69	−32	74/56	54	92	80	102	104	Absent for 7 years	Suspicious; uncooperative
		May 1938	27		125								Still absent	Working: domestic
Case 7 R. P.	♀	1936 March	21	5'5"	77	−26	104/70	82	114	118	95	88	Absent for 2 yr.	Variability of mood Emotionally unstable
		April 1938			81									
		May			110								Still absent	More stable; feels well
Case 8 A. S.	♀	1937 February	23	5'3⅜"	69¾	−18	80/58	134	148			124	Absent for 5 mos.; only 3 periods previous year	Intelligent; introspective; wilful; sensitive; refuses to cooperate
		1938 May	24		59		112/60						Still absent	

tary deficiency. Despite the normal appearance of secondary sex characteristics and the normal distribution of body hair, the latter diagnosis was favored.

After discharge she was given injections of antuitrin 1 cc. intramuscularly twice a week, from March to July 1932. Her appetite continued to increase.

On readmission to the hospital for ten days in April she was found to be eating 3,400 calories each day. Her weight was 73 pounds (33 kg.); the basal metabolic rate, −16 per cent; the blood pressure, 102 systolic, 52 diastolic. Her general appearance was much improved but she was still introspective and hypochondriacal.

Examination October 31, three months after antuitrin therapy was discontinued, showed a marked improvement in her mental attitude. The excessive desire for food had subsided and she was eating ordinary amounts. She was bright and agreeable and was taking part in games at school. She no longer displayed obsessions about her gastrointestinal tract. This improvement was maintained. Menstruation returned in November 1933 and was regular thereafter. Her weight in January 1934 was 86 pounds (39 kg.); height, 4 feet 8 inches (142 cm.); basal metabolic rate, −5 per cent; blood pressure, 112 systolic, 76 diastolic. Mentally and emotionally, she appeared normal. In view of the continued improvement after cessation of endocrine therapy it was felt that a diagnosis of anterior pituitary insufficiency was untenable and the diagnosis of anorexia nervosa was established.

The patient was seen again on February 19, 1938. She had been working in a factory for the past four years and had not missed any time owing to ill health. There had been no gastrointestinal symptoms whatever. Menstruation had occurred normally every four weeks during this time. Her height was 4 feet, 8¼ inches (142 cm.); weight, 99½ pounds (45 kg.); blood pressure, 122 systolic, 84 diastolic. The patient stated that she realized that her former illness was the result of a desire on her part to have things her own way in the home. Her two sisters and a brother, all older than herself, were living at home and would order her about. When she was sick her mother became very anxious and would take her part, aiding her in getting her own way. The two sisters and brother are now married and living elsewhere. Her life at home has been quite congenial since they departed.

Case 2.

D. K., a girl aged 18, first examined May 8, 1933, was in good health—weight about 108 pounds (49 kg.)—until the autumn of 1932, when she was sent to boarding school. Her menstrual periods ceased at that time.

Because of a coincident gradual increase in weight to 120 pounds (54 kg.) she began to restrict her diet, avoiding carbohydrates and fats. Progressive loss of weight resulted. Her appetite remained good but she began to complain of epigastric fullness whenever she ate more than a small quantity of food. She tired easily and worried greatly about constipation, which she believed was responsible for her symptoms. In January 1933 she menstruated once but had not menstruated subsequently. Since February, worry about her condition had led to difficulty in sleeping.

The patient was very thin but otherwise well developed; height, 5 feet 4 inches (163 cm.); weight, 91 pounds (41 kg.); temperature, 98.6 F.; pulse rate, 60 per minute; blood pressure, 98 systolic, 70 diastolic. There was no anemia. Her hands were cold and reddish blue. The colon was palpable and tender. Enquiry showed that the patient had always been ambitious, sensitive and conscientious. She had done well at school and was working very hard because she dreaded mediocre standing. Her mother suffered with paralysis agitans and the patient tended to be depressed when at home. A diagnosis of anorexia nervosa was made.

By June her weight had fallen to 88 pounds (40 kg.). She took high standing in matriculation examinations and returned to her home in the country, refusing to be admitted to the hospital for more complete investigation and treatment. During the subsequent year at home her weight gradually went down to 70 pounds (32 kg.). On investigation at another medical center in the summer of 1934 the basal metabolic rate was found to be −25 per cent; thyroid extract, 1½ grain (0.1 gm.) daily, was prescribed. In the autumn of 1934 the patient entered the university and following this showed gradual improvement. By Christmas her weight had increased to 93 pounds (42 kg.). When seen January 31, 1935, her weight was 100 pounds (45 kg.), she was eating well, and she had menstruated a few weeks before. She is now married.

Case 3.

R. V., a man aged 21, admitted to the hospital December 3, 1933, was in his usual state of good health until June 1931, when he commenced to lose his appetite. Desire for food gradually decreased and was associated with progressive loss of weight and a feeling of fatigue. There were no other complaints apart from an occasional sensation of nausea. During the interval of two and a half years from the onset, his weight decreased from 153 pounds (69 kg.) to 108 pounds (49 kg.). The patient was not inclined to discuss his condition in detail and did not appear greatly concerned about it. He explained that he had often tried to eat larger quantities of food but had found that whenever he took more than a small amount he was troubled with epigastric fullness and nausea.

The patient was well developed but extremely emaciated and was in no apparent discomfort. His height was 5 feet 9 inches (175 cm.) and weight 101 pounds (46 kg.). Hair distribution and secondary sex characteristics were normal for his age. The blood pressure was 95 systolic, 58 diastolic; the basal metabolic rate, −25 per cent. His sugar tolerance curve was low and flat (Table 1). There was no anemia. The pulse rate was from 64 to 85 per minute, the temperature from 97 to 98.6 F.

He had a good mentality; memory, perception and attention were not impaired. He was not depressed and appeared anxious to regain his health. Enquiry showed that he had always tended to be seclusive but, although he did not make friends easily, he never had difficulty in getting along with people. His parents and an older brother lived on a small farm. Two years previously the patient had been sent to a neighboring city to find work but he had not been successful. He made few friends and became dissatisfied with the idle life he was leading. He wished to return to the farm but his parents would not agree. The patient became worried about their attitude and jealous of his brother. It was at this time that he commenced to suffer from indigestion after meals, which consisted mainly of a feeling of fullness. To get relief he gradually cut down on his food intake. He stated that prior to his illness he ate very large meals and frequently ate between meals. To this excess he attributed the gastric disturbances which resulted in his present illness. He stated that there had been no loss of appetite but that he had a constant fear of the discomfort which invariably followed eating even a moderate quantity of food.

He was referred to the hospital as having Simmonds' disease. Because of the lack of evidence of gross endocrine dysfunction and the presence of an obvious psychological disorder, the extreme emaciation was believed to be due to anorexia nervosa.

The patient was assured that there was no organic disease and the nature of his symptoms was explained to him. A duodenal tube was passed and left *in situ* for thirteen weeks. Eight concentrated feedings of 260 calories each were administered at intervals of two hours daily. After his fear had been allayed that the stomach might be abnormally stretched, he showed steady improvement. In about two weeks' time he was encouraged to take nourishment by mouth as well as by tube. With the increase in food intake an irregular, low-grade fever developed and persisted for about two months.

Eight weeks after admission, his weight was 113½ pounds (51.5 kg.), the basal metabolic rate −29 per cent. The patient stated that he felt much stronger and eagerly anticipated his meals. He was more talkative than on admission and was frequently seen chatting with the other patients on the ward. The dextrose tolerance curve had become more normal (Table 1). When the duodenal tube was withdrawn the patient was eating a diet of 3,000 calories daily. His weight was 128 pounds (58 kg.) and the basal metabolic rate was −6 per cent.

On discharge from the hospital, March 30, 1934, his weight was 131 pounds (59 kg.), the basal metabolic rate −10 per cent. Mentally much improved, he regarded the future with optimism and was completely reassured regarding his digestive disturbances. Information received July 25, 1934, indicated that he was well, weighed 140 pounds (63.5 kg.) and was working happily on the farm.

Case 4.

D. G., a boy aged 13, admitted to the hospital January 24, 1934, was brought to the hospital by his parents because of loss of weight and a peculiar mental attitude toward food. He had developed normally until the spring of 1933, at which time he was a little heavier than most of his play fellows. The other boys called him "Tubby" and "Fat," which annoyed him greatly and resulted in several fist fights. He informed his parents that he was dieting to reduce weight. From that time on he took an abnormal interest in food. He talked about it constantly, with particular reference to the fat-producing ingredients of various dishes, and secretly took a "patent medicine" to aid in reducing. He would slip food into a paper bag between his knees during meals and afterward burn it in the furnace. It was noted that he would wipe the butter off his bread and put it on the undersurface of the seat of his chair. Over the period of a year his weight decreased from 115 pounds (52 kg.) to 79 pounds (36 kg.). His parents stated that during this time he had become suspicious of people and would sneak around the house listening to conversations on the assumption that people were talking about him. He had become greatly interested in music, which previously had not interested him at all. His aunt stated that the boy would go into the woods alone and pray to become thin, and that he had expressed an idea that his bedroom was holy.

Prior to his illness he had been healthy and strong, living happily with his parents and one older sister. He had done moderately well at school but preferred to stay at home and occupy himself with mechanical toys rather than play games with the other boys. His outside doctor had found his basal metabolic rate to be −39 per cent and for sixteen days prior to admission had been receiving 1 grain (0.065 gm.) of desiccated thyroid daily but had shown no improvement.

The patient was extremely emaciated; his height was 5 feet 4 inches (163 cm.), his weight 74¾ pounds (34 kg.). The secondary sex characteristics were normally developed for the age of the patient. There was no anemia. The basal metabolic rate was −45 per cent; the blood pressure, 108 systolic, 70 diastolic; the pulse rate, from 60 to 90 per minute; the temperature, from 97 to 100 F. The sugar tolerance curve tended to be rather low (Table 1).

It was ascertained that the father was an emotionally stable person with a good deal of understanding but that the mother was a highly strung, overly conscientious person who failed to take the boy's point of view into consideration and was constantly correcting him and endeavoring to make him conform to her standards. The patient had always been considered a nervous child, subject to impulses and full of short-lived enthusiasm for various interests. About two years previously his family moved to their present home in a different part of the city and, as the patient found difficulty in making friends in his new environment, he spent much time by himself. He stated that at first he intended to stop dieting when his weight fell to 100 pounds (45 kg.) but that he found it impossible to do so. He admitted being influenced by the thought that if he lost much weight and became very thin he would attract a great deal of attention. As a result, he made a study of food values and stated that he became angry and suspicious of people who tried to persuade him to eat the regular meals. In conversation he appeared to be bright and alert; memory, perception and attention showed no defects. He stated that the family, particularly his mother and sister, were against him and that they were ignoring him and leaving him at home rather than taking him to shows and other places of amusement. He had arrived at the conclusion that there was not much in life worth living for.

During his stay in the hospital the nature of the condition was explained to the boy and he rapidly accepted the fact that there was need for a greater food intake, but he went to the extreme and ate huge quantities of food, so that he vomited at times. His weight showed a progressive increase; twenty-four days after admission it had risen to 92 pounds (42 kg.). The basal metabolic rate was then −27 per cent. With the greater intake of food there was a low-grade fever ranging up to 100 F., lasting three weeks. During the next five weeks the intake of food was more moderate and there was but little change in weight. On discharge from the hospital, nine weeks after admission, his weight was 94 pounds (43 kg.) and his basal metabolic rate —29 per cent. It was arranged that he should be sent to a boarding school to get him away from the home environment. Improvement was uninterrupted and the patient did well at school, mixing with the other boys and showing no return of his former symptoms.

The diagnosis was between schizophrenia and anorexia nervosa. It was felt that the latter diagnosis was the more likely in view of the rapid response to treatment in the hospital away from the home environment.

The patient was seen April 11, 1938. He was feeling well and seemed active and happy. His height was 5 feet 11 inches (180 cm.); his weight, 159 pounds (72 kg.); the basal metabolic rate, —8 per cent. He was then 17 years of age and normally developed.

Case 5.

M. A., a girl aged 16, was admitted to the hospital September 24, 1934, complaining of amenorrhea of eighteen months' duration. Menstruation had commenced at the age of 11 and had been essentially normal until twenty months previously, when, after being scanty for two successive periods, it ceased entirely. She said that she felt well but that her appetite had been poor and that she had suffered from constipation for several years. She had been taking 1 grain (0.065 gm.) of desiccated thyroid daily for one year.

The patient was emaciated. Her height was 5 feet 5 inches (165 cm.); weight, 91 pounds (41 kg.); blood pressure, systolic 95, diastolic 60; basal metabolic rate, –28 per cent; pulse rate, from 45 to 70 per minute; temperature, from 96 to 98 F. The dextrose tolerance curve rose from an initial low level of 68 mg. to a peak of 220 mg., reached at the end of three hours (Table 1). Repeated a few days later, the curve was lower (Table 1). A barium sulfate enema showed tonus and haustration of the colon lacking to a moderate degree throughout. There was no anemia but the white blood count was 2,400, lymphocytes 31 per cent.

It was ascertained on enquiry that the patient weighed 135 pounds (61 kg.) at the age of 11 and became very self-conscious about her weight. The other children called her "Fatty," which annoyed her and evidently provided a basis for her curtailment of food intake since that time. She had always been very intelligent but inclined to fantasy. From the age of 4 she would occupy her time writing poetry, sketching and reading. She was always at the head of her class at school. She admitted daydreaming a great deal since the age of eleven and preferred solitude to the company of others. She stated that people annoyed her and that she found talking an effort. At various times she tried to increase her food intake, but this would result in a bloated feeling in the abdomen, which she attributed to constipation. Enquiry revealed that the constipation was associated with faulty habits and that she was relying on frequent laxatives. The patient stated that her home life was a happy one except for the attitude of her older sister, who was continually taunting her, making reference to the desirability of having a good figure and with this in view making a study of food values and diets. The sister was not fat and the patient thought her unreasonable to diet. The patient said that she had become acutely conscious of what other people ate. It would worry her when thin people left food on their plates or when obese people ate large amounts. This became an obsession with her.

The diagnosis was anorexia nervosa.

While in the hospital she usually was optimistic and cheerful. She spent her time reading books on philosophy and doing fancy work. Constipation was quickly relieved by instruction in proper habits and administration of liquid petrolatum. She was given a diet of 2,500 calories daily with 10 units of insulin one half hour before the midday and evening meals. No thyroid was administered while she was in the hospital. Soon she took most of the food offered and on discharge was taking approximately 2,300 calories a day. Her weight increased gradually to 102½ pounds, (46.5 kg.) over a period of eight weeks and her mental attitude steadily improved.

Following discharge from the hospital, November 10, 1934, she resumed thyroid therapy and took 1 grain (0.065 gm.) of desiccated thyroid daily until March 1936. The failure of this treatment to affect the basal metabolic rate materially is shown in Table 2. Seen in December 1935, she was in good spirits, eating well and weighed 119 pounds (54 kg.), but the menses had not yet returned. In May 1936 she weighed 150 pounds (68 kg.), having gained 24 pounds (11 kg.) in two months. Thyroid had been discontinued five weeks previously. The basal metabolic rate was now −17 per cent, the temperature 97.6 F., the pulse rate 54 per minute. The menses returned at this time and have continued normally ever since.

At present (May 1938) she feels well but is inclined to be nervous and easily upset. She is attending the university, working hard and doing well in her studies. Her height is now 5 feet 5¾ inches (165 cm.); weight, 139 pounds (63 kg.), basal metabolic rate, −17 per cent; blood pressure, 104 systolic, 68 diastolic.

TABLE 2
EFFECT OF ADMINISTRATION OF DESICCATED THYROID IN CASE 5

Date	Basal Metabolic Rate, %	Thyroid Medication
Sept. 6, 1934	−37	Desiccated thyroid, 1 gr. daily, Sept. 1933 to Sept. 24, 1934
Sept. 28, 1934	−28	
Nov. 5, 1934	−28	Receiving no thyroid
Jan. 5, 1935	−30	Receiving no thyroid
Jan. 26, 1935	−34	Desiccated thyroid, 1 gr. daily, Nov. 11, 1934 to March 1936
May 6, 1936	−17	Receiving no thyroid
March 17, 1938	−17	Receiving no thyroid

Case 6.

I. A., a woman aged 25, admitted to the hospital November 22, 1935, complained of loss of weight, strength and energy, with increasing fatigue during the previous year. For several months she had noted swelling of the lower extremities and abdomen and frequency of micturition, latterly associated with thirst. She had not menstruated since 17 years of age, at which time she weighed 102 pounds (46 kg.), her greatest weight. She had always been a small eater and disliked many foods, which included those of high caloric value. Because of attacks of frequency of micturition her physician had placed her on a markedly restricted diet, to which she attributed the rapid loss of weight.

Her home conditions were bad, her family being on relief. She lived alone with a semi-invalid mother, her father and a sister having died in recent years. The patient did all the housework.

The patient was extremely emaciated and pale; her weight was 69 pounds (31 kg.), her height, 5 feet 1½ inches (155 cm.). The secondary sexual characteristics were normally developed; head and body hair were abundant. There was edema of the feet, legs and thighs, and slight puffiness around the eyes. The hair and skin were dry. The temperature was from 96 to 99.7 F., heart rate from 70 to 90 per minute, blood pressure 74 systolic, 56 diastolic, hemoglobin 52 per cent, red blood count 3,000,000, white blood count 2,600. The twenty-four-hour output of urine was approximately 500 cc. daily, with specific gravity relatively fixed between 1.010 and 1.1014. Albumin was present occasionally in small quantities. The nonprotein nitrogen was 35 mg. per hundred centimeters of blood, serum protein 3.5 per cent, the basal metabolic rate, −32 per cent. The sugar tolerance curve was low and tended to be flat (Table 1). Electrocardiogram, voltage 6 mm.

The diagnosis was anorexia nervosa. It was believed that the edema and anemia were secondary to prolonged malnutrition.

During the one week the patient remained in the hospital she was unco-operative, refusing to eat an adequate amount of food, and was resentful and complaining in her attitude toward her attendants and visitors. Finally she went home against advice. On readmission a few weeks later the edema was more marked and the mental attitude worse. Her weight was 75 pounds (34 kg.), the increase believed to be due to edema. The serum protein was 4.5 per cent. The average caloric intake for one week was about 1,100 calories a day. Again she went home against advice.

At present (May 1938) she is working as a domestic outside the city. Her mother believes that she is well. Her weight is now 125 pounds (57 kg.). The menses are still absent.

Case 7.

R. P., a woman aged 21, admitted to the Psychiatric Hospital March 31, 1936, complained that she could not eat, was tired all the time, and that she cried a great deal. She stated that at about 8 years of age she commenced to become stout. At 13 years she weighed 160 pounds (73 kg.). Menstruation commenced at this time and was associated with considerable pain. The periods had never been very regular and stopped completely two years before admission. She became very conscious of her stoutness, especially of her large abdomen. Everybody teased her and called her "Fat." She had previously enjoyed swimming but about this time she noticed that her limbs felt numb and weak. She commenced to diet and from then onward lost weight. At the age of 16 she weighed 130 pounds (59 kg.) but people continued to tease her. At 17 years of age she became nervously upset because of fear that she might fail in her matriculation examinations. Since that time she had been subject to nervous symptoms and had existed in a state of mild chronic ill health. About one year before admission to the hospital she commenced to cut down her food intake to a marked degree. She lost weight rapidly and became increasingly easily fatigued. Little things at home bothered her and she lost all interest in reading and knitting which she had enjoyed formerly.

Examination was essentially negative, apart from the marked generalized emaciation. Secondary sexual characteristics were normally developed. Her weight on admission to the hospital was 77 pounds (35 kg.); her height,

5 feet 5 inches (165 cm.); the basal metabolic rate, -26 per cent. The sugar tolerance curve was flat (Table 1).

During her stay in the hospital the patient showed considerable variability in mood, at times displaying great apprehension and tearfulness and at other times being interested and cheerful. It was ascertained that there was a family background of religious fervor and that the mother was an emotionally unstable type of person and overly solicitous about the patient.

The diagnosis was anorexia nervosa.

The nature of her condition was explained to the patient and she was encouraged to eat an adequate diet. She co-operated well in this regard and engaged actively in occupational therapy. By April 14 her weight had increased to 81 pounds (37 kg.). She was feeling much better and showed a decided improvement mentally. She was bright, enthusiastic and interested in her progress. However, she was anxious to leave the hospital and was discharged April 18 to go and stay with her sister-in-law. Information received May 1, 1936, indicated that the patient adjusted herself well after leaving the hospital and was eating fairly adequate meals. The improvement continued and in June 1938 it was ascertained that she was well and happy. She has been working for two months as a dress designer. She is well developed physically, weighs 110 pounds (50 kg.) and is still gaining weight. The menses have not yet returned.

Case 8.

A. S., an active, alert, highly sensitive, wilful girl of 23, an only child, had fairly good health prior to 1934, at which time she weighed 112 pounds (51 kg.). Rather unhappy at the university, she gradually lost to a weight of 94 pounds (43 kg.) by the spring of 1936. She stated that during the preceding year the mistress of her boarding house had spread malicious tales about her carelessness of her health and refusal to eat. She felt this very keenly. Her appetite became worse and she began to vomit after eating without any associated nausea or discomfort. Her weight fell to 69 pounds (31 kg.) by February 1937. The menses occurred three times in the year 1935-1936. She has not menstruated since September 1936.

In February 1937 she was emaciated, active, alert and intelligent and stated that she felt well. The secondary sexual characteristics were normally developed. The blood pressure was 80 systolic, 58 diastolic, the basal metabolic rate, -18 per cent, the fasting blood sugar 134 mg. per hundred cubic centimeters; the sugar tolerance curve was incomplete but appeared to be flat (Table 1).

The diagnosis was anorexia nervosa.

The patient refused to come into the hospital. She went home, where she was unhappy, tried numerous types of therapy and is now worse than ever. Her own physician reports her weight to be 59 pounds (27 kg.), her blood pressure 112 systolic, 60 diastolic. He states that, though she claims to be feeling better, she is extremely emaciated and looks sick. She refuses to come to Toronto, fearing that she may be kept in the hospital.

Comment

It would appear that anorexia nervosa occurs almost entirely in people of psychoneurotic constitution. Most of them are intelligent, some to a marked degree; all are highly sensitive. Usually they are impulsive, wilful, introspective and emotionally unstable, but these qualities may not be very obvious. Associated with a sense of inferiority, they have a strong desire to prominence and dominance. Usually they are alert and optimistic but are resentful of control on the part of their family. Prior to the onset of anorexia they are often good mixers but with its development they frequently become seclusive. In only two cases did we obtain a history of a psychotic trend dating from childhood.

In persons with such a temperament as a basis, prolonged emotional disturbance may precipitate the development of this peculiar syndrome, which appears most commonly in the unstable period of adolescence and early adult life. In most of our cases there was an underlying discontent as the result of a failure of adaptation to the domestic situation. In four patients (2, 4, 5 and 7) the taunts of companions about a conspicuous obesity led to a psychologic repugnance for food which became a fixed habit. In others (cases 1 and 3) a morbid concern about minor symptoms referable to the gastrointestinal tract gave rise to a fixed fear of eating. In none did an acute emotional crisis precipitate the onset of symptoms. In only one case (case 6) was there a suggestion that therapeutic dietary restriction was a factor in the development of the condition. The other seven cases were definitely of the primary type. In none of our cases did we find evidence of any organic disease which might have been responsible for the symptoms.

The anorexia was peculiar in that it was not a simple want of desire for food such as is characteristic of wasting diseases but rather a morbid aversion to eating. It might be based on an abnormal desire to become thin, a desire to attract attention or gain sympathy, or a fixed belief in the inability of the stomach to hold any quantity of food (case 3), or a fear that ingestion of food would cause distressing symptoms. After a time this morbid anorexia became the habitual anorexia of undernutrition and starvation. It is evident that the morbid anorexia is a manifestation of an underlying psychological disorder. It should not be attributed to a secondary disturbance in function of the anterior lobe of the hypophysis or any other endocrine gland.

Amenorrhea

In the six female patients, as well as in many others reported in the literature, amenorrhea was an early symptom. It was present usually before the anorexia became marked and always before emaciation was extreme. In four of our cases the menses returned when improvement in nutrition and sense of well-being became well established. Neither of the other two patients co-operated but one has improved definitely in other respects, the other not at all. In no case was amenorrhea associated with loss of secondary sexual characteristics; the breasts remained wonderfully well developed, and axillary and pubic hair persisted in all. In reporting his fatal case, Lockhart (5) emphasized the fact that the breasts alone were not involved in the extreme generalized wasting. Libido is not grossly disturbed, although the state of chronic ill health may temporarily depress it. There is no atrophy of the external genitalia nor, as far as could be determined from examination, was there atrophy of other sexual organs.

It is generally recognized that change of environment and emotional disturbance may give rise to amenorrhea in apparently healthy young girls. Similarly, amenorrhea may be associated with many illnesses and with undernutrition (Sheldon, 7) in the absence of any demonstrable endocrine lesion. In some females the cycle appears to be easily interrupted, but little is known about the mechanisms by which this disturbance is brought about. When there is no other evidence of sexual dysfunction, it seems unreasonable to attribute the amenorrhea of anorexia nervosa to a gross disturbance in function of the adenohypophysis.

Low Basal Metabolism

In anorexia nervosa the basal metabolic rate is usually reduced, sometimes to very low levels. The reduction may be more apparent than real because of the inadequacy of normal standards for emaciated adolescents. The lowering of the basal rate is comparable to that observed in undernutrition from other causes and would appear to be secondary to the emaciation. In Simmonds' disease, on the other hand, the lowered rate, although aggravated by emaciation, is primarily the result of the underfunctioning of the thyroid gland secondary to pituitary insufficiency and, accordingly, it rises in response to thyroid therapy. In anorexia nervosa the basal metabolic rate rises toward normal with the improvement in nutrition, although not necessarily parallel to the gain in weight. It is notable that in two of our patients (cases 4 and 5) treated with desiccated thyroid there was no obvious effect on the basal metabolic rate and no improvement in their general condition (Table 2).

Blood Sugar Level

The blood sugar tolerance curves obtained in seven of the eight cases tended to be of two different types. Beginning at a relatively low fasting level, the curve might rise gradually to a peak between 170 and 220 mg. per hundred cubic centimeters at the end of two or three hours, failing to fall to the fasting level, i.e., the type of curve seen in healthy patients who have been starved or given a high fat diet for a few days (Sweeney, 9); or it might be low and flat, as seen in healthy people who have been on a high carbohydrate diet or in some patients with chronic undernutrition (Sheldon, 7), e.g., nontropical sprue. The two types might be seen in the same patient within a short time. Since it was not possible to control the many factors that may alter the dextrose tolerance, it seems wiser not to attach too great significance to variation in the curve. The fasting blood sugar was below 68 mg. per hundred cubic centimeters only once: patient 5 suffered from prolonged undernutrition with low serum protein and some generalized edema. Other fasting blood sugar readings in her case were 78, 59 and 69 mg. per hundred cubic centimeters of blood. It is noteworthy that, although the fasting blood sugar level tends to be low in anorexia nervosa, the fall is not to be compared with that frequently seen in Simmonds' disease, Addison's disease or hyperinsulinism, nor do the patients suffer symptoms of hypoglycemia. It would seem probable that the variations in carbohydrate metabolism are secondary to chronic undernutrition (Ross, 6; Sheldon and Young, 8).

Differential Diagnosis

Patients suffering from wasting diseases such as tuberculosis or tumors of various kinds are usually quite ill, complain of weakness and fatigue and have obvious physical signs long before they reach the degree of emaciation seen in patients with anorexia nervosa. The latter patients are characteristically restless and active, even when emaciation is extreme, and commonly they will not admit being ill. Their alarmed relatives bring them to the physician but the patients protest that they feel well.

Addison's disease is usually differentiated with ease by the characteristic weakness, pigmentation, crises of nausea and vomiting, and low blood sodium. In both conditions the blood pressure may be low. In Addison's disease there is no related fundamental psychologic disturbance, the anorexia is not a constant feature, and often emaciation is a late symptom. In one instance, however, an erroneous diagnosis of anorexia nervosa was initially considered in an emaciated adolescent without pigmentation. This diagnosis was doubted because no adequate psychological disturbance could be found to explain the anorexia and soon great fatigue and weakness with crises of nausea and vomiting pointed the way to a correct diagnosis of Addison's disease.

As a result of modern interest in the pituitary gland many cases presenting the picture of anorexia nervosa have been reported in the literature as cases of Simmonds' disease (extreme insufficiency of the anterior lobe of the pituitary gland). Superficially the syndromes closely resemble each other. In both, emaciation is a striking feature[5]. In both are found amenorrhea, lowered basal metabolic rate, altered

---

[5] It is true that emaciation may be lacking in Simmonds' disease, but this is exceptional.

sugar tolerance, low temperature and psychological changes. On careful examination, one finds that the syndromes are fundamentally different.

Simmonds' disease occurs most commonly and most typically in adult women who have had several children and who have previously had ordinary good health. The disease usually begins in the puerperium after a difficult labor associated with sepsis, postpartum hemorrhage or some complication. It may occur also when the anterior lobe has been destroyed by tumor, granuloma or trauma. There is no underlying psychoneurotic constitution or any precipitating emotional cause. The syndrome of anorexia nervosa develops in adolescents and young adults and occasionally in older persons who have a psychoneurotic tendency. Precipitated by an emotional disturbance, it is cured by psychotherapy.

As already mentioned, the anorexia of anorexia nervosa is a morbid aversion to eating, whereas in Simmonds' disease there is loss of appetite unassociated with emotion. In both, emaciation develops and with emaciation comes the appearance of senility, which, however, tends to be more marked in Simmonds' disease. The amenorrhea of Simmonds' disease is associated with loss of sexual function, loss of secondary sexual characteristics, falling out of axillary and pubic hair, and atrophy of the sexual organs. It persists unchanged in spite of therapy. In anorexia nervosa, amenorrhea occurs as a single symptom, important chiefly because of the concern it gives the patient and the patient's relatives, and not associated with other evidences of failure of sexual function.

The basal metabolic rate in Simmonds' disease is usually lower than in anorexia nervosa. Being due largely to underfunction of the thyroid gland, it responds more readily to the administration of small doses of thyroid than does the lowered rate of anorexia nervosa, which is secondary to emaciation. The blood sugar in Simmonds' disease is lower than in anorexia nervosa, and attacks of spontaneous hypoglycemia are common. In Simmonds' disease there is almost always anemia of moderate severity, which is unusual in anorexia nervosa.

Most striking is the difference in mental status. In Simmonds' disease the patient is dull and apathetic and shows intellectual impairment and usually gross changes in personality. In anorexia nervosa the patient is generally quick, alert, restless and intelligent but may become wilful, sensitive, impulsive and hysterical. Only in rare cases with gross psychotic manifestations does the mental state in anorexia nervosa in any way resemble that of Simmonds' disease.

The characteristic pathologic change in Simmonds' disease is an almost complete destruction of the anterior lobe of the pituitary gland with secondary atrophic changes in other endocrine glands, viscera and skin. There are few reports of post-mortem examination in cases of anorexia nervosa and the description of the endocrine glands in these is incomplete (Elliott, 3; Conybeare, 1). The available data suggest that there is no characteristic change in the endocrine glands. This opinion is supported by the unpublished detailed observations in a recent fatal case that has been brought to our attention. If anorexia nervosa were a "functional Simmonds' disease" there should be characteristic secondary changes in gonads and other endocrine glands.

The improvement in cases of anorexia nervosa, reported as such or as Simmonds' disease, has often been ascribed to the effect of administration of various endocrine preparations: insulin, thyroid, various female sex hormones and various pituitary preparations. Improvement occurring after pituitary therapy has often been taken as evidence of the correctness of the diagnosis of pituitary insufficiency (case 1). Actually the use of such preparations may be an effective, but not the most desirable, method of psychotherapy.

Treatment

The aims of treatment are to change the attitude of the patient toward food so that emaciation will be relieved through the ingestion of an adequate diet and to insure permanent recovery by eradication of the underlying mental conflict. The former often can be attained by change of environment, encouragement and suggestion, but if the second objective is to be realized, the psychological basis must be discovered and remedied if possible. Prolonged psychotherapy is often necessary before the patient fully understands the true nature of his illness and especially the effect that various environmental factors, past and present, have had on its development. This understanding is essential if the patient is to become properly adjusted to those disturbing associations in his daily environment from which there is no escape.

On commencing treatment it is desirable that the patient be removed to a hospital away from overly solicitous relatives and friends. Treatment in the public ward is to be preferred, because contact with other patients suffering from various organic diseases has a salutary effect on most patients with anorexia nervosa and makes the reassurance they receive more gratifying and significant. The well-ordered routine of a hospital, the optimism of doctors and nurses and the evidence of recovery around them have therapeutic value which, combined with freedom from the stress of their former environment, often results in rapid and striking improvement. To obtain the best results from psychotherapy it is essential that it be preceded by a most careful and thorough investigation of the patient. This is important both for the confidence it gives to the physician and for the reassurance of the patient. The life history of the patient should be obtained, with particular emphasis on his emotional reactions to his associates. The factors at the basis of the neurosis are sometimes quickly revealed, but often co-operation is imperfect and it is necessary to persevere in the search by questioning the patient's relatives and friends. Discussion should be continued until the patient understands clearly the connection between the psychological maladjustment and the development of his symptoms.

The patient should be reassured with the utmost confidence that no organic basis for the symptoms exists and he should receive an explanation of the relationship between emotional disturbances and the imbalance of the autonomic nervous system which may result. The manner in which the stomach adapts itself to gradual and persistent lessening of the food intake should be explained so that the patient's apprehension over the feelings of fullness which occur when he tries to increase his intake can be allayed.

The patient should be encouraged to eat, at frequent intervals, small but gradually increasing quantities of food of high caloric value. The caloric intake should be carefully calculated daily, and praise and encouragement given with each increase that occurs. When about 3,000 calories is being taken daily and gain in weight is evident, the frequency of the meals can be gradually lessened and the variety of food increased.

In some cases feeding by duodenal tube may be necessary in the early stages of treatment but usually the method outlined is all that is required. Insulin to stimulate the appetite should not be used except as a last resort. Similarly, nonspecific endocrine therapy should be avoided, because permanent results are more likely to be obtained if no artificial aids are employed.

During the patient's stay in the hospital every effort should be made to divert his thoughts from his obsession. The public ward is obviously more effective than a private room for this purpose. Occupational therapy is of great assistance, particularly if the hospital has a workshop available where skillful therapists may introduce a spirit of friendly competition with certain other patients in some work or game. By this means a feeling of achievement may be engendered which will go far to restore the confidence these patients need so badly and thus facilitate recovery.

Summary

The eight cases of anorexia nervosa that we have reported present the typical syndrome of emaciation, amenorrhea, low basal metabolic rate, low blood pressure and often rather low fasting blood sugar values with flat sugar tolerance curve. Although the syndrome bears a superficial resemblance to that of Simmonds' disease, it is actually quite distinct and different.

The syndrome of anorexia nervosa develops as a result of an underlying mental conflict and appears usually in the unstable period of adolescence, most commonly in intelligent girls whose emotional constitution and autonomic nervous control are unstable.

These patients respond well to proper psychotherapy. If the co-operation of the patient and the family can be obtained, cures should be effected for all patients placed in a suitable environment with the exception of those who have serious mental disease.

There is no specific endocrine therapy for this condition, but these patients, being of a hysterical nature, will often respond temporarily to the suggestion that goes with confident administration of a special extract. Actually such treatment should be avoided because permanent results are more likely to be obtained if no artificial aids are employed.

REFERENCES

1. Conybeare, J. J.: A fatal case of anorexia nervosa. *Guy's Hosp. Rep.*, 80:30, 1930.
2. Dunn, C. W.: Anorexia nervosa. *Lancet*, 1:723, 1937.
3. Elliott, T. R.: Pathological changes in the adrenal glands. *Quart. J. Med.*, 8:47, 1914.
4. Langdon-Brown, W.: Anorexia nervosa. *Lancet*, 1:473, 1937.
5. Lockhart, S.: Case of anorexia nervosa: Necropsy. *Lancet*, 1:31, 1895.
6. Ross, C. W.: Anorexia nervosa with special reference to the carbohydrate metabolism. *Lancet*, 1:1041, 1938.
7. Sheldon, J. H.: Anorexia nervosa with special reference to the physical constitution. *Lancet*, 1:369, 1937.
8. ―― & Young, F.: On the carbohydrate metabolism in anorexia nervosa. *Lancet*, 1:257, 1938.
9. Sweeney, J. S.: Dietary factors that influence the dextrose tolerance test. *Arch. Int. Med.*, 40:818, 1927.

PREPSYCHOTIC ANOREXIA

GRACE NICOLLE, M.B., B.S.
(1938)

The significance of the paper by Nicolle is that she again draws attention to the varied clinical psychiatric picture, stressing particularly the psychiatric elements. She attempts to implicate multiple factors with an emphasis on the primary endocrine disorder and suggests that the syndrome is connected with "primary ovarian failure, as Simmonds' cachexia is with primary pituitary failure." In a sense this is an attempt at a gross psychosomatic correlation. Nevertheless, the author's failure to clearly formulate basic concepts in the psychiatric field comes through in the somewhat confused presentation and conclusions.

Perhaps the discussion of Nicolle's paper by Dr. Paterson Brown is the best commentary on her methodology.

The title of this paper is perhaps ambiguous, and in its very ambiguity lies its object. That object is to discuss the function of the diagnostic label as illustrated in certain diseased conditions characterized by anorexia. It is an attempt to display the twofold nature of this function as a security for essentials of therapy and a stimulus to a review of causation.

Prepsychotic anorexia includes a range of cases the most typical being anorexia nervosa which has in turn been assigned to the pure psychoneuroses or to the incipient psychoses. I shall describe a case

Reprinted from *Proceedings of the Royal Society of Medicine*, 32:1, November 8, 1938.

labelled anorexia nervosa and pick out those characteristics which link it with allied conditions: much considerations may lead to deeper understanding and more fruitful treatment.

I select the case of Miss M. which I have been able to follow for some years and have had considerable opportunity to study. It corresponds in outline with the classical cases recorded by Sir William Gull and Charcot. The patient complained of nothing, but was brought for consultation by her parents, who were alarmed at her progressive loss of weight and her obstinate refusal to take adequate nourishment. The appearance of these cases is always arresting. My patient, Miss M., was then 19 years old: she was 5 feet, 6 inches in height and weighed 6 stone. Her condition had begun insidiously, but had been fully developed for a year, with complete amenorrhea. At this time she was 2 stone under normal weight and shrinking rapidly, though she had not reached such fantastic weights as 4 stone, which are frequently achieved. She had by no means reached the terminal stage of exhaustion, and was still indulging in riding, tennis, walking, which produced so little fatigue that every interval was filled with feverish attention to self-imposed household tasks. The energy expended in this way was maintained on a diet which scrupulously excluded anything nourishing. She allowed herself grapefruit and a little toast, and at meals made a pretence of eating a scrap of meat with green vegetables. An obstinate constipation was the result of this starvation, and she cheerfully resorted to large doses of purgatives.

I ask you to imagine Miss M. as a skeleton decently but inadequately clothed in a meager mantle of flesh, through which the bony prominences of every joint were clearly defined, as was the framework of limbs and thorax. The abdomen was concave and all swelling of the breasts had gone: The skinny neck looked unduly long and hardly capable of bearing the head, with its wizened deathly face and two dark burning eyes crowned by a tousled mop of glossy black hair. She was of mixed parentage: her father was a Greek and her mother Scotch, and from her father she inherited a typical modern Greek appearance and no small share of Southern fire.

She had been fully informed that her cure in the nursing home would involve separation from her family, but she never believed that her mother would abandon her. When she heard her mother get into the car she rushed to the window and tried to throw herself out with hysterical screams which were luckily drowned by the noise of the engine: She was left. From that moment she more or less gave in to be cured. Fortunately her parents were willing to acquiesce in a necessary isolation; this resolution was forced on them by their inability to deal with the patient's mental attitude. This was peculiar: Her natural shyness had become intensified and accompanied by scrupulosity and an unnatural solicitude for the welfare of others as long as she was left undisturbed in her regimen of exercise and starvation. Any interference with this immediately roused storms of remonstrance and actual violence, particularly against her mother.

After hearing the parents' account I felt the patient should be heard in her own defense, which was, however, totally unsatisfactory. She ascribed her behavior to the most trivial causes. She says she is quite well, eats almost excessively and certainly could not eat more as she is not hungry: She is not tired and exercise is essential if she is to eat at all: Everyone eats too much: There is nothing the matter with her, it is all the stupidity of other people as she never felt better in her life. She gives a baffling impression of offended dignity which admirably masks a most obstinate determination.

In the general management of this case the first essential of treatment is the restoration of nutrition, and all writers are agreed as to the methods, not always successful which should be employed for the purpose. This "distemper" was mentioned by Morton (16) as early as 1694 and again in 1789 by Nadeau (17), who graphically described "an amazing revulsion from food"; but little attention was paid to it till the last half of the nineteenth century. In 1868 Sir William Gull (8) drew attention to these cases, and in 1874 gave a full account of the successful treatment of several in the *Transactions of the Clinical Society* (9). Subsequently there have been many interested observers both here and abroad. There is general agreement on the two fundamentals of treatment: the first is isolation and feeding under strict supervision, and second is some form of psychotherapy. Isolation is essential in order to remove the patient from an environment which reacts emotionally to her condition and further to prevent interference of the parents in the treatment, for they cannot believe the consummate duplicity of their child, and if they do, ascribe it to moral perversion rather than mental disease. The patient protests with bland horror at the attendance of a special nurse and complains that no one trusts her and she will certainly eat all that is given her. But unless the nurse watches every mouthful disappear and remains beside the patient for a considerable time afterwards she will get rid of her food, down the water closet, the hand basin, or by concealment: She lies unblushingly, and it is only a steady increase in weight which can give assurance that deception is circumvented. The patient should be put to bed to restrain insensate exertion, and will even then leap in and out of bed at the least excuse. She should be given food at regular intervals and in increasing quantity. What the patient should be given at first must be regulated by the individual condition. The attitude of the physician, whose inflexibility must match that of the patient, should combine a benevolent assumption of authority. "I know and you don't," and a skillful evasion of all argument. This first stage is the most difficult, for the physician will be greeted by a recurrent demand for more liberty and less food, and though the patient apparently acquiesces, the sight of food is the signal for antagonism and tears.

The clinical manifestations of her state can be summarized under four heads: (1) Emaciation; (2) loss of appetite without digestive disturbance and reduction of food intake to a minimum; (3) persistent amenorrhea; (4) a peculiar mental state of euphoric type.

With emaciation and loss of appetite the possibility of a wasting disease should be considered. Tuberculosis in particular must be considered as undoubtedly some of these cases die of it. In Miss M.'s case such a possibility was easily excluded. Apart from a pulse rate of 44 and a systolic blood pressure of 88 she showed only one other point of interest, and that was the growth of hair on her body. There was a general distribution of downy hair on body and cheeks, while the arms and legs were covered with coarse dark hair and lines of similar hair extended from pubes to umbilicus. In front of the ears, in what might be called the whisker region, the down was long and dark, and in general the hair grew close round the face. The growth of hair has been noticed by Ryle and others, and together with the amenorrhea has suggested an endocrine disturbance. At this point comparison with another well-known wasting illness is suggested—that is Simmonds' cachexia. Since the original paper was published in 1914 the condition has been frequently described. Simmonds was first and foremost a pathological anatomist and his observations are based on post-mortem findings of destructive changes in the pituitary gland, so that the clinical picture has been associated with observed organic change; and it has been possible to institute cure by supplying the secretion which had failed through destruction of the gland. Careful observers have, however, recorded similar cases in which no organic change was found and in which a functional depletion of the gland must be accepted. It would be hard by superficial examination to distinguish in the middle stage between a case of Simmonds' disease and one of anorexia nervosa when certain later distinguishing features have not developed. The loss of appetite, the striking emaciation, and the amenorrhea, are all comparable. There are, however, important differences in the evolution of the two conditions and in the mental attitude of the patients. The onset of Simmonds' disease is abrupt, and that of anorexia nervosa is insidious. In the former loss of weight precedes the reduction in alimentation; in anorexia nervosa it is the result of the starvation. The amenorrhea is usually a late event in Simmonds' disease; in anorexia nervosa it precedes or is coincident with the mental change which produces refusal to eat. The age incidence in Simmonds' disease is more variable and less commonly associated with puberty: It is confined to females and often occurs after circumstances which might induce pituitary exhaustion, such as pregnancy with hemorrhage and prolonged labor. In the late stages of Simmonds' disease the teeth and hair fall out, a condition never noticed in anorexia. There is a profound difference in the patient's mental state. I have described the morbid energy and obstinacy of the anorexia, but these other patients show weakness, mental lethargy and somnolence, with a readiness to co-operate in treatment, though later delusions may make their appearance. I have consulted numerous authors in this connection. Sheldon (22), Hawkinson (10), Herman (11), Schulmann, Loeper and Fau (14), De Gennes, Delarue, and Rogé (6), and should like to make a few quotations from these sources; (1) That Simmonds himself thought that the cachexia was fundamentally mental in origin. (2) Sheldon considers Simmonds' cachexia and anorexia nervosa are fundamentally the same except for predisposition in the latter. (3) Here (in Simmonds' disease) the anorexia is a defense of the organism against food which it can no longer assimilate.

The long and interesting paper of De Gennes, Delarue and Rogé (6) describes a typical case of hypophyseal cachexia with a fatal termination. An autopsy revealed no gross or microscopic change in the pituitary but complete atrophy of the ovaries and suprarenal cortex and some alteration of thyroid structure. Reciprocal relationships exist between these glands and the pituitary though we are far from understanding their precise nature, and these authors urge the use of the Simmonds' syndrome to indicate the tentative state of our knowledge. In 1932 Baudouin, Lhermitte and Lerebouillet (3) reported the case of a young man presenting the symptoms of Simmonds' syndrome, where the autopsy revealed a tumor of the pineal. Endocrine disturbances can therefore be assigned as the cause of diseases which present strong affinities with anorexia nervosa. The endocrine basis of this latter is "unproven" but has been frequently adduced. Leopold Levi (13) and others regard it as due to thyroid deficiency and point to the slow pulse and low basal metabolic rate; but the cases described are not typical and on the whole thyroid has fallen into disuse.

Many observers are, however, satisfied that the whole pathology of anorexia nervosa is the pathology of a condition of starvation. I quote from Ryle's (21) masterly article in 1936: "It may be doubted if anorexia nervosa possesses a morbid anatomy, histology or chemistry of its own if we except those changes which come about as the result of starvation and a depression of the menstrual function." He, however, emphasizes the amenorrhea and the hirsuties and says of the former, "it accompanies the disease from the beginning and is an expression of the initial nervous trauma which accompanies the malady from inception to cure." He suspends judgment on their significance. In May of this year a paper was published by Wallace Ross (19) directed to proving that the pituitary gland has no relationship to this condition. It is easy to agree that the disturbances of carbohydrate metabolism on which he bases his argument can be fully explained as the result of starvation alone without any theory of glandular deficiency. The case which he quotes does not suggest the mental picture of anorexia nervosa, and as she was a girl before the onset of the menses his arguments are deficient in one vital particular. He summarily disposes of the significance of amenorrhea in these words: "In all probability, therefore, amenorrhea can arise either directly or as a consequence of wasting, independently of any special endocrine disorder." This was certainly the earliest supposition with regard to this feature of the malady, but later observers are almost unanimous in saying that many cases show an obstinate amenorrhea which persists long after appetite is restored. A French writer, Ballet (2), states: "As long as the patient has amenorrhea she is not cured. Even if she has become plump, relapses must be feared as long as the menses are not restored."

I should like to illustrate this point in the case of Miss M. She remained in the nursing home from August 1932 to the end of April 1933. During this time she put on 1 st. 10 lbs. in weight: She looked blooming and was living a normal life without special supervision. The tendency to compulsive exercise was gone and she had become much less seclusive. The menses had not reappeared since her last period in August 1931. After a short visit home she went to live in a family at one of the Universities to prepare for the entrance examination, as she wanted to study literature. At that time I had tried various pituitary and ovarian preparations with no success, and her mental condition still appeared unstable. In August 1934 I gave the patient a series of injections of progynon and proluton following Kauffmann's technique, and at the end of four weeks there were menstrual pains. A second series of dimenformon and progestin was followed by a period, the first she had had for three years. An immediate change for the better took place in her mental outlook and she expressed a joyful feeling of being a normal girl. I must not, however, minimize the fact that at this point she passed her entrance examination, no mean feat for a girl who had never had any proper schooling.

The mental state of these patients is of foremost interest, and it would be impossible to discuss it without facing the question of motive. I shall here tacitly assume that we accept Freud's theory of the unconscious and all his major affirmations but permit ourselves to question their universal validity.

The refusal to eat is no uncommon symptom in mental disease, and it is necessary to attempt some differentiation. Melancholics frequently refuse food, but their refusal can always be directly referred to their delusions of unworthiness. Patients in states of elation may exhaust themselves by neglecting their meals, but this is rather a result of the flight of ideas which carries them away heedless of consequences. The anorexic has no flight of ideas but rather a fanatical domination by one idea. Again patients suffering with paranoia will refuse their food, due to ideas that they are being poisoned. Anorexia nervosa was at first regarded as a form of hysteria or possibly hypochondria, but this was displaced in favor of a more serious classification as dementia praecox. The refusal to eat would then be regarded as part of a characteristic negativism. It may be noted that Robert Dubois (5) in 1913 published an account of a case which began as a typical anorexia nervosa and in ten years' time was a fully developed schizophrenia. Several French authors describe a type of case which evolves from hypochondriacal ideas about the digestive function fostered by the institution of diets and leading finally to loss of appetite and refusal of food. They may well be variants in a long series of allied conditions.

The differentiation between hysteria and anorexia nervosa is of the first importance as it must largely govern our selection of treatment. At the present moment I have two patients, one with anorexia nervosa and the other with hysterical abstention from food. The first has run a very chronic course with long periods of amenorrhea and no other symptoms. The second has always had regular periods, her breasts are normally developed, though the rest of her body is much reduced by starvation. She further presents alternatively attacks of asthma and urticaria. A monosymptomatic hysteria is a doubtful candidate for classification with that protean disease. The superficial mental attitude of the two patients is sharply contrasted. The hysteric makes parade of her inability to eat and undoubtedly eats when it suits her; the anorexic tries to dissimulate the fact that she does not eat. The hysteric desires to elicit sympathy. This is far from the anorexic, but she may enjoy in some less direct way her inability to tease and deceive those about her. I should say that the purpose of the anorexic to starve herself is of fundamental importance. This is illustrated by their different reactions to isolation: Emotional neutrality in the environment will make the hysteric eat in order to escape to one more congenial to her purposes, and we know she will eat when unobserved; not so with the anorexic who will only eat when under strict supervision. The hysteric welcomes attention from her environment directed to her disabilities, while the anorexic is mysterious and tries to evade inquiries. It is as though the hysteric plays a drama to her environment and the anorexic to herself. An analytical investigation in the case of this hysterical patient has produced a perfectly coherent picture of psychological causation. Her age is 32, old for anorexia. She was the eldest daughter of a marriage seemingly devoid of all emotional significance. The wife had money and land and the husband managed it. They belonged to an almost extinct race of minor landed gentry and both were devoid of emotion and imagination. The mother only wanted a son to inherit her property and had no use for two elder daughters, merely showing vague signs of life, when a son was born nine years after my patient. This child knew no tenderness or love from the mother, whose stupidity inflicted constant minor cruelties. She had no emotional rapport, no security. Her constitution was allergic and she soon discovered that her attacks of asthma were the only thing that roused her mother's attention. Her asthma lasted until adult life and disappeared during psychological treatment. In spite of her unfavorable surroundings she had a good deal of spirit, and after much opposition she escaped from home and qualified as a radiographer. Alas, having so escaped, she did not find herself capable of securing in the world the valuation she so sorely needed, nor was her work able to contribute much emotional satisfaction. She therefore never applied herself seriously to her profession, but fluctuated between work and home lest they forget her entirely. At home she obtained some satisfaction by causing anxiety about her asthma and the dangerous nature of her work. Presently her mother died, and then she transferred her operations to her father, who failed entirely to be moved by asthma. A new symptom was clearly needed, and at this point she began to starve herself. This proved efficacious and roused her father's attention by a curious echo from infancy. She had been difficult to feed. Her mother could not do it, and no satisfactory substitute could be found till, faced with the loss of his child, the father enlisted the services of a donkey, on whose milk this unhappy child survived. Frustrated and unhappy in later life, she wished to bring about the death from which she had been saved and by a method calculated to wring the hearts of the most stony parents. She stated her difficulty thus: "If only I were happy I could eat and be fat and how I long to be fat for that would mean I was happy." In spite of a great reduction in weight there was no loss of appetite in the strict sense. Many authorities on anorexia emphasize that the refusal to eat brings with it a loss of appetite which is physiological.

We can appreciate hunger and appetite as two conscious elements in physiological sequences. Hunger is awareness of the general need of the organism for fresh supplies of metabolic material, while appetite is the knowledge of the presence of, or memory of, suitable substances to meet the need. These two combined result in action—the ingestion of food. The thesis of Noguès', *L'Anorexie Mentale* (18), passes in review numerous theories of the physiology of hunger and the balance of evidence minimizes the role of gastric contractions as a primary cause of hunger; these localized sensations are, rather, an echo of a general cry for restoration. The arguments excellently presented in Wallace Ross' paper (19), which seek to explain anorexia nervosa on a basis of the physiology of starvation, appear too dogmatic. No doubt fluctuations in blood-sugar level are part of the mechanism by which we recognize our bodily needs, but we are still in the dark as to influences which may affect these signals. The condition of cellular metabolism must be fundamental and this is intimately associated with the activity of thyroid and ovaries and influenced by the circulation of toxins. Perhaps we may say that in true anorexia nervosa the loss of the sensation of hunger may be due to glandular interference with cellular metabolism, but that its real importance is that it enables the patient to pursue her morbid purpose without undue distress, rather than acting as a cause for perpetuating the fast. What then is this morbid purpose? In all cases I have seen, behind the trivial excuses offered, lurks a fanatical desire to be thin and a dread of obesity. Miss M. said: "I am terrified of getting fatter or even of not getting thinner." The psychoanalytic interpretation of this state of mind would regard fatness as the sign of indulgence in the pleasures of the mouth and that the intense guilt associated with these impulses must be penalized by starvation and purgation. Such mechanisms can be brought to light in analytic investigation of these patients, but their restoration to consciousness does not seem to produce an amelioration of the condition as in other compulsive states. They appear to exist apart and not to be charged with the profound affect latent in this condition. Obesity appears to be dreaded rather as an unbearable affront to narcissism.

Perhaps we can more fruitfully inquire into the circumstances attendant on the inception of the malady. One writer puts it thus: "the soil in which anorexia nervosa grows is adolescence." What is this "soil" of adolescence? We know its physiological instability and something of its psychological difficulties. It is to these latter I would first draw attention, and I should like to quote a passage which I recently encountered in a French novel, for in many ways the French have the most penetrating insight into feminine psychology.

The only satisfactory destiny for a woman is a happy marriage. Thus she is dependent on a man and she knows it very early. It is true that an adolescent boy suffers from feelings of impotence and inferiority, but he knows that the young man he will be by and by can do what he likes with his future. A girl fears the future. A boy knows his future will be what he wishes, while a girl knows that hers will be what a man wishes. During this period of adolescent uncertainty a girl is more prone to daydreams of happiness because, in advance, the achievement of that happiness is uncertain.

Stated more crudely—adolescent anxiety in a girl centers round doubts as to her ability to influence her environment to secure a mate. When an anorexic patient begins to confide her troubles they are always associated with doubts of sexual potency. She does not have periods like other girls, she does not experience the sexual thrills that others describe, she feels unable to attract boys. The majority of cases are to be found among the leisured or wealthy classes and among girls who have been spoiled and petted. Marriage is usually the only possibility visualized in their education, the only means of self-realization, the only claim recognized. Spoiling is the fostering of narcissism. Miss M., brought up abroad in the luxury of a white society employing native servants, was a little princess, and she expected a fairy-tale success. What are the likely reactions of a girl so nurtured when faced with a vaguely perceived inability to fulfil her sexual role? The situation will generate anxiety as surely as the threat of war to a community. There are not lacking other factors which stimulate her fears. Mothers with their eyes on the marriage market show anxiety about the amenorrhea and are not always guarded in their comments. Miss M. said to me: "I did not worry much about my periods till mother said, 'I couldn't let anyone marry you unless that comes right.' I knew I didn't have the same sex feelings as other girls. I began to think I was a freak."

The anorexic associates the plumpness of adolescence with her sense of sexual insufficiency and begins to try to remedy this obvious sign by dealing drastically with the fat. As soon as this mechanism is set in motion many secondary motives make their appearance and satisfactions are obtained by the revival of infantile partial sexual elements and by the mystification and annoyance of her parents. I have had opportunities for making prolonged attempts at analysis with these patients and have never been able to satisfy myself of a causal psychological sequence such as there is in my case of hysterical anorexia. The material appears in a much more disjointed way not bearing an adequate emotional relation to the picture, much as material is produced in certain schizophrenic cases. Paraphrenics and paranoid schizophrenics show discharges of affect connected with their delusional systems which are comparable in quality with the discharges encountered when we interfere with an anorexic. The hatred and aggression thus roused are not adequately discharged through a parent transference, as in the case of a hysteric, but remain, as it were, a primitive rage, the result of affronted narcissism.

I have just read a lucid and illuminating article by Mayer-Gross (15) on the early diagnosis of schizophrenia, and I should like to quote a few lines from it:

The normal emotions of affection and sympathy for the patient's nearest relatives and friends cool off or take on a quality of shallowness during a commencing illness. More primitive emotional reactions—for example fear or rage—are preserved longer.

This corresponds closely with the affective state in anorexia nervosa. Should we therefore think of this condition as a latent form of dementia praecox? It may well be as in the case of Dubois. Miss M.'s mental processes show a distinct schizoid savoring of mad genius: in an endeavor to present the cosmic implications of tragedy she soared away into the nebulous realms of modern physics and treated the fourth dimension with a familiarity Einstein might envy.

I believed that psychological treatment helped Miss M. by giving her more insight and developing less barbarous values, but I do not think she is stable, and I have been able to watch fluctuations of her mental condition closely following the state of her menstrual function. This has never been completely established, and at times she still requires ovarian hormones, to which she responds mentally and physically.

Earlier in this paper my perforce sketchy references to Simmonds' syndrome may have appeared to obscure rather than illuminate, but I hope that I have now clarified my line of thought. It leads me to the conclusion that anorexia nervosa is connected with primary ovarian failure as Simmonds' cachexia is with primary pituitary failure, the interrelationships of these glands allowing many variations of the essential picture. Noguès (18) in 1913 suggested the likelihood of ovarian failure, though at that time adequate substitutes were not available. In 1937 Vidart (24) published an admirably thoughtful article on mental anorexia and indicated ovarian therapy as one of the essentials of treatment. We do not know the relationship of ovary and pituitary to tissue metabolism, but I have noticed that when an anorexic regains normal weight she does not attain a graceful, attractive figure, but shows a tendency to puffy lumpiness. This might suggest thyroid deficiency but is unaffected by exhibition of the extract. Can we venture to postulate a faulty state of tissue metabolism which interferes with the normal signals governing the sensation of hunger and is due to the lack of essential hormones?

If therefore anorexia nervosa has its springs in the instability of the sex glands in adolescence, it would be reasonable to think that milder cases indicate only a functional retardation of development. The school and home environments may make too great physical and mental demands on these patients. Rest and realimentation in a neutral setting may allow spontaneous establishment of the menstrual function. More severe cases would indicate some constitutional factor of inherent gonad deficiency. The male cases reported appear to be of a severe type. Fatness is not a phase of development in boys as it is in girls at adolescence. The fat boy at this age is therefore more likely to be a glandular dyscrasia than the fat girl. A fear of fatness in a boy leading to self-starvation is therefore likely to be associated with profound gonad deficiency and to prove resistant to treatment.

It would be satisfactory to be able to place the abnormal hairiness of these patients in coherent relationship with the picture they present; this I cannot do. In the case of Miss M. there was a general distribution of downy hair and also coarse dark hair on the limbs, linea alba, and in front of the ears. The general distribution of downy hair is most commonly seen, and it tends to disappear when the patient is well. I have never seen any development of beard or moustache in these patients, as is common in schizophrenics and in women at the menopause. They do not present the anomalies of hair distribution recently described in association with a pathological state of the adrenal cortex. I do not know whether such hairiness is found in famine victims. It is certainly absent in the case of hysterical anorexia I mentioned, but it is seen in some cases of tuberculosis. It does not seem to indicate masculinization but rather a degeneracy or animalization.

My endeavor has been to show anorexia nervosa as a recognizable highlight in a series of varied conditions associated on the one hand with dementia praecox and on the other with definite endocrine disorder. Such a survey leaves everything in doubt, but this is a paper for discussion, and if it opens fruitful lines of thought its title and its purpose will be justified.

Discussion

Dr. Neill Hobhouse

I was very much interested by Dr. Nicolle's review of the various factors—neurotic, psychotic, and endocrine—which at different times have been held to underlie this disorder. Many of us who have seen these cases during a number of years have oscillated to some extent between them. We did not find it easy to explain them as purely neurotic, mainly because they were inclined to die. Then the idea of schizophrenic origin presented itself as a refuge from these difficulties. I was driven from this refuge when I first read Dr. Ross' *Enquiry into Prognosis* (20). Dr. Nicolle finds difficulty in accepting a monosymptomatic hysteria. It seems to me that a monosymptomatic schizophrenia with a recovery rate of eighty per cent is an idea still harder to assimilate. Then in recent years the idea of an endocrine basis came into prominence, and was strongly reinforced by the clinical resemblance between anorexia nervosa and Simmonds' cachexia.

I think it is beyond doubt that a condition of true pituitary cachexia exists, which includes the type of case described by Simmonds and also many which run a much more benign course and some of which respond to treatment by pituitary extracts. But I am firmly convinced that the disorder differs fundamentally from the type of case which Dr. Nicolle has described tonight and I do not believe that there is any valid evidence for attributing the latter to pituitary defect. I have observed some cases which were regarded by me and others as pituitary cachexia, and I very much doubt whether a real anorexia was an essential symptom. I remember particularly one case, a girl aged 19 with prolonged amenorrhea and emaciation. She was a poor eater, but to talk of anorexia would be exaggeration. She was perfectly co-operative and there was no difficulty in getting her to take a diet containing full calorie requirements, and on this entirely adequate diet she continued to lose weight. I believe that whereas in anorexia nervosa the wasting is the direct result of starvation, in Simmonds' disease this is not so; they may lose weight on an adequate diet just as does the thyrotoxic.

In a disorder such as anorexia nervosa where pathological evidence is lacking, but clinical features are remarkably constant, insight into its nature must best be obtained by a close evaluation of the latter. One of these features, though it is fully recognized seems to call for more explanation. If one considers the diets which these patients have usually been consuming before treatment, it is not only the quantity which is abnormal; they have a way of selecting a remarkable mixture of meat extractives and carbohydrate slops. The effect of feeding a normal individual on this diet would be twofold: it would lead to emaciation and it would cause dyspeptic pain. This is just what does not happen in anorexia nervosa; even though the alimentary condition is complicated by obstinate constipation which is dealt with by drastic purges, no pain is experienced. Sufferers from this disease do not feel the sensations of appetite, or the pangs of hunger or the dyspeptic pain which would normally be evoked by the existing conditions. In this complete unawareness of the sensations connected with nutrition I am reminded most of children suffering from pink disease, where there is undoubtedly a blocking of autonomic impulses by physical disease. In anorexia nervosa it seems obvious that there is a disturbance of function somewhere in the endocrine-autonomic system, but are there any grounds for locating it in the pituitary? Surely there is a block in the afferent impulses from the viscera, in the autonomic nerves, and these patients suffer from anesthesia and analgesia resulting from it.

When the disease progresses unfavorably the clinical picture passes on to one of starvation. But I am not sure that the picture is quite that of starvation from other causes. I have never observed in patients or in records the appearance of edema, or the development of ketosis with its resulting symptoms. It is possible that even in starvation the autonomic system of these patients does not function in the customary manner.

As to the nature of this blocking of afferent impulses, all the evidence available is against the presence of any physical disease. It seems therefore most likely that it is of the nature of dissociation, which brings the pathogenesis into the category of hysteria. I know that this view will be unacceptable to many psychiatrists, Dr. Nicolle among them, and I would like to put forward some considerations in defense of it. Dr. Nicolle discussed with great acumen the differential diagnosis of anorexia nervosa and manifest hysteria, and her remarks certainly carried conviction. But I would suggest that anorexia nervosa is of the nature of conversion hysteria which often does differ in much the same way from the more usual forms, and simply consists of a dissociation of certain neurones of a distribution corresponding with an idea. Those conversion hysterias which we see rather little of now, but which we saw much of in the War, were quite often monosymptomatic—at any rate until someone "cured" the symptoms; then they sometimes became polysymptomatic. My own belief therefore is that anorexia nervosa is primarily of psychogenic origin, that the patient becomes protected from the discomforts and pains of starvation by dissociation of afferent neurones, and that the ensuing bodily changes are purely secondary to inanition.

It seems to me that the idea of a primary ovarian failure, to which Dr. Nicolle inclines, must for the present remain in the balance. Ryle (21) commented on it as follows: "The occurrence of the disease in males and in women after the menopause reminds us that a primary ovarian dysfunction cannot very well be claimed as an essential cause of the disease." Unless we find grounds for believing that the cases described in males were something different from anorexia nervosa, I do not see how the validity of this statement can be disputed. I certainly think that one of the ways in which the elucidation of the pathogenesis of anorexia can best be served in the future will be by a critical investigation of any cases which may be observed in men.

The President, after congratulating Dr. Nicolle on her admirable paper, referred to cases of anorexia in which the main factor is a refusal to accept destiny. He referred to the speaker's anorexia in females as compared with males was attributable to the fact that the girl cannot look forward to shaping her own destiny in the same way that the youth can. In this connection he described a case of acute anorexia in an undergraduate aged 20, who had adopted starvation as a compromise form of suicide and as a protest against a destiny which biologically and functionally was completely unacceptable to him.

Dr. W. Paterson Brown

Dr. Nicolle has shown us the fear of sexual inadequacy in the anorexia nervosa patient. She has related the not eating to a fear of growing fat, and consequently sexually unattractive to the male. The explanation is superficial and inadequate, as it does not recognize the active repudiation of sexuality which is going on in these cases and which I should like to stress. At the deeper and more primitive level of the mind where this occurs the ingestion of food symbolizes impregnation and obesity pregnancy. In this connection it is interesting to reflect on those mental hospital patients for whom tube feeding has become a conscious sexual experience. I have myself come across two such cases while working at a mental hospital.

REFERENCES

1. Allbutt, T. C.: *A System of Medicine by Many Writers,* III & VIII. London: Macmillan, 1907 & 1910.

2. Ballet, G.: L'anorexie mentale. *Rev. gén. clin. thérap.*, 21:293, 1907.
3. Baudouin, A., Lhermitte, J., & Lerebouillet, J.: Un cas de pinéalome, absence de macrogénitosomie précoce. Le problème de la cachexie hypophysaire. *Rev. Neurol.*, 39 (i):388, 1932.
4. Charcot, J. M.: De l'isolement dans le traitement de l'hystéric. *Oeuvres Complètes*, III. Paris: Delahaye & Lescrosnier, 1887, p. 238.
5. Dubois, R.: De l'anorexie mentale comme prodrome de la démence précoce. *Ann. méd.-psychol.*, 4:431, 1913.
6. De Gennes, I., Delarue, J., & Rogé: *Bull. et mém. Soc. méd. d. hôp. de Paris*, 52:387, 1936.
7. Dejerine, J. & Gauckler, E.: *Les Manifestations Fonctionnelles des Psychonevroses, leur Traitement par la Psychothérapie.* Paris, 1911.
8. Gull, W. W.: The address on medicine. *This Volume*, pp. 104-127.
9. ———: Anorexia nervosa. *This Volume*, pp. 132-140.
10. Hawkinson, L. F.: Simmonds' disease. *J. Am. Med. Assn.*, 105:20, 1935.
11. Herman, C.: La maladie de Simmonds. *Rev. Franç. d'endocrinol.*, 6:301, 1928.
12. Lasègue, C.: De l'anorexie hystérique. *Etudes Médicales*, II. Paris: Asselin & Honzeau, 1884, p. 45.
13. Levi, L.: *Anorexie mentale et corps thyroide. Encéphale,* 17:507, 1922.
14. Loeper, M. & Fau, R.: Cachexie hypophysaire et anorexie mentale. *Monde méd.*, 17:875, 1936.
15. Mayer-Gross, W.: The early diagnosis of schizophrenia. *Brit. Med. J.*, 2:936, 1938.
16. Morton, R.: *Phthisiologia, or a Treatise of Consumptions.* London: Smith & Walford, 1694.
17. Naudeau, M.: Observation sur une maladie nerveuse accompagnée d'un dégoût extraordinaire pour les aliments. *J. de Méd. Chir. Pharmacie,* 80:197, 1789.
18. Noguès, G.: *L'Anorexie Mentale, ses Rapports avec la Psychophysiologie de la Faim.* T. Toulouse, 1913.
19. Ross, C. W.: Anorexia nervosa with special reference to the carbohydrate metabolism. *Lancet* 2:893, 1938.
20. Ross, T. A.: *An Enquiry into the Prognosis in the Neuroses.* New York: Cambridge University Press, 1936.
21. Ryle, J. A.: Anorexia nervosa. *Lancet* 2:893, 1936.
22. Sheldon, J. H.: Anorexia nervosa with special reference to the physical constitution. *Lancet* 1:369, 1937.
23. Venables, J. F.: Anorexia nervosa. A study of the pathogenesis and treatment of nine cases. *Guy's Hosp. Rep.*, 80:213, 1930.
24. Vidart, L.: L'anorexie mentale, *Gaz. d. Hôp.*, 110:861, 1937.

ANOREXIA NERVOSA:
A PSYCHOSOMATIC ENTITY

JOHN V. WALLER, M.D., M. RALPH KAUFMAN, M.D., AND FELIX DEUTSCH, M.D.
(1940)

Although Dr. W. Paterson Brown, in a clinical discussion of anorexia nervosa in 1938, called attention to the notion of ingestion of food as symbolizing impregnation, Waller, Kaufman, and Deutsch in 1940 emphasized that the "psychological factors have a certain specific constellation centering around the symbolization of pregnancy fantasies involving the gastrointestinal tract." In other words, "The syndrome involves not a physiological system, but rather a functionally co-ordinated unit subjectively important to the patient." They were impressed by the "oft repeated pattern of emphasis on food, alternate over-and undereating, conflict with the family and then precipitation of the syndrome of cachexia with apparent anorexia at the time of adjustment to adulthood and the regression to an infantile level." This promotes the symbolic equation of eating with sexuality, particularly with the fantasy of impregnation. The overeating and the alternating disgust for food represent a shift in the dynamic conflict. In the first, the impregnation fantasy is gratified, while in the second the ensuing guilt and anxiety forbid the intake of food. Other symptoms of the syndrome like amenorrhea and constipation are also viewed as reflecting the pregnancy fantasy.

They report in detail two cases, studied by intensive psychoanalytically oriented anamnestic interviews. In both cases the symbolism of eating as impregnation was quite clear and unambiguous; both patients expressed it in their own words in one way or another. Both patients were under the stress of rivalries and hostilities within and outside the family and regressed to centering the conflict around food. Both patients acted out in the somatic sphere the fantasy of oral impregnation.

The authors consider their cases as belonging to the syndrome of anorexia nervosa and hence do not enter into nosological discussions. However, they state: "The personality structure in both patients follows the lines recognized as compulsive-obsessive."

Generally the emphasis of the previous observers was on psychological factors in a nonspecific sense. The recognition was there to the effect that psychological and emotional factors played an important role in the genesis of the syndrome and that in some way these factors led to the reaction to food and that, by and large, the somatic manifestations were related primarily to the metabolic changes resulting from starvation. The authors attempt to utilize analytic concepts, especially in relation to the content of the fantasy, and to give meaning to the signs and symptoms of the syndrome, relating it to content and utilizing the generally accepted psychoanalytic hypotheses. In this way the signs and symptoms of the syndrome are shown to have specific unconscious meaning to the individual patient. The primary fantasy is thought to center around the significance of oral impregnation, and the signs and symptoms are shown to follow a pattern significant to that meaning.

It is of course necessary to assume that the pregnancy fantasy, though vital and essential for the formation of the syndrome and its characteristic symptoms, is only one factor in its evolution, one link in the chain of psychological events. These include open conflict between family and patient, preceding history of obesity and overeating, or emphasis on food and the problems of adjustment at puberty and early adolescence.

The authors were aware of overdetermination but oriented their presentation to stress the significance of symbolization in physiological functions. This led to a specific psychodynamic formulation in terms of acting out of a fantasy of function. Though the patients were not analyzed, their productions relating to sex and food intake were such as to warrant the assumption that unconscious mentation was affected by specific symbolization. In other words, the patients' remarks pointing to ideas of oral impregnation were merely indications or clues of underlying ideation.

The fantasy of oral impregnation, when pathogenic, activates or inhibits unconsciously phenomena of pregnancy. In anorexia nervosa we are dealing with fixation at or regression to oral level. Genital ideas are expressed orally and dealt with in terms of intake, output and rejection, as related to symbolic impregnation. The symbol formation is most important. The occurrence of amenorrhea carries further the symbolic assumption of impregnation.

The utilization of fantasy in somatic expression is an established mechanism in states of conflict. It is in this sense that specific fantasies are considered etiological for certain clinical syndromes. The prominence of a specific fantasy does not exclude other conflicts and corresponding defenses. As one of the mechanisms at play it can occur in multiform types of psychiatric syndromes ranging from neurosis to psychosis. It is also to be expected that the specific mental state can effect or color the impregnation fantasy. Thus the psychotic can include it in his delusional system.

A systematic analysis of this paper from the point of view of the eleven factors discussed previously (Psychogenicity, pp. 101-102) yields the following results.

1. Genetic factor. *Here we are immediately confronted by a methodological problem which involves the question as to whether it is really possible to obtain adequate data of a genetic nature through the anamnestic interview technique. This is a problem that is of great significance in this field. This paper demonstrates the deficiencies inherent in the anamnestic interview procedures since, although a fair amount of material is available concerning the development of the patient, nevertheless it is a unilinear rather than tridimensional picture that is presented. At best, a rather superficial knowledge of the early development of the patient is available. Very little material concerning the early life in terms of preconscious or unconscious fantasy, object relations and development is known. Therefore, it becomes necessary to extrapolate constructions from chronologically later experiences to the early phase of development. This is a limitation which is a fundamental one in any attempt to conceptualize the impact of early life experiences on the subsequent clinical manifestations.*

2. Occurrence of the trauma at an early age—at the undifferentiated core of oral phase. *Here again the lack of the kind of data obtained through the psychoanalytic procedure becomes glaringly apparent, since the anamnestic interview technique, as utilized in this paper, does not elicit this kind of material in depth. However, there are points in the history in Case 1 which make it plausible to assume an oral emphasis: (a) intense emphasis on food; (b) patient being the only girl in the family, and treated as a baby; and (c) traumatic episode at the age of one year when the patient choked on peanuts.*

Subsequent precipitating factors. *A series of possible precipitating factors relating to the function of eating appears in the history of Case 1: (a) The menarche at 12 concomitant with a desire for male companionship. There was a noticeable overeating. (b) Three years later, when she took up the first secret relationship with a boy friend, there was again overeating. (c) At 18, in the midst of a conflict with her family about a relationship to another young man, she begins to work in a candy factory where she was overtaken again by an overwhelming desire to eat. It was at this time that the clinical picture developed when the patient was unable to eat any other food aside from candy and developed a repulsion to food and nausea and, in addition, became amenorrheic and constipated. There was also a social-vocational conflict inasmuch as she wished to go to college and was disappointed when for economic reasons she could not do so.*

3. The failure to promote a solution of the disturbing situation by behavior or symbolic representation or even psychosis, at the ideational level leads to direct physiological expressions via autonomic pathways. *This point presents certain difficulties and demonstrates the problem of restrictive formulations. In regard to this the patient demonstrates a spectrum which runs from ideation to physiological response. Hypothetically she is reacting to an oral pregnancy fantasy, the gratification of which comes about through her candy eating. The reaction against the fantasy might be found in her repulsion to food and her nausea. Somatically she presents constipation and amenorrhea. Here again the absence of the kind of data which ordinarily can be made available*

through psychoanalytic procedure forces a speculation rather than a deduction based on convincing clinical data.[1]

4. Regression to an early level with corresponding methods of reaction. In this patient, as noted previously, the clinical symptom of overeating became manifest when the patient was confronted with a heterosexual conflict. There is evidence in the case record that this was resolved through the means of manifestations playing themselves out primarily at the oral level. In relation to the concept of regression, one might raise the question of the amenorrhea and ask what level of function or inhibition of function it represents. This is not only a regression to the oral level but involves a special type of orality, namely pregnancy through incorporation through the mouth. Therefore the consequences of the pregnancy fantasy may play themselves out in all other aspects of psychophysiological function associated with the idea of pregnancy. In this way, one sees the fantasy of function manifesting itself at the appropriate psychophysiological level which would in this instance include the absence of menses. The problem remains as to how these psychophysiological manifestations are mediated.

5. Adaptation principles which promote shifting and limiting of stress to certain organs and systems; This is essentially an energy distribution problem: This formulation raises many problems. Certainly at one point it relates to the choice of organ and organ systems. The basic psychodynamic formulation in the paper lies within this area, since the hypothesis is that the whole syndrome represents a fantasy of

---

Reprinted from *Psychosomatic Medicine*, 2:3-16, 1940.

[1] The question arises whether we are justified in postulating a failure of the thinking apparatus as a buffer system in patients suffering from so-called psychosomatic illnesses, in the sense that there is a hypothesis which states that there is an alternation between manifestations of symptoms which play themselves out primarily through the thinking apparatus and manifestations of symptoms and signs which play themselves out primarily in the soma and that there is a reciprocal relationship between symptoms in these two spheres. This raises the whole question of the hypothesis of ego strength and ego weakness in the sense that the ego as the executant of the psychic organism has the responsibility for the resolution of conflicts. One might formulate the problem in terms of energy distribution and the shifting valence intersystemically and intrasystemically. It also raises the problem of separating the various ego functions. It may be an error to relate ego strength or weakness in terms of a unitary function of the ego and similarly, in the utilization of the defenses, one is forced to the same conclusion that the defenses have to be studied both separately and in relation to each other, and that we can encounter primitive defenses in fairly integrated patients.

function and is a sequential progression of events expressed in system function language that signifies a conflict over oral impregnation. Here again the problem of the technique for eliciting data, namely the anamnestic, biographical versus the psychoanalytic, becomes of paramount importance. The over-all picture as outlined in the case history lends itself to the formulation. The details, however, which would be obtainable in psychoanalytic observation, are lacking.

6. The point at which the symbolic process enters the reaction or situation (a) as stimulus, (b) as giving secondary meaning. *This formulation raises the most interesting and intriguing problems in the whole area of psychosomatic medicine and of nosology. The data presented in the case history again demonstrate the problems inherent in the method utilized for the obtaining of data. At the risk of overevaluating the psychoanalytic method for obtaining data, one might say that if it had been possible to have these patients in analysis, the material obtained would have had more weight and consistency and would have lent itself to more convincing proof of the basic psychodynamic formulation. The data available in the case material seem to throw convincing light on the symbolic process entering the reaction as a stimulus. However, there is a suggestion that at puberty the patient was relating sexuality to eating and responded with overeating in a sexual situation. The clinical material with its symptomatology is of such a nature that it makes tenable the hypothesis that the syndrome reflects a conflict over the fantasy of oral impregnation.*

7. The abnormal distribution and utilization of sexual and aggressive drives. *From the point of view of the phenomenology at a descriptive level or formulation, the clinical material can be presented from this point of view. What seems to be lacking is a knowledge of the determinants of the energy flow at an unconscious level.*

8. The accumulation of nondischarged affect. *One of the earliest formulations in regard to psychophysiological functioning, regardless of the nosological category in which the end result manifests itself, is the concept of undischarged affect. This is illustrated by such terms as damming of libido and repressed affect. Early psychotherapeutic procedures such as catharsis and abreaction are also related to such a concept. One of Freud's earliest concepts was that all repressed affect could*

be changed into anxiety. This was essentially a physiochemical theory of anxiety. With the publication of "Inhibition, Symptoms and Anxiety" *there was a shift in emphasis and a change in point of view. Nevertheless to this day the energies or the economy of repressed affect plays an important role in the formulations dealing with symptom formation. Alexander utilized this concept logically in his presentation of psychosomatic illness. Repressed affect and attitudes manifest themselves either in parasympathetic or sympathetic function in the so-called vegetative neuroses. In the case material presented in the paper under discussion it is only by implication, rather than by specific clinical data, that the problem of the repression of the affect is a matter of concern.*

9. The position in and relation to family unit. *The anamnestic technique for the obtaining of the material is well illustrated by these case reports. Insofar as one deals with conscious or relatively preconscious data such material becomes available and relates to problems brought on by the mother's early and persistent emphasis on eating and later by strict regulation of sexuality and interference with the patient's sexual interest in adolescence. The patient's chronological position in the family is known; the relationship to siblings and parents and other such data lend themselves to an interpretation and formulation related to personality structure and the meaning of certain specific symptoms. Here again the lack of the kind of data available through the use of the psychoanalytic method is apparent. Nevertheless, the data available seem to have enough weight to make them utilizable legitimately in the ultimate formulation of the syndrome.*

10. The reaction to the socioeconomic situation. *The question of evaluating socioeconomic factors and their role in personality development and dysfunction is an intriguing one. This is especially true of the more recent emphasis of the so-called culturalist schools. The question of the specificity of socioeconomic factors relating to the basic syndrome cannot be answered from the clinical material available. The patients reported were of a lower economic group, and in one instance a particular episode seemed to be precipitated in relation to disappointment over inability to go to college because of financial reasons. The problem, however, is a much wider one since there is a relation-*

ship between socioeconomic factors and cultural patterns. Italian and Jewish maternal insistence on the importance of eating is not unknown. It has already been implied above that this insistence played a role in the patient's attitude toward eating. In the broad area of socioeconomic status it is evident from the many reports of patients with anorexia nervosa that individual patients may belong to all of the categories, and it would seem then that in itself socioeconomic status is not a basic etiological factor.

11. Quantitative factor of pathogenic elements. The material presented does not lend itself to a weighting of the factors. The final formulation, however, of the syndrome representing an organismic reaction to a fantasy of oral pregnancy, does give weight to a unique type of conflict situation and to the utilization of the symbolic process.

The breaking down of the clinical material into the above categories focuses clearly on the deficiencies of the material, since in each category lacunae become apparent. On the whole this approach presents a valid argument for the utilization of psychoanalysis as an instrument of observation, both at the phenomenological and psychodynamic levels. It will be demonstrated in the discussion of some of the later papers how the formulation presented in the paper under discussion is defective, since it apparently deals with only one major level of the total complexity. This is especially true in relation to the matter of overdeterminants, since the same manifestation or symptom may have many meanings. Although the genetic point of view is present and there is a review of the development of the individual in terms of pregenitality, nevertheless, the emphasis seems to be on the oedipal conflict which is rephrased in terms of oral impregnation.

The Clinical Syndrome known as anorexia nervosa has had an interesting nosological history. Interpretation of the etiological factors has varied from time to time, swinging from a psychological interpretation of the syndrome to an organic; it has been closely related to Simmonds' cachexia. More recently the emphasis has been placed upon the neurotic origin of the syndrome and we are in thorough agreement with this latter view. In addition, we believe there is a specific train of psychological events leading to the development and expression of this neurosis. The literature has been thoroughly and competently reviewed on a number of occasions and therefore will not be discussed in detail here.

One of the earliest references to "consumption of mental origin" was made by Richard Morton in 1694 (8). In his classical paper in 1874, Sir William Gull (6) discussed anorexia nervosa and reported another case in 1888 (5), stating, "these patients without apparent cause evince a repugnance for food, a perversion of the ego being the cause." Already in 1868 (4) he had maintained that certain cases of amenorrhea "may be the result of an intellectual disturbance." Sir Samuel Gee (3), in 1907, stated that after the return of appetite and gain in weight, "it may happen that the marasmus, constipation, amenorrhea and melancholy continue; a manifest proof that the disease is not the result of the anorexia." Other authors, among whom the most recent is Richardson (10), report clinical observations and theoretical discussions of this problem. Richardson particularly presents an excellent review of the literature, bringing out the development of the two viewpoints and emphasizing that the endocrinological approach was an "overspecialization" in which the patient was lost sight of. He presents his cases in chronological order of the development of the individual clinical course and through late developments in each case convincingly demonstrates the primary importance of the neurosis and the absence of, or secondary importance of, pathology related to the endocrine glands. On the whole, the modern point of view seems definitely inclined toward the psychogenesis of the clinical syndrome.

The generally accepted clinical syndrome of anorexia nervosa occurs in girls between the ages of twelve and twenty-one years, but may occasionally appear in the thirties and forties and is also reported to occur in young men. It consists of the following symptoms: First there is a complaint of loss of appetite, which, on closer examination, turns out to be a reaction of disgust toward food rather than a mere loss of appetite. This is followed by loss of weight, marasmus, or cachexia, complaints of constipation, exhaustion, weakness and irritability, and, in women, is always associated with amenorrhea of varying duration. During the course of the emaciation the skin texture may change; there is an apparent increase of hair over the body and there may be a loss of hair from the head. The secondary symptoms of cachexia are present. A point emphasized by some writers is that the degree of exhaustion is not so great as one would be led to expect by the amount of emaciation. There may be some mood changes.

On analysis of the syndrome there are three symptoms which stand out and which may at first sight be taken as primary: the reaction to food, the constipation, and the amenorrhea.

This, then, represents the somatic picture of the disease. The neurotic etiology has received but scant attention. Histories of the many cases reported in the literature, if they make any mention of the psychopathology, limit this phase to a brief description of the circumstance surrounding the precipitation of the clinical syndrome. Attempts to define the conflict situation have been made by Richardson (10), who maintained that the conflict centering around the relationship to the mother was important, and Farquharson and Hyland (2), who note "a fundamental failure of adaptation to the domestic situation." Further analysis of the literature reveals an amazing similarity in all the reported psychological circumstances. These may be grouped and then analyzed as follows:

1. There is an open conflict between the family and the patient. This is particularly true of the mother-daughter relationship. In a case reported by Stephens (11) as early as 1895, the fatal exacerbation of the anorexia followed upon the mother's resumption of frequent visits to her hospitalized daughter.

2. There is often a preceding history of obesity and overeating; this excessive eating may alternate with the anorexia. A very frequent history is that the patient was ashamed of being fat and then dieted until the cachectic stage appeared.

3. Peculiarities in the sphere of sex are characteristic; in the girl or woman, amenorrhea; in the male, impotence; in both, absence of sexual desire. The catamenial history may show all kinds of irregularities, but amenorrhea during the cachexia is universal.

4. The obesity and amenorrhea occur early in puberty at a time of attempted adjustment to the outside environment.

5. The anorexia, with the full-blown clinical syndrome, appears at a somewhat later period, when adjustments of immense psychological significance must be faced. These include leaving the family circle for college or boarding school, or, most often, a proposed marriage.

6. Parental pressure in the attempted solution of these problems adds further fuel to the perpetual internecine warfare.

7. Family history of neurosis or psychosis is encountered frequently. The peculiarities and characteristics of the older members of the family group will leave their impress on the personalities of the children. In this illness the neurotic behavior most frequently found in the parents takes the form of over-emphasis on the question of eating. If the history is taken from the mother, the patient is usually described as "always a finicky eater." If the history is taken from the patient, the mother is described as "oversolicitous and overbearing," particularly as regards matters of eating.

8. The secondary gains of the neurosis are frequently at a conscious level and the patient admits the desire for attention and sympathy and the attempt to divert the family notice from a supposedly more popular older or younger sibling.

This remarkable, oft repeated pattern of emphasis on food, alternate over- and undereating, conflict with the family and then precipitation of the syndrome of cachexia with apparent anorexia at the time of adjustment to adulthood, involving new ties outside of the family circle, and then regression to an infantile level, with loss of conscious sexuality, has led us to investigate the underlying psychopathology. A discussion of the psychological setting of the symptoms will lead to a detailed formulation.

The biological significance of food intake needs no elaborate discussion. However, what is often overlooked is that this need, having an original physiological basis, becomes intimately related with psychological factors and may assume a symbolic significance which has no primary relation to the problem of survival.

The infant, being totally dependent for the gratification of its needs upon the external world, soon develops psychological relationships to the individuals ministering to its needs, particularly the parents. The intake of food, or its rejection, assumes a significance in the expression of various emotional factors, and the infant uses the acceptance or rejection of the feeding to express varying emotional patterns. Frustration may lead to hostilities which are expressed in the rejection of food. Many of the feeding problems in infancy are understood when looked at from this point of view. Overemphasis on feeding by the parent or nurse may also create certain psychological patterns. Rejection of food, retention of food in the mouth, vomiting, all may express an attempt at a solution of a conflict with the environment. This is also true in relation to the function of evacuation; diarrhea, constipation and enuresis of childhood may serve psychologically to express certain conflict solutions. With the growth of the child, intake of food may assume even more elaborate symbolizations related not only to aggressive patterns of behavior, but also to patterns of sexual significance.

The comparison between psychological mechanisms seen in primitives and those seen in children has often been pointed out, and many authors, particularly in the field of psychiatry, have discussed these relationships. Among the myths of primitives are those dealing with magical forms of impregnation and birth. An excellent study was published by Hartland (7) in 1909 in which he cited numerous examples of such beliefs. For instance, Heitsi-eibib, a divine ancestor of the Hottentots, was born because a girl swallowed the sap of grass. Yehl, a quasi divine hero of British Columbia tribes, was born many times. He transformed himself in turn into a spear of cedar grass, a pebble, a drop of water, and was swallowed by the future mother. The Pueblo people of southwestern North America believed that their culture hero was born of a virgin who became pregnant from eating two piñon-nuts. This magical belief of pregnancy through eating is a very common fantasy in children and may continue unchanged, either consciously or unconsciously, throughout life. If one studies the concepts of children in relation to the origin of babies, one frequently comes across just such theories. Without entering into a detailed discussion of the psychological reasons for the acceptance and elaboration of such theories, one may state that they have a certain universality.

During the development of the child, certain emotional attitudes and relationships develop toward the parents. Under the pressure of training and education, there is a tendency to taboo natural biological expressions. This is particularly true in the sphere of sexuality and, for various reasons, the genital aspect of procreation is repressed. The curious child, however, is constantly seeking an answer to the question of where babies come from. Often the answer is couched in terms of just such symbolization as that seen in primitives. One has a baby by eating. In some of those children in whom feeding problems are of special significance, this then becomes an added factor. The fantasies centering around this problem are usually within the sphere of those things which the child is forbidden, implicitly and explicitly, to talk about. They may be repressed, but they retain their dynamic significance for the individual. These fantasies of oral impregnation are not necessarily confined to one or the other sex, but play an important role in the birth theories of all children.

There are certain crucial age periods in the development of all individuals. According to one school of psychology, the analytic, around the age of six there is a repression of certain conflicts centering around the family constellation; a satisfactory or unsatisfactory solution of the family conflict will color the future development accordingly. With the appearance of puberty, initiated perhaps by an upsurge based on endocrinological factors, there is certainly a need for a psychological reorientation and these older patterns of thought and behavior tend to recur. There is a need for a new adjustment during this period of great internal and external stress; old family rivalries and hostilities are revived. The girl, with the onset of the menses, enters upon her biological womanhood. In the normal development of the individual the adolescent identifies, in whole or in part with the parent of the same sex. There is a choice of many love objects outside of the family circle. New pressures are exerted by the environment. The normal girl weathers the puberty storm and develops into a non-neurotic woman. However, the person in whom certain neurotic patterns of behavior have been laid down in childhood has a tendency to regress to these same patterns in an attempt to solve the new conflicts which have arisen. Fantasies concerning sexuality recur with added intensity and the problem of child bearing recurs. The neurotic, who is tied with inextricable bonds to the family pattern again revives all the older conflicts and fantasies, among which may be those of impregnation through the gastrointestinal tract. To such an individual, then, the whole concept of sexuality and procreation is at this more primitive level. Activity centering around the mouth has not only the reality value of eating, but also a symbolic sexual significance centering particularly around ideas of procreation. The sexual function of the genitalia may be denied and a rather characteristic personality reaction occurs. All fantasies or activities connected with genitality are reacted to with guilt, disgust, or anxiety. Particularly at this time the autoerotic activity which is a recrudescence from childhood assumes great significance and is frequently reacted to with intense guilt. The fantasies associated with this autoerotic activity may be at a conscious level. Unconsciously the mouth and eating may play an important role. As in childhood, this adolescent uses eating or not eating also to express hostilities and aggressions to the family circle.

What is the result of these conflicting forces and the rather specific fantasy formations? The act of eating is now symbolically equated with sexuality, particularly with the fantasy of impregnation. Dependent on the quantity of guilt and anxiety associated with the fantasy of pregnancy and with aggressions within the family, there may be a complete rejection of eating which is understandable then only in terms of its symbolic significance and not of its original biological function. Now we can understand why there is more than a mere loss of appetite and actually a feeling of disgust. The obverse of this rejection of food is seen very frequently in a sort of compulsive ritualistic gluttony. With the shifting in the dynamics of the neurotic conflict, the gratification of these fantasies takes place at an unconscious level and the patient periodically indulges in an orgy of compulsive eating. Thus gratification of the fantasy of becoming pregnant may be expressed by overeating or gorging. When, however, guilt or anxiety arises in relation to his gratification, rejection of food ensues. The compulsive character structure of these individuals is further shown by many of the secondary symptoms. A characteristic finding of increased fluid intake serves the purpose of an obsessive ritual which serves the purpose of a cleansing and purification rite. This aspect of the syndrome will be demonstrated in the cases we are to report. In some instances this purification rite is not confined to fluid intake, but may show itself in an obsessive need for cleanliness, with an exaggerated handwashing, housecleaning, and neatness. These psychopathological manifestations are important in throwing light upon the level at which part of the conflict occurs. In the frank obsessional neurosis one frequently meets with such behavior.

As a correlate to the symbolic impregnation, one may perhaps understand the two other so-called primary symptoms in the syndrome: constipation and amenorrhea. Concomitant with the fantasies of oral impregnation goes the fantasy of a child in the abdomen. Here again one might cite many primitive beliefs. Constipation then becomes equated with the pregnant abdomen. This is rather clearly shown in the cases which we shall present. Again depending upon shifting factors of the structure of the neurosis, this constipation may alternate with diarrhea.

Following this line of thought, one may fit into the picture the amenorrhea. It is common knowledge that the menstrual cycle is profoundly influenced by purely psychological factors. The frequent temporary cessation of the menses in young women who fear pregnancy and also the menstrual irregularities which often occur the first few months of married life are in support of this concept. The relationship of menstruation to pregnancy is well known in our western civilization. The syndrome, schematically reconstructed, represents a symbolic wish to be impregnated. Eating is a denial of the wish and an acting out at an unconscious level of this fantasy. Naturally the significance of these factors varies with each individual and the quantitative interrelationship can be understood only on the basis of an intensive study of each case.

It seems that in the patients who develop anorexia nervosa the mother relationship plays a rather specific and significant role. The conflict between the mother and the child usually centers around the problem of food. Either the mother constantly overemphasizes the act of feeding or centers her disciplinary measures around this function. It may perhaps be significant that the mother's own psychological structure, to a certain extent, is evolved around her own relationship to food. This is a point which is of importance not only in relation to this specific problem, but to another and more general problem, the so-called inheritances of family characteristics. Perhaps what appears here is not an inherent or a constitutional trait, but rather the projection of a pattern in the parent onto the child. The conflict with the mother may often reach a great intensity and all the factors that enter into this relationship are not clear. The relationship to the father fits into the dynamics of the pattern of personality organization of the patient.

We have attempted in our discussion to demonstrate that the psychological factors which determine the etiology of the anorexia nervosa syndrome are not to be couched in general terms. We believe it is not sufficient to state that psychological conflicts and emotional factors enter into the picture, but rather that these psychological factors have a certain specific constellation centering around the symbolization of pregnancy fantasies involving the gastrointestinal tract.

Case 1

The patient, P. D., a nineteen-year-old girl of Italian extraction, entered the hospital, complaining of loss of appetite, loss of weight and weakness of nine months' duration. The history of her present illness, as it appeared in the house record, was as follows: The patient was well, weighing 120 lbs., until one year before admission. She had started to work in a candy factory and ate candy all day long; she stated that she therefore was no longer able to eat regular meals. After four months the loss of weight and weakness were so great as to necessitate a change in occupation. Despite the elimination of eating between meals, the weight loss and inability to eat continued. An occasional regular meal caused epigastric and abdominal distress, with flatulence and bloating. There was belching, but no vomiting or nausea. For several years preceding the onset of the illness the patient was constipated and resorted to frequent catharsis.

The menses were regular until one year previously, when they became irregular and scanty. For the six months preceding admission to the hospital there had been no menstrual flow.

Physical examination revealed a poorly nourished girl who appeared to have no distress. Except for evidence of recent loss of weight, the physical examination, including X rays of the chest, was entirely normal. Her weight on admission was 80.25 lbs. During her hospital stay it went down to 79.5 lbs. and then up to 81 lbs. The final clinical diagnosis of the ward service was anorexia nervosa.

The patient was subsequently studied more intensively and the following data were elicited: The patient was the only girl, the third of four siblings, whose three brothers were alive and well. The father was 48 and the mother 47 years of age. The patient had influenza in infancy and measles during early childhood. At the age of ten she had a tonsillectomy and at 15, an appendectomy. There had been no other physical illness.

Since earliest childhood there had been an emphasis, particularly on the part of the mother, who was rather stout, on the problem of eating. The mother stated that when the patient was one year old she gave her some peanuts and the patient choked. The mother has frequently told the daughter of this incident and has emphasized it a great deal in relation to eating, always cautioning her that she should be careful as to what she ate. The patient has shown a marked resentment against the mother, particularly because she had to eat everything that came to the table with no allowance for personal preferences.

Partly because she was the only girl in the family, she was always treated as the baby and shown special consideration by her parents and brothers. The father, a cobbler by occupation, to a certain extent emphasized this rule. The patient herself stated that she was aware throughout her life of being brought up in a manner entirely different from the American girls of her neighborhood; the mother's insistence on discipline caused a good deal of friction and resentment on the part of the patient. The father to a great extent supported the patient in her quarrels with the mother, except in one aspect, and that was in relation to sexual behavior. The family, including the two older brothers, paid a good deal of attention to her moral upbringing. She was not allowed to play in the street with her classmates and, as she grew older, strict rules as to her relationship with boys were set up by her parents. She stated that her only information on sex was gathered from schoolmates and an occasional book. She thought that pregnancy was simply a natural outcome of marriage.

At the age of twelve her menses appeared and about this time a desire for male companionship became manifest. It was during this time that the first evidence of compulsive eating became manifest. When she was eating large quantities of candy, she would become bloated and have nausea. Since her mother had warned her not to eat candy, she dared neither to comment to her on her observation, nor to ask whether she was correct in believing that a baby was growing in her stomach. She said in an interview, "Whenever I was alone I had to look at my stomach to see if it was not too big." She ate everything, to a point where she became distended, and as she stated during the interviews, she felt many times "as if she were pregnant." During this period she was not allowed to have anything to do with boys. Her entire life was guided by the mother who took her to school in the morning and called for her in the afternoon. On arrival home, she did the housework because she thought her mother was not sufficiently neat. During this period the patient was very obedient and it was not until she had entered high school that there occurred any conscious thoughts of disobeying her parents. The patient described herself as being very sensitive and ambitious, interested in obtaining an education and always trying to be an American and hence having certain ideas about life which her immigrant parents did not share.

At the age of fifteen she met her first boy friend and was sexually thrilled by his kisses and embraces. At this time she again had frequent episodes of compulsive eating, particularly in the afternoon. But it was not an urge like hunger. She merely kept on eating, apples, cake, etc., to the point of extreme discomfort and abdominal distention. She became more and more worried, afraid lest she might be pregnant. She lay down for hours, in order to listen to the movements and noises in her stomach, first indulging in eating and then waiting for something to happen. "How and from where could the baby come," she thought fearfully. Soon after meeting this boy the patient stopped overeating. Meetings were surreptitious and on several occasions were discovered by the father who lectured the patient severely. The thrill of sexual contact soon wore off and the patient became depressed after any sexual experience. She went with this boy for a year without telling her parents. When she finally did tell them the mother raised no objections, but the father disliked the boy and tried to break off the relationship. Once he accepted the boy, he wanted the patient to marry. The mother, however, discouraged any thought of marriage. During this period the patient relieved her sexual tension through masturbation which was accompanied by a great deal of guilt. The emphasis on cleanliness and neatness became exaggerated during this period.

Owing to financial conditions, the family had to move to a suburban town, which meant that the patient could not now enter college without the payment of a prohibitive tuition. She resented this a great deal and blamed her parents, especially because they did not agree to allow her fiancé to pay for her education. At the age of eighteen she began to work in a candy factory and at the same time her mother again made strenuous objections to the proposed engagement. An overwhelming desire to eat candy while at work now appeared and the patient could no longer eat any other food, the sight of which caused repulsion and nausea. At this time her amenorrhea occurred and the patient lost all sexual desire and excitability. She also became markedly constipated and gave this as another reason for her distaste for food. During this period of reduced food intake, the family, particularly the mother and brothers, attempted to force the patient to eat and this resulted in a constant series of arguments and a further limitation on her food intake. The constant emphasis upon eating grew so marked that the family checked on all the food she ate and the older brother complained at one time that she did not drink enough milk, since he had counted only fifteen glasses of milk during the preceding month.

Various factors interfered with marriage plans. The fiancé was a rather passive type of individual, very much attached to his own mother, was constantly running into financial difficulties because he had to support her and because of various other expenditures. The patient's mother, on the other hand, constantly objected to the proposed marriage. The patient, too, found various excuses for putting off the marriage. The real reason for this, as she stated, was that her amenorrhea had to clear up, since she felt that there was no possibility of having children as long as she suffered from amenorrhea. In addition, she feared her own reaction to sex although she had previously stated that she took for granted that the sexual part of life would come with marriage, and that she and her fiancé did not look forward particularly to this aspect of married life.

Although distinctly discomfited by her illness, the patient recognized certain gains from it. She was now the center of attention of the whole family group which gratified her wish to be babied and, also, relieved her jealousy of her brother, who being three years younger, had received a good deal of attention when he was an infant. She was jealous and objected very strenuously to her father's attention to her mother. She thought the world would be a better place to live in if she and her father were the only people in it.

Quite early in life, antagonism to the mother became quite conscious, especially since the mother had begun to live the patient's life for her and to interfere with her activities. Later, during the course of the interviews, the patient one day complained of continuous nausea and occasional upper abdominal pain of four days' duration. The pain was similar in nature to the distress caused by overeating at the age of fourteen, although the present episode was not related to overeating. It started with nausea after there had been a quarrel with the mother about the date of the proposed marriage. The mother wished her to postpone it again for a few more months. The patient insisted that, in spite of her fears about sexual intercourse, she was planning to get married as soon as possible in order to break away from the mother and planned, under any circumstances, not to live near the mother after her marriage.

During another recent interview, the patient stated that she had had diarrhea for four days and that this was the first time in some years that she had not been constipated. She felt slight bilateral breast pain which, previous to the present illness, was always associated with premenstrual periods, and felt hopeful because of this sign. The day before the interview, for the first time since the onset of the present illness, she was sexually excited for the whole day while she was in the company of her fiancé. That evening at supper time she had a return of her old anorexia, accompanied by the same feeling that she could not eat.

Briefly, then, the patient was a nineteen-year-old girl of foreign extraction in whom the relationship to eating had been constantly stressed throughout her life. With an episode in infancy which was constantly emphasized, her eating represented an actual danger to her. The onset of puberty and an interest in male companionship which ran counter to the wishes of the family marked the beginning of a compulsive eating ritual associated with fantasies of oral impregnation. Compulsive eating and emphasis upon cleanliness recurred, more directly, in connection with an attempt to make a heterosexual adjustment accompanied by direct sexual stimulation and autoerotic activity and, also, under pressure of a paternal censure. This was followed by marked anorexia, constipation, amenorrhea and loss of conscious sexual desire, as well as marked weight reduction. The parental and sibling reactions were motivated not only by the supposed interest in the patient but also by their own emotional problems.

Since discharge from the hospital the patient has gained some weight, but has had no return of her menses. Her present weight is 90.5 lbs. After the brief psychiatric investigation the patient stated that she felt much better, particularly as to her relationship with her family. Quarrels are few, as the patient definitely avoids them. She is biding her time until marriage brings geographical separation from her family. Since the patient has not achieved insight into the fundamental nature of the family conflict, it is likely that new situations, such as actual marriage or pregnancy will cause reprecipitation of the now partially suppressed clinical syndrome of anorexia nervosa.

Case 2

The patient, E. G., was a nineteen-year-old salesgirl, born in this country of European parents[2]. Her chief complaint on admission was loss of weight.

[2] The associative anamnesis of this case has been published by Felix Deutsch (1).

Her weight had dropped from 118 to 87.5 lbs. One year previously the patient weighed 118 lbs. and at that time began to eat compulsively all sorts of pastries and sweets. After a gain of 20 lbs., she consulted a physician because of being overweight. The basal metabolic rate was —28; thyroid medication was prescribed and, in addition, she restricted her diet voluntarily during this period. After the loss of 24 lbs., the basal metabolic rate still being —28, thyroid therapy was discontinued. However, the patient could not eat. She complained of loss of appetite and a great aversion to food. She ceased eating, and noticed that she drank a great deal of water, perhaps 16 glasses a day. This was not because of thirst, but because she had to do something to keep things out of her mind. The previous period of compulsive eating and gain in weight had also not been attended by hunger, but "to keep things away from my mind." At the time of admission her weight was 87.5 lbs. She gave a history of constipation dating back to her childhood and this she gave as one of the reasons for the lack of appetite. She complained of weakness and irritability, with an intensification of quarreling with her parents.

At the age of fifteen, since her menses had not yet appeared, oral endocrine therapy was resorted to and was followed by two scanty periods, one month apart. A year later this medication was repeated and another scanty flow resulted. Since that time she had had no menses. Related to her large fluid intake was frequent and copious urination.

Physical examination revealed an emaciated girl who appeared alert and intelligent and gave no evidence of distress. She was heavily made up, with rouged cheeks and lips and penciled eyebrows. Her breasts were well developed in spite of evidence of the recent extreme loss of weight. There was a marked hirsutism over the whole body, particularly of the arms and legs, which the patient attributed to the use of a depilatory. A thorough physical examination, including X rays of the skull and chest and laboratory tests, was completely normal. There was no evidence of hyperthyroidism.

The final diagnoses on the medical service were questions of Simmonds' disease, diabetes insipidus or anorexia nervosa.

Investigation revealed the following history: The patient was the eldest of three siblings, having two younger brothers. The mother was described as a somewhat obese, domineering woman, who forcefully managed the household and attempted to direct every move of her three children. The father was a somewhat passive tailor, given to frequent outbursts of temper. The family life was marked by strife and internal jealousies. There was a great deal of stress placed upon eating, especially by the mother, who provided special delicacies for the capricious palates of each of her children. She would follow the patient to school and there physically enforce the ingestion of the remainder of an unfinished breakfast. Later, when the patient began to put on weight, the mother constantly quarreled with her in an attempt to limit forcibly her food intake.

Some of the memories elicited during the interviews were of a type that one ordinarily has great difficulty in uncovering, but, as is sometimes characteristic in compulsive neurotic individuals, experiences which ordinarily are forgotten remain in the consciousness, although the related emotion may be displaced or repressed. In this connection the patient stated that she remembered, as a child of three, the birth of her first brother, which evoked marked and open hostility and a desire to replace him at the mother's breast. She remembered also that at this time she had ideas of running away with her father. At the age of six she thought that kissing was directly responsible for pregnancy. At this time she played "kissing" with another girl and a brother and sister of her own age. Between the ages of six and eight, she slept with her brother who was four years her junior. During the night, she would go to the kitchen, take food from the icebox, and bring it to her brother. They would then eat it together. From this time she dates her belief that eating was a causative factor in pregnancy, that from eating one got fat, and, finally, had a child. However, she thought this could only take place when people were married. Until the age of eleven, she spent part of each night in her parents' bed, in-between her father and mother, with the avowed purpose of keeping them apart.

Quarrels and recriminations were the rule, especially between the mother and herself, and there were many reciprocal threats of suicide. As early as her seventh year, the patient remembers standing on the sill of a window threatening to her mother that she would jump out. Death wishes against the mother were quite conscious and recurred frequently. The mother reacted to these quarrels with outbursts of crying and loss of appetite. The patient remembered frequent sexual activity, consisting of masturbation and genital play with children of both sexes, from an early period of life. These ceased abruptly when the patient became overwhelmed with a sense of guilt. The sexual activity was divorced from any knowledge of procreation, since the patient believed that procreation and pregnancy were, specifically and exclusively, brought about by the acts of kissing and eating. At the age of twelve, the patient suddenly became aware of the relation between genital sexuality and pregnancy. A neighbor had told her that intercourse was necessary for pregnancy and that all people practiced it. Until that time, she had thought that a child was a natural result of marriage. Her impression had been that eating and kissing were in some way directly connected with pregnancy and the thought that her own parents indulged in sexual intercourse disgusted her. This attitude was reflected in her eating habits, either in refusal of, or overindulgence in, food. Sometimes she ate everything in sight, not because she was hungry, but because of an insatiable craving. She would continue to eat until she felt pain in her stomach. Her stomach seemed very heavy and large, as if it were "sticking out." She then waited in fearful tension. She would look at her protruding navel and expect the appearance of a baby. On one occasion when she was distended, she was convinced that she had given birth to a baby boy, although she did not see it afterwards. She merely wondered why her child seemed to have no father. During recent years she had stayed up until two or three o'clock in the morning with the conscious intention of keeping her parents from having sexual intercourse; this behavior had become particularly intensified during the course of her illness. By remaining awake and having recourse to a ritualistic type of drinking, she forced her mother to stay awake with her, usually for the purpose of urging her not to drink so much, to eat, or to go to sleep.

With the persistence of the amenorrhea, the patient began to feel that she was abnormal and that her autoerotic practices of childhood were responsible for this abnormality. During this adolescent period her attitude toward genital sexuality was further colored by constant maternal admonition that sex was a dirty and vilifying thing. She had a marked interest in boys, however, and indulged particularly in kissing, with a good deal of enjoyment. Tongue-kissing always evoked a feeling of repulsion and nausea. During this period of awakening heterosexual interest and fully three years before the formal complaint of overeating, the patient already sporadically showed the signs of compulsive eating and ritual purification. Bouts of eating usually occurred in the afternoon immediately preceding a date with a boy in the evening. She would return from school and eat large quantities of cake, pastry, and candy to such an extent that her mother began to hide these things. She maintained that this eating was an attempt to overcome a "nervous feeling," evidently anxiety, and she would continue to eat until there was abdominal pain and distention, usually accompanied by fantasies of pregnancy. There was a concomitant marked increase in fluid intake and, at every meal or party, it was noticed that the patient drank three to four times as much fluid as her companions. Her rationalization was that, because of constipation, which had been present since earliest childhood, poisons had accumulated and these would be washed away by the large fluid intake.

At the age of sixteen the patient became attached to a boy, two years her senior, whom she described as impulsive and sexually attractive. There were marked parental objections to this boy and the father forbade her to see him, saying, "I would rather see her dead than married to him." The mother also forbade their meeting. She, however, would see him surreptitiously and indulged in a good deal of kissing. In spite of parental opposition, she continued her relationship for about a year; this resulted in quarrels and vilification particularly on the part of the father who, at times, attempted to hit her. Gradually, the boy drifted away.

With the break-up of this affair there was a definite change in the patient's behavior. She became seclusive, slept late in the morning, and began to eat even more. The increase in weight began shortly after this event. The patient stated that she ate continuously, because she felt a need to keep her mouth going and also that eating served the purpose of driving thoughts away from her mind. In spite of this, her fantasies continually centered about this boy.

About a year before admission to the hospital, the patient was introduced to a man eleven years her senior, whose economic status was secure. This man was quite settled, reserved, and distinctly unromantic. Her parents were "crazy about him." She, however, disliked him intensely. In spite of this she was forced to go out with him, although, whenever he touched her, she would shiver with disgust. Finally, some four months after the meeting, they were engaged to be married. One month after the engagement her fiancé attempted sexual intercourse with her in a rather crude way and she reacted with a feeling of nausea which has recurred every time the episode was recalled. After the engagement the patient's aversion to eating gradually began. This was not so much a lack of appetite as a distinct repulsion to food. Although her parents constantly emphasized the fact that her fiancé "would make such a good husband," she was exceedingly repelled by him, particularly because he reminded her so much of her father. The patient felt that sexual intercourse was unnecessary. After giving up the first boy, she became ashamed of her obesity. Later, when she had lost so much weight, one of the reasons for refusing to eat was a fear of aggravating the constipation and hence causing "piles." This fear was based on the fact that the mother had developed piles when she was pregnant with the patient. Another reason she gave for her illness was the jealousy of her female cousins who had always envied her beauty and social success.

During the last two months the patient quite consciously used her lack of eating to provoke the mother and, also, to test the loyalty of her fiancé. The father was very angry with her because of her loss of weight and, on some occasions, would accuse her of being ugly and like a skeleton; he wished she were dead rather than look the way she did. In the light of her "ugly appearance" the patient frequently wondered how long the fiancé would continue to love her and, if he did continue to love her in spite of her loss of beauty, this would be "true love." On leaving the hospital the patient continued her engagement and made plans to marry.

The alternation between bulimia and anorexia, in the patient's own words, expressing indulgence or refusal of the underlying fantasies or illustrating the interaction of her own and her mother's neuroses, became apparent in some of the interviews.

My mother would say something to me, if she was mad, like, "I want you to get out of this house," or, "I hate you," or "I don't want to see you before my eyes any more." She said these things because I didn't eat and she got disgusted. She wanted me to gain weight and I was losing. So that is the story. As soon as she would tell me to eat, I used to get so nervous that I couldn't eat.

Her reaction to her first boy friend, reflected in her eating habits, was put in the following words:

I liked him very much. I know that I shouldn't, but I couldn't help it. He liked what I liked and he was crazy about me. He was more emotional. He would give me a push and then take me in his arms and kiss me. Then I wanted to eat all the time. To have something in my mouth, so that I would be occupied, doing something. I did not want to think, so I used to eat. When my mother made me stop going with this boy, I used to eat to keep myself from thinking about him. But it certainly took me a long time and a lot of suffering, because I got so fat. I dreamt I had a child of his. I liked him and had to stop seeing him.

About the present boy friend, to whom she reacted with anorexia, she said: Now I have another boy friend, a nice boy. I didn't like him at first, although my parents liked him. I went with him because my parents said he was a wonderful person. I went with him on account of them. At the beginning it was terrible. I used to fight with my parents. I used to say I was not in love with him. And they said that I should keep on seeing him. I didn't care for him, I just didn't feel akin to him. He is so quiet, so settled, reserved and sure about his job. He kisses me, too, and takes me around, but he is different. I don't feel those emotions for him.

I was a pretty girl, but now I am skinny. Everything changed. My hair was oily and thick and now it is so dry and it is falling out. Hair on my hands, I never had it like that. And on my body too. I don't eat enough. I don't even care for my boy friend. He was here to see me this afternoon. If it was any other boy, well, I got so homely. He should not kiss me. I used to be pretty, but I kept on losing weight. But he kept on seeing me. He hopes now and my mother too.

Although her appetite and reaction to food improved, other compulsive symptoms remained, particularly the insistence upon a large fluid intake and staying awake late into the night.

It is of interest that in addition to the mother's reaction to quarrels by depression and lack of appetite, the youngest child developed vomiting and abdominal pain whenever the mother insisted on disciplinary measures.

In this patient the fantasies centering around impregnation through eating were present with particular clarity in her consciousness and persisted from her childhood.

In summary, the patient was a young woman of nineteen years, born in this country of European ancestry, who showed a cycle of compulsive eating with increase of weight, followed by a disgust for food with a marked weight loss, a persistent amenorrhea with only three scanty menstrual periods under endocrine therapy and a history of constipation dating back to childhood. There was also sexual activity, consisting of masturbation and genital play during early childhood, abruptly terminating at the age of eight because of a marked sense of guilt, with a recrudescence during puberty. However, her reaction to genital sexuality was one of disgust and nonacceptance. Sexual theories of procreation centered almost entirely around a fantasy of oral impregnation. Jealousy of her parents' sexual life was well marked and attempts to keep them separated were quite open. The mother's attitude toward the feeding problem, with an obsessive insistence upon eating, went back to the patient's earliest childhood, at which time the act of eating already symbolized impregnation. With the revival of her old neurotic difficulties as represented by her present illness, these old patterns again played an important role in the symptom formation. The present conflicts, which could not be solved normally because of the original unsatisfactory solution of the family problems, caused a regression to childhood with acting out of the old neurotic conflicts. The family constellation, centering around the problems of eating and the gastrointestinal tract, seemed also to play an important part in the choice of the patient's neurosis. The opportunity for a normal heterosexual adjustment by the patient, apparently attempted with her first boy friend, was frustrated by the reactions of her parents, particularly the father. This pressure played a part in driving the patient into an overt neurotic reaction and a revival of old patterns of behavior. It should be noted that the marked conflict and hostility with the mother played an important role.

The patient gained weight rapidly while in the hospital and continued to do so, but more slowly, during the first two months of the psychiatric study. During this period she was happier and had fewer quarrels with her family. The engagement to the older man was broken. After this initial improvement the patient began to regress, became seclusive, anxious, fought frequently with both parents, stayed up until five or six o'clock each morning, and began to decrease her non-too-large intake of food. At present the patient is preoccupied with thoughts of intercourse with, and rape by, every male, including her younger brother and uncle, with whom she has recently come in contact. It is felt that no improvement can be hoped for until the patient is given insight and placed in an environment removed from her mother.

Discussion

The parallels in the environment and in the fantasy life in both of these female patients is rather striking. In both patients there is a certain relationship to the father characterized by a need for affection and a resultant rivalry with the mother. It is important to note that the fantasy concerning the role of the gastrointestinal tract in the function of procreation is similar. The symbolism of eating as impregnation is quite clear and unambiguous; both patients, in their own words, express this in one way or another. The rivalries and hostilities which occur in the family and outside relationships are channeled into this overt conflict centering around food.

The compulsive, ritualistic behavior seen in both patients is related specifically to deep psychological mechanisms, the nature of which need not be discussed at the moment. One aspect, however, the ritualistic cleansing, is worthy of note. This is expressed by increased fluid intake or frequent washing of hands. The personality structure in both patients follows the lines recognized as compulsive-obsessive.

We see, then, a syndrome the main symptoms of which represent an elaboration and acting out in the somatic sphere of a specific type of fantasy. The wish to be impregnated through the mouth which results, at times, in compulsive eating, and at other times, in guilt and consequent rejection of food, the constipation symbolizing the child in the abdomen and the amenorrhea as direct psychological repercussion of pregnancy fantasies. This amenorrhea may also be part of the direct denial of genital sexuality.

The factors previously reported, as analyzed in the introduction, are all present in the two cases presented above, in addition to the similarity of the fantasy life and deep psychological mechanisms. The importance of each of these previously enumerated points varies with the individual under consideration; thus in Case 1 the older brother played a large role in the acting out of the family neurosis, whereas in the other case the role of the mother predominated in the environmental neurosis. Overeating and gluttony preceded the anorexia in each case and the latter also became manifest in each patient at the time of attempted marital adjustment.

The secondary gain in the neurosis is also quite clear. The illness allowed the patient to obtain affection, to be the center of the family, to work out hostilities, and to provoke the environment to certain acts of punishment which alleviated the guilt.

The problem of specificity of the syndrome, and the choice of the somatic locus in which the psychosomatic syndrome plays itself out, is a problem which still requires a good deal of investigation. Certain suggestions may be tentatively put forward. The syndrome involves not a physiological system, but rather a functionally co-ordinated unit subjectively important to the patient. In other words, it is not the system, but the functions in terms of the patient's fantasies, that are important. The role of the fantasy of oral impregnation in our patients is quite clear, with the mouth as the receptive organ of food symbolizing conception, the gastrointestinal tract symbolizing the womb and the cessation of menstruation being associated with pregnancy.

The pressure of the family constellation, with its complementary neurotic conflicts, played an important if not decisive role. In our own two patients, one can see clearly another element. With the onset of puberty, the opportunity for a normal heterosexual adjustment, with its usually correlated reduction of frustration and hostility toward the parental figures, was blocked. As a result of this frustration there was an intensification and revival of old conflicts and old patterns of behavior, so that the neurotic solution, involving regression to a childhood level, became the one of choice under the stress of internal and external circumstances.

REFERENCES

1. Deutsch, F.: The associative anamnesis. *Psychoanal. Quart.,* 8:354, 1939. Abstracted in *Psychosom. Med.,* 2:88, 1940.
2. Farquharson, R. F. & Hyland, H. H.: Anorexia nervosa, a metabolic disorder of psychologic origin. *This Volume,* p.   .
3. Gee, S.: *Medical Lectures and Clinical Aphorisms.* London: Oxford University Press, 1908.
4. Gull, W. W.: The address on medicine. *This Volume,* pp. 104-127.
5. ———: Anorexia nervosa. *This Volume,* pp. 139-140.
6. ———: Anorexia nervosa (Apepsia hysterica, anorexia hysterica). *This Volume,* pp. 132-138.
7. Hartland, E. S.: *Primitive Paternity. The Myth of Supernatural Birth in Relation to the History of the Family.* London: David Nutt, 1909.
8. Morton, R.: *Phthisiologia, or a Treatise of Consumptions.* London: Smith & Walford, 1694. Quoted by Ryle, J. A.: Anorexia nervosa. *Lancet,* 2:893, 1936.
9. Rahman, L.; Richardson, H. B.; & Ripley, H. S.: Anorexia nervosa with psychiatric observations. *Psychosom. Med.,* 1:335, 1939.
10. Richardson, H. B.: Simmonds' disease and anorexia nervosa. *Arch. Int. Med.,* 63:1, 1939.
11. Stephens, L. E. W.: Case of anorexia nervosa. *Lancet,* 1:31, 1895.

A PSYCHOSOMATIC STUDY OF ANOREXIA NERVOSA INCLUDING THE USE OF VAGINAL SMEARS

RUTH MOULTON, M.D.
(1942)

This clinical report of four cases with relatively long psychotherapeutic interviews led the author to confirm the hypothesis (Waller, Kaufman and Deutsch, 26) that in Anorexia Nervosa oral impregnation fantasies were dramatized through starvation, vomiting, and amenorrhea.

The vaginal smear technique of Papanicolaou and Shorr was used to investigate the endocrine ovarian status; the percentage cornification in the smear was used as an estimate of estrogen activity. The periods of cyclic vomiting were associated with increased cornification which is evidence of increased estrogen activity.

This study demonstrates the application of a newly discovered technique (Papanicolaou, 14) in the psychic and hormonal correlation of a psychosomatic disturbance. Thus the author was able to demonstrate that a woman with sexual conflict was more comfortable when her genital tract was in a "quiescent, more infantile, less differentiated state of sexuality, to correspond with her infantile state of mind."

Although the syndrome is explicable to the author on the basis of oral impregnation fantasies, she nevertheless attempted to correlate the physiology of the individual with the psychic state of the individual, and she found that when she gave one of the patients estrogen in order to bring on the menses, the tension was intensified. She therefore drew the conclusion that because there was a conflict over genital sexuality, i.e., the problem of pregnancy, the artificial intensification through hormonal therapy intensified the psychic conflict. This involves the question of whether the inferences the author made have any validity, and the whole problem of the hormonal cycle in relation to the psyche.

Does a fantasy related to pregnancy involve primarily genital sexuality as inferred by the author, or as her clinical material indicates, primarily focus on orality? If the latter is true, does any fantasy of function—in this instance, pregnancy—relate psychophysiologically to the basic functions involved in the physiology of pregnancy regardless of whether the fantasy of impregnation is per orum or per vagina?

The question raised by the second problem—the relationship of the hormonal cycle to the psyche—has been elaborated in great detail by the work of Benedek and Rubenstein (3). This paper is of value because the more refined techniques available at this time made possible certain types of observations and data at a level which was not heretofore possible. The correlative studies would seem to indicate that the psychophysiological response of the organism carried through in detail the pattern already observed in grosser form, namely, the somatic simulation of a pregnancy fantasy.

Anorexia nervosa is a fascinating syndrome which is particularly suitable to psychosomatic research because of the obvious metabolic and endocrine changes associated with the neurotic mechanisms. The correlation between the self-imposed starvation of the adolescent girl who has pregnancy fantasies and the accompanying physical changes, such as amenorrhea, is more accessible to investigation than more obscure psychosomatic interrelationships. Permanent therapeutic cures have been singularly difficult to achieve and not only has reversal of organic changes often been unsuccessful, but death has ensued.

The syndrome is essentially one of aversion to food, bodily vigor out of proportion to the extreme emaciation, amenorrhea or potency disturbances in the male, very low basal metabolism, low fasting blood

---

Reprinted from *Psychosomatic Medicine*, 4:62-74, 1942.

sugar, and many signs of dehydration. It is predominantly a disease of young women, although it has been described in men and older women. Since Gull's original description in 1874, many cases have been collected (4, 5, 12), and the literature has been adequately reviewed (16, 19). In the past, it has been a diffuse symptom complex, frequently confused with Simmond's disease, and the role of endocrines has been overemphasized in an attempt to find a tangible cause. This aspect has been recently discussed by Richardson (16). The possibility of an underlying pituitary anomaly has been pointed out by Sheldon (20), who stresses signs of sexual underdevelopment, masculine hirsuties, adolescent obesity, and asthenic habitus, which antedate the illness. He suggests either that the neurosis occurs in those with a constitutional predisposition to pituitary dysfunction, or that there is a "pituitary blackout of psychological origin." Modern emphasis has been on the psychogenic origin (15, 26). When mentioned in textbooks of psychiatry, it is usually considered to be a conversion hysteria. Nicolle (13) considers it a manifestation of latent schizophrenia, and shows how it differs from hysteria in that the patient does not want attention, is very negativistic, and really wants to starve. Recently, the obsessive-compulsive features have been stressed (26), and were found to be predominant in six of seven well-studied cases (15). Cases referred from a medical service to psychiatry are often simple anorexia as caused by superficial anxiety (15). Waller, Kaufman, and Deutsch (26) discuss carefully the specific psychological events leading to the neurosis, which they consider to be a psychosomatic entity with the symbolization of pregnancy fantasies through the gastrointestinal tract. They give two detailed cases, which show how the wish for oral impregnation leads to compulsive eating followed by the rejection of food and ritualistic cleansing due to guilt. Menses are suppressed as the result of pregnancy fantasies, and the child in the abdomen is expressed through constipation. Parental emphasis on food is outstanding, and desire for affection from the father leads to rivalry with the mother.

In order to study the mechanism of amenorrhea in anorexia nervosa, it was necessary to find a technic for evaluating the sexual endocrine imbalance in order to correlate the latter with emotional factors. Vaginal smears seem to be the only practical technic available for use over a long period of time. Papanicolaou (14) originally described the typical changes in women during the ovarian cycle as reflected in the histology of the vaginal epithelial cells. In brief, when estrogen predominated, the cells were intact, discreet, largely cornified, and associated with a few leucocytes. When progesterone predominated, the cells were folded, clumped together, fragmented, and associated with many leucocytes. Ovulation was marked by a sudden outpouring of leucocytes and a few erythrocytes. The estrogen effect is maximal at ovulation when the follicle ruptures, and premenstrually when new follicles are growing.

There is controversy as to the validity of the method and the question is raised as to whether smears are accurate criteria of active blood estrogen (7). However, endocrinologists have as yet found no satisfactory solution to the problem of how much estrogen found by any method is active and how much is merely an excretory product. There has been particular discussion as to whether ovulation can be determined by smears, but this is not a problem here, as the cyclic changes are themselves pertinent regardless of ovulation, which presumably would not be occurring with amenorrhea. Good correlation has been found between the histology of the vaginal mucosa as found on biopsy and the cytology on vaginal smears (8). Comparison has also been made with urinary estrogen assays (18). Another objection that has been raised is that estrus in animals cannot be regarded as an entity, but is of composite nature, as the ovary secretes several estrogenic hormones, some of which cause much more cornification of the vaginal smears than others (7). It has been suggested that cornification is secondary to hyperemia, as it can be induced by such nonspecific hyperemic agents as yohimbine (9). Since several estrus phenomena are related to hyperemia, it has been suggested that they must be under control of the parasympathetic nervous system, which might also cause symptoms of mental and emotional instability. This has many psychosomatic implications by giving a mechanism for the physical expression of emotional factors.

By the use of vaginal smears, Benedek and Rubenstein (3) studied the correlation of ovarian activity with psychodynamic processes. In the estrogen-dominated follicular phase of the cycle, there was increased heterosexual desire of an active nature, which might be expressed by the neurotic in a defensive or masochistic way. Progesterone dominance was associated with passive, receptive ideas and pregnancy fantasies. Physiologically, the changes which occurred then are in preparation for pregnancy should fertilization have taken place, so it seems reasonable that psychic conflicts over pregnancy should be greatest at that time. In the secondary peak of estrogen preceding menstruation, the active heterosexual tendency recurs often combined with the tendencies characteristic for the diminishing progesterone production. The premenstrual withdrawal of progesterone is correlated with eliminative tendencies. This might be expressed as genital eliminative tendency, such as fantasies of labor and childbirth, fantasies of bleeding from the genitals; it might be expressed also by oral elimination —nausea and vomiting—or by elaborations of anal eliminative tendency.

Method of Study

This study was originally conceived because of the interesting correlation discovered in Case 1, namely, that cyclic vomiting occurred monthly, apparently at the time of the missed menstrual period. The patient had a well-formed hysterical pattern, that was modified very little by psychotherapy and could be observed over a long period of time lasting from March 1940 to August 1941, a total of 18 months. The patient was weighed every two days and a careful chart kept of her mood, activities, appetite and symptomatology. Psychiatric interviews were four to five times weekly during the first six months, and then three times a week with casual visits more frequently. Vaginal smears were started in August 1940 and were taken by a nurse daily until October 16, 1940. On November 1, they were continued at the rate of three per week until July 1941, except for the month of January, when they were again done daily, in attempts to find signs of ovulation, which were lacking. Rectal temperatures were also taken at the time of the smear (6 A. M.) in view of Rubenstein's work (17) showing that there is a drop of basal body temperature at the time of ovulation, followed by a characteristic rise. A premenstrual rise in temperature is also described. Of the first five months before smears were taken, only the chart for May 1940 is reproduced as being typical, in that its biphasic weight curve correlated with two vomiting attacks.

The smears in Case 1 showed evidence of moderate continuous estrogen activity, as the cells were of the intermediate type rather than of the basal type, and were distinct, well-formed, and partly cornified. The percentage of cornification was taken as the best and only quantitative measure of the level of estrogen activity, and cyclic increases in this were found to coincide with, or just precede, vomiting attacks. The quiescent level of cornification between attacks was 2-10 per cent, with definite increase during attacks to 25-40 per cent. These peaks are indicated on the graph of Case 1. They were thought to be of significant magnitude because they consisted of at least a 20 per cent increase in cornification, while the margin of error in estimating each smear was about 5 per cent as shown by rechecking. In an attempt to achieve objectivity, the smears were read and the percentage of cornification recorded without any reference to date or nursing notes as to clinical symptoms. It was only after cyclic variation in the vaginal smears was found, that correlations between the two separately collected series of data were attempted.

All intramuscular injections were given in the buttock and made to appear identical to the patient. Sterile sesame oil injections were first given in November 1940 as a control for future endocrine injections. Testosterone was then given to neutralize the effects of estrogen, as this action of the latter has been described by Shorr (21). By this means the vaginal smear can be reversed; the cells become basal in type, and cornification with other signs of estrogen activity disappears. This is what happened with this case, and basal cells were seen in the smear for twenty days following cessation of testosterone.

Smears were also taken three times a week on Case 3 for five months, but no cyclic changes were found, the smears being of the atrophic type, described as being typical of primary amenorrhea and severe secondary amenorrheas (22). Only a small percentage of the amenorrheas studied by Shorr and Papanicolaou were of the follicular type with irregular cyclic changes as in Case 1. Smears were taken for 15 days on Case 2, and unfortunately had to be stopped because of her discharge. Cases 2 and 4 were not treated psychotherapeutically by the writer. All smears were stained by the new modification of the Masson trichome technic described by Shorr (23). The smears were made with the use of a glass pipette as originally described by Papanicolaou (14).

Case 1

This sixteen-year-old girl entered the hospital in March 1940 because of periodic attacks of vomiting since the age of twelve and one half. Her background was one of quarreling and deprivation in the lower East Side slums. Her parents were foreign-born orthodox Jews. The father was a hypochondriacal mental defective who was irritable, mildly psychotic, and unemployed for years. The mother was a deaf mute who spoke only almost unintelligible Yiddish, and was domineering and overprotective. The nine-year-old brother had borderline intelligence, and the patient was found to have an Intelligence Quotient of 84. Her physical development had been slow, with teething at twelve months, walking at fifteen months, and enuresis persisting for years. Her childhood was very unhappy, with an inconsistent nagging mother who obviously preferred the brother and forced the patient to act as her interpreter and carry the responsibility of shopping for the family. The child was embarrassed about both parents, although she pitied her mother. All of the relatives looked down on the family, and patient always felt "like mud under their feet." Her only social opportunities were through settlements, where she was shy, fearful, and resentful. She was suspicious of hospitals, as her previous experiences had been futile.

Examination showed a disheveled, forlorn girl, undernourished and of asthenic habitus. She was interested only in her somatic complaints, constantly whined, answered questions coherently but with much evasiveness and blocking. Her weight was 82 lbs. She had never weighed over 90 lbs. and had not menstruated since December 1938. Muscular development was poor; hands and feet were abnormally small; breasts were quite small; there was excess hair on the upper lip and back. Vaginal examination merely showed a hypoplastic uterus. Barium meal revealed moderate intestinal hypomotility, and a film of the heart showed it to be abnormally small. There was a tendency to right axis deviation in the electrocardiogram. Basal metabolic rate was –25 to –30. X rays of chest, skull, and spine were normal, as were blood and urine studies. Acne of the face was marked, but was seen to clear up considerably between vomiting attacks. These lasted from three to eight days and occurred twice a month for the first four months. Short sporadic attacks were definitely precipitated by a visit from the family, as the patient was thereby reminded of "disgusting things at home that make me nauseous." Visits were then curtailed for as long as three months at a time.

The attacks followed quite a uniform pattern. For days before, the patient would be overactive, loud, aggressive, hypercritical, and quite talkative, compared with her usual shy sullenness. Her appetite would be increased, especially for sweets, and occasionally she would gorge herself. Prodromal restlessness caused her to pace the floor, looking glum and depressed, with no interest in the environment. Loss of appetite would be followed in a day by nausea, dryness of the mouth, and a bad taste as though she would "have to spit." There would be a "sticking sensation" in the chest, the throat would feel blocked, and the stomach "glued together" or "full as though there were something inside that had to come out." There would also be a "sticking or burning sensation" in the vagina, perspiration about the perineum, and complaint of vaginal discharge, occasionally noted to be blood-tinged. Patient often wondered if this came out of the rectum. Abdominal pain occurred, which was likened to menstrual cramps, and the patient said that "gas came out" of her vagina. Loose stools occurred two to four times a day at first, but after vomiting started, there would be constipation. Vomiting at first was spontaneous, but was then induced by drinking large quantities of water and by putting the whole hand down the throat and moving it back and forth rhythmically. She bent over double while walking and curled up in bed in the fetal position. The burning sensation in the stomach was relieved by vomiting. Sometimes the patient would move her hips up and down on the bed in a definitely erotic way, and occasionally exposed herself, although she was usually excessively modest. Her general behavior was most infantile, as she sought attention in obvious ways, begged for medicine, for injections and for more water. When secluded in order to prevent excessive drinking, she would often be very noisy and bang on the door. As the attack wore off, she complained of fullness in the head, of being unable to think, of feeling dead and "not human." In several of the later attacks, she was dazed, unapproachable and had a clouded memory for the period, as though in a hysterical twilight state.

The sexual fantasies underlying this characteristic behavior pattern were slowly worked out, although the patient was very resistant and would accept their significance only when she felt well. Hypnosis was tried by several physicians, but was actively resisted by the patient. Sodium amytal was used to facilitate interviews twice. The most important dynamic material was the following: The first memory was of seeing her brother's circumcision when she was four years old. Soon after, when at a convalescent home to gain weight, she cried from homesickness and refused food. Her brother was dead when she came home, and she never forgave her family for lying to her about it. At the age of five, she was very upset by seeing her father undressed, and would beg her mother to sleep with her because she was afraid. She had a fear of burglars, particularly once when she heard a noise in her father's bedroom. She objected strenuously to going to school and vomited her breakfast every morning for several years, so that her mother would bring her food in the middle of the morning. The brother now living was born when she was eight years old; she had wanted a sister and was very jealous of the pampering the mother gave him. She recalled with horror a little girl spitting in her mouth, but dates her oral conflict to an episode occurring at the age of twelve and one half. A man watched her and stuck his tongue in and out of his mouth, whereupon she ran away for fear he would kidnap her and put his penis in her mouth. Shortly after this, while in the country with her aunt, she remembered the incident and vomited the next day for the first time since the age of eight, whereupon she had to come home. Two minor attacks occurred that fall. The next spring, on the first day of her first menses, March 10, 1937, a "janitor slapped me on the behind and I thought I would have a child." The next periods were on April 25 and June 21, and she vomited on two of these three. Vomiting then occurred with her periods, or in place of them, until the last one on December 18, 1938. Since then they were precipitated by excitement, and became so frequent that she had to stop in her second year of high school in May 1939.

To complete the fellatio fantasy, the patient explained that she thought that if a girl were merely touched by a man during her menses, she would become pregnant. She had believed in oral impregnation, thinking that the baby grew in the stomach and had to be cut out. Vomiting, she knew, was a sign of pregnancy, and she thought of it as a means of getting rid of the "sticky" semen and of the baby that made her stomach feel full. She later thought that urine, feces, and babies all came out through one opening. When asked to draw a picture of the stomach, she connected it crudely with the vagina in front and the rectum behind.

There were two attacks in each of the first four months, averaging from days 8-12 and 24-28 each month. (See graph for month of May 1940.)

This suggested a relation to the two main peaks of the ovarian cycle, ovulation and menstruation. The second attack was most severe, and the first one was dropped out beginning July 1940. The September attack was delayed and extended into the first of October; thereafter the main attack was at the beginning of each month. Control injections of sterile oil were begun November 26. The patient was very suggestible, and had previously been told that injections would ameliorate symptoms and induce menses. Two days later she had a mild attack, probably due to a visit from her family. Eighteen days later, after the eighth injection, she menstruated for the first time in two years. There was merely a scanty flow of brown, hemolysed

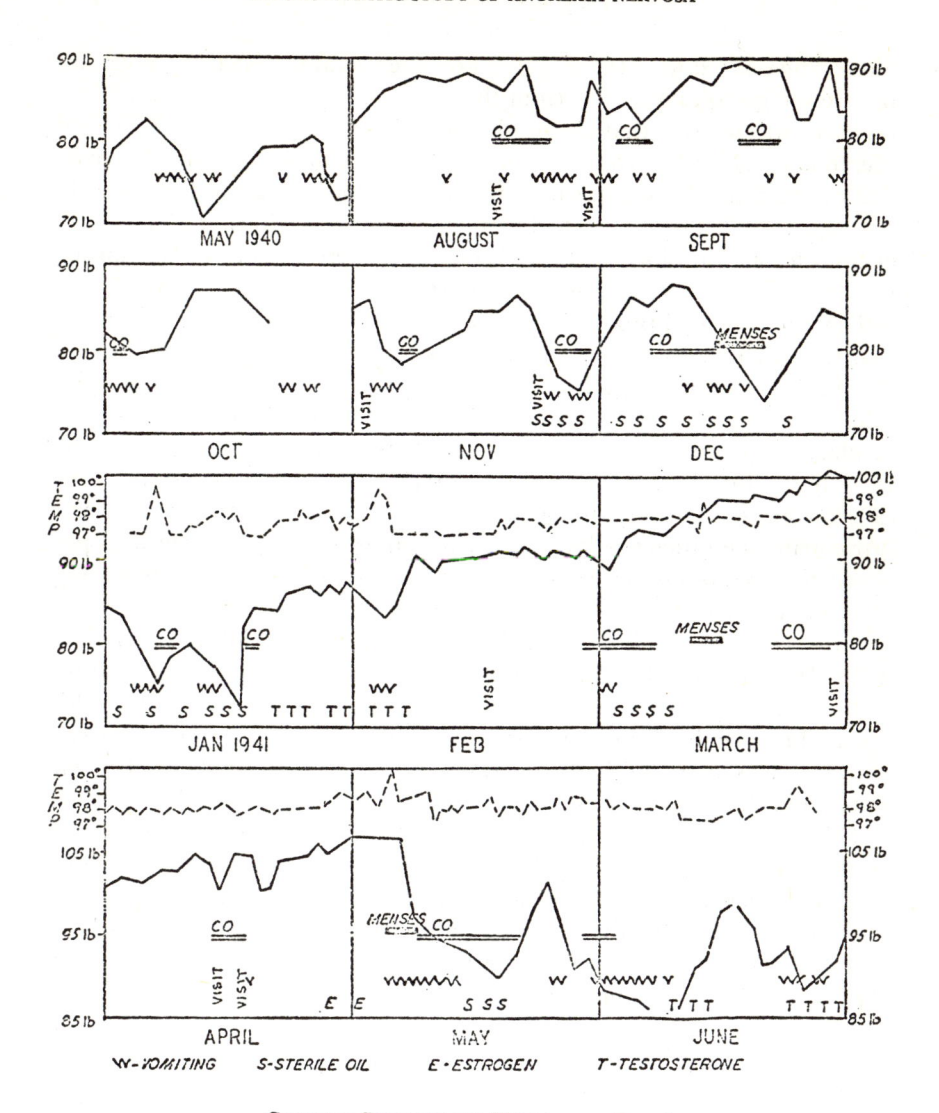

CHART OF PROGRESS AND THERAPY IN CASE 1

The solid line represents the weight in pounds as plotted against days of the month. Basal body temperature each morning for last six months is shown by the dotted line across the upper part of the graphs. Vomiting attacks are represented by a series of v's, vvv. Visits with relatives are indicated by the word "visit." Intramuscular injections are shown by the letters S, E, T, given so as to seem the same to the patient. Marked peaks of increased cornification in the vaginal smear are labeled CO and the duration shown by the double line. Symptoms and anorexia were marked during most of May 1941, even when actual vomiting was absent.

blood. She reacted with the fear that now she was able to become pregnant in case she got sperm on her from the chairs or from boys' hands. Embarrassment was so great that she blushed whenever spoken to, as she thought everyone detected her condition by odor and sight. Sterile oil was given during the January attack, which was shorter and milder, but menses did not recur. From January 20 to February 7, nine injections of 25 mg. each of testosterone propionate (Ciba Perandren), were given. Vaginal smears became very atrophic, with many basal cells and no cornification. The last of February, she had prodromal signs, but fought the attack off with more than usual control and only vomited twice the first two days of March. During the menstrual period that followed, she was symptom-free, presumably for the first time since the menarche. Improvement was then spectacular; weight rose to 106 lbs.; the family visit did not upset her, and she went home for the first time since entry thirteen months before. This caused vomiting for only twelve hours, April 17. During this period of improvement, the quiescent level of cornification, which had been 2-10 per cent before testosterone was given, was raised to 15-20 per cent during March and April.

On April 28 and May 1, she was given 1 mg. of estradiol diproprionate (Ciba, Di-ovacyclin). On May 4, vomiting began following severe cramps, and was more severe than any time in the preceding year. Menses also began. The peculiar conversion symptoms of burning, etc., did not occur until two days later, and in ten days, weight fell from 105 to 89 lbs. For ten more days, she refused to eat or get up although vomiting did not occur, and she seemed completely disillusioned. She begged for injections and sterile oil was finally given. Following this, she was well for four days, and then lapsed back into her vomiting pattern which continued another two weeks. Cornification in the smear had been from 50-80 per cent from May 5-14, and cells had been of the high follicular type. Cornification did not fall below 20 per cent until testosterone was given in June, in order to complete the experiment and relieve acute symptoms. Three injections of testosterone were given; vomiting ceased and weight began to rise after the first injection. However, when transferred to a convalescent floor, she again relapsed. This time, five injections of testosterone had little effect and she did not improve until she was moved back to the former floor, where she wanted to be, as she was accepted more by the other patients, and could adjust with less effort. She then remained well in July until the time she was to go to camp. She wanted to go very much, but this again was a threat to her delicate adjustment on a childish level. She was still unable to accept the psychogenic nature of her illness during an attack, and had no insight, confidence, or spirit of co-operation except when well. In her words, she was "just too stupid to catch on."

Case 2

This patient was a very capable and intelligent twenty-nine-year-old newspaperwoman, who had had attacks of vomiting for four years following a salpingectomy. She grew up in the East Side slums, suffering physical abuse from a domineering father from whom she ran away at the age of sixteen. Vomiting had occurred in childhood and recurred once following an abortion at age twenty-three. She later tried to conceive and found she was sterile. Four years before entry, a salpingectomy had been done for pain, and when patient learned that she was permanently sterile, she became "hysterical" and had a severe vomiting attack. Attacks became more frequent, usually a month apart, and were often related to premenstrual tension. There were two hospital admissions, a year apart, and both times patient entered in severe attacks with menses overdue. The only other attack observed was also premenstrual, although there were many menses without symptoms after therapy began. In an attack, she bent over double, drank much water compulsively, and vomited innumerable times a day. On examination, hair was abundant on the legs and of masculine pelvic distribution. Basal metabolism was -3 per cent and -9 per cent. There were no other physical findings, except weight of 93 lbs. instead of a normal of 120 lbs.

Under therapy, she discussed her great resentment of the feminine passive role which her father had forced on her mother. Her fear of pregnancy was based on resentment of this brutal father, yet she had a tremendous desire for it, wanting to "feel my breasts grow very large until the milk spurts from them," as she considered pregnancy the only worthwhile contribution a woman could make. Menses were associated with rape and childbirth trauma, and during three consecutive periods, she had fantasies of castrating men "to make up for their breeding and not menstruating." She wanted a penis herself, and had wanted to castrate her father to prevent his impregnating her mother. She had vomited when her father forced food on her as a child, and could not eat bananas, which she associated with a penis. She wanted to be close to her mother's breast because he had rejected her. Vomiting was a rejection of her father and was used to prevent marital intercourse. Ideas of oral impregnation were recalled, and in a dream a tremendous nipple was used as a phallic symbol, and was thrown away by a baby. Patient was discharged to a private analyst in a state of remission, having been hospitalized five months the first time and three months the second. Weight gain was from 88 to 110 lbs. Unfortunately, vaginal smears could only be taken for two weeks before discharge, and are discussed below.

Comment

The second case is given as a comparison with the first, as the vomiting attacks were descriptively very similar in the two cases. Vomiting in both represented rejection of the incorporated phallus and the feared oral pregnancy, which was an aggressive attack as well as a masochistic expiation. This is similar to the mechanisms in Masserman's case (11). There was ritualistic compulsive cleansing with water, as described by Waller, Kaufman and Deutsch (26). The aggressive taking, and the passive receiving, aspects of eating, have been differentiated by Alexander (2) as two types of oral dependence, the wish for which may be denied by vomiting. The latter was induced manually by Case 1 in a rhythmic masturbatory way. Both cases were considered predominantly hysterical, with conversion symptoms, which they played up to the maximum for attention. Neither had any trouble eating between attacks, and Case 1 even gorged during the prodromal period, in contrast to the last two cases where there was a persistent phobia for food without vomiting. In spite of these similarities one was an adolescent girl with borderline mentality and the other a married woman of high intelligence. In thirty-three cases in women under thirty, Ryle found only one married (19).

Vomiting attacks were primarily premenstrual in both cases. The few smears taken in Case 2 following a period were normal in the follicular phase. Cornification was 60-90 per cent during the first few days, when patient was getting over an attack and still vomiting; it then dropped to 25-35 per cent when she was well. This proves nothing, but is suggestive, since it is similar to the correlation shown more clearly in Case 1. Here, all vomiting attacks were found correlated with marked increase in cornification in the smears (exceptions on the graph are May 1940 before smears were started, and the end of October when smears were stopped for fifteen days). This endocrine response was inhibited in February and June by giving testosterone. These attacks were originally twice a month, apparently correlated with the ovulatory and premenstrual peaks of estrogen. Then there was only one at the beginning of the month, definitely premenstrual in December and March. The December menstrual period, the first since December 1938, seems to have been precipitated by suggestion with sterile oil. Testosterone was given to neutralize the estrogen, with dramatic improvement for three months the first time, and more transient improvement later. Two injections of estrogen caused the most prolonged attack observed with cornification and hysterical symptoms for a month. The patient seemed to respond with her hysterical pattern to the uterine cramps and possibly other sensations from her sexual organs, resulting from the estrogen. It is possible that she might have an unusual physical response to a small dose of estrogen, but certainly a normal, non-neurotic person would never have this psychologically significant overreaction. Testosterone gave complete freedom from uterine cramps, and a regressive vaginal smear. One would expect a patient with great sexual conflict to be more comfortable when not reminded of her problem by any sexual sensations, even though these might not be any greater than those unnoticed by a normal person. Such a patient would be more comfortable with her genital tract in a quiescent, more infantile, less differentiated state of sexuality, to correspond with her infantile state of mind. It is interesting to note that the following dream occurred in Case 1 after estrogen was given and her breasts were slightly larger. She dreamt of herself as being nine years old and being mauled by older boys because of sexual development beyond her years, which she wished she did not have. She said afterwards that she was happiest at that age, when she was sexless.

No endocrine status could be considered a specific prerequisite to attacks, as these were also caused by emotional disturbances, such as visits from unwelcome relatives. A higher level of estrogen was tolerated in March, as well as menstrual period. Apparently the marked improvement in the month and a half since testosterone had encouraged her to more mature control. Thus estrogen could only be acting as a precipitating agent whose removal might temporarily help, but could not cure the patient.

The weight curves in Case 1 are interesting in respect to work that has been done on premenstrual edema. Monkeys show increased weight and swelling of the sexual skin preceding estrus, which is related to estrogen activity. There is a sharp increase in the excretion of urine with the subsidence of swelling after ovulation and again with the onset of menses (10). Peaks of estrogen occur with peaks of urine excretion. A study of 42 healthy women showed that 30 per cent gained over 3 lbs. during the menstrual cycle with the maximum just before the period (24). Cases have been reported in which there was a gain of 10-14 lbs. premenstrually, with headaches, increased spinal fluid pressures, occasional choked discs, and vomiting in one. Diuresis occurred with the onset of menses and anterior pituitary hormone gave improvement. The pattern remained following hysterectomy and unilateral ovariectomy. Nothing is given concerning the psychiatric status of the patients (25). It has been thought that this phenomenon of water metabolism might be controlled by the pituitary through the sympathetic nervous system, and might be responsible for many premenstrual complaints. Frank (6) has described premenstrual tension as being associated with high blood estrogen and decreased urinary estrogen output. Most of this patient's change in weight was associated with loss of food and water by vomiting, but increased excretion of water and dehydration were associated with increased cornification on the vaginal smears. Marked cyclic changes were found in the urine excretion by Dr. A. Barnett, whose unfortunate death recently made publication of these records impossible. Urine excretion was excessive during attacks, but was of normal type in February, March and April.

Interpretation of the curve of basal body temperature in Case 1 is not clear. Definite upswings above 99 degrees occurred twice during attacks, once during menstruation without an attack, once during menstruation with vomiting, and also when there was vomiting during testosterone injection. Increase in temperature is described premenstrually (17), but there is usually a drop during estrogen activity. It is possible that increased temperature during vomiting is merely the result of dehydration.

The next cases are given as examples of a different type of clinical picture without conversion symptoms or vomiting, but with a persistent phobia for food.

Case 3

This sixteen-year-old girl was hospitalized from August 1940 to February 1941, because of anorexia for six months, with weight loss from 130 to 70 lbs. The father was a tense, emotionally inadequate man, harassed by work, and unable to give adequate affection. The mother was emotionally unstable, inconsistent in her discipline, and alternated between nagging and overprotection. A nine-year-old sister had many phobias and was infantilized by the mother. The patient had four mastoid operations in childhood and poliomyelitis at age three, with residual atrophy and limp of the left leg. Her awareness of this defect was exaggerated by the overanxious mother. The patient was quite successful in grade school, writing poetry, editing a newspaper, composing plays. She was "bossy" with friends and obviously "spoiled." She was socially unhappy in high school and concentrated on getting superlative grades. A year before admission she dropped her friends, studied compulsively, overate, and was almost obese. Her mother was working, and the patient had increased household duties, including cooking. At Christmas 1939, she became convinced that she had flunked and refused to return to school. She began to diet and lied profusely about eating, forcing food on her sister. Menses stopped in February 1940, and she began to express hatred toward everyone, especially her mother. She gained a few pounds in June under threat of tube feeding in a private sanitarium, but lost again in July, when receiving insulin in another hospital.

Examination here showed such emaciation that her activity seemed remarkable. Acetone odor and dehydration were evident. There was excess soft hair over the upper arms and legs, and the left leg was shortened an inch with anterior tibial paralysis. Blood pressure was 84/72 and pulse was weak. Basal metabolism was -31 and -27. Blood sugar was 69 mg. per cent. Other laboratory work, including X rays of skull, was negative. The patient was completely oriented with an intelligence quotient of 121. She was ingratiating and almost euphoric, but very evasive and demanding. She was given a trial period of ten days with no emphasis on her eating, but weight fell from 70 to 66 lbs., and tube feedings were ordered, following meals which were not eaten. These were explained to her as a temporary emergency measure, but she dreaded them and only six were necessary. She was carefully watched as she would do away with food in any way possible, and was completely unreliable. Disciplinary management was handled separately by another physician, to aid transference and to prevent the therapeutic interview from being devoted to quibbling over orders.

Psychotherapy fell into three stages, the first being six weeks of extreme resistance. Four pounds were gained on initiation of tube feeding, but she then purposely stopped gaining, as she did not wish to get well. She was afraid of being fat like her mother and thought that fat exaggerated the difference between her two legs. There was real anxiety about eating, as she felt she could not swallow, would choke, and that her stomach was too small. She used Orthodox Jewish customs as an excuse, although she had not followed them previously. Food that came from animals, such as meat, milk, and eggs, was particularly revolting to her, as she had a fear of animals throughout childhood. "Slippery, slimy" food was most disgusting, as it was associated with pus from her mastoids, mucous in her throat, and finally with semen. This discovery had a remarkable beneficial effect, and initiated the period in which she actively participated in looking for emotional conflicts.

A second six-week period was one of exploration and improved attitude, but of little weight gain. She discussed her tremendous resentment toward her mother and her whole environment, where she felt "squelched." She had no friends, was afraid of boys, and the race for grades did not bring her happiness; she could only escape by wanting to fail. She blamed her mother (rightly in many respects) and determined to get revenge and attention by being an invalid. Food had been used as a bribe, and refusing to eat was always a method of punishing her mother. She had been a poor eater until her sister was born, and then overate to get more sweets than her sister, just as she wanted more love. She would munch food while studying to alleviate anxiety and loneliness. She concluded that rejecting food meant rejecting her mother, whom she hated and yet was dependent on. The physician was often seen as a threat, who might take her away from her mother. She wanted more love from her father, resented his interest in the mother, and had death dreams about the latter. Fears were recalled from childhood of being kidnapped by strange men who hid in her bedroom, or by women who bribed her with food. Enuresis and fear of the dark persisted until eleven years of age. There were fears of being bitten by a dog, and in adolescence she dreamt of riding a horse, falling off, and having it land on top of her. Her concept of sexual relations was sadistic and she feared physical affection. She admitted early ideas of oral impregnation and feared that fat on her abdomen meant pregnancy. Mushy food was disgusting, and she would pack it dry in the roof of her mouth and spit it out later. Food was finally associated with feces, and at this point she began to eat as though starved. She dreamt of being in a town made of food; the road was gingerbread, oatmeal poured out of a volcano, houses were made of cake, shoes of meat, a brook of milk with chocolate mud, and a woods of mint leaves. With the help of her mother, she was able to eat her way out through the walls and escape. This was interpreted as eating her way out of the hospital which is what she proceeded to do.

The last stage was one of rehabilitation, lasting from November till the patient was discharged in February. She gained 20 lbs. in a month, with final stabilization at 100 lbs. There was transient edema of legs and face, due to low serum protein. Basal metabolism rose to −8 and hairiness on legs and arms disappeared. She took piano lessons, modeled, knitted and edited a hospital newspaper. In December she tried returning to an outside school, but left the first day in a panic. She insisted that she would never return to a high school, but this was worked through as being another rejection of her mother. In February, she went to a commercial high school, joined clubs, made friends, and went out on dates with boys. Discussions centered around her domineering attitude at home, her fear of being unable to face the outside world, and her new, more mature, relation to her mother. She was resistant to deeper therapy, begged to go home, and agreed to continue therapy in clinic. She refused to return after four visits, although her mother continued social service interviews. She began to refuse food, and gradually lost weight to 80 lbs. Compulsive baking and cooking became more pronounced. She was recently readmitted, a year after her first admission, weighing 75 lbs. Her aversion to food had never returned, but her conflict with her mother had been so severe, that she expressed the desire to learn to support herself so that she could live in a girls' club apart from her family. She admitted continued insincerity during her previous hospitalization in order to "get back to home and mother."

Vaginal smears were done three times a week from the beginning of the second phase of therapy in October till clinic contact was broken in March. The first smears were of the atrophic type found in menopausal women and castrates, with many deep staining basal cells, mucous, and leucocytes. Gradual improvement in the smear was noted after Christmas, following the gain in weight. There was slight regression when patient was considering return to outside school in January, but there were no other cyclic changes. Beginning February 3, seven injections of 1 mg. estradioldiproprionates each, were given at the rate of two a week. There was no reaction except cramps two to three hours after each dose. Smears became highly follicular with 90 per cent cornification when last dose was given on March 10. Four days later, she began to menstruate for the first time in a year. Clinic contact was broken just at this time, and menstruation may have been a causal factor in her flight, although the accumulating strain of living at home two weeks must have been as important. The patient might have returned had not the mother, who was jealous of the doctor's influence, threatened readmission frequently. There have been no menses since.

Case 4

This fourteen-year-old girl was hospitalized from January to June 1940 because of inability to chew or swallow food for 18 months, since eating caused anxiety. Menses had been absent for two years and weight had dropped from 104 to 52 lbs. Both parents were oversolicitous, and the mother had been in a sanitarium for fourteen months because she became hysterical and suicidal over the patient's illness. There were two healthy daughters, aged seventeen and thirteen. The patient had been scholastically brilliant (intelligence quotient of 140), a good cellist and pianist, and wrote very well. Tube feedings were started in a hospital. The father learned to pass the tube and did so on his daughter at home about seven times a day for over a year. The girl did all the cooking and housework, nursed her sisters, lost all of her outside interests, and thus completely fulfilled the role of her mother. When tube feedings were stopped, she lost weight to 48 lbs. and became mute. When seen here three months later, she was completely oriented and alert, with no signs of physical abnormality, endocrine imbalance, or vitamin deficiency.

For the first five months in the hospital, she was tube-fed daily by different doctors. She said that "only daddy can put it down without hurting," and took it with passive disgust, meanwhile making obviously erotic pelvic movements. There was great resistance during the first six weeks of psychotherapy, and she merely expressed guilt about causing her mother's illness. The next three months she was much freer, realizing first aggression against her mother, and then death wishes. She recalled many pleasant associations with her father, a feeling of being "filled up" in his presence, a desire to keep her mother away from him, and the fact that illness had always meant the pleasure of being able to sleep in the same room with him. She wrote out many dreams during this period, some of which contained cavalry rushing at her with spears. On reaching 85 lbs., she again became resistant, and her mother returned home as well. She wanted to flee from therapy, so decided to eat without tubing. She did so, and the parents insisted on taking her home when she weighed 68 lbs. There have been two known relapses since. No vaginal smears were done.

Comment

These two cases are quite similar in many ways. Both were talented adolescents with a high intelligence quotient, whose starvation was so persistent and serious that it reached suicidal degree. They were both very resistant to psychotherapy, but were clever enough to attain spectacular external improvement in order to gain discharge, after which they returned to their old pattern. In both instances, therapy fell naturally into three stages parallel to those in Alexander's case (1). At first there was tremendous overt resentment against the therapist, which the patient gradually realized was ineffective; a phase of partial cooperation followed and some dynamic material was uncovered until there was a real threat to the core of the neurosis; finally, there was a flight from therapy by "eating their way out of the hospital." This was done by means of sudden voluntary overeating in Case 3 and a resolve to give up tube feedings in Case 4. From then on no dynamic material appeared, but resistance became more subtle, and with the help of misguided parents, the goal of discharge was gained. The parents were largely responsible for severing the clinic contact and precipitating premature discharge. They were deeply involved in the pattern of their child's illness because of their own neurotic tendencies and concern with gastrointestinal functions. This has also been stressed by Rahman (15). It was most marked in the father who tube-fed his daughter seven times a day for a year. Another conspicuous factor was the rivalry with the mother and the girl's attempt to take her mother's place.

Discussion

These four cases of anorexia nervosa are related in that pregnancy fantasies are dramatized through the food-taking and menstrual functions. Symptomatology was cyclic and predominantly premenstrual in the first two cases, while the second two showed persistent amenorrhea. Menstruation, with its associations of pregnancy, was obviously a threat in all four, and was reacted to violently or repressed. The common purposes of starvation are to prevent the onset of menses, prevent pregnancy, and prevent growing up, which means facing men and marriage. Eating was erotized as there were ideas of oral impregnation and oral incorporation of the father's phallus. It was therefore associated with guilt and anxiety, so that eating was avoided entirely by the last two cases and followed by vomiting in the first two, as a means of expiation and restitution of the incorporated object. Thus, both types of case represent stages in a process with the same basic psychosomatic correlations.

However, the four cases are not related, in that they do not belong to the same diagnostic category of the orthodox classification of the neuroses. The cyclic vomiting partakes primarily of the nature of a conversion symptom, and the patients were of hysterical nature in other respects, demanding a great deal of attention and functioning primarily on an oedipus level. On the other hand, the last two cases more nearly approached anxiety hysteria, as there was a real phobia against the mere taking of food, as eating was associated with anxiety. Compulsive phenomena are seen in the ritualistic cleansing and the compulsive baking and cooking in Case 3. The latter have been pointed out previously, but the phobic phenomena have been overlooked.

Vaginal smears were useful in this study for research rather than therapy. Increased ovarian activity in Case 1 was clearly shown to be associated with increased symptomatology (vomiting) and conflict. In Case 3, relapse was simultaneous with the first observed menstruation, which was artificially induced, although this might have been accidental and dependent on discharge. Premenstrual tension in Cases 1 and 2 seemed to precipitate hysterical vomiting and give rise to pregnancy fantasies. If ovarian activity or sensations from the sexual organs, such as uterine cramps, are psychologically intolerable to the patient, it is no wonder that estrogen given in Cases 1 and 3 precipitated symptoms instead of alleviating them. Estradiol has been reported to have improved appetite, induced menstruation, and possibly facilitated recovery in one case successfully treated with psychotherapy over a long period (15). In the days before hormone therapy, clinicians remarked that recovery was not to be trusted until menses returned. It does not follow that artificially induced menstruation would cure the patient. Smoother recovery has been noted in an unreported case when menstruation was allowed to occur spontaneously, although this took time. A pessimistic attitude toward hormone therapy is not intended, but at present we do not seem to know enough about its various effects on the patient.

Therapy in anorexia nervosa is most unsatisfactory. Not one of the cases reported is well at the time of writing, although the last three were discharged as well once and later relapsed. There is no evidence in the literature of good results with anterior pituitary hormone, and thyroid medication may cause sudden loss of weight as the low basal metabolism serves a protective function (15). There is little rationale for the use of insulin, as hypoglycemia may already exist (4). One injection of insulin was given to Case 3, who bitterly complained, with good reason, that insulin did not overcome her fear of eating and her appetite was already painfully strong. Good results have been reported with bed rest, small frequent feedings, and constant nursing attention (1, 5, 19), but one wonders how much of this improvement is due to gratification of infantile cravings for attention and oral dependence. The erotic gratification from tube feedings was well illustrated here in Cases 2 and 4.

The need for prolonged psychotherapy in a hospital seems to be great, because of the resistance of the patients and the neuroticisms of the parents. On the basis of these four cases, a period under a year seems inadequate. Careful social service work with the parents is of great importance. Long hospitalization is necessary, not only because of parental attitudes and environmental factors, but also because adolescents can not be expected to manage a difficult therapeutic situation while living at home.

Summary

Anorexia nervosa is discussed as a psychosomatic entity in which fantasies of oral impregnation are dramatized through starvation, vomiting, and amenorrhea. Four cases are presented, two with premenstrual cyclic vomiting of hysterical conversion nature, and two with complete amenorrhea and a persistent phobia for food.

The vaginal smear technic of Papanicolaou and Shorr is used to investigate the endocrine ovarian status, and the percentage cornification in the smear is used as an estimate of estrogen activity. Smears done for a year on a case of cyclic vomiting showed that hysterical vomiting was associated with increased cornification; the pattern was interrupted by testosterone and precipitated by estrogen. Menstruation occurred for the first time in two years following suggestion through control injections of sesame oil. A case of persistent anorexia without vomiting showed atrophic smears, which improved with weight gain; estrogen induced menstruation, but may have increased conflict.

There is no evidence that physical therapy does more good than harm, and prolonged psychotherapy is favored in cases with good intelligence and co-operation. Long hospitalization in adolescents is recommended because of extreme resistance and neurotic parental attitudes.

REFERENCES

1. Alexander, G. H.: Anorexia nervosa, *R. I. Med. J.*, 22:189, 1939.
2. Alexander, F.: Influence of psychological factors upon gastrointestinal disturbances: Symposium. *Psychoanal. Quart.*, 3:501, 1934.
3. Benedek, T., and Rubenstein, B. B.: Correlations between ovarian activity and psychodynamic processes. *Psychosom. Med.*, 1:245, 461, 1939.
4. Berkman, J. M.: Functional anorexia and vomiting—Relation to anorexia nervosa. *Med. Clin. N. Amer.*, 23:901, 1939.
5. Cross, E. S.: Diagnosis and treatment of anorexia nervosa. *Med. Clin. N. Amer.*, 23:541, 1939.
6. Frank, R. T.: The hormonal causes of premenstrual tension. *Arch. Neurol. Psychiat.*, 26:1053, 1931.
7. Freed, S. C., Mesirow, S. D., and Soskin, S.: Composite nature of the estrus phenomenon. *Endocrinology*, 21:731, 1937.
8. Geist, S. H., and Salmon, U. J.: Evaluation of human vaginal smears and histology of vaginal mucosa. *Amer. J. Obstet. Gynaec.*, 38:392, 1939.
9. Hechter, O., Lev, M., and Soskin, S.: Relation of hyperemia to action of estrin. *Endocrinology*, 26:73, 1940.
10. Krohn, P. L., and Zuckerman, S.: Water metabolism and the menstrual cycle. *J. Physiol.*, 88:369, 1937.

11. Masserman, J. H.: Psychodynamics in anorexia nervosa and neurotic vomiting. *Psychoanal. Quart.,* 10:211, 1941.
12. McCullogh, E. P., and Tupper, W. R.: Anorexia nervosa. *Ann. Intern. Med.,* 14:817, 1940.
13. Nicolle, G.: Prepsychotic anorexia: *Proc. Royal. Soc.,* 32:153, 1939.
14. Papanicolaou, G. N.: Sexual cycle in the human female. *Amer. J. Anat.,* 52:519, 1933.
15. Rahman, L., Richardson, H. B., and Ripley, H. S.: Anorexia nervosa. *Psychosom. Med.,* 1:335, 1939.
16. Richardson, H. B.: Simmonds' disease and anorexia nervosa. *Arch. Intern. Med.,* 63:1, 1939.
17. Rubenstein, B. B.: Relation of cyclic changes in vaginal smear to temperature and BMR. *Amer. J. Physiol.,* 119:635, 1937.
18. Rubenstein, B. B., and Duncan, D. R. L.: A technic for assay of estrogen by evaluation of human vaginal smears and comparison with urinary estrogen assay on the mouse uterus. *Endocrinology,* 28:911, 1941.
19. Ryle, J. A.: Anorexia nervosa. *Lancet,* 2:893, 1936.
20. Sheldon, J. H.: Anorexia nervosa with special reference to physical constitution. *Lancet,* 1:369, 1937.
21. Shorr, E., Papanicolaou, G. N., and Stimmel, B. F. S.: Neutralization of ovarian follicular hormone in women by simultaneous administration of male sex hormone. *Proc. Soc. Exper. Biol., N. Y.,* 38:759, 1938.
22. Shorr, E., and Papanicolaou, G. N.: Action of gonadotropic hormones in amenorrhea as evaluated by vaginal smears. *Proc. Soc. Exper. Biol. N. Y.,* 41:629, 1939.
23. Shorr, E.: A new technic for staining vaginal smears. *Science,* 91:579, 1940.
24. Sweeney, J. S.: Menstrual edema, preliminary reports. *J. Amer. Med. Assn.,* 103:234, 1934.
25. Thomas, W. A.: Generalized edema only at menstrual period. *J. Amer. Med. Assn.,* 101:1126, 1933.
26. Waller, J. S., Kaufman, M. R., and Deutsch, F.: Anorexia Nervosa. *Psychosom. Med.,* 2:3, 1940.

ANOREXIA NERVOSA:
REPORT OF A CASE

SANDOR LORAND, M.D.
(1943)

It should be noted that the case reported by Lorand is one that has been in psychoanalytic treatment on a daily basis for some two and a half years, with a successful termination. Therefore, the data available to him, unlike the data presented by Waller, Kaufman, and Deutsch (7), were more comprehensive and tridimensional. Although in this rather short report, it was obviously impossible for the author to present these data in detail, it would seem that the fantasy of oral impregnation was present and was of importance in the psychodynamics of the patient's total reaction. He was able to report that the earliest oral relationship to the mother was a determining factor in the patient's later development and threw a good deal of light on the subsequent course of her personality structure. It provided a basis for her oral impregnation fantasy and also for the vicissitudes of her relationship to her mother. In this sense, they seemed to give added dimension to the case presentation, in contrast to the earlier paper referred to where, although orality was discussed, the data were not sufficient to demonstrate its earliest roots.

However, in a critical review of the case as presented, one wonders whether Lorand had worked out with the patient the various elements of the fantasy of function relating to oral impregnation, and what its relative importance was in this specific case. Although Lorand writes about the utilization of the gastrointestinal tract to represent earlier feelings "concerning mother, father, sister, brother, and representatives of the outside world," in this paper it is not clear how this is mediated. In a sense then this still leaves one with the fundamental problem in psychosomatic medicine.

The clinical syndrome of anorexia nervosa and its attendant complexities have been the subject of recent psychological study by various authors. Case histories were presented in some detail, conclusions drawn as to the interpretation of the symptoms, and suggestions made for therapy.

In this study I will omit reviewing the extensive literature which has been comprehensively cited in recent publications (4, 5, 6, 7). I will also omit a detailed discussion of the possibilities of diagnosis on the basis of obsessive, compulsive, and depressive features which were noted by many of the observers, and lead to the various descriptive diagnoses.

Nearly all the investigators emphasized correctly the factor of the child-parent relationship, especially the relationship to the mother, as the most important factor in the disease. Comprehensive formulations were given in the study by Waller, Kaufman, and Deutsch (7). They stressed, correctly, the importance of the interaction of environment and the personality organization of the patient in anorexia nervosa.

In support of certain theoretical assumptions made in previous studies, as well as to illustrate the deeper psychodynamics and therapy, clinical material is presented from the psychoanalysis of a patient suffering from anorexia nervosa who had been under daily treatment for two and one half years.

In this patient this symptom complex seemed to indicate a serious disturbance. It was an expression of many conflicts besides those which referred to the sexual sphere—which some investigators maintain the outstanding or main symptom. There was a deeper struggle going on within the patient—a struggle involving not only fight and defense against sexual drives, but drives which were more diffuse and pertained to disturbances in the whole personality structure. These referred mainly to the very early period of the patient's attachment to her

---

Reprinted from *Psychosomatic Medicine*, 5:282-292, 1943.

mother, and successful therapy resulted from the solution and working through of this early attachment in detailed analytic therapy.

Unquestionably, the distorted and powerful sexual aspect of the oedipus fixation operated to cause the patient's difficulties. But the early, strong oral tendencies were found largely responsible for her inability to cope with reality and sexual function.

What was once an oral desire for the breast and food, became a craving for all that could be taken in and eaten up, the mother's breast, everything the mother possessed, including the father. As this oral craving suffered increasing frustration by the mother, it became directed toward the father, charged with the same fear and guilt which were created in infancy by the frustrating mother.

The patient was in her early twenties. She had been under medical care for many years. Prior to her analysis, she had been for two weeks in a university clinic and was sent away without any suggestion for medical treatment. In the clinic, she had been receiving injections for amenorrhea.

The family physician referred her to me with complaints characteristic of the anorexia nervosa symptom complex: disgust with food, loss of appetite and taste for food, periodic vomiting—especially if she tried to force herself to eat. Accompanying symptoms were excruciating pains in the epigastrium and lower abdomen, and periodic amenorrhea. She also complained of increased growth of hair on the torso, face, lips, arms and thighs; occasional constipation; feeling of cold and depression most of the time. Her symptoms could be considered in three important groups: first, peculiar reactions to food; second, disturbances in bowel functions; and third, menstrual disorders and amenorrhea. This arrangement was also emphasized by Waller, Kaufman, and Deutsch (7).

All these symptoms had been more or less present for about ten years. Her illness started at twelve when she had crying spells and feelings of depression. She lost weight from time to time because of disgust with food, but gained easily after the symptoms subsided. Before she was twelve she had many emotional setbacks, felt unhappy, and had difficulties in school. She liked her teachers and was a good student, but was afraid of the other children and hated them because they would laugh and play and she was unable to join them. She would go home from school in a nasty temper. In high school the same situation prevailed. She always had the feeling of not belonging with other children. She had always been fussy about eating. After every meal, she used to lie on her stomach across a chair to get relief from pressure. However, her disturbance did not become very severe until she was twelve. The first occurrence took place when the family moved from one neighborhood to another. She did not like the people there, rebelled, and told her mother she hated it. She became moody, cried a great deal, and lost her appetite. These moods and crying spells became permanent. Menses started first at fourteen, but they were never regular. Because of frequent abdominal pains, appendectomy was done when she was eighteen, but proved to be an unnecessary procedure. A plastic nose operation to improve her appearance had also been performed without her parents' previous knowledge, and before she started analysis.

When she started analysis she was going through one of her periods of depression and crying spells. For days she was unable to take solid food. At night, when everyone was asleep, she would go to the icebox and eat lightly. She attributed her condition at that time to a steadily growing tension and resentment toward her mother. She felt her mother was neglecting the home for her social engagements which kept her away most of the day. This state of affairs was nothing new, but seemed to grow worse. It infuriated the patient because it made her ashamed of having such a mother and because her father was neglected.

From the outset of the analysis her behavior was childish, and her carriage, voice, mode of speech were all playful and coquettish. During this time she was not able to bear much frustration, and so was given every freedom possible to encourage the display of her feelings. In the first few months, appointments were changed according to her wishes, and ingenuity was needed to keep her from running away in the middle of an analytical hour because of intense rage and unhappiness. She was on the verge of quitting treatment whenever she became enraged by her mother, father or sister.

When she was in a bad temper with her mother she felt like grabbing and choking her. She described her mother as a cold woman, always nagging and shouting at father and the children, and particularly at her. She accused her mother of neglecting the children, and said she could not believe her mother's protestations of affection. Her mother claimed that she nursed her for five months, wanted to do so longer, but that the patient refused to take the breast. At the same time she would express her disgust at the act of suckling babies. The patient commented, "Probably I did not want to take something that was not given with love. Kids sense love that early as dogs sense the people that love them."

She complained that her mother, being a simple woman with little cultivation, was always impatient with her. This was proof that her mother did not want her. Then too, her mother often cursed and ridiculed her, and expressed the hope that the patient would have children like herself so that she might know the torture she had caused her mother. At the same time, the patient felt self-compunction and guilt. She was sarcastic and termed every word she uttered a "worm." She was constantly resentful and aggressive, and at the same time suffered self-depreciation, guilt, pains, crying, and depression.

The mother's attitude toward her created constant anxiety in childhood so that she was shy, retiring, morose, and brooding. The patient, when a child, became convinced that her mother was dangerous because there were varying and unconstant attitudes toward the oldest child, the sister, and the youngest, her brother, and toward herself. Toward her father, whom she considered maltreated by mother, the patient was at times sympathetic, but ambivalence developed very early and she distrusted both parents. As a result, she could not express tender emotions. She schooled herself to appear composed so as to conceal her need for dependency and parental love. Thus she attempted to spare herself disappointment.

In her early childhood she also felt unwanted because her parents had wanted a boy. When the boy was born, she was envious and jealous. The growing boy, admired for his appearance, made her feel ugly and inferior. The mother had told the patient that when she was two years old she was ashamed to take her on the street for fear that people would comment on her skinny and ugly child. She frequently questioned her mother as to whether she was a stepchild, and was disappointed by the negative reply.

She repeatedly expressed the thought that parents should be dead before children are born. She went on to say, "I felt I wanted only to hate, then I felt I wanted only to love—then I didn't want anything." Life was difficult for her because she felt she was vulnerable and afraid of crying. She said she hated everybody around her at home so that she could not eat. Her mother threw the food at her, and she wanted it served appetizingly. Mother repeated to her many times that "mothers should never be born because they suffer so much."

Her relationship to her father was very ambivalent, and there was a long struggle in analysis until she reached an attitude of at least tolerating father. He was domineering, argumentative with mother and cruel in his business. Nevertheless, he could be more tender at times than her mother. She recognized in herself certain resemblances to her father: critical and sarcastic attitudes, tone of voice, and expression of the eyes.

Her father once forced her, in the presence of other people, to eat eggs, which she promptly vomited on him, soiling his suit. He never seemed satisfied with her. He was always interfering with her, telling her what to eat and what to do. He taught her to be stiff and formal in his presence. He always came home from business in bad temper.

Once she served her father a glass of water, and thought at the same time, "I hope you choke on it." Then in guilt she tried to nullify it by thinking, "I hope you don't choke on it." Such thoughts tortured her constantly, and her inability to escape from them made her desperate. At other times, however, she was sympathetic toward him. As analysis progressed, her thoughts and fantasies about him showed more and more confusion of concern, contempt, attachment, and rejection. Her jealous concern with her father, and also her fear of her brother, whom in dreams she often identified with her father, her conscious fears that in his excitement he might rape her became more and more obvious.

Long after the disturbed feelings toward her mother diminished, the emotional problem caused by her father remained active. It was not until the end of the second year of analysis that she was able to sit through a meal with him. When the meal was over, she was at ease and relaxed, whereas previously such an occurrence would sometimes bring on abdominal pains, stomach symptoms, and eating difficulties that would last for days.

Competition and rivalry with the sister from earliest childhood were important factors in her illness. Before her brother was born, she was aware of the partiality shown her older sister, particularly by her father. Her mother mentioned many times that when the patient was born her sister, then over two years of age, wanted to kill her with a big stick and throw her out of the window. At the age of two, the patient kept herself meticulously clean, while the sister, at that time four, was still soiling herself. In school the patient was bright, while her sister was dull. In later years the patient developed intellectual pursuits and tried to be more attractive in her appearance, for the sister was heavy-set and the patient wanted to remain just the opposite. The patient said, "So long as my sister was present, I was not allowed to be an individual." After her sister was married, she tried unconsciously to make her brother-in-law admire her, and did succeed in making him very fond of her. At times he even compared her with his wife to the patient's advantage. Once when she noticed he was sexually attracted to her, she became at once panicky and enraged at him. She understood the situation, as she herself had become aware that her brother-in-law behaved in many aspects just like her father. In business and politics, with money and friends, etc., he was boastful, pretended importance, and she saw clearly that both the rage and panic really related primarily to her father. That insight gave her a more tolerant attitude toward her sister.

The same jealousy and competitiveness were present in relationship to her brother, but here there was also a protective motherly attitude. She remembered her brother's birth when she was five, and how she visited the hospital to see him. Her parents were very happy to have a boy, but she said he looked like a little animal. During adolescence her brother used to tease her by singing a song that he made up, "You are wrong; you are an accident," which she thought he must have heard from their parents. She was resentful because both brother and sister had nice names but her name was ugly. She stated that it was unfortunate that she was not able to talk when a baby and object to her name. She identified herself very definitely with him when he was severely punished by father, for at such times it was proof to her that father did not love any of the children, and then she felt justified in hating him.

In discussions of sexual matters, she was shy and resentful. In the second year of analysis, she fell in love with a young man, whom, after a few weeks of courtship, she intended to marry. Then she talked of sexual matters more freely. Prior to that time, she would talk about her love and children and the wish to have them, but she preferred that they be "test-tube" babies. During this courtship she enjoyed for the first time intimate contact with a man, sitting on his lap, and kissing him. This was also the first time she could truly admit her hunger for affection and desire for dependence upon a man.

She had been aware of desiring men for some years, although it usually happened when she felt depressed, miserable, and alone. She then engaged in "petting parties" mostly because it enabled her to be close to someone. She also wanted to be nice to the men who desired petting, as if in payment for the attention thus secured. She feared to dress attractively because she would be annoyed by men who would become attached to her. This she wished to avoid, for fear of hurting them. There was guilt for causing them discomfort which she thought they must have felt. At other times, however, there was an active impulse to hurt them, and sometimes when kissing, she bit them. It gave her a peculiar pride to joke about her own body, which attracted men, and to joke about her breasts, which she termed "handmade" by petting.

It was apparent that her seeming ignorance about sexual matters was merely the result of deep repression. As a matter of fact, she knew a great deal about them, and knew from experience about genital sensations. However, she rejected the knowledge in order not to be disturbed by it. She expressed repeatedly the desire to be sexless, and when father talked about her getting married, she wondered about it because father and mother's union was unhappy. She knew they never liked each other. Fear of getting hurt in coitus and in childbirth added to the conflicts. Being close to her *fiancé* made her constantly conscious of reality. More and more, she experienced the feeling of being a woman, which she thought was bad for her because she feared losing her head. She was afraid to let him know she wanted him. Because she desired constant affection, she was terrified at the possibility of losing it. She described her need for love as a hunger, which in fantasies revealed the relationship to hunger for food. She indulged more freely in loving and being loved, and permitted herself passionate feelings. Nevertheless, she was seized by fear whenever her wedding plans were discussed, because she felt that marriage would deprive her of a defensive independence which had been the pattern of her past strivings.

Analysis at this stage served as a gratification which she desired to retain. Unconsciously it meant being spared from taking decisive steps. She had never dared to take a final step or to express an opinion, and this indecision made her always doubtful and speculative about what to do, and fear prevented her from carrying out any plans. It gave her gratification to talk and to be listened to, both of which she had never before experienced. When she first came for treatment, it was the opportunity of having a place to cry which kept her in analysis. Such attention as she thus got had been given only to her brother and sister. In the analytic relationship she wanted basically to be feminine, to be conquered by a masculine man. On the other hand, she wanted to be different and handle sex in her own way because of her fear of dependence. However, as her desire for dependence became more conscious, she showed more inclination to accept the fundamental feminine wish. During this period she very often talked about her *fiancé* as the ideal and independent man of the world capable in his profession. She was horrified at the thought that he might take money from her father. Yet if they were to marry and live in the city it would be necessary to accept money from her father. This circumstance turned her love to boundless hatred. Again her father would exercise his power over her with money. This she hated and therefore decided not to marry. She recognized too, that since her love was an attempt to solve her problems "in flight" it could not remain permanent. Her reaction to this situation once again brought her strong basic conflicts with father into the foreground.

She was depressed, postponed her marriage plans, cried for a few days feeling as though she would never get better. However, she did not have any eating difficulties and slowly her depression subsided. She began to feel happier and more at ease at home. Slowly her behavior changed and though it happened spontaneously, she became more and more aware of acting differently. She understood more clearly, at this time, the emotional factors which caused her to be sick, and she tried consciously to carry out certain of her plans, in spite of some hesitation. For instance, an old wish of hers to go back to school had caused her much unhappiness because of the fear that she would not be able to remain there. She solved it this time with a splendid result. She went back to take courses at college, and though her first visit to the registrar's office was a very hard task because she felt like running out, breaking down and crying, she stuck it out, and thereafter all went well. She enjoyed the courses, and even the new friendships with some of the girls. She became aware once again of her popularity with men, and began to enjoy their companionship, even though her fear of attachment to them still persisted. Going out with men whenever she had a date still created problems for her. She was disturbed when anticipating dining out with them. At frequent intervals pains, menstrual-like, even though she had just menstruated, would occur. She recognized quite fully, however, that all these symptoms on such occasions related to sex.

Through analysis of her dreams at this period, the fundamental points in her development could be understood and related to her. All the dreams cited occurred in the second year of analysis. Before that, she did not take the trouble to remember dreams. She thought they were silly and, even if she told one occasionally, refused to discuss it and rejected any interpretation which was attempted. By this time, as she learned to comprehend the reasons for her fears and symptoms, she dared to face more of her fantasies and feelings and was more willing to remember her dreams and to discuss them. She acknowledged them, became more convinced, and was able to handle her problems through the understanding she derived from them.

Her concern, attachment to, and fear of father were illustrated in the following dream: "I was giving father his slippers." The same night she dreamed also, "I saw father stepping out of a car with a blonde girl."

The associations to these dreams dealt with her jealousy of father, her thoughts about the married life of her parents, and father's unhappiness. She also discussed the possibility that her mother caused father's unhappiness at home, which forced him to find solace in business, and possibly in the company of other women. Some of her distrust of all men was based on these doubts about father. She also understood why father did not like her, for she nagged him as her mother did. The significance of giving the slippers to father was quite obvious to her. It expressed her deep jealousy of mother, competition with mother for father's affection, and her desire to keep him home and make him comfortable, which the patient tried quite often to do by preparing his favorite dishes for which he would praise her.

There were frequent dreams about babies. She was consciously fond of them and desired to have them, but fear and guilt prevented her from freely indulging in such fantasies. The following dreams deal with this problem.

Two babies were brought to our house. Two more beds were put in my room. The little baby was like a puppy. His feet were not like feet, his walk not like a walk, and his hands were not like hands. There was a big dog chasing everybody.

In connection with this dream, all the jealousy, envy, and unhappiness concerning sibling rivalry came to the fore. The first signs of improvement in analysis came when her parents moved to a new apartment (at the analyst's suggestion) where she got her own room and no longer had to sleep with her sister. This problem of sleeping with sister, with mother constantly entering the room, created many bitter hours for the patient. In the dream, she once more repeats her conscious memories about the youngest child after birth, when he appeared to her like a little animal; she also reassured herself of superiority to this baby. The big dog chasing everybody in the dream referred to father, whom she many times thought of as a dog, and also to men in general. It revealed also the fear of sexual approaches by men.

The anxieties concerning sexual involvements with men had its deepest roots in the strong desire to have a baby, which was accompanied by fear and guilt because of her attachment to father and competition with mother. The following dream is a good illustration of this problem:

I am driving with father in a car. He had an accident. I asked him not to drive wildly. Then I got out of the car and met many girls from the school, but I had to get back in the car. I was reluctant. I was afraid.

She started her associations by stating, "I was an accident. Too bad that parents had to have more children after my birth." Her father was actually a careless driver, but never had an accident. Many times when they would ride together in the car, she was embarrassed because she did not know what to say to him, and he too apparently reacted that way. She understood the sexual significance of the dream, and talked about her fear of riding with men, because they wanted to put their hands all over her, yet at times she encouraged advances, only to repel them once they were started. In the dream, there was also an attempt to return to school, to play with girls, to avoid the danger of growing up, and of facing sex. She was reluctant, but finally did step into the car which was actually her conscious attitude at that time, for she became more willing to accept her feminine role.

As she attempted more and more to adjust herself to her corrected ideas about sex, anxiety dreams dealing with sexual matters became more frequent. One of them is of special importance because it occurred in a menstrual period which was preceded by abdominal pains of a week's duration. It is of importance that at this time her amenorrhea ceased, her menses having appeared regularly for several months.

The discussion of her menstruation continued with the subsequent dream:

The maid servant had a fur hat, and suddenly there appeared little leopards in the fur. There were many women in the room and all had leopards. I took one in my arm. It bit me. None of the women were bitten.

In her associations she talked about her earlier disgust with hair around her genitals. At puberty, she tried to pull the hair out, but at the same time she was proud of the upper half of her body, especially the breasts, which she accentuated by her way of dressing. She had always suffered physically when menses did not appear. Not menstruating made her feel like an "it." Yet she always had a dreadful apprehension of menstruation. She fantasied exploding with blood gushing all over her, leaving her lifeless. On the other hand, she feared that if she did not menstruate she might explode. She expressed the whole conflict by saying "I want to bleed in order not to explode, but I am afraid to bleed because of the fact that all the blood will flow away."

She expressed the wish to be a woman like others and to have sexual intercourse, but also the fear of the damage of being bitten. Being bitten referred to her fantasies about her own castration, which made her reject the lower part of her body as unattractive, "freakish."

She related a dream which she called the dream about the cannibals:

I am in the woods, little nude people—cannibals, savages, are all around —I climb on the tree.

She started her associations with something she did not want to talk about. Months ago, during the summer on the beach, she saw by accident the penis of one of her boy friends. She felt disgusted talking about it. It looked red, like a chunk of raw meat. She could not understand how women could be attracted by sex. She felt "gypped" by that observation, as in childhood when she bought prize packages though she knew she would be fooled. How can women be attracted to men when they know they will be cheated? Then she talked about eunuchs and hermaphrodites, sexual anomalies about which she had read lately. At times she felt herself like a cannibal, having a desire to strangle, yank out the penis. She felt that way particularly after being passionate during petting. At this time her petting was quite extensive, everything short of sexual intercourse, and it made her afraid to be so passionate.

She complained in the course of this hour about frequent persistent diarrhea which she was embarrassed to mention. She was surprised by this symptom which she could not remember ever having experienced before, for as a rule she was constipated.

The dreams made it evident that this sudden change of constipation to diarrhea seemed to be a last attempt to solve her problems of going out with men, for just a few days before she proudly announced, "Do you want to know how much better I am?" and said that she had a blind date. Although she hated to go out, she had no disturbance before the date, and ate her dinner. She chose where to go, how to go, and was hungry enough to eat with the man. It seems as though she could no longer use oral symptoms as an excuse for not going out. She unconsciously used the diarrhea as an attempted escape. On a deeper level, these symptoms signified masculine strivings, as Alexander (1) has indicated. Urinary frequency expressed the same masculine strivings, and in addition, masturbatory tendencies forcing preoccupation with her genitals which she previously tried to disown.

To illustrate the general improvement, two additional dreams are cited to clarify the psychodynamics of her symptoms. One day while commenting that hair on her face and thighs was disappearing, she suddenly remembered a recent dream:

An old man is using electrolysis on my face. I was afraid it would leave scars, we were in mother's bedroom in the old house. He removed few hairs.

Starting her associations, she mentioned that when she wakened that morning she looked in the mirror, saw that she had gained weight, and suddenly thought, "Could I be pregnant? Could going out so many times, and indulging in petting, have caused me to become pregnant?" Then she remembered that at thirteen, while in the country, she was frightened by a woman who was pregnant, and told her that good country air helps women to get pregnant. The old man in the dream was a friend of the family, a cheapskate, a pest. He always objected to giving his children anything. On the dream night, at a card game at home, her sister lost to father, and when the sister's husband wanted to pay the loss, father insisted the money be paid by sister. He enjoyed making her pay because she was stingy. The patient in associating then continued, "I am glad sister cannot have a baby. I am mean, I know, but if someone has to have a baby, I want to have it." In this light, the whole dream could be understood. The electrolysis performed in mother's bedroom really referred to her primary wish in the oedipus situation: Hair is masculine. She wanted to be made a woman by father in mother's bed and have a baby by him. Her fears of the scars refers to the fear of permanent punishment which would accompany these guilty gratifications.

The next dream is of importance because it shows the extent of her improvement in the transference relationship:

I had an appointment at twelve for my analytic hour. I forgot it, and it was late. I called your office and you said it does not matter because you were going fishing. Your voice was faint and getting weaker and weaker. You told me that you were poisoned. I wanted to tell you to be careful, you must live, instead of which I said be careful, M. must live. (M. is the name by which patient was called when she was a child; later it was changed.) Then you ceased to talk and I felt panicky. I looked for a telephone number to call your home.

Then she remembered that there was an additional part with which the dream started, which was something like the following:

You told me you have broad shoulders and you do not like it. I reassured you that I do like it. Then you asked me whether I think of men these days, and I said I do, and I also think about you.

Her associations to this dream brought out the many thoughts and feelings which she had about analysis itself, Freud, analysts in general; criticism, scorn in the past, but how later she learned to trust the analysis because of the experience of patience and kindness. In the dream when she tells the analyst that he must live, she was exceedingly embarrassed, because it was an admission of identification of the analyst with the kind of father she would have liked to have had. That is why she called herself "M," which she abandoned at fourteen. The problem of the analyst being poisoned brought up ideas about his unfaithfulness and consequent contraction of some disease. This led straight to the problem of sexual intercourse and pregnancy, which meant being poisoned. Further associations referred to the ideas that her life was poisoned by father by his constant watching and disapproval of her. The first part of the dream, which she remembered later, shows clearly her attachment to and her preoccupation with the analyst, which at that stage of analysis she was ready to acknowledge. She also referred to vaginal sensations other than pain. At times rather vague, they became definitely pleasurable. She also noticed when dancing at times, that she had a slight vaginal secretion.

Her greatest improvement at that time was the wish to live. She watched herself when crossing streets, and did not think of accidents as she once did. She could experience the same emotions for days in succession, which never had happened before. No confusion resulted from unpleasant occurrences. She described her feelings as something new. She was not afraid of her parents, spent weekends with them, and went driving alone with father. She no longer felt guilty in accepting things from her parents, and could spend her money freely. She was not embarrassed to kiss father on the cheek. If he kissed her five or six times she was not afraid. She talked more about the responsibility of growing up, but feared it. She said, "I can see into people's minds better now, and it frightens me." She was still afraid of asserting herself at home, even when she was right, because there were always five opinions against hers, and it seemed useless to stand up against so many adversaries. But she now says, "I won't sit back and take it any more. I am old enough to make up my own mind."

Of her two parents she concluded her mother was the more normal. She said her father was "remarkably good" at times, and very gracious, but everybody feared him. She concluded her family was not really mean, but very dull, and incapable of love, therefore she would have to seek love elsewhere. She could now evaluate her entire situation and her relationship to her parents. As to her relationship to analysis, her own words will describe it best. She said, "I feel very grateful to you for not feeling sick any more, and the days are not torture any more."

Discussion and Formulation

The manner in which her symptoms developed during the formative years, and in which they could first be changed, then partially eliminated in the course of analysis, gives us insight into the powerful opposing forces in her unconscious. As a result of the analysis of this case, which ended in a satisfactory recovery, and also in review of the cases and formulations of Waller, Kaufman, and Deutsch (7), and also Rahman, Richardson and Ripley (6), it seems justifiable to draw conclusions as to the emotional development and type of personality structure which appear characteristic of cases showing the symptom complex, anorexia nervosa.

To understand the meaning of the symptoms of the case under discussion, it is well to remember that a neurotic symptom is a substitute for a desire which cannot be gratified because of external or internal reasons. In this case, all the disturbances seem to have as their primary cause the reactions to the mother's attitude from earliest infancy. The whole symptom complex centered around the problem of how to deal with her, and later with the indifferent father. They were the two people who made her, as she termed it, "starve."

There were periods during her analysis when sensations in the mouth, stomach, and abdomen reactivated emotions which could be traced to the earliest years. Her whole psychic development could be understood in the light of the emotional ties to her parents.

Every child's problem centers around the relationship with parents: avoiding anxieties and frustrations which are caused by them, and then changing these frustrating attitudes into supporting, reassuring, and loving ones, thereby eliminating anxiety. The patient's illness and symptoms point in the same direction. She remained to a great extent infantile, defending herself from anxieties which were revived by growing up.

In her early childhood, she remembers being like a little beast who wanted to eat up and tear up everything and everybody. Her jealousies started with sibling rivalry as early as the age of two. At this early age, her father became linked with her oral cravings. From then on, these desires carried sexual charges. The desires which primarily concerned mother's breast, food, and getting love from mother became in later stages identified with desires to have everything mother possessed—including father's love. This, in turn, was associated with early ideas of oral impregnation.

The disturbances concerned with eating were connected with an unconscious concept of the poisonous content of food, and this idea related to fantasies of oral impregnation; thus the ideas that food could harm just as does pregnancy and sexual intercourse were formulated. These early experiences in relation to food and love, and the accompanying confusion, caused hostility and consequent guilt feelings which she tried to expiate with intense masochism. In depressed phases, she had suicidal impulses and strong wishes to die. When miserable with abdominal pains and unable to eat, she consoled herself by repeating, "It won't last long, tomorrow I will die." In her deepest unconscious, her inability to eat expressed her wish to waste away and die. Something of that tendency was also emphasized by Rahman, Richardson and Ripley (6). They considered the patient's starvation as an aim to kill the "gross" or the "physical" in the patient. The self-punishing tendencies in her symptoms were outstanding. She recognized them as representing simultaneous punishment of her parents as well. They wanted love when she no longer could give it. Instead, she gave resentment and caused worry. Her symptoms were also an attempt to win affection. For now, in her illness, she became the center of anxious attention as never before.

The analysis of this patient proved without question that the oral symptom—her reaction to food—served to realize other fantasies which were of primary importance to the patient. In a symbolic way, eating was equated with sexuality, just as in instances noted by previous authors, especially Waller, Kaufman and Deutsch (7), and Rahman, Richardson and Ripley (6). All symptoms centering around eating could really be transposed to her problems of sexuality. In the deepest layer, there was the primary desire for impregnation, to become fat, to have a big abdomen. The guilt, however, associated with that desire, resulted in the expression of the opposite, namely a denial by expulsion or vomiting out the stomach content, all of which indicated the danger of "getting fat." The fantasy of oral impregnation was clearly proven in the course of analysis when she used as a defense nausea and loss of appetite to prevent her dates with men. The fear of being poisoned by food expressed the same fear of pregnancy, but at the same time it concealed hostility against her parents, which she expressed by vomiting. It was retaliation for their "poisoning her life."

The disturbance of bowel function, constipation, was in the service of the same unconscious fantasies. While the oral symptoms meant intake and conception, constipation realized the wish of permanent impregnation. The intestinal tract was definitely symbolic to her of the womb, and functioned like it in some respects.

The jealousy and envy, which started with feeding, became attached to the problem of sibling favoritism. In this way, it also became connected with love and sex. She was precocious in childhood, but genital sexuality had become repulsive to her because of the whole early childhood oedipus involvement. Unconsciously, she had good reason to reject all men and sex. In analysis, she realized that she really had no aversion to men, but only to marriage. That was the problem against which she had to protect herself because of the implication of pregnancy and also because of her observations of the unhappy marital life of her parents. She also had to reject genitality because of her fear of being exposed. She considered herself abnormal because from early childhood she had always ailed and complained. This she connected later with sexual disorders. With the onset of menstrual disturbances, she was sure that this was so. She ceased to menstruate. Amenorrhea expressed denial of femininity. At times, she wanted to be an "it," neither man nor woman, but a sexless child. The fear of exploding when not menstruating, was derived from guilt and the consequent fear of being pregnant, having a baby, being injured, and dying. Not menstruating had the aim of concealing her abnormality, which meant to her being a woman.

Freud's statement that "the prolonged feeling of tension and dissatisfaction and nongratification, and at the same time, early and frequent exposure to the outer world, produces fear and resentment," can readily be applied to the patient. Her social and sexual passivity was the continuation of her infantile passivity which resulted from early fears and which later served as a defense. She felt herself to be an unwanted child, and that was the root of all her fundamental distrust of everyone and everything. This I consider a very important factor in her case. It differs from the findings of Rahman, Richardson and Ripley (6), who report that in their cases the parents wanted the children but the difference can probably be explained by the fact that they obtained the history from the parents. I think the history as revealed by the patient, particularly in deeper investigation, revealed the fact that this patient felt herself to be "unwanted."

The symptoms were all elaboration and acting out in the somatic sphere. The somatic sensations which were so closely bound up with emotions in infancy and early childhood became a carrier of all kinds of emotional involvements. Feelings concerning mother, father, sister, brother, and representatives of the outside world could elicit disturbances in the gastrointestinal tract. Emotional reactions against people, which could not be verbalized, would attempt expression through the same channels which were employed for this purpose in early childhood. All the bitterness and pain which related to the earliest disappointments by mother, and which were primarily bound up with feeding, care, affection, remained the source of her permanent distrust of everybody. "If I cannot trust mother or father, how can I trust anyone?" She tried to utilize, in the solution of her emotional conflicts, organs which were especially sensitive to psychic stimulae. This corresponds to the formulation of Felix Deutsch (2). Her whole gastrointestinal tract, to which system in her unconscious the whole abdominal content belonged, including the womb, was used to express and to reject cravings which included pregnancy and the defense against it. They also served to express love and hate in the same manner as every individual uses the intake of food and excretion as a means to express love, obedience, rejection, and hate, in the course of early development. Deutsch (2) writes about his cases, "The food intake symbolizes the taboo fantasies. The food problem became the nucleus of the neurosis."

Therapy

The treatment of anorexia nervosa, I believe, should be conducted along psychoanalytic lines. However, the analysis will differ from the so-called classical psychoanalytical treatment because such patients find it difficult to develop a transference relationship. This patient constantly fought the expression of tender feelings in analysis as she did in her social relationships. She set in motion unconscious forces as defenses against dangers which tender relationships would create. Her main defense was keeping all her reactions, especially sexual ones, infantile. As she herself said, she had to learn too early to take care of herself. Her parents' attitude drove her to early intellectual maturity. She had to become a precocious child to cope with the difficulties to which she was exposed. She therefore developed a weakness of the ego, which was always ready to give up easily, and which was patterned on the very early developmental stage, when, for reasons of environment, the child cannot get a strong grasp on its parents. In order to develop a transference relationship, various means have to be employed. When such dependence does develop, one must be very careful not to spoil it, because a fundamental distrust of the patient is constantly ready to reassert itself. She stated: "I was an aggressive child, nasty, and always fighting with everyone. Then I became submissive, beaten into submission. Now I am afraid that I could very easily become nasty again, and so I cannot form any attachment because I cannot tolerate being hurt."

If the patient is too weak to stay in the home environment, the treatment should take place in a sanitarium, at least until the patient becomes ambulatory. It is necessary at times to apply direct educational influences, just as one does in the analysis of children. The slowly developed dependence will enable us to utilize Freud's fundamental technical advice, "remembering, repetition, and working through." Repetition is displayed in acting out and emotional discharge in the analytical situation, which then automatically helps the patient to recollect early situations and reactions, thus allowing working through so that the patient may constantly re-evaluate her thoughts, feelings, and actions as an approach to development of maturity.

The aim then, in therapy of this type of case, is to reduce the severity of the superego so that the patient has more feeling of inner freedom and more flexibility in the outer world with more capacity to enjoy it. Fear of punishment plays a prominent part in character formation of the child. Primarily, this punishment comes from parents. Later, the fear becomes an inner one, a fear of the superego. The stronger this fear, the stronger the hostility against the punishing and frustrating parents, so that guilt increases and becomes harbored in the unconscious. This could be constantly observed in the patient in shifting phases of analysis. She had developed a severe superego as a result of the inverted aspect of infantile aggression. Then, too, the parents really were severe. Deprivation of love is also regarded as punishment and may therefore have the same effects in the vicious circle of fear, aggression, and guilt.

The externalization of aggressive and tender feelings in the analytical situation becomes an important factor because the patient gets for the first time the opportunity to dare to think, talk, and act freely, without being punished, so that feelings of guilt slowly diminish. Thus the ego becomes strengthened as the patient learns to accept impulses previously considered forbidden and guiltful.

This is a very slow process. To become more self-reliant and enjoy things with less guilt depends on the successful reduction of the severity of the superego. As her whole environment had an important bearing on the development of her neurotic symptoms, her reaction pattern to the environment had to be changed so that she could develop the insight which she expressed by stating that her parents were really good people but dull and incapable of loving her. Since she could not get love from them, she would seek it in the outside world.

In summarizing, I feel the successful analysis of this case clarified sufficiently the psychodynamics of the whole symptom complex, so that one may draw conclusions as to other cases of the same type.

The following points are of outstanding importance:

1. This patient, suffering from anorexia nervosa, felt herself to be an unwanted child as a result of frustrations by parents—especially the mother.

2. She developed a very severe superego as a result of the inverted aspect of infantile aggression resulting from her feeling of "not belonging."

3. The feeling of being unwanted and the severe superego made identification very difficult, and the result was weak ego structure.

4. Puberty in this patient was characterized by vivid and extremely painful revivals of infantile relationships to father and mother, making adjustment as faulty at this period as it was in early childhood, because the ego was still immature.

5. To establish a diagnosis is extremely difficult in such cases because some patients show milder symptoms than others, and their personality structure is not so deeply involved. Whatever other symptoms are present, one symptom is common to all, and that is depression. Also

common to such cases is the fact that their symptoms are those of hysterical conversion, and their character structure shows outstandingly infantile and hysterical trends. From the therapeutic aspect, depression is one of the most difficult symptoms to handle and is responsible for the strong wish of these patients to die.

The symptoms express the following meanings:

1. Loss of appetite: Food implies oral and sexual gratification identified with early fantasies of impregnation. Thus are revived strong feelings of guilt necessitating denial by rejection of food (7). Food usually is excessively charged with importance in an environment where a patient develops anorexia nervosa. It is the vehicle of love and also of punishment. In this case, food was a constant topic of conversation and the focus of family interests.

2. The denial of adulthood in general and especially in sexuality: Adult problems cannot be handled because of constant preoccupation with the problem of food around which the earliest difficulties of the child centered. This preoccupation also excludes adult adjustment to sexual needs. Then too, genitality has to be denied because of desires and guilt centering around the early oedipus relationship.

3. Wasting away: It expresses strong suicidal desires. (This is the end result of the inverted aspect of infantile killing impulses against parents—particularly the mother—which were so outstanding.)

4. Menstrual disturbances: Cessation of menstruation is an attempt to eliminate the problem of being preoccupied with genital function which in adulthood implies thoughts of sexual relationship and pregnancy. At times amenorrhea means permanent impregnation, and then again complete rejection of femininity. These are defenses against oedipal guilt.

5. Guilt and atonement: Since the symptoms are used to obtain revenge and attention, they become charged with guilt; at the same time the suffering acts as expiatory self-punishment.

REFERENCES

1. Alexander, F.: The influence of psychologic factors upon gastrointestinal disturbances. *Psychoanal. Quart.*, 3:501,1934.
2. Deutsch, F.: The choice of organ in organ neuroses. *Int. J. Psychoanal.*, 20:252, 1939.

3. Dunbar, H. F.: *Emotions and Bodily Changes.* New York: Columbia University Press, 1938.
4. Magendantz, H., & Proger, S.: Anorexia nervosa or hypopituitarism? *J. Am. Med. Assn.*, 114:1973, 1940.
5. Moschcowitz, E.: *Anexoria Nervosa.* Anniversary volume for Robert Tilden Frank. St. Louis: C. V. Mosby, 1937, p. 359.
6. Rahman, L.; Richardson, H. B.; & Ripley, H. S.: Anorexia nervosa with psychiatric observations. *Psychosom. Med.*, 1:335, 1939.
7. Waller, J. V.; Kaufman, M. R.; & Deutsch, F.: Anorexia nervosa: A psychosomatic entity. *This volume*, pp. 245-273.

PSYCHODYNAMISMS IN ANOREXIA NERVOSA AND NEUROTIC VOMITING

JULES H. MASSERMAN, M.D.
(1941)

Masserman's patient, a thirty-five-year-old woman, presented a clinical syndrome characterized by severe anorexia, marked weight loss, cachexia with characteristically unimpaired energy and activity, intractable vomiting after food intake, which led to the diagnosis of Anorexia Nervosa even though "less determinative criteria, such as loss of hair and amenorrhea were not present." (One can question the loss of hair as a factor in anorexia nervosa.) Masserman attempted to minimize the importance of the absence of amenorrhea in his patient, and he argued that "it could easily be conceived that had the patient's rejection of this aspect of femininity and her castration fears been even greater than they were at the time, her menses instead of becoming merely scanty and painful might have been suppressed as completely as they had been previous to the age of sixteen."

In Masserman's analysis of the patient, he arrived essentially at the following psychodynamic formulation: "The vomiting appears to be a symbolic rejection and restitution of the father's phallus, orally incorporated in an attempt to render exclusive her basic passive dependence on the mother; however, the symptom also expresses an aggressive attack on the thwarting parents, masochistic expiation and other psychic overdeterminants." In reference to the oral impregnation fantasy, Masserman states: "While similar associations in my patient might have been traced to deeply repressed fantasies of impregnation by father's incorporated phallus, it must be stated that further material explicitly relevant to this complex did not appear in the analysis."

A number of interesting questions might be asked in relation to the above presentation and formulation. The first problem is a diagnostic one. In the patient presented, the vomiting and anorexia were prominent with a limitation on the intake of food and resulting loss of weight. There are many possible variables relating to food intake at different levels. Therefore, when any one of these levels is implicated with resultant noneating, the physiological concomitant would be a loss of weight. Does this sequence of events justify a diagnosis of anorexia nervosa? Phenomenologically the emphasis on weight loss without any loss of energy is reminiscent of the original clinical descriptions of Gull and Lasègue. Nevertheless, the sequence of not eating, loss of weight, cachexia, does not justify an inevitable diagnosis of anorexia nervosa. If one holds to the concept of a syndrome in medicine, and indeed Masserman states, "it should be nevertheless made clear that the psychoanalytic findings in this patient are not necessarily applicable to every case of anorexia nervosa since the term has a broad medical rather than a specific psychosomatic connotation," the problem arises as to what is understood by a syndrome. A broader medical base as opposed to a specific psychosomatic connotation is perhaps a contradiction in terms, since it is difficult to visualize such a broad, medically based syndrome without a specific psychosomatic significance. The variation in the psychological constellation in each instance will make for different reasons for not eating. The consequences of the not eating may be the same. On this basis one might question the diagnosis of anorexia nervosa in Masserman's patient, since if the syndrome anorexia nervosa presents a psychophysiological acting out of a specific oral impregnation fantasy as expressed in a fantasy of function reaction, then although the weight loss would be explicable on the basis of limitation of food intake, the other aspects of the syndrome, namely amenorrhea and constipation or diarrhea, would not necessarily relate to the limitation of food intake but would play out the other aspects of the fantasy. This might serve then as a differential between the classic anorexia nervosa syndrome and other syndromes which have a different etiological emphasis resulting in noneating as *such. Thus the case of Masserman might be considered as a regressive hysterical reaction related to orally determined conflicts at an initial oedipal level.*

In these days of poignant insecurity, reactive aggressiveness, intense ambivalence toward authority and other manifestations of direct pregenital determinants in social behavior, it is significant from a psychosomatic viewpoint that functional disorders of the gastrointestinal tract appear with great frequency and have become the subject of intensive medical and psychoanalytic interest and research. Recent studies at the Chicago Institute for Psychoanalysis (8) have demonstrated the relationship of gastric and colonic dysfunction to neurotic attitudes of excessive passivity or reactive hostility, especially in insecure, dependent individuals who feel themselves frustrated and threatened in their familial or social milieu. With specific regard to gastric dysfunctions, Brosin, Palmer and Slight (18) have recently summarized the psychiatric literature dealing with the highly interesting syndrome of anorexia nervosa. These authors, in their conclusion that no "single psychiatric entity adequately describes all members of the group," confirmed the necessity of a psychodynamic rather than a purely phenomenological investigation of such organ neuroses. In the case about to be presented in which a medical diagnosis of anorexia nervosa had been made, psychoanalysis revealed with relative clarity the relationships of unconscious genital and especially pregenital psychodynamisms to certain character traits and also specifically to gastric and other dysfunctions. The case is believed to be of general interest and therefore to merit a special report.

CASE REPORT

The patient, a thirty-five-year-old, unmarried girl with a diminutive, boyish appearance and a diffident, overingratiating manner, stated that she came for psychoanalysis primarily because she had been troubled for the preceding five years by nausea or actual vomiting whenever she attempted to dine in the presence of a man and, more recently, even when she merely thought of such a situation. The patient with some difficulty had been able

---

Reprinted from *The Psychoanalytic Quarterly*, 10:211-242, 1941.

to continue her work as a stenographer, but to circumvent her symptoms she had found it necessary during the last four years to avoid the company of men altogether, to forego almost all cultural and recreational pursuits and to live in self-imposed isolation with her widowed mother as her only close companion. The patient also complained of recurrent "chills," headaches and attacks of diarrhea but regarded these and other symptoms as of relatively minor importance. Nevertheless, in view of the failure of past medical treatment, her many harassing personality limitations and the deepening discouragement in regard to her occupational, marital and social prospects, she had decided to try analysis as a last therapeutic measure.

The youngest of three sisters, the patient was born into a middle-class family in an eastern European city. When she was two years old her father departed for America. She was left in the care of her doting mother, a forceful, independent, ambitious, but emotionally unstable individual, who apparently at first indulged her youngest daughter greatly, as the patient recalled that the first few years of her life in Europe had been exceedingly happy. However, she soon learned that the family was really being supported by a paternal uncle, from whom she was taught to expect—and sometimes even to beg—not only her little luxuries but also the very clothes and food she required.

It is significant that only two unpleasant memories persisted from this period: in both instances *elderly men had offered her food* and then attempted to approach her sexually, and on both occasions she had been *too frightened to tell her mother.*

When the patient was five years old the family left Europe and rejoined the father in America. On the initiative of her ambitious mother, the patient was then placed on a regime of training that, it was hoped, would make her a famous violin virtuoso. She took readily to this plan, practiced arduously and began to delight in exhibiting herself in many little recitals arranged by her mother. Up to about the age of her menarche she took pride in helping with the housework and seemed especially interested in the preparation of food for the family. She was frankly ashamed of her father who had never acquired what she considered an adequate American culture and whose work as a tailor she regarded as a handicap to her anticipated social position as a musical prodigy. However, when at about fourteen the mediocrity of her talent became apparent even to her mother, the intensive musical training was discontinued. At this time the patient became consciously aware that the mother had shifted her favor to the eldest sister who had on her own merits achieved greater social and occupational success. She reacted to the withdrawal of her mother's support by becoming outwardly more aggressive to her mother and sisters and for a time even taking the father's part in the many domestic quarrels. During this period, significantly, she began to prefer boyish clothes, adopted various athletic pursuits and became a disciplinary problem at school, which she left at the age of fifteen. She then secured a series of positions which she held with fair success until the time of her analysis, although beneath a façade of independence and self-sufficiency she continued to be shy and hypersensitive, highly limited in her social contacts and interests, and almost exclusively immersed in the minutiae of the household and family relationships.

In tracing through the origins of her somatic symptoms during the initial anamnestic interviews, the patient recollected that her first attack of nausea had occurred at the age of twelve when a boy whom she admired had offered her a piece of cake at a party. After this episode, eating in the presence of men often induced vague abdominal discomfort or mild nausea and diarrhea—reactions which became definitely worse after the death of her father when she was eighteen. In relation to such memories, however, she emphatically denied that she had acquired any sexual knowledge or had experienced even a single erotic fantasy until her menarche at sixteen, at which time her mother "explained" sexual intercourse to her in a depreciatory manner and stringently warned her against the "animal intents" and seductive activities of men.

The patient's symptoms took their present form at the age of twenty-five under the following circumstances. During her first prolonged separation from her mother, she was visiting the summer home of her middle sister and was there introduced to her first prospective suitor. At first she disliked the man but then began to feel a guilty erotic attraction toward him. One evening, after dinner with him during which the patient felt peculiarly tense and uncomfortable, she permitted some sexual play, but when he began to caress her breasts, she began to experience unusual severe nausea and abdominal discomfort. She immediately informed the man that she never wished to see him again and the next day, in compliance with a sudden compelling desire, she returned to her mother's home. She remained relatively symptom-free for a period, but only by the device of avoiding almost all heterosexual contacts. At the age of thirty she "fell in love" with the son of her employer but found herself able to accept his attentions only through the strict observance of certain conditions: sex play had to be non-stimulating, her breasts could not be touched and, most imperative of all, the man *was not permitted to mention food or drink in her presence,* let alone invite her to indulge in them; otherwise she would develop severe nausea and sometimes vomit.

Such ritualistic defenses sufficed for several months, but later became much more elaborate. She soon found it necessary to forbid her *fiancé* even to telephone her while she was having a meal at home lest severe nausea, emesis or diarrhea ensue. Vomiting became frequent despite all precautions, a persistent anorexia set in and her symptoms became so severe that in a few months she lost thirty-two pounds without, however, corresponding loss of strength or energy. Her family naturally regarded her condition as of serious physical import, urged her to quit her job and finally induced her to enter a well-known diagnostic clinic. Thorough physical, laboratory and roentgenological examinations showed completely normal findings. A diagnosis of anorexia nervosa was made and the patient was discharged by the internist with the admonition to lead a "more active and normal life."

Significantly, the patient informed her mother that the doctor had obviously meant to specify heterosexual indulgence, but that she would virtuously refuse to follow any such recommendation no matter what the penalty in ill health might be. The whimsical result of these protestations was that her mother took the patient's misinterpretation at its face value, disregarded her professed scruples and insisted that the patient begin having sexual intercourse with her *fiancé* immediately, on pain of being disowned by the family; in fact the mother actively arranged the details of moving the patient into an apartment for the greater convenience of the couple. During the seven months that the liaison lasted the patient's symptoms improved somewhat and she regained considerable weight, although she remained sexually inhibited, was excessively dependent upon and demanding of her lover, and found it difficult to eat in his presence. Moreover, when he finally deserted her to marry another girl who possessed the added attractions of greater emotional maturity and considerable wealth, the patient's anorexia, vomiting and diarrhea promptly reappeared and once again became severe and disabling. Pleading her lack of control of these symptoms, the patient then gave up all further attempts at sexual or other emancipation and returned to live with her mother. For a time she seemed comparatively content, but since her social isolation and various disabilities eventually became burdensome both to herself and her family, she yielded finally to their repeated urgings and applied for analysis.

Physical, laboratory and X-ray examinations preceding the analysis again revealed essentially normal findings. The patient's intelligence quotient on the second Stanford Revision of the Binet-Simon scale was 134. It is of interest that her responses to the Fantasy Test (43), given for the purpose of a preliminary psychodynamic survey, accurately anticipated the essential determinants of some of the patient's main unconscious reactions as later revealed in the analysis. Thus, in association to a stimulus picture of a monstrous eerie dragon issuing from a cave in a mystic canyon, she produced a very unusual fantasy in which she identified herself with this threatening phallic symbol, yet anxiously represented it (herself by projection) as a depreciated, helpless, oral-incorporative creature (a caterpillar) which, after a brief contact with the dangers and anxieties of the outside world, gladly regresses to the security of the mother's womb:

Here's a little caterpillar that wanted to seek his fortune and he left his nice, cozy, warm, little home for the great, big world. (I don't know what else to say. Wait till I embellish this a little.) Somehow or other he was beset by dangers wherever he went, rocky paths to cross, dangerous enemies to pass, no food in sight and so he finally stopped and pondered: "This great, big world I was trying to find doesn't seem to be remarkable after all. Maybe I should have thought twice instead of giving up that nice, comfortable, cozy, little place I left and maybe it wouldn't be too late to turn back now." And so dear children, even though you don't see him returning, that's what he did and he's content to stay where he is, the big outside world no longer having any fascination for him.

Course of the Analysis

The patient's initial transference was one of a self-conscious, puerile flirtatiousness in which significant oral components and naïve regressive fantasies were early expressed. Typical associations in the first three hours were the following:

This... is like a first date, because I get the same sort of sick [nauseated] feeling.... Mother certainly has a queer daughter.... Once when I was four years old and sick she brought me a doll.... I'm not so sure of things when I'm out with a man.... I won't keep this up if it makes me feel nauseated.... Why did even thinking of B [patient's lover] make me sick to my stomach?... I hope I'll be able to come tomorrow.

True to these indications and despite simple, reassuring interpretations that she might be tempted again to react with vomiting as an escape from uneasiness over erotic or hostile feelings mobilized in the analytic situation, the patient spent the weekend after her tenth analytic hour vomiting almost continuously and insisting to her family that this proved the analysis to be not only useless but probably actually harmful. However, the patient's mother, apparently again sensing the patient's intense unconscious guilt and her need for explicit maternal solution, strongly urged resumption of the treatment. The patient therefore returned and for some twenty hours thereafter defended herself against her highly ambivalent genital and oral transference by picturing the analyst as a haughty, cold, unapproachable individual, or an unprincipled seducer sure to be thwarted by her strong moral resistance, or else—even more damningly—as an unsympathetic confidant who did not give her adequate support and solace. Closely connected with early oral fantasies was a series of dreams which indicated, with the naïveté of initial analytic material, the patient's desire that the analyst present her with a male organ with which to please and win her mother. In fact, the only defense she summoned was to regard the oral incorporation of the phallus—which she fancied her mother wanted her to have—as unpleasant and *nauseating*.

Dream
I reached for a hat.... It went over a partition, but a man gave it back to me. I wore it and brought my mother and sister some cookies which I hoped would please them. Then mother gave me a frankfurter and I ate it, but I said it tasted terrible, like pork.

Associations
[Hat] Men's hats. A new hat makes me feel self-confident. [Man] You. I came back to the analysis to please mother. [Frankfurter] My mother and sister always joke about their being penises; I like to eat them, but this morning the thought made me sick. [Pork] I don't let myself eat it, but *mother* always fed us well.

As may be expected, she did not at this time develop further these early indications of deep oral conflicts, but instead erected a categorical defense to the effect that she was not really a weak, dependent child who must please her mother in order to secure food and protection, but was instead an able, self-sufficient and even potent individual who, incidentally, needed no analysis. However, when she ventured the ultimate bravado of dreaming that her father and mother were dead, and that she was a famous violin virtuoso with the rest of the world at her feet, her reactive guilt was so great that she recollected a firm resolution of childhood *to swallow poison* if ever she were bereaved of her parents. Aggressive material also appeared in more frankly anal forms of attack:

I want to be very destructive—tear things up and throw them out the window.... Your couch cover is filthy.... I hate all teachers.... Once in high school class I let wind from my rectum and it made a terrible noise. I was so embarrassed I quit school and never went back—I decided to study music instead.

In further masochistic reaction against hostile urges directed mainly toward the analyst as a father figure, the patient brought the following dream:

A man sang love songs in German to a woman who was with him on a balcony. I said I understood German too, so he came down and beat me.
Associations: Dad used to sing love songs to mother. Germans are terribly cruel—they kill people. [Balcony] Our home bedroom.

These and other associations indicated that the dream expressed competitive identification with the mother but that in reaction the primal scene was conceived so sadistically that the patient's gratification was far outweighed by an overwhelming fear of female genitality. Analysis of this fantasy also led to a franker expression of reactive castrative impulses toward father figures (as expressed in increasingly critical remarks about her boss, the analyst, and other men) accompanied, as usual, by a retreat in fantasy to the welcoming safety of the mother. This was typified a few days later in another dream:

Men lay in hospital cots all bandaged up like with mumps.... I dreamed of my Dad, who's dead.... Then there was an avalanche and I was in danger, but finally I was at home with my mother all cozy and warm.
Associations: [Hospital cots] My father died there. [Mumps] Makes men sterile. [Avalanche] Danger. [Cozy with mother] Warm, clean house on Friday night and the wonderful meal mother used to feed us.

In connection with other covert avowals of aggressions against the father and retreat to the mother the patient remembered a fantasy which had recurred frequently between the ages of about eight and sixteen: She was not her father's daughter and he had found her in her mother's garden. However, when the origin of such fantasies of virgin birth in early rejections of her father was explored, she defended herself for a period against recollecting predominantly oral hostilities toward him by maintaining that in her girlhood it had actually been her "happy task" *to bring him his meals,* especially (sic) during the frequent parental quarrels.

Positive oedipus memories also appeared, but with so little guilt as to make it obvious that these recollections of genital attractions toward the father were really defenses against great hostility toward him. For instance, as early as the first month of her analysis the patient brought a (screen?) memory that one day, at about the age of ten, she had actually encouraged her mother to leave home after a quarrel, and that night had "innocently" entered her father's bed "to make up for mother"—although this, she hastily added, had only made his grief all the greater. Nevertheless, as the reasons for her actual renunciation of men and the regressive flight to the mother were further analyzed, the patient was led to face her jealousies of the father not only on a superficial genital, but also on more significant pregenital levels. The characteristic features of the patient's oral conflict then appeared more clearly: whereas she could admit her ostensibly erotic temptations toward her father or his surrogates with little difficulty (she dreamed frankly of marrying her cousin, "which would be as bad as marrying my father"), she nevertheless wished to renounce her oral-aggressive wishes to incorporate her father as a mother substitute and at the same time eliminate him as an envied, thwarting rival. Consecutive fragments of her defensive associations at this stage are self-explanatory:

I fear marriage because I can't cook like my sisters and it wouldn't be right to let my husband feed *me*. . . . Often when I sat down to a meal, if the phone rang for a date I wouldn't be able to eat any more. I remember my father urged me to eat on fast days, but I just couldn't because I'd get nauseated. When B [former lover] kissed me after a meal I vomited all that night. . . . Once when I was fourteen mother went away and Dad cooked my meal.... I also vomited all that night too.... I also avoid marriage because my teeth bleed at night and that would be embarrassing [an indication that assumption of an adult feminine role would necessitate masochistic self-punishment for oral biting aggressions and would also symbolize self-castration.]

Yet more directly symbolic of her oral guilt, the patient cancelled several hours *to get treatment for a "painful mouth and throat"* although no organic basis for these paresthesias was ever found by a competent oral surgeon. From a psychosomatic standpoint it was also interesting that periods of reactive aggression toward the analyst, conceived as a rejecting parent figure, were characteristically accompanied by urges to vomit, defecate, or urinate during the hour, whereas genital urges (which were less guilt-charged and which the patient characterized lightly as "hot ideas") were reacted to only by minor bodily "chills" and subjective tremors. In this connection she clearly recalled that she had habitually slept with her mother until she came to America, that she had then greatly resented the fact that her father joined her mother in bed, that she had insisted on continuing to share this bed until she was eight years old, and that even at that age she had energetically resisted being sent to sleep with her sister because at that time she "wanted to keep on being warm and cozy with Mother and Dad." Moreover, the substrate of this material in deep oral attachments to her mother and jealousies against the *first* father image in her life, her uncle, soon appeared in other associations:

My uncle in W—, where I lived until I was four, didn't like me and was mean to me because I took up mother's time—but mother said I should be nice to him because he was the breadgiver; once she even refused to feed me until he could bring us more food.... I think my boss should leave me this money, because Dad never provided enough for us.

At this time the material also began to deal with the specific nature of her incorporative desires toward men, namely, to acquire their penises as a symbol of the masculinity desired by her mother and thereby eliminate them as competitors and displace them homosexually in her mother's affections. Such desires were soon indicated with increasing clarity in a multitude of dreams and associations. For instance, in the seventy-eighth hour, the patient reported the dream: "I aroused my sister R. sexually and didn't know whether to be glad or contemptuous." In this dream the sister was definitely associated with the mother and the patient granted herself the power (phallus) to arouse a mother figure sexually, yet wished to depreciate that same power because of the accompanying guilt over its acquisition.[1] Early (screen?) memories also came to the fore:

In W— when I was in a hospital a nurse passed by with a tray of buns that I wanted. I then asked the doctor to get me one and he promised, but instead he stuck a needle in my stomach and it hurt.

Similarly, the object she desired to incorporate from her father appeared in the next dream, in which, after a reiteration of her anxious rejection of the female role and a denial that she had ever been robbed of a fantasied penis, she allayed her anxiety by self-reassurance that she knew how to handle masculine appurtenances even though she did not openly despoil their envied owners—the analyst with the pencil and the little boy with the spear:

A man who was with my father wanted to sleep with me, but I refused because people were looking. Then I thought a burglar had gone through my clothes and taken something, but found he hadn't. I then helped my nephew to select a tie that I liked and saw a Buddha with a pencil attached that I wanted. Then I was showing a little boy to hold a spear and be a knight!

While this material was being worked through the patient showed considerable clinical improvement: she no longer spent nearly all her free time with her family; she permitted herself a greater number of social and recreational outlets in mixed company and she even dined out alone on one occasion with an elderly male acquaintance. To test her newly found freedom (and also apparently in a more or less con-

---

[1] The corollary or obverse interpretation of this bisexual dream, namely, that the patient reversed the sexual roles and depreciated femininity, is equally characteristic of the patient's neurosis.

scious effort to please the analyst to whom she had concurrently strong maternal transference) she even ventured at this meal to eat strawberries despite her conviction, born of invariable experience, that she would break out in hives if she did so. To her surprise, however (as well as to my own when she reported it), she felt no nausea at the meal and suffered no ill effects afterward.

But much still remained to be analyzed. For one thing, the patient unconsciously continued to reject femininity in favor of deeply guarded fantasies that despite her own guilt-charged rejection of the fantasy of the oral acquisition of the phallus, she had somehow actually acquired a penis which was of value in cementing her exclusive solidarity with her mother and which therefore had to be cherished and defended from all threats of castration. An amusing instance of this, related to many dreams and fantasies in which burglars had unsuccessfully attempted to search and rob her clothes or her room, was the following. One day, the patient playfully began to count the cylindrical buttons on her dress to the accompaniment of the familiar childhood chant of "Doctor, lawyer, merchant, chief." Suddenly she stopped in manifest consternation: the word "thief" had come out on the button over her genitals! During this period she also professed great concern that her breasts "were so very small," whereas her nose "was so very large"— both ideas having the import of a denial of matronly or feminine qualities.[2] In the same significant connection, she frequently added that her mother had always admired her "boyish figure." In this period also she became interested in various girl friends whom she suspected of being homosexual, was jealous that R. ("the most mannish" of her sisters) was living with her mother, and stated wishfully that the latter was "disappointed because I can't get a raise and take care of her myself." However, a beginning resolution of both her homosexual and heterosexual oral conflicts, arising from a partially relenting internal-

[2] These preoccupations with her bodily form at times approached the intensity of a "dominant idea" (Benedek, 14) that not only must she abjure adult feminine activities, but she also must not look like a woman. While this idea was never stated explicitly, the analytic material indicated that an ego-syntonic obsession of this nature may have contributed to the overdetermination of her vomiting and diarrhea, in as much as these symptoms tended to keep her thin, sallow and heterosexually unattractive and thereby protected her from situations in which her oral aggressions and reactive fear of men would be mobilized.

ized maternal superego, appeared in her hundred and sixty-eighth hour in the dream:

> Mother offered me a sausage, and I again spit it out saying, "I don't eat pork!" Then my mother said I could have men if I liked.[3]
> *Associations:* [Sausage] penis. [Have men] You buying me a meal.

After this initial working through of guilt over phallic incorporative fantasies, the patient could for the first time pleasurably visualize the analyst buying her food; moreover, in the next hour the defenses were sufficiently penetrated to permit the patient to have the sudden fantasy of *eating the analyst's penis*—a desire which, of course, had not been interpreted in specific terms previously. Similarly, feelings of nausea in subsequent hours were often associated with explicit ideas of having eaten and then vomited the analyst's or some other man's penis. In this connection the patient also mobilized material relative to her rejection of femininity and the fantasied identification with men in order to displace the father in the mother's favor. For instance, the patient remembered that whereas she had had no compunctions about entering the bathroom while her father was naked (as though she also were a man), she "had always been ashamed" to expose her breasts or pubic region to her mother "because I always felt there was something wrong with my shape"; likewise, menstruation always made her feel "hurt" or deficient (castrated) in some way. Similar material led to the formulation of the patient's castration anxiety on the basis of a feared retaliation for the aggressive oral incorporation of the father's penis—an act which must therefore be partially expiated in compulsive vomiting. For instance, the patient felt *very nauseated* and almost vomited on reading that Ethiopian slave boys were castrated and that *savages ate testicles to become more masculine*. An even more direct reference to the oral method of incorporating the phallus was revealed in a dream to the effect that her cousin's penis was filled with peas (as though it were edible) and that then her own vagina began growing them—to which she associated that once, after eating pea

---

[3] Material relevant to this dream indicated that at a deeper level the patient also desired to castrate her thwarting, aggressive, phallic mother, and therefore dreamed of the latter's forgiveness and indulgence.

soup prepared by her father, she had become nauseated and had vomited severely. At this point the patient was finally able to formulate an explicit and basic fantasy previously deeply hidden:

Any man to me is really more like food. . . . I feel like a cannibal when I eat with one. . . . I get nauseated and vomit. . . . The same thing happens when I see babies feeding at the breast. . . . I never could stand that sight; I can't even yet.

From this and similar material the patient then formulated another previously inexpressible fantasy arising from fear of retaliation for her oral aggressions toward men: if she permitted herself to be "feminine" and had sexual relations with a man, *somehow she would be physically hurt* by him. This masochistic concept she then elaborated by assertions that her mother "had suffered and lost her health [sic] through sexual intercourse"; by specific phobias of menstrual blood, dentists, operations, etc., by an anxious play on the analyst's name as meaning "knife-man" and by a peculiarly displaced obsession that "If I parted my hair in the middle [i.e., exposed my vagina for intercourse] I would become bald [castrated]." During this period the patient also felt compelled to urinate forcefully both before and after each hour, as though this characteristically aggressive and boyish activity had a definitely reassuring value for her.[4] Moreover, for the first time she could remember what she had really been acutely aware of throughout early childhood, namely, that both her mother and father had been greatly disappointed that the patient, their last child, had not been born a boy. Her conciliatory longing for her father and her jealous oral castrative reactions toward him were then simultaneously expressed in a "duplex" dream:

1. A man had a dog I wanted to pet.
2. I had a little dog that I cherished, and I protected him from a bigger dog. A negro couple were going to bed and I felt alone. A man came along and I avoided him. But my mother and sister petted the bigger dog and I was mad.

[4] Cf. Alexander (7), Gerard (30), and Van der Heide (54) on the symbolism of urination as a penis fantasy in girls.

Associations: [Dog] Penis. [Pet the dog] I would like to own a big dog. [Big dog] It threatened my dog. [Negro couple] My father and mother have crinkly hair [depreciated parents]. [Mother and sister played with bigger dog] I felt jealous and wanted to chase him away but I was afraid.

In response to the appropriate interpretations of such dreams and their related material, the patient then produced a wealth of deeper fantasies relative to her wish to acquire the penis by oral incorporation. For instance, an anxious dream about herself as "a little boy becoming a little girl" (refeminized by the analysis) was followed by a reassuring one in which the patient concealed her genitals in a public bath, and was then *willingly fed by a man with "almonds"* (association: "nuts, testicles") *and "chocolate"* ("feces—penis—bad taste in my mouth like before I vomit"). Likewise, her desire to use the orally acquired penis to seduce her idealized mother away from the father was epitomized in a dream of limpid clarity:

Ginger Rogers and Tyrone Power were making love, and I was in the way. There was some danger, but I went to a room in my mother's house and got some chocolate and nuts [rebirth as a male?]. I gave these to Ginger Rogers, and she was pleased. She paid no more attention to Tyrone Power and he disappeared.

To this dream the patient again associated that when she had slept in her parents' bed she had felt particularly displaced and jealous *when her father fondled her mother's breasts* (oral jealousy). Chocolate was again associated to feces and penis (depreciated phallus) and "nuts" frankly represented testicles. Moreover, not long thereafter the partial renunciation of this same desire to incorporate a phallus even to please her mother was indicated in the third and final dream of the "frankfurter" series:

My mother once again gave me a cut up frankfurter that looked good to eat, but this time my father was there and I gave it to him because I felt it belonged to him.

Concurrently, the anal components of her aggressive and incorporative fantasies about her father also appeared more openly: for instance, the patient played with the phrase "eliminating father" and reported that whereas she no longer vomited, thoughts of sexual intercourse still occasionally induced diarrhea. To this she associated a childhood concept that intercourse was performed per rectum, in connection with persistent fantasies that her feces at the same time eliminated and substituted for an anally incorporated penis—an organ which, in specific relation to her father's phallus, was always conceived as "dirty" and "soiling." Strong feelings of disgust with all mucous and "slimy" things were also specifically associated with a revulsion to obsessive thoughts of fellatio and with a fantasy the patient had had of swallowing semen during possible oral contacts with her father's penis while she was sleeping in the parental bed.

With the self-punitive, "undoing" and possibly restorative aspects of the patient's vomiting and diarrhea thus disclosed, the analysis could then also attack the overdeterminations and positive cathexes of these symptoms. These were, in brief, the function of the vomiting and diarrhea as disguised expression of oral and anal aggressions, the significance of these symptoms as reactions to coprophilic impulses, the masochistic gratification and various secondary gains (sympathy, indulgence, protection, etc.) the patient derived from them, and finally, their unconscious use in frustrating the analyst while the patient acted out fantasies of infantile narcissistic omnipotence in the tolerant and receptive analytic situation. At present (300th hour) her analysis is not as yet complete, but the following clinical improvements seem well established: the patient is for the first time of her own volition living apart from her family and is successfully pursuing extrafamilial friendships and interests. The vomiting has ceased, the diarrhea is infrequent and mild, and the other minor symptoms have disappeared. The patient now experiences little or no difficulty in eating with men, is experiencing satisfactory sexual relationships, and is cultivating suitors with a view to eventual marriage and the establishment of a home.

Formulation

In fairness to this and other psychoanalytic "formulations" it may be conceded at the outset that no simple running account of the emotional development of any individual can give really adequate consideration to the multiplex interplay and changing vector balance of the psychic forces operative even in childhood, let alone their multitudinous adjustments to the realities of later life. In the present case, nevertheless, the analysis seemed to justify a fairly specific reconstruction of the nature and development of at least the main libidinal trends and typical ego defenses, not only because these appeared with relative clarity in the analytic material, but also because the patient was permitted by circumstances to act out many of her childhood neurotic patterns in her daily life until the time of her analysis. The psychodynamic origins of her outstanding personality deviations and neurotic symptoms may therefore be reconstructed as follows:

The patient's primary oral attachment to her mother, represented in the formula "to be loved is to be fed" and by the *Ursymbol* of sole possession of the maternal breast, was early intensified and fixated as her main libidinal drive by a number of intercurrent factors: her puny, delicate physique, the indulgences by her mother as the youngest child, her jealous rivalry with her elder sisters, the early departure of her father from the family, and the subsequent insecurity and poverty of her childhood. This passive overdependence on the mother, however, was threatened when she learned that the providing member of her immediate circle was really a paternal uncle who fed and clothed the entire family. Obviously, this posed what may be termed the patient's first major problem: how to divide her allegiance between this intrusive man and her mother without incurring the latter's jealousy and prejudicing her primary desire for the transcendent security of the suckling. The child's problem was further aggravated by the fact that the uncle obviously resented her presence in the mother's home. To the first three years of the patient's life, then, belong the pregenital screen memories of running to her mother with feelings of guilt when men tempted her *by offering her food* and the fantasy of summoning "a nurse carrying buns" (breasts) in preference to a "doctor who might hurt her." To the latter part of this period, moreover, may belong the patient's earliest wishes actually to acquire a penis and thus, by becoming the little boy her mother expressly desired, to secure for herself the latter's exclusive support and protection. However, these early conflicts gave rise to relatively little anxiety, inasmuch as the patient appears to have left Europe at the age of five in a fairly secure oral receptive relationship with her mother. Unfortunately, when the family rejoined the father in America her position was more gravely threatened, which led to a series of emotional reactions and countercathexes that determined the patient's subsequent character neurosis and furnished the basic psychodynamisms of her symptomatology. Thus, the patient's continuous desire for oral dependence on her mother, coupled with her need to remain physically close to the latter even in the parental bed, made the patient for a number of years an actual witness of the primal scene, the most harrowing and "disgusting" detail of which she characteristically remembers as her father's fondling of the mother's breast. On the other hand, the patient's misunderstood persistence as an obtrusive third party in the marital relationship apparently also aroused the mother's suspicion and jealousy, with the result that the mother reacted not only by showing preference for the patient's eldest sister (the most "masculine" of the daughters) but also by punishing the patient in a number of highly traumatic ways—including a reiteration of her disappointment that the patient had not been born a boy. In this manner, the mother in turn became for a time no longer a protective and all-providing figure, but an unreliable, rejecting, fickle person who, until she was won back, would not provide complete security. Concurrently, the patient's anxieties were accentuated by the emerging genital components of her oedipus impulses which, strengthened but at the same time rendered extremely guilt-charged by her nightly physical contacts with the father in the presence of the mother, themselves increased her guilt and fear and therefore pressed for adequate ego defenses. The urgent problem faced by the patient at this juncture was then: how resolve this now complex and highly conflictful emotional situation and escape the dangers that seemed to threaten on every side?

The patient's initial attempt at solving her dilemma seems to have been simply to shunt the energy of her genital desires back to the *oral* sphere, transfer her dependent attachment from the temporarily unreliable mother to her kindlier father, and substitute in her typically passive receptive fashion the desire to feed from him (possibly, in an early misconception of anatomical equivalence, from his discharging penis) in lieu of the withdrawn maternal breast that had now been pre-empted by the father. In accordance with the lag in her libidinal development and the persistence of strong oral urges, this relationship at first constituted what might be termed an emotionally anachronistic "oral oedipus"—namely, the emergence for a period of predominantly oral receptive desires directed to the father with concomitant fear of retribution by the mother who at the same time—because of the patient's need for such a fantasy—was wishfully conceived to be jealous of the loss of the patient's dependent devotion (cf., her self-reassuring statements of her mother's indulgence when she resisted other oral temptation). Nevertheless, the positive genital oedipus fantasies, continually stimulated as they were, could not long remain completely repressed, so that she began to wish more or less consciously to be not only the parental suckling, but also to displace her mother as the father's mistress. (This genital oedipal phase is related to the transient fantasies, predominantly prepubertal, of displacing the mother in the father's bed.)

This, however, was likewise an untenable situation, since the patient, still passive and insecure and now conceiving herself helplessly adrift from her accustomed receptive relationship to her mother, found no really safe refuge in the father, whom she soon perceived to be as vacillating and as subservient to the mother as she herself was. There remained then only one alternative for the patient's weak, anxiety-ridden ego: a repression of the hostile part of her ambivalence and a final strategic retreat to an oral passive relationship to the only strong personality in the family, the mother, who must therefore again be won at all costs. But now certain modifications even in this libidinal relationship were necessary inasmuch as the patient's oral desires in response to repeated frustration, had changed vectorially from a merely passive receptivity to an actively attacking incorporation, as expressed in the unconscious fantasy that *if her mother no longer willingly gives her the breast or the father his phallus, she must aggressively take them for herself*. Moreover, the second portion of this fantasy—the symbolic desire for her father's penis—was now overdetermined by her wish to displace the father in an exclusive homosexual relationship with her mother, a relationship designed to supplement and strengthen the primary oral dependent one. It was in this manner, then, that her main conflicts assumed their final form, since primitive cannibalistic fantasies such as the oral incorporation of breast and penis were so charged with guilt that not only repression but nearly every other ego defense from denial to sublimation needed to be summoned to assure the indirect discharge of their cathected energy. She therefore began to be governed both alloplastically and autoplastically by a number of interrelated emotional syllogisms which, as stated, were reflected not only in her symptoms but also in her distinctive character traits and reality maladjustments up to the time of her analysis. Some of these syllogisms, for the sake of simplicity of presentation, may be formulated separately as follows:

1. REGRESSION

Since all levels of libidinal satisfaction above that of primal oral attachments to the mother appeared to be beset by dangers and anxieties, the patient renounced nearly all her ambitiously aggressive and genital strivings and devoted her life to resuming and making secure the only comparatively safe relationship she had ever known—a passive infantile dependence on the mother.

a. *Genital Renunciation*

She surrendered her transient oedipal wish to pre-empt the father from the mother. In fact, she foreswore all outward semblance of genital or other possessive desires for all men and indulged in such relationships only if and when they were not only permitted but demanded by the mother. At all other times, the patient by unconscious compulsion made herself in both appearance and behavior actually unattractive to men.

b. *Pregenital Mechanisms*

Anal-sadistic depreciation and masochism. The patient obsessively conceived of all genitality as obscene (forbidden) or dirty (aggressive and depreciated). In this sense she regarded everything her father touched as contaminated, as shown in many compulsions and fantasies, particularly in relation to his discharging penis. In the same manner she conceived the fantasy of sexual intercourse as a frightening anal attack, and equated the phallus with a column of feces which she could then not only herself possess, but also eliminate aggressively by diarrhea whenever threatened with the passive role in heterosexuality. Beneath these concepts, however, was an important element of masochistic gratification in her vomiting and other symptoms and in the few traumatic genital contacts that, with the mother's express consent, she had permitted herself.

Defense of secondary narcissism. In deference to the mother's expressed desires, the patient made a pretense of apparent emancipation from her, but only in ways that served really to cement their relationships. For instance, she studied music and played it showily as the mother desired, yet never sufficiently well to become independently proficient. Similarly, she held a job and made just sufficient money to help support the mother—but never enough to justify living apart from her.

2. "PENIS WISH"

Still other defenses against anxiety were necessary since the mother once undeniably had discarded the patient in favor of the father's phallus and thus had severely traumatized the patient's narcissism. To emasculate and displace the father and at the same time regain the mother she therefore erected and cherished a fantasy that she also had a penis, acquired by oral incorporation from the father. Moreover, to preserve this fantasy that she had masculine attributes, she had to conceal her femininity. She therefore professed pride in the smallness of her breasts and the "boyish figure" she hoped her mother admired, yet she always avoided letting the latter see her naked and penisless. She played tomboy until her menarche which was delayed until sixteen, and even in her adolescence walked into her father's bath as though on equal terms with him. Later, she raged against menstruation and feared dentists, operations, and all other castrative threats however indirect their connotation.

3. ORGAN NEUROSES: VOMITING AND DIARRHEA

Finally, only through adequate self-punishment and specific restitution, could she allay the obsessive guilt over desires that had led to the fantasy of the oral (and anal) incorporation of the penis.

a. *Talion fear*

Because she hated the father for displacing her with the mother and then in turn thwarting her both orally and genitally, and because she therefore also wished to castrate him, she became fearful of physical retribution by all men and manifested this fear by chills, palpitation, and various neuromuscular disturbances in their presence.

b. *Fantasy of oral rejection and restitution*

More specifically in relation to the main determinant of the vomiting, if she dared actually to take food in the presence of a man and thus repeated the symbolic act of oral castration of the father, she immediately experienced disgust and eliminated the phallus (more deeply, the breast—cf., nausea at the sight of infants feeding) by vomiting and diarrhea. This she did not only in masochistic gratification and to deny deep cannibalistic desires but also *to restore* what once in fantasy she had actually wished to incorporate.

Such then were the main vortices of emotional conflict in the patient's character and organ neuroses. Unfortunately, the defects of the formulations are readily apparent: they are necessarily short and oversimplified; they assume a specificity of libidinal expressions and ego defenses not completely substantiated by the abbreviated account of the analysis; they artificially telescope into "crucial" episodes of the patient's life emotional actions and reactions that were probably worked through over long periods, and finally, they represent under separate rubrics various economically indissoluble intrapsychic mechanisms that really bore to each other a constantly varying relationship in determining the patient's internal and external adjustments. Only two considerations extenuate these difficulties: first, that the "emotional logic" of the unconscious is in reality relatively direct and elemental; second, that even in the description of complex intrapsychic reactions the limitations of language unfortunately demand that only one topic be dealt with at any one time. It is hoped that despite these limitations the nature and derivations of the patient's main psychosomatic characteristics have been indicated.

Discussion

From the medical standpoint, the question naturally arises: was the diagnosis of anorexia nervosa "correctly" made in this patient? The answer obviously depends on how rigidly delimited this syndrome is considered to be.[5] At the time of her admission to the medical clinic five years before analysis the severe anorexia, marked weight loss, cachexia with characteristically unimpaired energy and activity, intractable vomiting after food intake and absence of any positive indication of organic disease were almost pathognomonic of the syndrome of anorexia nervosa as originally described by Gull, although it must be remembered that other less determinative criteria, such as loss of hair and amenorrhea, were not present. However, with particular respect to the menstrual function, it could easily be conceived that had the patient's rejection of this aspect of femininity and her castration fears been even greater than they were at the time, her menstruation, instead of becoming merely scanty and painful, might have been suppressed as completely as it had been previous to the age of sixteen. Finally, her partial symptomatic recovery after her hospitalization does not invalidate the diagnosis, since anorexia nervosa is often a phasic disorder[6] and, as has been noted, the unconsciously reassuring psychotherapy she received from her physician and her mother, combined with the special environmental arrangements made for her (removal from the home, expressly permitted heterosexual outlets, etc.) temporarily relieved some of her pressing emotional conflicts. It should nev-

---

[5] The author has elsewhere discussed the general nonspecificity of medical-psychiatric "diagnoses" (42, 43).

[6] Wilbur and Washburn (55) in a two-year follow-up study of ninety-seven patients with functional vomiting studied at the Mayo Clinic, reported "cure" or improvement in over 70 per cent. For other clinical reports illustrating the wide variety of formulations and methods of therapy, cf. Pischer (48), Middleton (46), Hill (32), Morgan (47), Hurst (33), Kiefer (38), Stengel (53), Smith (52), Wilbur (55), and Berkman (15). The clinical psychiatric aspects of severe vomiting have been especially well reviewed by Meyer (45).

ertheless be made clear that the psychoanalytic findings in this patient are not necessarily applicable to every case of anorexia nervosa, since the term has a broad medical, rather than a specific psychosomatic connotation (Brosin, Palmer and Slight, 18 and Alexander, 11).

REVIEW AND DISCUSSION OF THE LITERATURE[7]

As early as 1892, Freud, in a paper with Breuer, mentioned "chronic vomiting and anorexia carried to the point of refusal of food" as being of psychic origin, and stated that "a painful affect, which was originally excited while eating but was suppressed, produces nausea and vomiting, and this continues for months as hysterical vomiting [which] accompanies a feeling of moral disgust." Freud (27), in his *Interpretation of Dreams* (1900) also speaks of a patient who had chronic vomiting both in fulfillment of and self-punishment for a fantasy of being continually pregnant by many men. The possible roots of oral conflicts are then further traced in *Three Contributions to the Theory of Sexuality* (1905), as follows:

One of the first.... pregenital sexual organizations is the oral, or, if one will, the cannibalistic. Here the sexual activity is not yet separated from the taking of nourishment,[8] and the contrasts within it are not yet differentiated. The object of the one activity is also that of the other; the sexual aim then consists in the incorporation of the object into one's own body, the prototype of identification, which later plays such an important psychic role [28].

In 1911, Ernest Jones developed another thesis with regard to neurotic vomiting, namely, that the symptom expressed a rejection of an incorporated penis, conceived as an incestuous pregnancy. In effect, Jones (37) agreed with Melanie Klein that little girls "enjoy taking

---

[7] An excellent review of the literature and of the present psychoanalytic concepts of the gastrointestinal neuroses, seen in manuscript by the author after the present article was prepared, is the chapter on "The Gastrointestinal Neuroses," by F. Alexander in S. Portis' *Diseases of the Digestive System*. Philadelphia: Lea & Febiger, 1941.

[8] In this connection, Starke speaks of the withdrawal of the mother's breast as the "primal castration."

the penis into the body.... to make a child from it." Similarly, Ferenczi attributed the vomiting of hyperemesia gravidarum to an attempt on the part of the patient simultaneously "to deny the genital localization" of the pregnancy and to give up "the phantasied 'stomach-child'." In another place (26, p. 326) Ferenczi also recognized that vomiting may be a reaction to coprophagic fantasies, as expressed in my case by expulsive oral rejection of the dirty, distasteful penis.[9] While similar associations in my patient might have been traced to deeply repressed fantasies of impregnation by the father's incorporated phallus, it must be stated that further material explicitly relevant to this complex did not appear in the analysis.

Abraham, in his study of The Development of the Libido (5) dealt with the unconscious desires of the melancholic patient for the oral incorporation of the lost and ambivalently loved object and stated that the refusal of food in depressive states could be traced to the corresponding cannibalistic guilt. That this mechanism was operative in my patient was indicated by her prolonged refusal of food and frequent vomiting during the several months of depression after the death of her father. It is significant, however, that mere anorexia was apparently insufficient to expiate the guilt attached to her previous aggressive

---

[9] In such fantasies the equation mother equals penis is often also depreciatingly and aggressively expanded to penis equals feces (cf. Abraham 4, p. 485 et seq.) so that primary oral incorporative fantasies are reacted to with nausea, disgust and vomiting.

The primitive psychosomatic reaction of removing dangerous (incorporated) substances through diarrhea and vomiting has been called by Rado the "riddance principle" and is described by him (49) as follows: "Control of pain is directed toward eliminating the source of suffering, if necessary even by the sacrifice of a part of one's own body. Such conduct reveals a principle ingrained in the organization of all animals, including man. In the phylogenetic scale of increasing differentiation and complexity of organization there gradually become apparent many reflexes designed to eliminate pain-causing agents from the surface or inside of the body. The scratch reflex, the shedding of tears, sneezing, coughing, spitting, vomiting, colic bowel movement are but a few well-known instances of this principle of pain control in our bodily organization. This principle I have called the "riddance principle" and its physiological embodiments of the "riddance reflexes."

Following the experimental demonstration by Cannon of the intimate interrelationships of emotional states and gastric motility, it has been demonstrated clinically that gastric peristalsis increases during hunger (22) and either ceases or is reversed during strong emotions and *especially in disgust* (50, 51). However, as Alexander (9) states in his *Medical Value of Psychoanalysis*: "Even psychogenic vomiting itself may not always express anything psychological, for example, disgust, although conditions in the stomach which led to vomiting may have been called forth by psychological factors." For a brief review of the psychosomatic aspects of vomiting, cf. Dunbar (25), pp. 311-315.

incorporative fantasies toward the lost father, so that vomiting as a symbolic restitution was also economically necessary.

More directly germane to the present study is a series of papers published in 1934 on *The Influence of Psychologic Factors upon Gastro-Intestinal Disturbances* by various members of the Chicago Psychoanalytic Institute (8). In his introductory section to this symposium, Alexander pointed out that in patients with gastric neurosis characteristic attitudes of "parasitic receptiveness" are thwarted by internal or external circumstances and therefore become colored by oral aggressivity and strong narcissistic protests over feelings of inferiority. As a result, unconsciously weak, orally dependent patients adopt a defensive façade of great personal self-sufficiency, an exaggerated attitude of helpfulness toward others and a superficial optimism[10] that they in turn will always be provided for—traits characteristic of my patient. In the same symposium, Catherine Bacon described a woman with a gastric neurosis who was a frequent witness of the primal scene in her childhood, had intense rivalry with a sister, marked ambivalence to her thwarting mother and strong early heterosexual inhibitions. Bacon's analysand resembled mine in other ways: she associated genital sexuality with eating and "when her oral desires were thwarted by external frustration, she went into a rage the content of which was a desire to attack the penis of the thwarting object and incorporate it."

A corresponding case of a forty-one-year-old woman who suffered from a recurrent duodenal ulcer was reported by George Wilson,[11] who found that his patient had a "retaliation fear because of the castration wish. . . . The oral dependent attitude toward the mother was transferred to a wish to incorporate the penis orally . . . due not only to resentment and fear but also to the wish to own something, the possession of which pleased the mother. . . . She wanted to possess a penis with which she can please the mother as the father does and in consequence

---

[10] Cf. Abraham (4).

[11] That corresponding unconscious mechanisms (compulsive disgorgements and restitution of gastric contents) are operative in male patients with gastric neuroses is indicated by the analyses of patients reported by Harry Levey and by Maurice Levine (8). In Levine's patient the relationship of vomiting and diarrhea to the neurotic character structure is especially well demonstrated.

continue to receive from her."[12] One other comparison is noteworthy: in both patients, pregenital conflicts were manifested mainly in gastrointestinal dysfunctions, whereas genital ones were expressed symbolically in the neuromuscular system. To illustrate: Wilson's patient, while working through the reawakened guilt over incestuous relations with her brother, suffered from various muscular pains and disturbances of locomotion; whereas my patient reacted to heterosexual fantasies with characteristic paresthesias (vaginal itching, pilomotor "chills," etc.) and sensations of generalized muscular tremors.

The various psychogenic roots of the patient's diarrhea have not been treated as fully in this discussion as have those of the dysgeusia, nausea and vomiting, not only because the latter were more significant in her case from the standpoint of psychosomatic investigation but also because the subject of colonic dysfunctions has already received extensive theoretical consideration in the psychoanalytic literature, particularly by Abraham (2, 3), Jones (36) and by the members of the Chicago Institute (8). More specifically from a clinical standpoint, Alexander (8) cites the case of a female patient in whom "the diarrhea, apart from the meaning of restitution, had also the narcissistic significance of masculine activity and expressed the masculine strivings of the patient." Similarly, Wilson (8) found that in women with colitic diarrhea the symptoms signified a rejection of femininity, in that the female role was conceived to be either parasitically oral-receptive or else too aggressively castrative in significance. Freud (28) postulates that on a deeper level the diarrhea may also represent the anal elimination of an incestuous pregnancy. However, it may be well to point out that in my patient the diarrhea which developed in reaction to fantasied or actual threats of heterosexuality had the significance not only of a conciliatory gift to the mother and a guilty elimination or restitution of the penis *per anum* as well as *per os*, but at other times also represented a jealous and sadistic attack on the analyst or other

---

[12] Felix Deutsch (24) attributes the rejection of food in two cases of anorexia nervosa that he analyzed to early concern on the part of the mother as to the patient's food intake and "stabilization of phantasies around the gastrointestinal tract" after "maternal rejection." While, as Deutsch contends, this would lead to the "choice" of the gastrointestinal tract to express the patient's neurosis, the psychodynamism described does not seem sufficiently clear to be regarded as *pathognomonic* of anorexia nervosa.

parent imago for fantasied thwarting in the oral or genital spheres (2). A corresponding explanation for the patient's urinary urgency as symbolic of masculine aggressivity may be found in Freud's Interpretation of Dreams (p. 512). From an economic standpoint, therefore, the patient's various symptoms—vomiting, diarrhea and urinary urgency—served as channels for an autoplastic discharge through the eliminative functions of various guilt-charged aggressive or erotic impulses which the patient, because of fear and guilt, was inhibited from expressing in alloplastic social behavior.

Summary

The analysis of a patient with character difficulties, neurotic vomiting and diarrhea, and the syndrome of anorexia nervosa is outlined. The organic dysfunctions are shown to be somatic manifestations of a highly complex personality disorder arising from severe early emotional conflicts, especially in the oral sphere. The most important specific psychodynamism of the vomiting appears to be a symbolic rejection and restitution of the father's phallus, orally incorporated in an attempt to render exclusive her basic passive dependence on the mother; however, the symptom also expresses an aggressive attack on the thwarting parents, masochistic expiation and other psychic overdeterminants. These and other psychosomatic reactions are considered in relation to the present psychoanalytic concepts of the various gastrointestinal neuroses.

REFERENCES

1. Abraham, K.: The spending of money in anxiety states. *Selected Papers*. London: Hogarth Press, 1927, p. 299.
2. ———: The narcissistic evaluation of excretory processes in dreams and neuroses. *Selected Papers*. London: Hogarth Press, 1927, p. 321.
3. ———: Contributions to the theory of anal character. *Selected Papers*. London: Hogarth Press, 1927, p. 370.
4. ———: The influence of oral erotism on character formation. *Selected Papers*. London: Hogarth Press, 1927, p. 393.
5. ———: A short study of the development of the libido. *Selected Papers*. London: Hogarth Press, 1927, p. 418.

6. Alexander, F.: *Psychoanalysis of the Total Personality.* New York: Nerv. & Ment. Dis. Monograph Series, No. 52, 1930.
7. ——: The relation of structural and instinctual conflicts. *Psychoanal. Quart.,* 2:181-207, 1933.
8. ——, et al.: The influence of psychologic factors upon gastro-intestinal disturbances: a symposium. *Psychoanal. Quart.,* 3:501-588, 1934.
9. ——: *The Medical Value of Psychoanalysis.* New York: Norton, 1936, p. 197.
10. ——, et al.: Culture and personality: a round table discussion. *Am. J. Orthopsychiat.,* 8:602, 1938.
11. ——: Gastro-intestinal neuroses. In: *Diseases of the Digestive System* by S. Portis. Philadelphia: Lea & Febiger, 1941.
12. —— & Menninger, W. C.: The relation of persecutory delusions to the functioning of the gastro-intestinal tract. *J. Nerv. & Ment. Dis.,* 84:541-554, 1936.
13. Bacon, C.: Typical personality trends and conflicts in cases of gastric disturbances. In: The influence of psychologic factors upon gastro-intestinal disturbances: a symposium. *Psychoanal. Quart.,* 3:558-573, 1934.
14. Benedek, T.: Dominant ideas in the relationships to morbid cravings. *Int. J. Psychoanal.,* 17:40-51, 1936.
15. Berkman, J. M.: Functional anorexia and functional vomiting; relation to anorexia nervosa. *Med. Clin. N. A.,* 23:901-912, 1939.
16. Blitzsten, N. L.: Psychoanalytic contributions to the conception of disorder types. *Am. J. Psychiat.,* 94:1431-1439, 1938.
17. Breuer, J. & Freud, S.: On the psychical mechanism of hysterical phenomena. In: Freud, S.: *Collected Papers,* I, London: Hogarth Press, 1924, p. 25.
18. Brosin, H., Palmer, W. F., & Slight, D.: Anorexia nervosa. Unpublished manuscript.
19. Cannon, W. B.: The movements of the stomach studied by means of the Röntgen rays. *Am. J. Physiol.,* 1:38, 1898.
20. ——: The influence of emotional states on the functions of the alimentary canal. *Am. J. Med. Sci.,* 137:480, 1909.
21. ——: *Mechanical Forces of Digestion.* London: E. Arnold, 1911.
22. —— & Washburn, A. L.: An explanation of hunger. *Am. J. Physiol.,* 29:441, 1912.
23. Carmichael, H. T., & Masserman, J. H.: Results of treatment in a psychiatric out-patient department. *J. Am. Med. Assn.,* 113:2292-2298, 1939.
24. Deutsch, F.: Choice of organ in organ neurosis. *Int. J. Psychoanal.,* 20:252, 1939.

25. Dunbar, H. F. *Emotions and Bodily Changes.* New York: Columbia University Press, 1938.
26. Ferenczi, S.: *Theory and Technique of Psychoanalysis.* New York: Boni & Liveright, 1927, p. 326.
27. Freud, S.: Interpretation of dreams. In: *The Basic Writings of Sigmund Freud.* New York: Modern Library, 1938, p. 512.
28. ———: *Three Contributions to the Theory of Sexuality.* New York: Nerv. & Ment. Dis. Pub. Co., 1910.
29. ———: Transformation of instincts with special reference to anal-erotism. *Collected Papers,* II. London: Hogarth Press, 1924, pp. 164-171.
30. Gerard, M.: Child analysis as a technique in the investigation of mental mechanisms. *Am. J. Psychiat.,* 94:653-662, 1937.
31. Gull, W. W.: The address on medicine. *This Volume,* pp. 104-127.
32. Hill, L. W.: Glucose and insulin in the treatment of recurrent vomiting. *Med. Clin. N. A.,* 10:1329-1337, 1927.
33. Hurst, A. F.: Hysterical vomiting. *N. Y. Med. J.,* 111:95, 1930.
34. Jones, E.: *Papers on Psychoanalysis.* Baltimore: William Wood, 1938.
35. ———: The relationship between dreams and psychoneurotic symptoms. In: *Papers on Psychoanalysis.* Baltimore: William Wood, 1938, pp. 277-282.
36. ———: Anal erotic character traits. In: *Papers on Psychoanalysis.* Baltimore: William Wood, 1938.
37. ———: The phallic phase. In: *Papers on Psychoanalysis.* Baltimore: William Wood, 1938.
38. Kiefer, E. D.: A treatment for persistent vomiting. *Surg. Clin. N. A.,* 11:329-336, 1931.
39. Klein, M.: *The Psychoanalysis of Children.* London: Hogarth Press, 1932, pp. 269 ff.
40. Levey, H. B.: Oral trends and oral conflicts in a case of duodenal ulcer. In: The influence of psychologic factors upon gastro-intestinal disturbances: a symposium. *Psychoanal. Quart.,* 3:574, 1934.
41. Levine, M.: Pregenital trends in a case of chronic diarrhoea and vomiting. In: The influence of psychologic factors upon gastro-intestinal disturbances: a symposium. *Psychoanal. Quart.,* 3:583, 1934.
42. Masserman, J. H. & Carmichael, H. T.: Diagnosis and prognosis in psychiatry. *J. Ment. Sci.,* 84:894-946, 1938.
43. ——— & Balken, E. R.: The psychoanalytic and psychiatric significance of phantasy. *Psychoanal. Rev.,* 26:343-379 & 535-549, 1939.
44. Meng, H.: Anorexia nervosa. *Int. Ztschr. f. Psychoanal.,* 20:439-458, 1934.
45. Meyer, F. M.: Nervous vomiting and its psychotherapy. *München. med. Wchnschr.,* 83:96-97, 1936.

46. Middleton, W. S.: Sauerkraut in treatment of vomiting. *Wisconsin Med. J.,* 25:554-559, 1926.
47. Morgan, I.: Cyclic vomiting. *Med. J. Australia,* 2:524-532, 1930.
48. Pischer, J.: Deep breathing in treatment of neurotic vomiting. *Bull. Acad. de Méd. Paris,* 86:43, 1921.
49. Rado, S.: Developments in the psychoanalytic conception and treatment of the neuroses. *Psychoanal. Quart.,* 8:427-437, 1939.
50. Schindler, R.: Die Psychoneurosen des Verdauungstraktes. *Ber. üb. d. II. Allg. ärztl. Kongr. f. Psychotherapie,* Leipzig, 1927, pp. 184-194.
51. Schwab, M.: Die Ursache des unstillbaren Erbrechens in der Schwangerschaft. *Zentralblatt f. Gynäk.,* 45: 956-958, 1535-1536, 1921.
52. Smith, C. H.: Recurrent vomiting—etiology (especially in relation to migraine) and treatment. *J. Pediat.,* 10:719-742, 1937.
53. Stengel, E.: Periodic incoercible vomiting as equivalent of depressive phase of manic depressive insanity. *Med. Klin.,* 29:1612-1613, 1933.
54. Van der Heide, C.: A case of pollakiuria nervosa. *Psychoanal. Quart.,* 10:267-283, 1941.
55. Wilbur, D. L. & Washburn, R. N.: Clinical features of functional and nervous vomiting. *J. Am. Med. Assn.,* 110:477-480, 1938.
56. Wilson, G.: The transition from organ neurosis to conversion hysteria. *Int. J. Psychoanal.,* 19:23-40, 1938.

CONCLUSION

THE MOUNT SINAI SEMINAR GROUP

As the participants in this discussion review the work presented in this volume, it can be seen that the approach to the problems of psychosomatic conditions has shown a development over the past century. Hopefully, we have documented the outline and nature of the progressive development.

What can be seen is that over the century there has been a gradual refinement of concepts concerning psychosomatic medicine. Gull, writing a hundred years ago, could speak only of the role of emotional and psychic factors as a cause of disease. He was seeking etiologic factors as was the attempt in his time and, while recognizing that emotions play a role in some way, he could not be more specific than that in his statements. In contrast, writers of the past decade (Waller et al., Lorand, Masserman), in considering the same aspect of the role of psychic factors more clearly, pinpoint the problem in terms of unconscious mental functioning, involving unconscious fantasies, shifts of psychic energies, etc.

This change is more than a difference in terms. Rather, it represents a shift from a general proposition to a study of the more specific means whereby that general factor is carried out. This changing approach in the field of psychosomatics parallels the shifting emphasis in medicine in general in which the search for understanding has led to attempts at understanding the function of specific biochemical systems of the body organs. Also involved in the changing emphasis of the role of psychic factors is a growing recognition of the mind as an organ of the body whose functioning is integrated into the total organismic adaption. Thus psychic factors play a role at all stages of the development of a disease state, a role which may vary in importance at given stages of the development of the state, but is present at all times. Regarded in this manner, it is not necessary to search for psychic factors as the etiologic agent in certain conditions, and to ignore them completely in other states. It becomes a question of how large a role, or how small, psychic factors play at a given point in the progression of the disease state.

Since the work of Freud it has become increasingly evident that the more that is known about an individual's psychic functioning, the more precise a researcher can be in evaluating the total personality involved in a disease process. We are still in a period of collecting data and correlating new observations in the fields opened up by Freud's discoveries. Not all researchers are at the same level of development, nor is there universal agreement even on the tools of research in this field. Yet there are increasingly more data and observations which seem to confirm the trend to examination of the specific mental content, including energy changes, defensive maneuvers, etc., to determine the total mode of adaption of an individual. Included in such a concept is the awareness that health or disease are relative terms which reflect the total homeostatic balance of forces within the organism to re-establish the previously existing homeostatic adaption.[1] Such attempts may not succeed in restoring the previous state but may rather end in a new and different level of adaptational balance. This also may be regarded as a successful outcome for the individual organism, even if society or the outside environment may not so regard it.

The ultimate goal that we strive toward as physicians is to be able to intervene in a disturbance of adaptation, to bring about a restoration of a homeostatic state which serves the needs of both the individual and his environment. To achieve this, however, requires more detailed knowledge of the functioning of mind, body and environment than we now possess, although we have made considerable progress in the past century.

---

[1] M. R. Kaufman: The problem of psychiatric symptom formation. *J. Michigan State Med. Soc.*, 57:71-76, 86, 1958.

The editors hope that the reprinting of the original papers with the accompanying commentary has fulfilled the basic premise of the Introduction. The gradual evolution of psychosomatic concepts has been demonstrated. This involves progress from an early stage at which there was recognition of fairly nonspecific psychological factors to a stage where highly specific psychological constellations at the conscious, preconscious and unconscious levels are demonstrable. The work of Sigmund Freud made this evolution possible since, up to his time, the role of the unconscious, even though hinted at and recognized, could not be utilized as an integrated systematic factor in health and disease.

The syndrome of anorexia nervosa seems to us to be a happy choice as a paradigm of the integration and interrelationship of all the facets of psyche and soma. The growing trend toward cellular biology makes it even more evident that psychological factors assume increasing significance on all levels of organismic function, and that the "mind" functions as the great integrator.

BIBLIOGRAPHY

ABBATE, F. E.: Endocrine psychiatry of anorexia nervosa. *Med. panamer., B. Aires*, 12:299-309, 1959.

ABT, I. A.: Anorexia in infants. *Med. Clin., Chicago*, 1:493-504, 1915.

AGGELER, P.M.; LUCIA, S. P.; & FISHBON, H. M.: Purpura due to vitamin K deficiency in anorexia nervosa. *Am. J. Digest. Dis.*, 9:227-229, 1942.

AGNEW, L. R. C. & MAYER, J.: Mechanism of anorexia in vitamin-deficient hyperphagic animals. *Nature, London*, 177:1235-1236, 1956.

ALAJOUANINE, T.; VILLEY, R.; NEHLIL, J.; & HOUDART, R.: Appetite disorders and rhinencephalon; with special reference to a regressive case of obesity due to hyperphagia secondary to temporal lobectomy for epilepsy. *Rev. neurol., Paris*, 96:321-323, 1957.

——— ——— ——— & ———: Appetite disorders and rhinencephalon; with special reference to a case of regressive obesity due to hyperphagia secondary to temporal lobectomy for epilepsy. *Presse méd.*, 65:1385-1387, 1957.

ALBEAUX-FERNET, H.; CHABOT, J.; & GELINET, M.: Research on hormonal functions in 29 cases of mental anorexia and functional thinness of young girls. *Sem. hôp. Paris*, 35:1000-1003, 1959.

ALBERT-CREMIEUX & DONGIER, M.: Statistical observations of families in which mental anorexia has occurred. *Ann. méd. psychol., Paris*, 114 (1):639-641, 1956.

ALDRICH, C. A.: Common type of anorexia seen in run-about children. *Bull. Menninger Clin.*, 8:185-187, 1944.

ALEXANDER, G. H.: Anorexia nervosa with emphasis on psychotherapy. *Rhode Island Med. J.*, 22:189-195, 1939.

ALLIES, F.: Fatness and polyphagia in leukemia. *Mschr. Kinderh.*, 106:237-239, 1958.

ALLIEZ, J.; CODACCIONI, J. L.; & GOMILA, J.: Mental anorexia in men. *Ann. méd. psychol.*, Paris, 112(2):697-711, 1954.

ALLISON, R. S. & DAVIES, R. P.: Treatment of functional anorexia. *Lancet*, 1:902-907, 1931.

ALTSCHULE, M. D.: Adrenocortical function in anorexia nervosa before and after lobotomy. *New England J. Med.*, 248:808-810, 1953.

AMSLER, R.: Causes and treatment of anorexia in infants. *Concours méd.*, 78:865, 1956.

ANAND, B. K.; DUA, S.; & SHOENBERG, K.: Hypothalamic control of food intake in cats and monkeys. *J. Physiol.*, 127:143-152, 1955.

Anorexia. *Nutrit. Rev.,* 11:271-273, 1953.
Anorexia in childhood. *Internat. Med. Digest,* 39:121-124, 1941.
Anorexia nervosa. *Clin. Rev., Pittsburgh,* 3:60-68, 1935.
Anorexia nervosa—psycho or somatic. *Nutrit. Rev.,* 17:138-139, 1959.
ANSTREICHER, K.: Anorexia nervosa; a case report. *Delaware Med. J.,* 31:239-243, 1959.
ARNHOFF, F. N.: A case of anorexia nervosa in a 16-year-old girl. *J. Clin. Psychol.,* 13:194-196, 1957.
BAKWIN, R. M.: Feeding difficulties in early childhood. *Med. Clin. North America,* 31:688-695, 1947.
———: Poor appetite in young children. *J. Pediat.,* 31:584-586, 1947.
BALDUZZI, E.: Psychopathological aspects of mental anorexia. *Arch. psicol. neurol. psichiat.,* 14:176-179, 1953.
———: The syndrome of mental anorexia; clinical contributions. *Riv. sper. freniat.,* 77:441-471, 1953.
BARTELS, E. D.: Studies on hypometabolism; anorexia nervosa (in relation to Simmonds' disease). *Acta med. scandinav.,* 124:185-211, 1946.
BARTSTRA, H. K. G.: Anorexia nervosa; case. *Nederl. tschr. geneesk.,* 92:750-757, 1948.
BAUER, B. & POHL, W.: Anorexia nervosa. *Zschr. ärztl. Fortbild.,* 50:839-841, 1956.
BAUER, J.: Endocrine aspects of sprue; relation to pituitary syndrome in anorexia nervosa. *J. Trop. Med.,* 42:245-250, 1939.
BEAMER, W. D. & THOMAS, J. E.: Effect on appetite in dogs of pyrogenic substances in intravenous infusions. *Gastroenterology,* 27:347-352, 1954.
BECK, J. C. & BROCHNER-MORTENSEN, K.: Prognosis in anorexia nervosa. *Acta med. scandinav.,* 149:409-430, 1954.
BEECH, H. R.: An experimental investigation of sexual symbolism in anorexia nervosa employing a subliminal stimulation technique; preliminary report. *Psychosom. Med.,* 21:277-280, 1959.
BENEDETTI, G.: Diagnosis and therapy of so-called psychoendocrine cachexia; from primary anorexia to Simmonds' disease. *Clin. terap.,* 8:457-484, 1955.
———: Psychoanalysis of mothers in therapy of anorexic children. *Helvet. paediat. acta,* 11:539-561, 1956.
BENSI, H. W.: Emaciation as a problem of holistic medicine. *Med. Klin., Berlin,* 50:49-54, 1955.
BERGOUIGNAM, M.: L'anorexie mentale. *Sem. hôp. Paris,* 32:2983-2985, 1956.
BERKMAN, J. M.: Anorexia nervosa; anorexia, inanition, and low basal metabolic rate. (Thesis.) *Minneapolis: University of Minnesota,* 1930.
———: Anorexia nervosa, anorexia, inanition, and low basal metabolic rate. *Am. J. Med. Sc.,* 180:411-424, 1930.

———: Anorexia nervosa, anterior-pituitary insufficiency, Simmonds' cachexia and Sheehan's disease; including some observations on disturbances in water metabolism associated with starvation. *Postgrad. Med.,* 3:237-246, 1948.

———: Anorexia nervosa; diagnosis and treatment of inanition resulting from functional disorders. *Ann. Int. Med.,* 22:679-691, 1945.

———: Functional anorexia and functional vomiting; their relation to anorexia nervosa. *Med. Clin. North America,* 23:901-912, 1939.

———: Some clinical observations in cases of anorexia nervosa. (objections to desiccated thyroid therapy.) *Proc. Mayo Clin.,* 18:81-86, 1943.

———; OWEN, C. A., JR.; & MAGATH, T. B.: Physiological aspects of anorexia nervosa. *Postgrad. Med.,* 12:407-418, 1952.

———; WEIR, J. F. & KEPLER, E. J.: Clinical observations on starvation edema, serum protein and effect of forced feeding in anorexia nervosa. *Gastroenterology,* 9:357-390, 1947.

BERLIN, I. N.; BOATMAN, M. J.; SHEIMO, S. L.; & SZUREK, S. A.: Adolescent alternation of anorexia and obesity. *Am. J. Orthopsychiat.,* 21:387-418, 1951.

———; ———; ———; & ———: Adolescent anorexia and obesity. In case studies in childhood emotional disabilities, Vol. 1, ed. George E. Gardner. *New York: American Orthopsychiatric Assn.,* 1953.

BILLIOTTET, J. & GOASGUEN, P.: Rapid cure of mental anorexia by neurovegetative inhibition. *Bull. Soc. méd. hôp., Paris,* 70:571-574, 1954.

BIRLEY, J. L.: Anorexia nervosa. *St. Thomas Hosp. Gaz.,* 34:204-208, 1933.

BIRNIE, C. R.: Anorexia nervosa and its treatment. *Med. Press,* 207:360-362, 1942.

———: Anorexia nervosa treated by hypnosis in out-patient practice. *Lancet,* 2:1331-1332, 1936.

BLANC, A.: Treatment of anorexia in children. *Méd. Infant,* 66:59-63, 1959.

BLISS, E. L. & BRANCH, C. H. H.: Anorexia nervosa: its history, psychology, and biology. *New York: Hoeber,* 1960.

——— & MIGEON, C. J.: Endocrinology of anorexia nervosa. *J. Clin. Endocrinol. Metab.,* 17:766-776, 1957.

BOND, D. D.: Anorexia nervosa. *Rocky Mountain Med. J.,* 46:1012-1019, 1949.

BORJESON, M. & WRETLIND, A.: The protein metabolism in anorexia nervosa. *A.M.A. Arch. Gen. Psychiat.,* 1:283-287, 1959.

BORNICHE, P.; BRANDEL, M.; CANLORBE, P.; & SCHOLLER, R.: Effect of a synthetic carnitine compound on the blood during therapy of post-infectious anorexias in childhood. *Sem. hôp. Paris,* 34:2515-2517, 1958.

BREMENER, S. M. & FEDOTOVA, L. V.: Control of loss of appetite in pulmonary tuberculosis. *Vopr. pitan.*, 14(4):26-30, 1955.

BRETON, J. & MARS, F.: Anorexia that was not mental. *Presse méd.*, 65: 1888, 1957.

BRICKNER, R. M.: Appetitive behavior and sign stimuli in human life. *A.M.A. Arch. Neurol. Psychiat.*, 72:92-107, 1954.

BROBECK, J. R.; LARSSON, S.; & REYES, E.: Electrical activity of hypothalamic feeding mechanism. *J. Physiol.*, 132:358-364, 1956.

BROCK, J.: Poor appetite in children. *Deut. med. J.*, 7:16-22, 1956.

BROSER, F. & GOTTWALD, M.: Symptomatic psychoses in pituitary insufficiency. Also a contribution to the question of anorexia nervosa at puberty. *Nervenarzt*, 26:10-20, 1955.

BROSIN, H. W.: Anorexia nervosa; case report. *J. Clin. Endocrinol.*, 1: 269-271, 1941.

——— & APFELBACH, C.: Anorexia nervosa; case report with autopsy findings. *J. Clin. Endocrinol.*, 1:272-275, 1941.

BROWN, W. L.: Myth, phantasy and Mary Rose. *St. Barth. Hosp. J.*, 33: 98-102, 115-117, 133-136, 1926.

——— & CROOKSHANK, F. G.: Anorexia nervosa. *Med. Press*, 131:308-310, 1931.

——— YOUNG, J. C.; GORDON, G.; & BEVAN-BROWN, C. M.: Anorexia nervosa; a discussion. *London: C. W. Daniel*, 1931, pp. 11-51.

BRUCH, H.: Role of emotions in hunger and appetite. *Ann. New York Acad. Sc.*, 63(1):68-75, 1955.

BRUCKNER, W. J.; WIES, C. H.; & LAVIETES, P. H.: Anorexia nervosa and pituitary cachexia. *Am. J. Med. Sc.*, 196:663-673, 1938.

BRULL, L.: Dietetic aspects of mental anorexia. *Rev. méd. Liège*, 11:249-250, 1956.

BRUNECKY: Anorexia in children. *Česk. pediat.*, 10:33-35, 1955.

BRUSCH, C. A. ET AL.: Clinical evaluation of appetite depressants. *Delaware Med. J.*, 26:295-296, 298, 1954.

CAMPOS, P. C.; LAWAS, I.; MANIPOL, V.; & CLEMENTE, A. C.: Anorexia, weakness, restlessness and parkinsonism associated with hypokalemia following radioactive iodine therapy. *Philippine J. Surg.*, 14:254-259, 1959.

CANELLAS, R. R.: The appetite as the maintainer of physical and mental vitality in adults. *Med. españ.*, 41:21-34, 1959.

———: Treatment of anorexia nervosa in mental patients. *Ther. Umsch.*, 16:385-390, 1959.

CANLORBE, P.; DELTOUR, G.; BORNICHE, P.; & SCHOLLER, R.: Attempted treatment with a stable derivative of carnitine; its action on digestive functions and weight increase. *Sem. hôp. Paris*, 32:1780-1783, 1956.

CARLANDER, O.: Pica and iron deficiency. *Sven. läk. tidn.*, 55:387-391, 1958.

CARMODY, J. T. B. & VIBBER, F. L.: Anorexia nervosa treated by prefrontal lobotomy. *Ann. Int. Med.*, 36:647-652, 1952.

CARPENTER, K. J.: Concept of "appetite quotient" for interpretation of ad libitum feeding experiments. *J. Nutrition*, 51:435-440, 1953.

CARR, J. W.: A case of anorexia nervosa. *Proc. Roy. Soc. Med.*, 4:80-81, 1911.

CARRYER, H. M.; BERKMAN, J. M.; & MASON, H. L.: Relative lymphocytosis in anorexia nervosa. *Proc. Mayo Clin.*, 34:426-432, 1959.

CARSTENS, J. E. G.: Children with poor appetite. *Nederl. tschr. geneesk.*, 83:478-482, 1939.

CENTELEGHE, E.: Mental anorexia with report on two cases. *Minerva med.*, 50:3665-3668, 1959.

CHAFFEY, W. C.: A case of anorexia nervosa. *Rep. Soc. Study Dis. Child., London*, 3:257-258, 1902-1903.

CHALMERS, T. M.; KEKWICK, A.; & PAWAN, G. L.: Treatment of anorexia nervosa by ethyl-nortestosterone. *Proc. Roy. Soc. Med.*, 52:514-515, 1959.

CHEBAT, H.: L'obésité, maladie de l'appetit. *Paris: A.G.E.M.P.*, 1955, pp. 48-51.

CHIMENES, H.: Mental anorexia followed by diabetes mellitus; case. *Presse méd.*, 63:382, 1955.

CIOFFARI, M. S.: Weight gain through sedation (pentobarbital derivative) in malnourished children. *J. Michigan Med. Soc.*, 53:183-184, 1954.

CLAYTON, R. S. & GOODMAN, P. H.: Roentgenographic diagnosis of geophagia (dirt eating). *Am. J. Roentgenol.*, 73:203-207, 1955.

CLOW, F. E.: Anorexia nervosa. *New England J. Med.*, 207:613-617, 1932.

COLE, M.: Anorexia nervosa; review. *Med. Ann. District Columbia*, 25: 605-615, 650, 1956.

————; STRAIGHT, B.; ROBINSON, M.; & LOURIE, R. S.: Anorexia nervosa. *Clin. Proc. Child. Hosp., Wash.*, 14:49-63, 1958.

COLLINS, W. J.: Anorexia nervosa. *Lancet*, 1:202-203, 1894.

CONYBEARE, J. J.: Fatal case of anorexia nervosa. *Guy's Hosp. Rep.*, 80: 30-33, 1930.

COOPER, M. M.: Pica, a survey of the historical literature, . . . the present study of pica in young children. *Springfield, Ill.: C. C Thomas*, 1957.

CORSINO, G. M. & EUTIZI, D.: Contribution to the etiopathogenetic problem of mental anorexia; report of a case with traumatic etiology. *Riv. sper. freniat.*, 83:685-690, 1959.

COWARD, N. B.: Anorexia in children. *Nova Scotia Med. Bull.*, 23:1-7, 1944.

CRAIG, J. O.: Oral factors in accidental poisoning. *Arch. Dis. Childhood*, 30:419-423, 1955.

CREMIEUX, A.: Les difficultés alimentaires de l'enfant: Les anorexies mentales infantiles et juvéniles. *Paris: Presses Universitaires de France*, 1954.

CROSS, E. S.: Diagnosis and treatment of anorexia nervosa. *Med. Clin. North America*, 23:541-552, 1939.

DALLA VOLTA, A.; COTELLESSA, G.; & RESTA, G.: Precocious breast and hair development associated with psychogenic disorders in child with anorexia; case. *Minerva pediat.*, 5:895-900, 1953.

——— MERLINI, M.; & ZECCA, G.: Anxiety neurosis and cachexia due to secondary anorexia following tonsillectomy and excision of adenoids. *Arch. psicol. neurol. psichiat.*, 17:877-903. 1956.

——— MERLINI, G.; & ———: Recent findings on a case of anxiety neurosis with anorexia. *Arch psicol. neurol. psichiat.*, 18:334-342, 1957.

DALLY, P. J.: Carotenaemia occurring in a case of anorexia nervosa. *Brit. Med. J.*, 5133:1333, 1959.

DAVIS, H. P.: Anorexia nervosa; case. *Endocrinology*, 25:991-995, 1939.

DECOURT, J.: Anorexia nervosa; psycho-endocrine cachexia of puberty. *Deut. med. Wschr.*, 78:1619-1622, 1661-1664, 1953.

———: Anorexia nervosa; psycho-endocrine cachexia of adolescence. *Strasbourg méd.*, 5:233-247, 1954.

———: La anorexia nervosa. *Rev. méd. cubana*, 67:165-178, 1956.

———: Mental anorexia in days of Lasègue and Gull. *Presse méd.*, 62:355-358, 1954.

DE GENNES, L.: Les anorexies mentales. *Gaz. méd. France*, 62:1705-1715, 1955.

DEL CASTILLO, E. B.; TRUCCO, E.; ROMERO, J. A.; & O'FARRELL, J. J.: Anorexia nervosa and enlargement of the salivary glands. *Medicina, B. Aires*, 19:11-16, 1959.

DEL PONTE, E.: Mental anorexia and poly-hormonal therapy; clinico-therapeutic study. *Minerva med.*, 46:67-75, 1955.

DE VINK, L. P. H. J. & DE VAAL, O. M.: Nervous anorexia, pituitary cachexia and atrophy of pilar system. *Nederl. tschr. geneesk.*, 93:3410-3415, 1949.

DIEKNEIER, L.: Disease and artistic pictures of Margaretha Weiss, the girl prodigy of Speyer. *Kinderärztl. Prax.*, 27:107-115, 1959.

DOWSE, T. S.: Anorexia nervosa. *Med. Press & Circ.*, 32:95, 147, 1881.

DREYER, P.: Anorexia during puberty; case. *Kinderärztl. Prax.*, 24:118-119, 1956.

DRUMMOND, D.: A case of anorexia nervosa. *Northumberland & Durham Med. J.*, 4:7-8, 1896.

DUBOIS, F. S.: Anorexia nervosa; a re-evaluation of the problem. *J. Insur. Med.*, 5:18-20, 1949-1950.

———: Compulsion neurosis with cachexia (anorexia nervosa). *Am. J. Psychiat.*, 106:107-115, 1949.

DURAND, C.: Psychogenesis and therapy of mental anorexia. *Helvet. med. acta*, 22:368-380, 1955.

EATON, L.: Simmonds' disease or anorexia nervosa. *Quart. Bull. Indiana Univ. Med. Center*, 9:60-63, 1947.

EDGE, A. M.: A case of anorexia nervosa. *Lancet*, 1:818, 1888.

EDWARD, C. H.; MCSWAIN, H.; & HAIRE, S.: Odd dietary practices of women. *J. Am. Dietet. Assn.*, 30:976-981, 1954.

EISSLER, K. R.: Psychiatric aspects of anorexia nervosa demonstrated by case report. *Psychoanal. Rev.*, 30:121-145, 1943.

EITINGER, L.: Anorexia nervosa. *Nord. Med.*, 45:915-918, 1951.

ELKINTON, J. R. & HUTH, E. J.: Body fluid abnormalities in anorexia nervosa and undernutrition. *Metabolism*, 8:376-403, 1959.

EL-TAWIL, T.: Ideal as repression versus satisfaction of appetites. *Egypt. J. Psychol.*, 8:33-47, 1952.

EMANUEL, R. W.: Clinical diagnosis, prognosis and treatment of anorexia nervosa. *Postgrad. Med. J.*, 32:238-242, 1956.

———: Endocrine activity in anorexia nervosa., *J. Clin. Endocrinol.*, 16:801-816, 1956.

———: A study of the body weight in anorexia nervosa. *Postgrad. Med. J.*, 33:73-77, 1957.

ENGELHARDT, J.: Prolonged diarrhea in children. *Nederl. tschr. geneesk.*, 99:602-605, 1955.

ESCAMILLA, R. F.: Anorexia nervosa or Simmonds' disease? Notes on clinical management with some points of differentiation between the two conditions. *J. Nerv. Ment. Dis.*, 99:583-587, 1944.

——— & LISSER, H.: Simmonds' disease (hypophysial cachexia); clinical study with review of literature; differentiation from anorexia nervosa by statistical analysis of 595 cases, 101 of which were proved pathologically. *J. Clin. Endocrinol.*, 2:65-96, 1942.

ESSER, M.: Pathophysiology of perverted choice of food in small children. *Schweiz. med. Wschr.*, 87:385-387, 1957.

EVANS, J. C. G.: Anorexia nervosa. *Lancet*, 1:268-269, 1939.

FALK, W.: The value of lysine in the treatment of malnutrition and lack of appetite. *Harefuah, Tel-Aviv*, 56:183-184, 1959.

FALSTEIN, E. I.; FEINSTEIN, S. C.; & JUDAS, I.: Anorexia nervosa in male child. *Am. J. Orthopsychiat.*, 26:751-772, 1956.

FARQUHARSON, R. F.: Anorexia nervosa. *Illinois Med. J.*, 80:193-200, 1941.

—— & HYLAND, H. H.: Anorexia nervosa; metabolic disorder of psychologic origin. *J. Am. Med. Assn.*, 111:1085-1092, 1938.

FAURE, H.: Nutritional cirrhosis in Morocco. *Algérie méd.*, 62: 737-740, 743-744, 1958.

FERON, J. A. A.: L'anorexie mentale; position actuelle du problème. *Paris: D. P. Taib*, 1956, pp. 42-44.

FERRIO, L.: Efficacy of a stimulating and anabolic preparation with embryonal lipid base in relation to various methods of administration. *Gazz. med. Ital.*, 112:150-152, 1953.

FORCHHEIMER, F.: Anorexia nervosa in children. *Arch. Pediat.*, 24:801-810, 1907. Also: *Arch. Pediat.*, 68:35-45, 1951.

FORSSMAN, B.: Anorexia nervosa with electrolyte disorders. *Nord. med.*, 54:1373-1377, 1955.

FRANDSEN, S. & JACOBY, P.: Eating problems in children. *Acta Paediat.*, Suppl. 83:61, 1951.

FRAZIER, S. H., JR.; FAUBION, M. H.; GIFFIN, M. E.; & JOHNSON, A. M.: A specific factor in symptom choice. *Proc. Mayo Clin.*, 30:227-236; discussion, 236-243, 1955.

FRIEDLANDER, A.: A case of anorexia nervosa in an infant. *Interstate Med. J.*, 13:446-669, 1906.

FRIEDMAN, G. D.: Trois cas d'anorexie mentale chez l'homme. *Genève Université Faculté de Médecine.* Thèse, M.D. No. 2227, 1954.

FRYER, J. H.; MOORE, N. S.; WILLIAMS, H. H.; & YOUNG, C. M.: Interrelationship of energy-yielding nutrients, blood glucose levels and subjective appetite in man (studies on obese subjects). *J. Lab. Clin. Med.*, 45: 684-696, 1955.

—— —— —— & ——: Satiety values of isocaloric diets for reducing, with special reference to glucostatic theory of appetite control. *J. Am. Dietet. Assn.*, 31:868-875, 1955.

GAILEY, A. A.: Pica. *Practitioner*, 178:749-751, 1957.

GALETTI, P. M. & LABHART, A.: Thyroid function in mental anorexia. *Helvet. med. acta*, 22:536-539, 1955.

GALLINEK, A.: Syndrome of episodes of hypersomnia, bulimia and abnormal mental states. *J. Am. Med. Assn.*, 154:1081-1083, 1954.

GARDNER, J. E. & TEVETOGLU, F.: The roentgenographic diagnosis of geophagia (dirt-eating) in children; a report on sixty cases. *J. Pediat.*, 51:667-671, 1957.

GARLAND, J.: Appetite loss in infancy and childhood. *New England J. Med.*, 200:1135-1141, 1929.

GASTAUT, H.: Eating behavior disorders in psychomotor epileptics. *Rev. neurol., Paris*, 92:55-62, 1955.

—— ROGER, J.; & GIOVE, C.: Olfactory, gustatory and appetite disorders in psychomotor epileptics. *Ann. méd. psychol., Paris,* 113 (1):177-206, 1955.

GAULHOFER, W. K.: Inhibition of excessive appetite in mental patients by preludin. *Nederl. tschr. geneesk.,* 102:2508-2510, 1958.

GAUTIER, A. & JEANDET, J.: Note on the treatment of anorexia in infant and child with B-OM. *Praxis, Bern.,* 46:506-507, 1957.

GEE, S. J.: Nervous atrophy (atrophia nervosa; anorexia nervosa). In medical lectures and aphorisms. *London: Oxford University Press,* 1908, pp. 40-48.

GEISLER, E.: The problem of puberal anorexia. *Psychiat. Neurol. med. Psychol., Leipzig,* 5:227-233, 1953.

GEORGI, F.: On partial functional disorders associated with liver disease. *Bibl. paediat., Basel,* 58:675-684, 1954.

GERO, G.: An equivalent of depression: anorexia. In: affective disorders, ed. P. Greenacre. *New York: International Universities Press,* 1953, pp. 117-139.

GIANAKON, H. G.: Anorexia nervosa; a study of residential treatment. *J. Kansas Med. Soc.,* 58:159-163, 1957.

GIBERTI, F.: Mental anorexia; clinical and therapeutic study of case. *Gior. psichiat. neuropat.,* 82:69-76, 1954.

GIERTHMÜHLEN, F.: Vitamin B in pediatrics. *Med. Klin., Berlin,* 51:2137, 1956.

GIFFIN, M. E.; FRAZIER, S. H.; ROBINSON, D. B.; & JOHNSON, A. M.: The internist's role in successful treatment of anorexia nervosa. *Proc. Mayo Clin.,* 32:171-182, 1957.

GILLESPIE, R. D.: Treatment of functional anorexia. *Lancet,* 1:995, 1931.

GINZBERG, R. & BRINEGAR, W. C.: Appetite and constipation in advanced life: psychological and statistical evaluation of a county home survey in Iowa. *Am. J. Digest. Dis.,* 21:267-272, 1954.

GIUSTA, G. & GIUSO, J. R.: New medical therapy of anorexia in neurosurgical patients. *Sem. méd., B. Aires,* 114 (Suppl. 7):179, 1959.

GLAZEBROOK, A. J. & PROSEN, H.: Compulsive neurosis with cachexia. *Canad. Med. Assn. J.,* 75:40-42, 1956.

GLEDITSCH, E.: Pica in iron deficiency anemia. *Tskr. Norske laegeforen.,* 79:398-399, 1959.

GOITEIN, P. L.: Potential prostitute; role of anorexia in defense against prostitution desires. *J. Crim. Psychopathol.,* 3:359-367, 1942.

GOLDSTEIN, L. S.: Norethandrolone and reserpine; a study of treatment of nervous, underweight children. *Arch. Pediat.,* 76:196-199, 1959.

———: A nutritional approach to growth failure in children; a preliminary report. *Internat. Red. Med.,* 169:371-375, 1956.

GOTTESFELD, B. H. & NOVAES, A. C.: Narco-analysis and sub-shock insulin in treatment of anorexia nervosa. *Digest Neurol. Psychiat.*, 13:486-494, 1945.

GRAY, E. L.: Appetite and acclimatization to high altitude. *Mil. Med.*, 117:427-431, 1955.

GREENBERG, M.; JACOBZINER, H.; MCLAUGHLIN, M. C.; FUERST, H. T.; & PELLITERIO, O.: A study of pica in relation to lead poisoning. *Pediatrics*, 22:756-760, 1958.

GREENBLATT, R. B.; BARFIELD, W. E.; & CLARK, S. L.: Use of ACTH and cortisone in treatment of anorexia nervosa. *J. Med. Assn. Georgia*, 40:299-301, 1951.

GREENWALD, H. M.: Anorexia nervosa. *Am. Med.*, 23:875-880, 1928.

GRIFFITH, J. P. C.: A case of anorexia nervosa in an infant. *Arch. Pediat.*, 25:321-323, 1908.

GRIMSHAW, L.: Anorexia nervosa; a contribution to its psychogenesis. *Brit. J. Med. Psychol.*, 32:44-49, 1959.

GROBIN, W.: Anorexia nervosa; a somatic disorder. *Canad. Med. Assn. J.*, 79:674, 1958.

GROSSMAN, H.: Étude endocrinienne de 12 cas d'anorexie mentale. *Paris: R. Vesin*, 1957, pp. 67-69.

GROSSMAN, M. I.: Integration of current views on regulation of hunger and appetite. *Ann. New York Acad. Sc.*, 63(1):76-91, 1955.

GULL, W. W.: The address on medicine. *Lancet*, 2:171-176, 1868.

———: Anorexia nervosa. *Lancet*, 1:516-517, 1888.

———: Anorexia nervosa (apepsia hysterica, anorexia hysterica). In a collection of the published writings of Sir William Withey Gull. *London: New Sydenham*, 1894, pp. 305-314.

———: Anorexia nervosa (apepsia hysterica, anorexia hysterica). *Trans. Clin. Soc. London*, 7:22-28, 1874.

HACK, H. J.: A contribution to the pathological anatomy of anorexia nervosa. *Endokrinologie*, 38:56-67, 1959.

HAGEDORN, H. C.: Anorexia nervosa. *Acta med. scandinav.*, 151:201-208, 1955.

HAGGENMULLER, F.: Appetite and digestive disorders in children. *Hippokrates*, 27:155-157, 1956.

HANSEN, C. E.: Therapy of anorexia nervosa. *Ugesk. laeger*, 118:1368-1369, 1956.

HARRIS, S. C.: Clinically useful appetite depressants. *Ann. New York Acad. Sc.*, 63 (1):121-131, 1955.

HAWKINGS, J. R.; JONES, K. S.; SIM, M.; & TIBBETTS, R. W.: Deliberate disability. *Brit. Med. J.*, 4963:361-367, 1956.

HELD, R. & CHERTOK, L.: Anorexie mentale et potomanie; considérations psychosomatiques. *Sem. hôp. Paris*, 35:1649-1652, 1959.

HENNEQUET, A.: Les anorexies du nourisson. *Concours méd.*, 78:4195-4203, 1956.

HERMAN, W. J.: A depression expressing itself in loss of appetite and extreme emaciation. (Cabot case, 15172.) *New England J. Med.*, 200: 895-896, 1929.

HERNANDEZ, H.: Treatment of anorexia and denutrition in children. *Rev. españ. pediat.*, 14:553-570, 1958.

HERTZ, H.: Nervous anorexia. *Acta med. scandinav.*, Suppl. 266:523-527, 1952.

HICKISH, G. W.: Pellagra in an English child. *Arch. Dis. Childhood*, 30: 195-196, 1955.

HIRSCHMAN, J.: Pathologic transformation. *Arch. Psychiat.*, 192:369-382, 1954.

HOLECKOVA, E. & FABRY, P.: Hyperphagia and gastric hypertrophy in rats adapted to intermittent starvation. *Brit. J. Nutr.*, 13:260-266, 1959.

HOLLANDER, A. G.: Ineffectiveness of isoniazid as appetite-stimulator. *Dis. Chest*, 27:674-676, 1955.

HOLLANDER, F.; SOBER, H. A.; & BANDES, J.: A study of hunger and appetite in a young man with esophageal obstruction and jejunostomy. *Ann. New York Acad. Sc.*, 63 (1):107-120, 1955.

HURST, A. F.: Anorexia nervosa. In the British Encyclopaedia of medical practice, Vol. I. London: Butterworth, 1936, pp. 598-600.

IANDOLE, C.: Appetite and hunger. *Policlinico, sez. prat.*, 65:710-714, 1958.

ILLINGWORTH, R. S.: Food refusal in children. *J. Roy. Inst. Pub. Health Hyg.*, 14:384-386, 1951.

JACCOTTET, M.: Mental anorexia or renal disorder? *Internat. Zschr. Vitaminforsch., Bern*, 28:72-79, 1957.

JACOBZINER, H. & RAYBIN, H. W.: Lead poisoning and pica in children. *New York State J. Med.*, 59:1606-1610, 1959.

JANOWITZ, H. D. & HOLLANDER, F.: Time factor in adjustment of food intake to varied caloric requirement in dog; precision of appetite regulation. *Ann. New York Acad. Sc.*, 63 (1):56-57, 1955.

JORES, A.: Anorexia nervosa as endocrinologic problem. *Acta endocrinol.*, 17:206-210, 1954.

———: Psychosomatic symptoms as seen in a case of anorexia nervosa. *Wien. med. Wschr.*, 108:1062-1065, 1958.

KAGAN, H.: Anorexia in severe inanition association with a tumor involving the hypothalamus. *Arch. Dis. Childh.*, 33:257-260, 1958.

KAPLAN, D.: Hyperthyreose im kindesalter kombiniert mit letaler pubertätsmagersucht. *Diss. Med. Bern*, 1955.

KAPLAN, H. I. & KAPLAN, H. S.: The psychosomatic concept of obesity. *J. Nerv. Ment. Dis.*, 125:181-201, 1957.

KARPINSKI, W.: Clinical aspects and therapy of digestive disorders and loss of appetite in nurslings and infants. *Medizinische*, 22:834-836, 1956.

KAY, D. W.: Anorexia nervosa; a study in prognosis. *Proc. Roy. Soc. Med.*, 46:669-674, 1953.

────── & LEIGH, D.: Natural history, treatment and prognosis of anorexia nervosa, based on study of 38 patients. *J. Ment. Sc.*, 100:411-431, 1954.

KLOTZ, H. P. & LAMBROSO, P.: Clinical, pathogenic and therapeutic aspects of mental anorexia: concept of "abiorexia." *Sem. hôp. Paris*, 31:440-445, 1955.

KOFMAN, I. & SILBERKASTEN, A.: Findings on various stimulants of the child. *Sem. méd., B. Aires*, 111:727-734, 1957.

────── & WEINSTEIN, M.: Androstanolone in infantile inappetence and dystrophy. *Sem. méd., B. Aires*, 110:596-604, 1957.

KUHN, R.: Existential analysis of anorexia mentalis. *Nervenarzt*, 24:191-198, 1953.

KUNERT, W.: Treatment of anorexia nervosa by special feeding cures. *Ther. Gegenwart*, 97:216-221, 1958.

L., G.: Treatment of insane persons who refuse to eat. Pathology of the distaste for food. *Lancet*, 1:319-320, 1842-1843.

LABOUCARIE, J. & BARRES, P.: Clinical, pathogenic and therapeutic aspects of anorexia nervosa; report on 50 cases. *Évolut. psychiat.*, 1:119-146, 1954.

LAMOTTE, M. & HIMBERT, J.: Unusual appetite provoked by abnormal gastric contractions associated with pancreatic tumor; case. *Sem. hôp. Paris*, 32:2740-2741, 1956.

LANTUEJEUL, P.: Anorexia in the first months of pregnancy. *Progr. méd., Paris*, 85:403-404, 1957.

LANZKOWSKY, P.: Investigation into the aetiology and treatment of pica. *Arch. Dis. Childh.*, 34:140-148, 1959.

LASEGUE, C.: On hysterical anorexia. *Med. Times & Gaz.*, 2:265-266, 367-369, 1873.

LAUNAY, C.: Anorexie mentale des grandes enfants et des adolescentes. *Gaz. méd. France*, 62:177-186, 1955.

────── TRELAT, J.; VERLIAC, F.; & LEFEBVRE, (MME): Mental anorexia in the small infant and behavior in the play room. *Arch. fr. pédiat.*, 13:858-879, 1956.

LEBLOND, S. & BUTAS, N.: Neurohypophysial thinness. *Laval méd.*, 18:1360-1371, 1953.

LEEDE, C. S.: Anorexia nervosa; hypoglycemia or hypoadrenia. *Northwest. Med.*, 27:233-238, 1928.

LEMUET, G.: Present aspects of geophagism in Morocco; relative to 300 cases. *Maroc. méd.*, 35:933-940, 1956.

LERNER, M.: Hypnoanalysis in case of psychogenic anorexia and vomiting. *Acta neuropsiquiat. argent.*, 2:308-312, 1956.

LEWIS, B. W.; COLLINS, R. J.; & WILSON, H. S.: Seasonal incidence of lead poisoning (with reference to pica) in children in St. Louis. *South. Med. J.*, 48:298-301, 1955.

LIEBNER, E. J.: A case of Lindau's disease simulating anorexia nervosa; a roentgenologic report. *Am. J. Roentgenol.*, 78:283-288, 1957.

LJUNGGREN, H.; IKKOS, D.; & LUFT, R.: Studies on body composition. III. Body fluid compartments and exchangeable potassium in females with anorexia nervosa. *Acta endocrinol.*, 25:209-223, 1957.

LÖFFLER, W.: Mental anorexia. *Helvet. med. acta*, 22:351-367, 1955.

LÔO, P.: Anorexie mentale, maladie de Simmonds, maladie de Sheehan. *Ann. méd. psychol., Paris*, 113 (1):369-375, 1955.

—— & DUFLOT, J.-P.: Digestive disorders, their form and conditioning. *Ann. méd. psychol., Paris*, 116 (2):553-556, 1958.

—— & ——: Anorexia nervosa. *Ann. méd. psychol., Paris*, 116 (2): 734-750, 1958.

LOPEZ, I. J.: Obesity and leanness as ways of life. *Rev. iber. endocrinol.*, 3:179-190, 1956.

LORAND, S.: Anorexia nervosa; case. *Psychosom. Med.*, 5:282-292, 1943.

LÖVEGREN, E.: Psychogenic anorexia in children. *Finska Lak.-sallsk. Handl.*, 73:115-120, 1931.

LÖVEI, E. & BONA, E.: Anorexia nervosa. *Zschr. ges. inn. Med.*, 12:749-753, 1957.

LUFT, R. & SJOGREN, B.: Disturbed electrolyte metabolism in two cases of nervous anorexia. *Acta endocrinol.*, 17:264-269, 1954.

LUKAS, K. H.: Therapy of emaciation in female. *Zschr. Psychother.*, 6: 159-173, 1956.

LURIE, O. R.: Psychologic factors associated with eating difficulties in children. *Am. J. Orthopsychiat.*, 11:452-466, 1941.

MACDOUGALL, I.: Case of oesophageal carcinoma (in patient with anorexia nervosa). *Brit. Med. J.*, 4629:686-687, 1949.

MACKENZIE, E. P.: The treatment of anorexia. *J. Pediat.*, 53:189-197, 1958.

MACKENZIE, S.: On a case of anorexia nervosa vel hysterica. *Lancet*, 1: 613-614, 1888.

MAGENDANTZ, H. & PROGER, S.: Anorexia nervosa or hypopituitarism? *J. Am. Med. Assn.*, 114:1973-1983, 1940.

MAJOOR, C. L.; WIJDEVELD, P. G.; & VAN MUNSTER, P. J.: Diuretic disorders in a patient with anorexia nervosa. *Nederl. tschr. geneesk.*, 101:1839-1841, 1957.

MARQUES, A.: Psychologic aspects of alimentation. *Hospital, Rio de Janeiro*, 46:549-554, 1954.

MARSHALL, C. F.: A fatal case of anorexia nervosa. *Lancet*, 1:149-150, 1895.

MARTIN, F.: Pathology of neurologic and psychiatric aspects in certain deficiency manifestations with digestive and neuroendocrine disorders; changes of central nervous system in so-called mental anorexia of young girls; 2 cases. *Helvet. med. acta*, 22:522-529, 1955.

MARTINOTTI, G.: Therapy of psychic anorexia. *Lav. neuropsichiat.*, 13:121-139, 1953.

MASHANSKII, F. I.: Symptom of aversion to sweet and fatty foods in cysticercosis of the fourth ventricle. *Vopr. neirokhir.*, 20 (6):41-43, 1956.

MASSERMAN, J. H.: Psychodynamisms in anorexia nervosa and neurotic vomiting. *Psychoanal. Quart.*, 10:211-242, 1941.

MATHIS, M.: Anorexia nervosa in a small child. *Cah. Psychiat.*, 13:57-62, 1958.

MATTER, W. & BOLIKOWSKI, S.: Post-infectious anorexia and its treatment by atmospheric depression; airplane and caisson. *Méd. aéronaut.*, 9:19-24, 1954.

MAZEL, Y. I. & SHESSOL, E. Y.: Clinical aspects and pathogenesis of psychogenic anorexia. *Klin. Med.*, 18:105-111, 1940.

MCCULLAGH, E. P. & TUPPER, W. R.: Anorexia nervosa. *Ann. Int. Med.*, 14:817-838, 1940.

MELLINKOFF, S. M.; FRANKLAND, M.; BOYLE, D.; & GREIPEL, M.: Relationship between serum amino acid concentration and fluctuations in appetite. *J. Appl. Physiol.*, 8:535-538, 1956.

——— ——— & GREIPEL, M.: Effect of amino acid and glucose ingestion on arterio-venous blood sugar and appetite. *J. Appl. Physiol.*, 9:85-87, 1956.

——— ——— ———; SHIBATA, H. N.; & DIXON, W. J.: Post-prandial blood amino acid patterns in patients with hepatic anorexia. *Gastroenterology*, 32:592-599, 1957.

MENGHI, P. & FANTUZZI, B.: The so-called anorexic infant and its ponderal growth. *Minerva nipiol.*, 7:59-62, 1957.

MEYER, B. C. & WEINROTH, L. A.: Observations on psychological aspects of anorexia nervosa; report of a case. *Psychosom. Med.*, 19:389-398, 1957.

MEYROUD, M.: Infantile anorexia of children and psychosomatic medicine. *Rev. med. Suisse Rom.*, 75:241-260, 1955.

MICHAUX, L. & GEORGES-JANET, L.: Factor of mental anorexia of adolescents; repudiation of material cares; affirmation of pure intellectualism. *Presse méd.*, 64:181-183, 1956.

MILLER, D.: A case of anorexia nervosa in a young woman with development of subcapsular cataracts. *Trans. Ophth. Soc., U. K.*, 78:217-222, 1958.

MILLICAN, F. K.; LOURIE, R. S.; & LAYMAN, E. M.: Emotional factors in etiology and treatment of lead poisoning; pica in children. *A.M.A. J. Dis. Child.*, 91:144-149, 1956.

MITCHELL, S. W.: Gastro-intestinal disorders of hysteria. In lectures on diseases of the nervous system, especially in women. *Philadelphia: Henry C. Lea's Son & Co.*, 1881, pp. 201-216.

MOGTADER, M.: Feeding during the sucking stage of ECT. *Psychiat. Quart.*, 30:458-463, 1956.

MOMMSEN, H.: Child without appetite. *Medizinische*, 42:1496-1499, 1956.

MONNET, M. P.: Anorexia in the infant. *Lyon méd.*, 87:451-460, 1955.

MORINI, A. & MENOZZI, R.: Geophagia and Banti syndrome. *Clin. Pediat.*, 36:537-558, 1954.

MORLOCK, C. G.: Anorexia nervosa. *Proc. Mayo Clin.*, 14:24-28, 1939.

MOULTON, R.: Psychosomatic study of anorexia nervosa including the use of vaginal smears. *Psychosom. Med.*, 4:62-74, 1942.

MÜLLER, H.: Pubertal anorexia in young girls. *Med. Klin., Berlin*, 51:209-212, 1956.

MYERS, B.: The treatment of anorexia nervosa in children. *Practitioner*, 113:351-357, 1924.

MYERS, J. W.: Mental anorexia simulating pituitary cachexia; case. *Southwest. Med.*, 23:367-368, 1939.

NEMIAH, J. C.: Anorexia nervosa; a clinical psychiatric study. *Medicine*, 29:225-268, 1950.

─────: Anorexia nervosa; fact and theory. *Am. J. Digest. Dis.*, 3:249-274, 1958.

NICHOLSON, M.; KEITEL, H.; WILLIAMS, J.; MILLICAN, F.; LOURIE, R. S.; LOPRESTI, M.; STEVENS, H.; & GUIN, G. H.: Pinealoma with associated hypernatremia and symptoms of anorexia nervosa. *Clin. Proc. Child. Hosp., Wash.*, 13:133-145, 1957.

NICOLLE, G.: Prepsychotic anorexia. *Proc. Roy. Soc. Med.*, 32:153-162, 1939.

NILES, G. M.: Anorexia. *South. Med. J.*, 1:376-379, 1908.

NOVLIANSKAIA, K. A.: A prolonged pathological reaction in puberty; anorexia nervosa in adolescents. *Zh. Nevropat. psikhiat., Moscow*, 58:861-866, 1958.

Nutrition Society: The psychology of eating. *Lancet,* 1:326-327, 1953.

NYIRO, G.; FORNADI, F.; & BARTOS, V.: Case of anorexia nervosa cured by serial electroshock therapy. *Ideg. szemle,* 11:99-102, 1958.

OPPENHEIMER, B. S.: Simmonds' disease versus anorexia nervosa; case with necroposy findings. *J. Mt. Sinai Hosp.,* 10:640-650, 1944.

ORCHARD, N. G.: A case of anorexia nervosa in an infant. *Arch. Pediat.,* 31:367-370, 1914. Also: *New York State J. Med.,* 14:36-38, 1914.

ORTEGA, C. L. & MICHELLI, J. J.: Treatment of infantile anorexia with a combination of reserpine with vitamins B12, B1 and intrinsic factor. *Sem. méd., B. Aires,* 115 (Suppl. 16):376-381, 1959.

PALMER, H. A.: Beriberi complicating anorexia nervosa. *Lancet,* 1:269, 1939.

PALMER, J. O.; MENSH, I. N.; & MATARAZZO, J. D.: Anorexia nervosa; case history and psychological examination data with implications for test validity. *J. Clin. Psychol.,* 8:168-173, 1952.

PARADEE, I.: Cachexia (anorexia) nervosa. *Med. Clin. North America,* 25:755-773, 1941.

PARKER, H. L.: Anorexia nervosa. *Irish J. Med. Sc.,* pp. 289-294, 1940.

PATEL, J. C.: Symptomatic relief. IV. Loss of appetite. *Ind. J. Med. Sc.,* 11:268-273, 1957.

PFLANZ, M.: Symptomatic psychoses associated with emaciation. *Nervenarzt,* 26:397-398, 1955.

PIJADE, R.: Rare case of polyphagia with transitory gastric dilation. *Voj. san. pregl., Belgrade,* 15:572-574, 1958.

PLAYFAIR, W. S.: Note on the so-called anorexia nervosa. *Lancet,* 1:817-818, 1888.

PLESHETTE, N.: Pica-bezoar simulating intestinal obstruction during pregnancy. *Harlem Hosp. Bull., N. Y.,* 6:137-140, 1953.

POROT, M.: Isoniazid and its psychological effects. *Ann. méd. psychol., Paris,* 112 (1):161-183, 1954.

POSNER, L. B.; MCCOTTRY, C. M.; & POSNER, A. C.: Pregnancy craving and pica. *Obst. Gyn. N. Y.,* 9:270-272, 1957.

POTACS, W.: Amino acids as stomachic drugs. *Neue Oesterr. Zschr. Kinderh.,* 2:229-231, 1957.

PRYOR, H. B.: Factors involved in combating the hunger strike in children. *Am. J. Dis. Child.,* 41:249-261, 1931.

PUECH, A.; COMBIER, C.; PAGES, A.; & MIMRAN, R.: Psychogenic cachexia with pseudoalteration of the field of vision; failure of ACTH therapy; remarkable results of insulin therapy. *Montpellier méd.,* 44:130-132, 1953.

PUNCERNAU, R.: Kleine-Levin syndrome; probable case. *An. med. (espec.),* 41:130-138, 1955.

QUERIDO, A.: Physiopathology of anorexia nervosa. *Nederl. tschr. geneesk.*, 92:660-663, 1948.

———: Simmonds' disease or/and anorexia nervosa. *Geneesk. Gids*, 25:265-268, 1947.

RACHEV, L.; MARINOV, D.; GIZOV, G.; IANEVA, T.; & DAMIANOVA, M.: Anorexia in preschool children. *Suvrem. med., Sofia*, 5 (11):10-16, 1954.

RAHMAN, L.; RICHARDSON, H. B.; & RIPLEY, H. S.: Anorexia nervosa with psychiatric observations. *Psychosom. Med.*, 1:335-365, 1939.

RAMOS, F. E.: Appetite and its effect on the development of children. *Hispalis med.*, 15:489-500, 1958.

RANDOLPH, T. G.: The descriptive features of food addiction; addictive eating and drinking. *Quart. J. Alcohol*, 17:198-224, 1956.

RANK, B.; PUTNAM, M. C.; & ROCHLIN, G.: Significance of "emotional climate" in early feeding difficulties. *Psychosom. Med.*, 10:279-283, 1948.

RECAGNO, URRUTI, E. R.; TISMINESKY, J.; & DE TISMINESKY, E. K.: Infantile anorexia organic and psychic foci. *Prensa méd. argent.*, 45:1676-1678, 1958.

REISS, M.: Unusual pituitary activity in case of anorexia nervosa. *J. Ment. Sc.*, 89:270-273, 1943.

RICHARDSON, H. B.: Simmonds' disease and anorexia nervosa. *Arch. Int. Med.*, 63:1-28, 1939.

———: Simmonds' disease and anorexia nervosa. *Trans. Assn. Am. Physicians*, 52:141-145, 1937.

ROITH, A. I.: Extreme sensitivity to insulin. *Brit. Med. J.*, 4874:1305-1306, 1954.

ROLLA, E. H.; & GRINBERG, L.: Anorexia nerviosa y claustrofobia. *Rev. psicoandl., B. Aires*, 13:486-490, 1956.

ROSADINI, I.: Action of 4-chlorotestosterone acetate in anorexia nervosa. *Minerva med.*, 50:3001-3003, 1959.

ROSE, J. A.: Eating inhibitions in children in relation to anorexia nervosa. *Psychosom. Med.*, 5:117-124, 1943.

ROSENKÖTTER, L. & WENDE, S.: Electroencephalographic findings in Kleine-Levin syndrome. *Monatsschr. Psychiat. Neurol.*, 130:107-122, 1955.

ROSS, C. W.: Anorexia nervosa with special reference to carbohydrate metabolism. *Lancet*, 1:1041-1045, 1938.

ROSSIER, M.: Certain aspects of treatment of anorexia in adults. *Praxis, Bern*, 48:269-271, 1959.

ROSSIER, P. H.; STAEHELIN, D.; BÜHLMANN, A.; & LABHART, A.: Alkalosis and hypokalemia in mental anorexia (hunger alkalosis). *Schweiz. med. Wschr.*, 85:465-468, 1955.

ROSSINI, R.: Brief consideration on the pathogenesis and nosographic position of mental anorexia. *Riv. sper. freniat.*, 83:36-43, 1959.

ROTH, O.: Accidents and anorexia mentalis. *Zschr. Unfallmed.*, *Zurich*, 50:307-313, 1957.

ROUX, J. A.: Use of isoniazid in certain anorexies of nurslings. *Pédiatrie*, 10:68-70, 1955.

RUDOLFER, N. DA S.: Un caso de anorexia nerviosa. *Rev. psicoanál.*, *B. Aires*, 13:491-497, 1956.

RYLE, J. A.: Anorexia nervosa. *Lancet*, 2:893-899, 1936.

────── et al.: Discussion on anorexia nervosa. *Proc. Roy. Soc. Med.*, 32:735-746, 1939.

SABRIE, C. R.: Polycis: nutritional auxiliaries. *Rev. internat. Serv. santé Armées*, 32:431-434, 1959.

SAINZ DE LOS TERREROS, C.: Anorexia. *Acta pediat. españ.*, 13:863-873, 1955.

SCHLUTZ, F. W.: The problem of chronic anorexia in childhood. *J. Am. Med. Assn.*, 94:73-77, 1930.

SCHWARTZMAN, J.: Testosterone (androgen); effect on anorexia and underweight in children; review of 19 cases. *Arch. Pediat.*, 71:99-110, 1954.

SCOTT, W. C. M.: Notes on the psychopathology of anorexia nervosa. *Brit. J. Med. Psychol.*, 21:241-247, 1948.

SEREBRINSKY, B.: Psychic anorexia. *Prensa méd. argent.*, 42:2387-2395, 1955.

SEVIN, J. C.: Contribution a l'étude de l'anorexie mentale. *Paris: R. Foulon*, 1957, pp. 69-74.

SEXTON, D. L.: Diagnosis and treatment of anorexia nervosa. *Ann. West. Med. Surg.*, 4:397-401, 1950.

SHAPIRO, F.: Anorexia in infancy and childhood. *Arch. Pediat.*, 44:175-180, 1927.

SHELDON, J. H.: Anorexia nervosa with special reference to physical constitution. *Lancet*, 1:369-373, 1937.

────── & YOUNG, F.: Carbohydrate metabolism in anorexia nervosa. *Lancet*, 1:257-259, 1938.

SIEBENMANN, R. E.: Anorexia nervosa with hypokalemia; fatal case. *Schweiz. med. Wschr.*, 85:468-471, 1955.

──────: Pathologic anatomy of anorexia nervosa. *Schweiz. med. Wschr.*, 85:530-537, 1955.

SIFNEOS, P. E.: A case of anorexia nervosa treated successfully by leucotomy. *Am. J. Psychiat.*, 109:356-360, 1952.

SILBERKASTEN, A. & KOFMAN, I.: Comparative value of various stimulants in pediatrics. *Sem. méd.*, *B. Aires*, 111:774-785, 1957.

SMALL, S. M. & MILHORAT, A. T.: Anorexia nervosa; metabolism and its relation to psychopathologic reactions. *Am. J. Psychiat.*, 100:681-685, 1944.

SMITH, D. E. & TYREE, E. B.: Attempts to provide the rat with nutrition during post-irradiation anorexia. *Radiation Res.*, 4:435-448, 1956.

SMITH, J. W.: Case of anorexia nervosa complicated by beriberi. *Acta psychiat. neurol.*, 21:887-900, 1946.

SMITH, M. H.: Anorexia nervosa complicated by vomiting and pain; new point in diagnosis and new method of treatment. *J. Florida Med. Assn.*, 6:58, 1919.

SMITH, W. I.; POWELL, E. K.; & ROSS, S.: Food aversions; some additional personality correlates. *J. Consult. Psychol.*, 19:145-149, 1955.

SNOW, I. M.: Curative effect of rest in children with persistent loss of appetite. *J. Am. Med. Assn.*, 51:1917-1920, 1908.

SOKOLOVA, T. S.: Causes of anorexia in young children and measures of their correction. *Pediatriia, Moscow*, 3:16-22, 1959.

SOLEZ, C.: Overeating and vascular degeneration; excesses causing insufficiencies. *J. Am. Geriat. Soc.*, 6:873-879, 1958.

SOMMER, B.: Puberty emaciation as a somatopsychic disorder of the maturation crisis. *Psyche, Stuttg.*, 9:307-327, 1955.

SONG, C. S.; PEARSON, W. N.; & DARBY, W. J.: Effects of anorexia and x-irradiation on vitamin B6 excretion in rats. *Am. J. Physiol.*, 184:309-311, 1956.

SOROL, R. V.: Enuresis and nervous anorexia. *Prensa méd. argent.*, 43:441-442, 1956.

SPENCE, A. W.: Anorexia nervosa. *St. Barth. Hosp. J.*, 52:129-130, 1948.

SPROCKHOFF, O.: Loss of appetite in children. *Münch. med. Wschr.*, 101:118-119, 1959.

SQUIRES, A. H.: Emotions and the diet. *Canad. Hosp.*, 35:70; passim, 1958.

STAFFORD-CLARK, D.; SIM, M.; TIBBETTS, R. W. & ALLEN, C.; & DEW-JONES, J. A.: Anorexia Nervosa. (Correspondence.) *Brit. Med. J.*, 5093:446-447, 1958.

——— & WILLIS, J. H.: Anorexia nervosa. *Brit. J. Clin. Pract.*, 13:533-540, 1959.

STAEHELIN, D.; REBER, K.; & BÜHLMANN, A.: Acid-base equilibrium in mental anorexia. *Helvet. med. acta*, 22:530-535, 1955.

STÄUBLI-FRÖHLICH, M.: Problems of anorexia nervosa. *Schweiz. med. Wschr.*, 83:811-817, 837-841, 1953.

STEPHENS, D. J.: Anorexia nervosa; endocrine factors in undernutrition. *J. Clin. Endocrinol.*, 1:257-268, 1941.

STEPHENS, L.: Case of anorexia nervosa; necropsy. *Lancet*, 1:31-32, 1895.

STEVENEL, L.: Red pepper, a too little used therapeutic agent for anorexia, liver congestion and various vascular disorders (hemorrhoids, varices). *Bull. Soc. path. exot., Paris,* 49:841-843, 1956.

STIMMING, H. J.: Treatment of emaciation. *Med. Klin., Berlin,* 52:833-834, 1957.

STOLZ, H. R.: Resistance to eating among preschool children. *California & West. Med.,* 40:159-163, 1934.

STOWE, F. R., JR. & MILLER, A. T., JR.: The effect of amphetamine on food intake in rats with hypothalamic hyperphagia. *Experientia, Basel,* 13:114-115, 1957.

STUNKARD, A. J.: Untoward reactions to weight reduction among certain obese persons. *Ann. New York Acad. Sc.,* 63 (1):4-5, 1955.

——— GRACE, W. J.; & WOLFF, H. G.: The night-eating syndrome; a pattern of food intake among certain obese patients. *Am. J. Med.,* 19:78-86, 1955.

SUNDERMAN, F. W. & ROSE, E.: Serum electrolytes; changes in serum and body fluids in anorexia nervosa. *J. Clin. Endocrinol.,* 8:209-220, 1948.

SURMONT, H.: Different forms of nervous anorexia. *Medicine,* 1:603, 1920.

TAYLOR, S.: A case of anorexia nervosa. *West London Med. J.,* 9:110-112, 204-207, 1904.

TEITELBAUM, P.: Sensory control of hypothalamic hyperphagia. *J. Comp. Physiol. Psychol.,* 48:156-163, 1955.

——— & STELLAR, E.: Recovery from failure to eat produced by hypothalamic lesions. *Science,* 120:894-895, 1954.

TELLES, W.: Loss of appetite in infants. *Rev. brasil. med.,* 15:104-106, 1958.

TEVETOGLU, F.: Treatment of common anemias in infancy and childhood with cobalt-iron mixture including case report of iron deficiency anemia due to geophagia. *J. Pediat.,* 49:46-55, 1956.

THOM, H.: Psychosomatic aspects of anorexia nervosa. *Med. Klin., Berlin,* 53:1985-1989, 1958.

TIEMANN, F.: Symptomatology of anorexia nervosa, its differential diagnosis and treatment. *Med. Klin., Berlin,* 53:329-335, 1958.

TOLSTRUP, K.: Psychogenic anorexia and hyperorexia among siblings. *Acta paediat.,* 41:360-372, 1952.

———: Want of appetite in children. *Copenhagen: Munksgaard,* 1957, pp. 189-195.

TORRES, UMANA C.: Anorexia. *Rev. colomb. pediat.,* 16, (Special No.): 34-40, 1957.

TUCKER, W. I.: Lobotomy case histories; ulcerative colitis and anorexia nervosa. *Lahey Clin. Bull.*, 7:239-243, 1952.

TUSTIN, F.: Anorexia nervosa in an adolescent girl. *Brit. J. Med. Psychol.*, 31:184-200, 1958.

TYSON, R. G.: Anorexia nervosa; an unusual case study. *Permanente Found. Med. Bull.*, 10:315-318, 1952.

VAGUE, J.: Should the concept of anorexia nervosa be restricted or extended? *Presse méd.*, 66:659-660, 1958.

────── PAVIER, G.; & TORRESANI, J. L.: Nervous thinness in brother and sister. *Ann. endocrinol., Paris*, 18:393-396, 1957.

VAN BALEN, G. F.: Anorexia nervosa and hypophysial emaciation. *Acta med. scandinav.*, 101:433-450, 1939.

──────: Simmonds' cachexia, hypophysial emaciation and anorexia nervosa. *Nederl. tschr. geneesk.*, 83:905-914, 1939.

VAN BIEMA, H. R.; KOEK, H. C.; & SCHREUDER, J. T. R.: Hysteric anorexia resembling Simmonds' disease; case. *Nederl. tschr. geneesk.*, 85:58-60, 1941.

VANDERBILT, UNIVERSITY HOSPITAL STAFF CONFERENCE: Anorexia nervosa. *J. Tennessee Med. Assn.*, 46:330-337, 1953.

VAN PUTTEN, L. M.; VAN BEKKUM, D. W.; & QUERIDO, A.: Influence of hypothalamic lesions producing hyperphagia, and of feeding regimens on carcass composition in rat. *Metabolism*, 4:68-74, 1955.

VAZ, E. J.: Anorexia. *Ind. J. Med. Sc.*, 11:765-766, 1957.

VENABLES, J. F.: Anorexia nervosa. *Clin. J.*, 59:544-548, 1930.

──────: Anorexia nervosa; a study of the pathogenesis and treatment of nine cases. *Guy's Hosp. Rep.*, 80:213-226, 1930.

VENTURA, J.: Adrenocortical influence on appetite and somatic catabolism. *Arch. med. exper.*, 18:261-271, 1955.

VIEIRA DA SILVA, C.; SCHERMANN, J.; & CAPRIGLIONE, L.: Mental anorexia and diabetes (discussion of clinical case no. 20). *Arq. brasil. med.*, 43:384-386, 1953.

VIGNEC, A. J.; MOSER, A.; & JULIA, J. F.: Treatment of chronic enuresis, poor weight gain, and poor appetite in institutional children. *Arch. Pediat.*, 74:119-130, 1957.

VINTHER-PAULSEN, N.: Senile anorexia. *Geriatrics*, 7:274-279, 1952.

WALL, J. H.: Anorexia nervosa. *Bull. New York Acad. Med.*, 32:116-126, 1956.

──────: Diagnosis, treatment and results in anorexia nervosa. *Am. J. Psychiat.*, 115:997-1001, 1959.

WALLER, J. V.; KAUFMAN, M. R.; & DEUTSCH, F.: Anorexia nervosa; psychosomatic entity. *Psychosom. Med.*, 2:3-16, 1940.

WEIDENTHAL, D. T.: Anorexia nervosa. *Ohio Med. J.*: 55:664-667, 1959.

WEILL, J.: Mental anorexia in pediatrics. *Progr. méd., Paris,* 83:8-12, 1955.

———— BERNFELD, J.; & PAUMELLE, P.: Treatment of a mental anorexia by isoniazide. *Bull. Soc. méd. hôp., Paris,* 69:496-506, 1953.

WEIPPL, G.: Anemia with geophagia in early childhood. *Arch. Kinderh.,* 160:142-146, 1959.

WEISS, E.: Psychosomatic aspects of dieting. *J. Clin. Nutrition,* 1:140-148, 1953.

WHITE, L. E. & HAIN, R. F.: Anorexia in association with a destructive lesion of the hypothalamus. *A.M.A. Arch. Pathol.,* 68:275-281, 1959.

WHITE, W. G. & MOEHLIG, R. C.: Differentiation of anorexia nervosa and pituitary cachexia; case. *J. Michigan Med. Soc.,* 49:665-667, 1950.

WILD, E.; SCAZZIGA, B. R.; and REYMOND, C.: Metabolic disorders in mental anorexia. *Helvet. med. acta,* 22:540-543, 1955.

WILLIAMS, E.: Anorexia nervosa; a somatic disorder. *Brit. Med. J.,* 5090: 190-195, 1958.

WILSON, D. C.; RYMARKIEWICZOWA, D.; & WHITE, W. M.: Anorexia nervosa with special regard to insulin therapy. *South. Med. J.,* 39:408-416, 1946.

WILSON, R. R.: Case of anorexia nervosa with necropsy findings and discussion of secondary hypopituitarism. *J. Clin. Pathol.,* 7:131-136, 1954.

ZIMBLER, M.: Anorexia mentalis. *Delaware State Med. J.,* 13:112-117, 1941.

INDEX

Abdominal disease, 111
Abercrombie, J., 113, 121
Abraham, K., 345, 347, 348
Abramson, H. A., 28, 32
Activity, excessive, 158
Adaptation, 88, 99
   and conversion hysteria, 85
   and energy distribution, 102
   and health, 178
   and memory, 96
   as cause of disease, 100
   homeostatic mechanism, 93
   preformed tools of, 95
   principles of, 249
   total mode of, 353
Addison, T., 116
Addison's disease, 177
   differential diagnosis, 221
Adenohypophysis, functional disturbance of (Farquharson and Hyland cases), 219
Adler, A., 90
Adolescence, instability of, 225, 237
Adrenal insufficiency, 176, 177
Adrenal system, effects of rage on, 75
Affect, nondischarged, 250
Aging of tissues, variability in, 105
Aggression and hatred, 238
Aggressivity, masculine, and urinary urgency, 347
Alexander F., 1, *56-77*, 251, 286, 296, 318, 334 n., 344 n., 346, 347, 349
   on emotional tension, 91
   vector concepts, 97
Alexander, G. H., 293, 296

Alimentation, function of, 159
Allbutt, T. C., 243
Allen, N. H., 29, 32
Allergy, 54
Amenorrhea, 112, 202, 203, 225, 253, 275, 276
   and constipation, 259
   and emotions, 24
   and fear of pregnancy, 25
   and puberty, 254
   and ulcer, 19
   anxiety regarding, 238
   Farquharson and Hyland cases, 219
   Lorand case, 314
   Moulton cases, 293
   Nicolle's case of Miss M., 228, 232
   significance of, 233
   Weizsäcker's case of Mrs. H. Q., 184
Amnesia, 159
Anabolism and catabolism, 88
Analysis
   and understanding of the psychosoma, 50
   effect on drug intake, 52
   psychosomatic course of treatment, 48
   treatment of the whole person, 53
   see also psychoanalysis
Anamnesis, 51
Anamnestic interview, limitations, 247
Anatomic alteration, basis of diagnostic medium, 39

377

INDEX

Anderson, D., 44
Angina pectoris, 22, 23
  pseudo, 54
Angioneuritis, emotional determinant in, 23
Animals, psychic system in, 96
Annales médico-psychologiques, 9
Anorexia and psychotherapy, 32
Anorexia nervosa, cases of
  Charcot's Angoulême girl, 160-163
  Farquharson and Hyland, 8 cases (Table 1) 204-218
  Grote and Meng case 1, 169-170; case 2, 170-176
  Gull's cases: Miss A., 132-133; Miss B., 134-136; Miss C., 136-138; K. R. 139
  Lasègue's diagrammatic sketch, 145-155
  Lorand case, 300-311
  Masserman case of vomiting, 322-326
  Medvei and Schur's six cases, 199-201
  Moulton case 1, 278-285; case 2, 285-286; case 3, 289-292; case 4, 292
  Nicolle's case of Miss M., 228-233; two cases, 234-236
  Waller, Kaufman, Deutsch case of P. D., 260-264; case of E. G., 264-271
  Weizsäcker's case of Mrs. H. Q., 183-186; case of Mrs. V. Q., 186-191
Anxiety, 17, 147, 276
  and eating (Moulton cases), 294
  and nondischarged affect, 10, 251
  and seasickness, 21
  castration (Masserman case), 333
  effect of French Revolution on Parisians, 11
Anxiety hysteria, Moulton cases, 294
Anxiety neurosis, 15, 16

Apepsia, hysteric, 123
  Gull's case, 135
Appetite
  and hunger, 183
  effect of mental states on (Gull's cases), 136
  failure of, 203
  false, 145
  lack of, 129, 130, 131
  perversions of, 144
  rhythm of, 193
  Weizsäcker's case of Mrs. H. Q., 184
Arteriosclerosis and emotions, 23
Aschoff, K. A., 45
Ashwell, S., 24, 32
Asthma
  amelioration by hypnosis, 30
  and gaining attention (Nicolle's two cases), 235
  and psychosis, 28
  bronchial, 178
  description of, 29
Ataxia, locomotor, 105, 114
Attitudes
  and physiological substrate, 89
  contradictory, 196
Auenbrugger, L. J., 8 n.
Autointoxication, theory of, 16
Autonomic nervous system, 96
  and emotional disturbance, 224
  and emotional tensions, 91

Bacon, C., 346, 349
Bacon, F., empiricism of, 41
Bacteriology, 42
Baillie, M., 39, 114
Ballantyne, H., 20, 32
Ballet, G., 244
Barker, L., 32
Barnett, A., 288
Barthez, A., 9
Basedow's disease, 182
Batty, R., 13

INDEX

Baudouin, A., 232, 244
Beard, G. M., 15, 31
Beaumont, W., 6, 17, 18, 32
Behavior
  and physiological substrate, 89
  "brain" concept of, 12
  compulsive ritualistic (Waller, Kaufman, Deutsch case of E. G.), 271, 272
  psychoanalytic theory of, 10
Benedek, T., 101, 275, 277, 296, 332 n., 349
Bergmann, G. von, 75, 77, 165, 198
Berkman, J. M., 296, 343 n., 349, 356, 357
Bernard, C., 11, 12, 40, 42, 99, 129
Bichat, M. F. X., 9-14 *pass.*
Bilz, R., 197
Binet, A., 16
Biochemistry, advancing methodology of, 38
Biological contradiction, 195
Biophysics, advancing methodology of, 38
Birch, S. B., 21, 33
Blindness, hysterical, 84
Blitzen, N. L., 349
Blood pressure, 16, 225
Blood sugar level, 225
  Farquharson and Hyland cases, 220
  fluctuations in (Nicolle's two cases), 236
Bodily behavior and instinctual drives, 55
Body and mind, 70, 352, 353
Body and personality, 68, 77
Body ego, structural organization of, 48
Boston Society for Medical Improvement, 13
Boullaud, J. B., 22
Brain
  and nervous system, 7
  dynamic change in, 15
  pathological anatomy of, 64
  tumor of, 111
Breuer, J., 13, 31, 349
  on chronic vomiting, 344
Brigham, 18, 33
Bright, R., 39
Brinton, W., 19, 33
British Journal of Dental Science, 27
Brodie, B. C., 33
"Brodie's knee," 13
Bronson, E. B., 27, 33
Brosin, H., 322, 349
Broussais, F. J. V., 17, 33
Brown, W. P., 227, 243, 245
Brown-Séquard, C. E., 11, 12, 13, 129
Brunton, L., 23
Bulimia, 131
  Weizsäcker's case of Mrs. H. Q., 184

Campbell, F. W., 22, 33
Cancer
  and anxiety, 13
  local origin of, 116
Cannibalistic fantasies
  and dental disturbances, 84
  Masserman case, 340
Cannon, W. B., 345 n., 349
Cardiovascular system, 22
  and inhibited rage, 76
Carmichael, H. T., 349
Cartesian interactionism, 7
Case histories
  Charcot's Angoulême girl, 160-163
  Farquharson and Hyland, eight cases (Table 1) 204-218
  Grote and Meng case 1, 169-170; case 2, 170-176
  Gull's case of Miss A., 132-133; case of Miss B., 134-136; case of Miss C., 136-138; case of K. R., 139

Case histories *(cont.)*
  Lasègue's diagrammatic sketch, 145-155
  Lorand case, 300-311
  Masserman case, 322-326
  Medvei and Schur's six cases, 199-201
  Moulton case 1, 278-285; case 2, 285-286; case 3, 289-292; case 4, 292
  Nicolle's case of Miss M., 228-233; two cases 234-236
  Waller, Kaufman, Deutsch, case of P. D., 260-264; case of E. G., 264-271
  Weizsäcker's case of Mrs. H. Q., 183-186; case of Mrs. V. Q., 186-191
Castration anxiety (Masserman case), 333
Catabolism and anabolism, 88
Cause and effect, theory of, 41, 42, 204
Cell stenosis, 43
Cellular biology
  growing trend toward, 354
  introduction into medical science, 9
Cellular metabolism, 43
Cellular pathology, 41
Central nervous system and unity of organism, 69
Cerebral activity and reflex action, 15
Cerise, L., 9, 33
Champneys, F. H., 25, 33
Channing, W., 30, 33
Character structures, specific for various diseases, 91
Character traits and erotogenic zones, 89
Charcot, J. M., 66, 156, 157, 164, 228, 244
  case of Angoulême girl, 160-163

French school of psychiatrists, 13
hysterical elaboration of local injury, 31
Chaussier, F., 9
Chicago Psychoanalytic Institute, 322, 346
Chronic invalidism, psychological treatment of, 30
Churchill, F., 25, 33
Clarke, L., 114
Claudicatio intermittens, 54
Cleanliness, obsessive need for, 258
Clinical medicine
  development of, 40, 41
  importance of, 107, 109, 110
Cobb, S., 128
Colonopathies, psychological causation of, 21
Comprehensive medicine, education in, 32
Compulsive phenomena, Moulton cases, 294
Conditioning, 96, 97
Conflict, mental
  unconscious (Lorand case), 312
  underlying anorexia nervosa syndrome, 226
Conversion hysteria, 58, 92, 93, 242, 276
  and adaptation, 85
  bodily symptoms from emotional conflict, 71
  symptoms of (Moulton cases), 286
Constipation, 144, 203, 253
  and amenorrhea, 259
  and diarrhea, 21, 259
  Lorand case, 314
Constitutional predisposition to pituitary dysfunction, 276
Contractility, 9
Conversion
  and displacement symptoms, 14
  pregenital, 90
  symptom formation, 81

Convulsions, infantile and senile, 113
Conybeare, J. J., 223, 226
Cooper, A. P., 13, 33
Coronary vasoconstriction, use of nitroglycerine, 23
Creighton, C., 10, 11, 33
Cullen, W., 12
Curschmann, H., 172

Darwin, C., 14, 99
Death, longing for, 192
De Blegny, N., 9
Defenses
 ego (Masserman case), 338
 of nausea (Lorand case), 313
 psychic, 98
Defensive attitude and unconscious anxiety, 51
De Gennes, I., 231, 232, 244
Déjerine, J. J., 32, 244
Delarue, J., 231, 232
Denny, J. H., 16 n., 33
Dental disturbances
 and mental strain, 27
 and oral-erotic fantasies, 84
Dentistry, psychosomatic implications, 27
Dependent tendencies and nutrition, 76
Depression, 253
 and refusal of food (Masserman case), 345
 Lorand case, 313
Dermatoses, neuropathic, 27; *see also* Skin disease
Descartes, R., Cartesian interactionism, 7
Deutsch, F., 1, 47, 90, 91, 102, 131, 176, *245-273*, 276, 286, 298-300, 312, 318, 247 n., 349
Diabetes
 etiology of, 59
 orality in, 1942

Diagnosis
 and alleviation of symptoms, 127
 and anatomic alteration, 38, 39
 and pathology, 119
 and urinalysis, 124
Diarrhea, 144
 and constipation, 21, 259
 and masculine strivings, 347
 and ulcerative colitis, 100
 infantile and senile, 113
Digestive organ disturbances, 143, 144
Disease
 abdominal, 111, 123
 acute idiopathic, 111
 alteration of form and function, 36
 and emotion, 8
 causal relation of environmental factors to, 44
 cerebral, 121
 described as neurosis, 12
 febrile, 117, 118
 investigation of, 108
 localization of, 62
 mesenteric, 123
 of the chest, 123
 role of psychic factors in, 353
 Virchow's view of, 41, 78
Disease, mental, and metabolic disturbances, 16
Disease process, psychological factor in evaluation of, 3
Disorders of unknown origin, 75
Dissociation, 14, 242
Donders, F. C., 11
Dreams
 and early oral fantasies (Masserman case), 327
 in endogenic *magersucht*, 181-197
 intermediary role of, 195-196
 pregnancy fantasies in, 166
 symbolic language of, 194
 utilizing manifest content of, 166

Drug intake and analysis, 52
Dubois, P., 79, 80, 102, 164
Dubois, R., 234, 244
Dubois-Reymond, E. H., 28
Ducheme, G., 114
Ductless glands, discovery of, 69, 70
Dunbar, F., personality profiles for psychosomatic syndromes, 91
Dunbar, H. F., 1, 319, 345 n., 350
Dunn, C. W., 204, 226
Duodenal tube, feeding by, 225
Duodenal ulcer, 346
Dysmenorrhea, vasomotor neurosis, 25
Dyspepsia, 151
 and mental excitement, 18

Eating
 and anxiety (Moulton cases), 294
 and genital sexuality, 346
 and impregnation, 258
 and pregnancy, 256
 and sexuality, 245, 250
 aversion to (Farquharson and Hyland cases), 219
 emphasis on, 251, 252
 fear of (Farquharson and Hyland cases), 218
 psychological influences on, 128
 symbolism of (Waller, Kaufman, Deutsch case of E. G.), 271
 symbolizing pregnancy, 131
Ecological interreaction, 99
Eczema
 and emotions, 26
 infantile and senile, 113
Edema
 premenstrual (Moulton cases), 288
 Weizsäcker's case of Mrs. H. Q., 184
Edes, R. T., 30

Educational influences, direct application of, 316
Ego, weakness of (Lorand case), 316
Ego defenses (Masserman case), 338
Ego functions, 95, 96, 97, 249 n.
 and autonomous energy, 79
Ego structure and feeding stimulus, 48
Ego-syntonic obsession and vomiting, 332 n.
Electricity, lessening in bodily resistance to, 16
Elimination, oral and anal, 278
Elliott, T. R., 223, 226
Emaciation, 225
Embolism, 40, 120
Emmet, T. A., 13
Emotional components in organic dysfunctional behavior, 50
Emotional conflict, 203
 and conversion hysteria, 71
 basis of psychoneurosis, 76
Emotional disturbance
 and autonomic nervous system, 224
 as precipitating factor (Farquharson and Hyland cases), 218
Emotional life
 disturbances of, 64
 normal psychosomatic correlations in, 49
Emotional reactions
 and gastrointestinal disturbances (Lorand case), 315
 and menstrual disturbances, 25
Emotional states and gastric motility 345
Emotional suffering, 177
Emotional tensions and autonomic nervous system, 91
Emotional traumata and endocrine disturbances, goiter, 76

382

INDEX

Emotions
  adaptive functions of, 99
  and amenorrhea, 24
  and arteriosclerosis, 23
  and blood pressure, 16
  and bodily changes, 1
  and body functions, 77
  and circulation, 11
  and disease, 8
  and feeding, 255
  and gastrointestinal system, 17
  and lessening in bodily resistance to electricity, 16
  and nervous hyperirritability, 129
  and physiological changes, 58, 70
  and the heart, 22
  and the skin, 26
  consequence of, 160
  influence on the uterus, 26
  physical expression of, 113
  reactivated (Lorand case), 312
Endocarditis, 118
Endocrine disturbances
  and emotional traumata, 76
  Nicolle's case of Miss M., 232
Endocrine glands
  discovery of systems, 58
  pathology related to, 253
  role of, 276
Endocrine-autonomic system, disturbed function of, 242
Energy
  distribution in adaptation, 102
  economics of, 3
  storage in neurons, 15
Energy, autonomous and ego functions, 79
Energy flow, concept of, 94
Energy, neural and pathological changes, 129
Enuresis, 256
Environment
  and personality, 87, 299
  causal relation to disease, 44
  conflict with, 256
  emotional neutrality in (Nicolle's two cases), 235
  influence of figures in, 153
  interaction with, 58
  reaction pattern to (Lorand case), 317
Enzymatic processes, interference with, 43
Epigastric distress, 203
Epilepsy, 122
Epiphenomenal conception of mind, 7
Epistemology of the eighteenth century, 41
Erotogenic zones and character traits, 89
Erythromelalgia, 23, 24
Esquirol, J., 8 n.
Estrogen activity, estimate of, 274
Etiology, of anorexia nervosa 157
  changes in concepts, 73-75
  somatic and neurotic, 253, 254
Eulenburg, A., 22, 28
Euphoria and nutrition, 193
Evolution of medicine and philosophical climate, 41
Ewald, C. A., 20
Excitomotor acts and reflex action, 10, 129
Exophthalmic goiter, 30
Experimental psychology and psychiatry, 16
Eye, tumescence of, 94

Fainting, 146
Falconer, W., 8, 33
Family
  attitude toward patient, 149
  patient's removal from, 77
  pressure of constellation, 273
Farquharson, R. F., *202-226*, 254, 273, 361

Farquharson and Hyland, eight cases (Table 1) 204-218
Fasting, selective, 151
Fatigue, suppressed feeling of, 158
Fau, R., 231
Fazio, E., 25
Fear
  and skin disease, 26
  cause of disease, 9
  expression in the organism, 49, 50
  of retaliation (Masserman case), 342
Fear neurosis, 16
Fechner, G., 57
  experimental school, 68
Federn, P., 90
Feeding
  and expression of emotions, 255
  overemphasis on, 259
Feeding stimulus, foundation of ego structure, 48
Feelings, externalization of (Lorand case), 317
Fellatio, obsessive thoughts of (Masserman case), 336
Fenichel, O., pregenital conversion, 90
Ferenczi, S., 1, 85, 100-103, 176, 345, 350
  libidinal withdrawal, 84
  organ neurosis, 86
  psychosomatic interrelations, 80
Feuchtersleben, E. von, 9, 33
Fixation and the libido theory, 100, 101
Food
  abstinence from (Weizsäcker's case of Mrs. V. Q.), 187
  and depression (Masserman case), 345
  and fear of poisoning (Lorand case), 313
  and fear of pregnancy (Lorand case), 313
  and mother's love (Lorand case), 312
  and pregnancy fantasies (Moulton cases), 293
  progressive repugnance toward, 148
  rejection of, 256
  selective intake of, 154
Food, ingestion of, 243
  symbolic significance, 255
  symbolizing impregnation, 245
  variables relating to, 321
Forensic psychiatry, menstruation as extenuating circumstance, 24
Frank, J., 8 n.
Frank, R. T., 288, 296
Freed, S. C., 296
French Revolution, emotional effect on Parisians, 11
Freud, S., 1-4 *pass.*, 10-16 *pass.*, 353
  character traits and erogenous zones, 89
  chronic vomiting, 344
  diarrhea, 347
  hysteria, 31
  libidinization, 94
  prolonged nongratification, 314
  psychoanalysis and mental disturbance, 65, 66
  psychoanalytic psychology, 102
  psychosomatic interrelationships, 80-84 *pass.*
  repressed affect, 250, 251
  theory of the unconscious, 233, 234
  urinary urgency, 347
Frigidity, mental, and impotence in men, 25
Function
  inhibition of, 94
  psychic aspect of, 78
Function, pathological, and pathological structure, 74
Functional disturbance, 58

Functional disturbance (*cont.*)
  and organic disturbance, 73
  and psychotherapy, 72

Gastralgias, 144
Gastric dysfunction and neurotic attitudes, 322
Gastric irritation and neuroses, 17
Gastric motility and emotional states, 345
Gastric pain, 143, 146
Gastrointestinal behavior, anal and oral type of, 49
Gastrointestinal disorders and emotional reactions (Lorand case), 315
  and patient's emotional life, 50
  and pregenital conflicts, 347
  influence of psychologic factors on, 346
  psychotherapy for, 32
Gastrointestinal functions and neurotic tendencies (Moulton cases), 293
Gastrointestinal neuroses, 344 n.
Gastrointestinal tract
  and pregnancy fantasies, 245
  effect of emotion on, 17
  fantasies role of (Waller, Kaufman, Deutsch, case of E. G.), 271
  gastritis, 20
  utilization of, 298, 299
Gee, S., 253, 273
Geist, S. H., 296
Genital conflicts and neuromuscular system, 347
Genitalia
  denial of (Lorand case), 318
  denial of sexual function, 258
  renunciation of (Masserman case), 340
Gerard, M., 334 n., 350
Gestalt psychology, 57, 68

Glomerulonephritis, investigation of, 45
Gluttony, 258
Goal of medicine, 46
Goals in therapy, 353
  analytic, 53
  attitude toward food, 223
Goiter
  and emotional traumata, 76
  etiology of toxic, 59
  exophthalmic, 30
Gonad deficiency, 240
Greenacre, P., 90
Greenough, R. B., 19, 33
Gregg, A., 56, 63, 77
Grinker, R. R., 97, 100, 102, 103
  multiplicity of factors in psychosomatic phenomena, 91
Groddeck, G., 1, 86, 87, 176
Grote, L. R., 165, *167-180*, 181
Grote and Meng cases
  case 1 treated with insulin, 169-170
  case 2 insulin failure, 170-176
Guilt
  and self-indulgence, 236-237
  cannibalistic (Masserman case), 345
  reactive (Masserman case), 328
Guilt feelings
  Lorand case, 313
  specific expression of, in the organism, 49, 50
Gull, W. W., 4, *104-127*, 128, 129, *139-140*, 203, 228, 229, 244, 253, 273, 321, 343, 350, 352, 264
  case of Miss A., 132-138
  nerve force, 95
Gull's cases
  Miss A., 132, 133
  Miss B., 134-136
  Miss C., 136-138
  K. R., 139
Gull-Lasègue syndrome, 141

Gynecologic operations and postoperative psychoses, 30

Haematemesis, 112, 143
Haemoptysis, 112
Hair, distribution of, 240
Hall, M., 10, 12, 129
Haller, A., 9, 11, 12
Hamilton, W., 15 n.
Hansen, G., 176
Hartland, E. S., 256, 273
Hartmann, H., 79, 95, 103
Harvard Medical School, 31
Harvey, W., 38
Hatred and aggression, 239
Hawkinson, L. F., 231, 244
Hay fever, psychosomatic implications of, 28, 29
Haygarth, J., 9, 33
Headache, 27, 28
　and tumor, 122
Health and adaptation, 178
Heart
　and emotions, 22, 23
　disease of, 197
　emotionally conditioned disturbances of, 71
Heberden, W., 22
Hebra, F., 27
Hechter, O., 296
Heiman, M., *198-201,*
Heinroth, J., 8 n.
Hendrick, I., 100
Henle, F. G. J., 39
Henry, F. P., 24, 33
Hereditary determination of nervous system irritability, 14
Hereditary predisposition, 14
Herman, C., 231
Hill, L. W., 343 n., 350
Hinsie, L. E., 80, 103
Hippocrates, 4, 38, 104
Hirsuties, masculine, 276

Nicolle's case of Miss M., 232
Histochemistry, applied to cellular abnormality, 40
Histology, introduction into medical science, 9
Histopathology, progress in, 45
Hobhouse, N., *240-243*
Holmes, O. W., 31, 34
Homeostatic mechanism, 93
Hormonal aspects, 167
Hormones, ovarian, 239
　and psychic system, 101
　therapy, 172
Hospitalization, prolonged (Moulton case), 295
Huchard, H., 23, 34
Hunger
　and appetite, 183
　physiology of, (Nicolle's two cases), 236
Hurst, A. F., 343 n., 365
Hydrotherapy, Charcot's case of the Angoulême girl, 162, 163
Hygiene and therapeutics, 124, 125
Hyland, H. H., *202-226,* 254, 362
Hyperacidity
　and migraine, 21
　and neurasthenia, 20
　and psychological stress, 21
Hyperemesis gravidarum and psychotherapy, 178
Hyperinsulinism, 221
Hyperirritability and emotion, 129
Hypertension
　etiology of, 59
　psychosomatic implications of, 23
Hypnosis, effect on asthma, 30
Hypnotic suggestion and cutaneous lesions, 27
Hypochondria and suggestive therapy, 54
Hypochondriasis, 92
　and hysteria, 155
Hypoglycemia, 221

INDEX

Hypophyseal cachexia, Nicolle's case of Miss M., 232
Hysteria
  and "Brodie's knee," 13
  and patient's mental disposition, 155
  and pregnancy, 26
  etiology of, 14
  influence of environment on, 150
  major symptoms of, 156-159
  origin of, 13
  treated by psychotherapy, 32
  variability in, 1942
Hysteric apepsia, 123
Hysteric passion, 8
Hysterical anorexia, 159, 203
  prognosis, 153
  third stage of, 152
Hysterical blindness, 84
Hysterical conversion, onset of symptoms, 92
Hysterical inanition, 144
Hysterical localizations, 151
Hysterical patients, 16
Hysterical reactions, 14
  psychosomatic meaning of, 13
Ideas expressed in speech, 70
Ideation, 78
  verbal and nonverbal, 79
Identification with parent of the same sex, 257
Impetigo and emotions, 26
Impotence in men and mental frigidity, 25
Impregnation, fantasies of (Masserman case), 345
Infectious diseases
  and neuroses, 130
  and personality, 50
Insanity and gastric irritation, 17
Insomnia, psychosomatic determinants of, 8 n.
Instincts, the motor force of psychic life, 81

Instinctual drives
  and bodily behavior, 55
  repression of, 82
Instinctual life, physical correlates in developmental stages of, 49
Insulin therapy, 168
Internal medicine and psychoanalysis, 47-55
Intestinal infection among members of the same family, 50
Irritability and irritation, 9
Isolation
  Nicolle's case of Miss M., 229, 230
  therapeutic benefits of (Charcot's Angoulême girl), 162

Jaccoud, S., 28
Jacobi, A., 8
Jackson, H., 14, 15, 34, 100, 114
Jackson, J., 18, 19, 34
Janet, P., 3, 13, 14, 16, 103, 156-159
  dissociation theory, 81, 82
Jejunum, immunity of, 105
Jones, E., 45, 344, 347, 350
  character traits and erotogenic zones, 89
Joslin, E., 20, 34
Journal of Psychosomatic Medicine, 1

Kaltenbach, R., 21, 34
Kant, I., 41
Kaufman, M. R., *198-201, 245-273,* 276, 286, 298-300, 312
Keiller, A., 26, 34
Kelp, L., 28, 34
Key, E. A. H., 20
Kiefer, E. D., 343 n., 350
Kiernan, F., 30, 34
Kirkes, W. S., 120
Klein, M., 90, 344, 345, 350
Klemperer, P., *36-46,* 78
Knight, F. I., 29, 34
Koch, R., 40, 74

387

Koffka, K., 57, 68
Kohler, W., 57, 68
Kraepelin, E., 16, 65
Krafft-Ebing, R., 24
Krieger, F. J., 25, 34
Kris, E., 79
Krohn, P. L., 296
Kronecker, K. H., 11
Kussmaul, A., 11, 20

Laennec, R. T. H., 22, 29 n., 39
Langdon-Brown, W., 204, 226
Langley, J. N., 12
Lasègue, E. C., 135, 156, 157, 203, 244, 321
  on hysterical anorexia, *141-155*
Lasègue's diagrammatic sketch of anorexia patient, 145-155
Laycock, T., 14, 15, 34, 129
Learning, 96, 97
Le Gallois, J. J. C., 17
Letterer, E., 44
Lev, M., 296
Levey, H., 346 n., 350
Levi, L., 23, 24, 232, 244
Levine, M., 346, 350
Lhermitte, J., 232
Libidinal cathexis and organ changes, 93
Libidization and somatization, 94, 95
Libido
  and injury to erotogenic zones, 85
  development of (Masserman case), 345
  fixation at various levels, 100
  theory of, 80, 81
  withdrawal of, 84
Life, affirmation and denial of, 166
  altered aim of, 194
  positive attitudes toward, 193
Linnaeus, C., 12
Lipodystrophies, 167
Localization of disease, 62

Locke, J., 41
Lockhart, S., 219, 226
Locomotor ataxia, 105, 114
Loeper, M., 231, 244
Lorand, S., *298-319*, 352, 367
Lorand case, 300-311
Louis, P., 17
Love
  and food (Lorand case), 313
  deprivation of (Lorand case), 317
  object choice, 257
Lublin, A., 168, 169
Lucae, S. C., 11, 34
Ludwig, K., 40
Lupus erythematosus, systemic anatomic studies of, 45
Luys, J. B., 12

Magendantz, H., 319
Magersucht (anorexia), 167-180
Mal de mer and anxiety, 21
Marasmus, 253
Margetts, E. L., 8 n., 34
Masserman, J. H., 286, 297, *320-351*, 352
Masserman's case of neurotic vomiting, 322-326
Mayer-Gross, W., 238, 244
McCullogh, E. P., 297
Medical psychology, 60
Medical school education, 46
Medical treatment, historical perspectives, 60-63
Medicine, nineteenth century, 4, 10
  particularist concept in, 62, 63
  scientific system in, 38
  somatopsychic, 17
Medvei, C. V., 165, 166, 198-201
Medvei and Schur, six cases, 199-201
Melancholy, 253
Memory
  and adaptation, 96
  unconscious, 48
  unconscious organic, 10

INDEX

Meng, H., 165, *167-180*, 181, 350
Menninger, K., 97, 103
Menses, cessation of, 131
Menstrual cycle, influence of psychological factors on, 259
Menstrual disturbances and emotional reactions, 25
"Menstrual insanity" and forensic psychiatry, 24
Menstruation
　absence of, 198
　and pregnancy fantasies (Moulton cases), 293
　cessation of, 152, (Lorand case) 318
　vicarious, 112
Mental attitude, 198
Mental disease and metabolic disturbances, 16
Mental disposition and hysteria, 155
Mental excitement and dyspepsia, 18
Mental frigidity and male impotence, 25
Mental functioning, laws of, 3
Mental mechanisms
　dissociation, 14, 242
　effects of, 71
　learning, 96, 97
　Masserman case, 340
　regression, 93, 100, 101, 249, 255
　repression, 14, 76, 82
Mental status in Simmonds' disease and anorexia nervosa, 222
Mental strain and tooth decay, 27
Mentation, unconscious, 247
Mesirow, S. D., 296
Mesmer, 7, 8
Mesmerism, 8
Metabolic and endocrine changes, 275
Metabolic disorder, 204
　and mental disease, sexual functions, 16
　and neuroses, 130
Metabolism, 182, 193
　carbohydrate, 232
　cellular; Nicolle's two cases, 43, 236
　faulty tissue, 239
　low basal, (Table 2) 220, 225, 275
　variations in, 98
Meyer, A., 3, 87, 88, 89; *see also* Psychobiology
Meyer, F. M., 343 n., 350
Michaels, J. J., 100
Microbiology, 42
Micro-organisms, pathogenic, 74
Middleton, W. S., 353 n., 350
Migraine, etiology of, 27, 28
　and hyperacidity, 21
Mind
　and anxiety, 10
　and heart, 22
　and psychic aspect of function, 78
　as the great integrator, 354
　complexity of, 67
　definition of, 80
　early nineteenth-century conception, 7
　epiphenomenal conception, 7
　influence on body, 8
　influence on vascular system, 11
　ruling over the body, 70
　see also Psyche
Mind and body, 63, 87, 352, 353
　interrelation of, 6
　medicine of, 7
　parallelistic position, 7
　psychophysiology of functioning, 12
　relationships, 12
Minor, L. S., 24
Moellendorff, W. von, 28, 34
Morgagni, G. B., 39, 40, 46
　anatomical observations, 38
　association of disease symptoms and organ changes, 41

389

Morgagni, G. B. *(cont.)*
  localization of disease, 62
Morgan, I., 353 n., 350
Morton, R., 244, 253, 273
Moschcowitz, E., 319
Mosso, A., 16
Mother
  and child, 259
  dependence on (Masserman case), 337, 338
  oral relationship to, 298
  reaction to (Lorand case), 312
Mother, frustrating, role of, 300
Mother's love and food (Lorand case), 312
Moulton, R., *274-297*, 369
Moulton's cases
  case 1, 278-285
  case 2, 285-286
  case 3, 289-292
  case 4, 292
Mount Sinai Seminar Group, *1-5, 78-103, 128-131, 352-354*
Mouth, sexual significance of, 257, 258
Muller, H. J., 97-103
Munro, H., 14

Nadeau, M., 229, 244
Narcissism
  and neurosis (Weizsäcker's case of Mrs. V. Q.), 191
  fostering of, 237
  secondary defense of (Masserman case), 341
Narcissistic personality, skin manifestations of, 49
Nasse, C. F., 8 n.
Nausea as a defense (Lorand case), 313
Need, the meaning of, 183
Nephropathies, investigation of glomerulonephritis and others, 45
Nerves, influence on blood vessels, 11
Nervous irritability, 12
Nervous stimulation, reactions to, 11
Nervous system, 18
  anatomical and functional organization of, 15
  and brain, 7
  autonomic, 12
  divisions of, 10
  evolution and dissolution of, 14
  idiopathic influence of, 8
  over-irritability of, hereditarily determined, 14
Nervousness and neurosis, physiopathology of, 12
Neumann, E., 8 n.
Neurasthenia, 15
  and chronic invalidism, 31
  and hyperacidity, 20
  and the sympathetic nervous system, 31
  see also Psychosomatic diseases
Neurological integration, 15
Neurology, advances in, 69
Neuromuscular system and genital conflicts, 347
Neurons, energy stored in, 15
Neuropathic dermatoses, 27
Neuropathology, 14, 105, 112
Neurophysiological research, 12
Neurosis
  alteration of, 28
  and gastric irritation, 17
  and inner tension of narcissism (Weizsäcker's case of Mrs. V. Q.), 191
  and nervousness, 12
  and nutritional, metabolic, or infectious diseases, 130
  and organic process, 52

Neurosis *(cont.)*
  and reflex irritability, 129
  and the chronic invalid, 30
  family history of, 255
  of puberty, 176, 177
  primary importance of, 253
  reflex, treated by surgical aggression, 13
  secondary gain in, 272
  sexual, 84
  traumatic, 31
  vasomotor, reflex, and trophic, 10, 11
Neurotic attitudes and gastric dysfunction, 322
Neurotic patients, psychoanalytic study of, 71
Neurotic symptoms, meaning of, (Lorand case), 312
Neurotic tendencies and gastrointestinal functions (Moulton cases), 293
Newton, I., 41
Nicolle, G., *227-244*, 276, 297, 369
Nicolle's cases
  case of Miss M., 228-233
  two cases, 234-236
Nineteenth-century Medicine 10
  changes in, 4
  "somato-psychic," 8
Nineteenth-century psychotherapy, 31
Nitroglycerine and coronary vasoconstriction, 23
Noguès, G., 236, 244
Nosological history of anorexia nervosa, 252
Nutrition, 182
  and euphoria, 193
  and excitation of vasomotor nerves, 11
  and function, 126
  and pregnancy, 166
  function of and dependent tendencies, 76
  see also Weizsäcker's case of Mrs. V. Q.
Nutritional diseases and neuroses, 130

Obesity
  and puberty, 254
  in adolescence, 276
  dread of (Nicolle's two cases), 236
  preceding anorexia, 254
Obsessive-compulsive features, 276
Obstetrical medicine, psychosomatic thinking in, 26
Occupational therapy, 225
Oedipal conflict, 252
Oedipus fixation, 300
Oken, L., 112
Oliver, J., 45
Oppenheim, H., 31
Oppolzer, J., 19, 20
Oral aggressivity, 346
Oral components, expression of (Masserman case), 326
Oral conflicts, possible roots of (Masserman case), 344
Oral fantasies, early, and dreams (Masserman case), 327
Oral impregnation, 131, 246, 247, 257, 259
  Lorand case, 312, 313
  Moulton case, 294, 298
Oral incorporation
  of breast and penis (Masserman case), 340
  of father's phallus (Moulton cases), 294; Masserman case, 333
"Oral oedipus" (Masserman case), 339
Oral pregnancy, fear of, (Moulton cases), 286
Oral rejection and restitution, fantasy of (Masserman case), 342

Oral tendencies, early, 300
Orality of diabetes, 142
Organ changes and libidinal cathexis, 93
Organ neurosis, 86, 90, 91
  functional disturbance, 58
  gastric, intestinal, cardiac, 72
  Masserman case, 342
  psychotherapy in, 59
  treatment of choice 54
Organ psychosis, 165, 166, 177
Organic alterations and developmental disturbances in the instinctual life, 49
Organic disease
  and psychoneurosis, 73
  as secondary gain, 54
Organic dysfunctional behavior, emotional components in, 50
Organic need to be sick and unconscious conflicts, 52
Organic symptoms
  and psychic complexes, 48
  emotionally conditioned, 52
  recurrence of, in analysis, 53
Organoneurotic disorders, suggestive therapy for, 54
Ovarian activity and psychodynamic processes, 277
Ovulatory cycle and psychic system, 101

Pallor, 146
Palmer, C. D., 25, 322
Papanicolaou, G. N., 274, 276, 277, 279, 297
Parallelistic position, 7
Paralysis
  in hysterical anorexia, 159
  treated by psychotherapy, 32
Paraplegia, 114, 115
Parents
  pressure by, 255
  social service work with, 295

Parker, L., 18, 19, 34
Parry, C. H., 22
Particularist concept, 62, 63
Pasteur, L., 40, 74
Pathogenic micro-organisms, discovery of, 74
Pathologic anatomy
  basic observational principle of, 44
  correlation of clinical symptoms with structural alterations, 39
  experiments on thrombosis and embolism, 40
  in modern medicine, 36-46
Pathological changes and neural energy, 129
Pathology
  comparative, 110
  role in diagnosis, 119
Pathoneuroses, 84
Patient as indivisible whole, 60
Penis wish (Maserman case), 341
Peptic ulcer, character structure for, 91
Perkins, E., Perkinism, 9
Personality, 67
  and body, 77
  and course and duration of infectious disease, 50
  and environment, 87, 299
  and socioeconomic factors, 251
  and the central nervous system, 69
  definition of, 57
  meaning of, in disease, 31
  profiles, 91
Phallus, father's
  oral impregnation by (Moulton cases), 294
  oral incorporation of (Masserman case), 333
Philosophical climate and evolution of medicine, 41
Phobias, 15
Phrenology, 15 n.

Physiological changes and emotions, 58
Physiological substrate, and attitudes and behavior, 89
Physiology, general, 9
  methods of, 37, 38
Physical changes in emotional situations, 71
Physical symptoms and unconscious conflicts, 54
Pischer, J., 343 n., 351
Pituitary
  anterior lobe insufficiency, 198-201
  dysfunction, constitutional predisposition to, 276
  exhaustion (Nicolle's case of Miss M.), 231
Plethysmograph, circulation testing device, 16
Pluegge, H., 197
Portis, S., 344 n.
Pregenital conflicts and gastrointestinal dysfunction, 347
Pregenital conversion, 90
Pregenital determinants in social behavior, 322
Pregenital mechanisms, Masserman case, 340
Pregnancy, 26
  and eating, 256
  and hysteria, 26
  and nutrition, 166
  fear of, and amenorrhea, 25
  vomiting of, 21
  Weizsäcker's case of Mrs. V. Q., 190
Pregnancy fantasies, 272
  and food taking (Moulton cases), 293
  and gastrointestinal tract, 245
  and menstrual functions (Moulton cases), 293
  in dreams, 166

Premenstrual tension, Moulton cases, 294
Primary process, 3
Primitives, myths of, 256
Prepsychotic anorexia, 227-244
Prince, M., 3, 13, 16, 35, 229
Proger, S., 319
Pruritis, psychological aspects of, 27
Pseudocyesis, 26
Psyche
  and soma, unity of, 1
  definition of, 80
  organization of, 3
Psychiatry
  and experimental psychology, 16
  pre-Freudian, 57
  role in modern medicine, 64
  stepchild of medicine, 65
Psychic cathexis, 53
Psychic complexes and organic symptoms, 48
Psychic constellation, primacy of, in anorexia nervosa, 128
Psychic defenses, 98
Psychic factors, role of, 2
Psychic system
  and hormonal systems, 101
  and ovulatory cycle, 101
  in humans and animals, 96
  species specificity, 98
Psychic trauma and organic symptoms, 51
Psychoanalysis, basic treatment concept, 51
  and internal medicine, 47-55
  as a theory of personality, 66
  historical view of development, 66, 67
  method of observation, synthetic influence of, 68
Psychoanalytic treatment
  and clinical improvement (Masserman case), 336
  first approach, 165

Psychoanalytic treatment *(cont.)*
  Lorand case, 315
Psychobiology, 87, 88, 89
  fused relationship of phenomena, 47
  of the individual, 99
Psychodynamics, 131
  and ovarian activity, 277
  see also Anorexia nervosa cases
Psychodynamisms
  and certain character traits, 322
  and gastric dysfunctions, 322
  in anorexia nervosa, 320-351
Psychogalvanic reflex, 16
Psychogenic motivation in anorexia, 142
Psychogenic organic disorder, 59
Psychogenic origin, 242
Psychogenicity, 78-103
  importance of, 5
  of anorexia nervosa syndrome, 164
Psychological behavior and blood circulation, 16
Psychological disturbance, basic factor in causation, 204
Psychological factor
  in evaluation of disease, 3, 4
  overemphasis on role of, 36
Psychology
  gestalt, also nonmedical synthetic trend in, 57, 68
  united with medical science, 9
Psychoneurosis
  and emotional conflict, 76
  and organic disease, 73
  Dubois' use of the term, 79
  need for treatment, 65, 66
Psychoneurotic constitution of anorexia nervosa patients (Farquharson and Hyland cases), 218
Psychopathology, 14
  physiology of, 8 n.

Psychophysic parallelism, 49
Psychophysiological experiments, 16
  initial observations of phenomena, 130
  interrelations, 10
Psychosexual development, 92
Psychosis
  and asthma, 28
  following gynecologic operations, 30
Psychosomatic body schema, 48
Psychosomatic concepts, historical development of, 2
Psychosomatic conditions, development of, 352
Psychosomatic correlation, 227
Psychosomatic diseases, 17
  concepts of, 54
  factors in choice of, 101, 102
  neurasthenia, 15
  phases of, 3, 4
  syndrome, 128, 275, 276
  see also Anorexia nervosa cases
Psychosomatic medicine
  a new approach to causes of disease, 70, 71
  basic concept of, 47
  conceptual development of, 166
  definition of, 3
  first appearance of, 56
  in the nineteenth century, 6-35
  operational approach, 3
  principles in physics, thermodynamic, 15
  systematized studies in, 1
  with experimental and empirical body of knowledge, 17
Psychosomatic relations, specificity of, 196, 197
Psychosomatic unit, 90, 91
  and regression, 101
Psychotherapy
  and change in attitudes, 178

INDEX

Psychotherapy *(cont.)*
  and *hyperemesis gravidarum,* 178
  entrance into medicine proper, 72
  for various disorders, 32
  importance of (Grote and Meng cases), 172, 173
  in the nineteenth century, 31
  need for prolonged treatment, 223, 295
  Nicolle's case of Miss M., 229
  resistance to (Moulton cases), 293
  response to, 225
  results of, case of Marie Y., 179
  transference, positive, in, 52
  treatment choice, 52
Puberty
  adjustment problems of, 246
  and amenorrhea, 254
  neuroses of, 176, 177
  obesity, 254
  psychological reorientation at, 257
Punishment
  fear of (Lorand case), 316
  need for, 49, 50
Putnam, J. J., 13, 30, 32, 34

Raciborski, A., 25
Radioactive substances, effects on body, 44
Rado, S., 345 n., 351
Rahman, L., 273, 293, 297, 312, 313, 314, 319, 371
Raynaud, M., 23, 35
Raynaud's disease, 24
Reflex action
  and excitomotor acts, 10, 12, 129
  concept extended to cerebral activity, 15
Reflex irritation, 12
Regression, 93, 249
  and adaptation, 100
  and psychosomatic units, 101
  to infantile level, 255

Masserman case, 340
Regulative principle of Virchow, 40
Reil, J. C., 8 n., 9
Reizkoerper Therapie, 178
Repression
  effects of, 71, 76
  of instinctual drives, 82
  purposeful, 14
Research, neurophysiological, 12
Respiratory disturbance, and dependent tendencies, also sexual wishes, 76
Response, individual variability of, 105
Rheumatic fever, 118
Rheumatism, 119
Richardson, H. B., 253, 254, 273, 276, 297, 312, 313, 314, 371
Richmond Penitentiary, 25
"Riddance Principle," 345 n.
Ripley, H. S., 312, 313, 314, 319
Rokitanski, C., 20, 37, 39, 63
Rosen, G., 6
Ross, C. W., 221, 226, 244, 371
Ross, T. A., 241, 244
Ross, W., 232
Rossbach, M. J., 21, 35
Rougnon, N. F., 22
Royal Medical Society in Edinburgh, 22
Rubenstein, B. B., 101, 275, 277, 297
Ryle, J. A., 204, 231, 232, 243, 244, 286, 297, 372
  primary psychogenicity of the syndrome, 163, 164

St. Martin, A., 17
Salmon, U. J., 296
Salpêtrière, Pinel ward of, 32
Savage, G. H., 28, 35
Schindler, R., 351
Schizophrenia, 234
  paranoid, 238
Schultz, J. H., 176

395

Schur, M., 165, 166, 198-201
  six cases (with Medvei), 199-201
Schwab, M., 351
Schwann, T., 41
Schwimmer, E., 27, 35
Sears, G. D., 30, 35
Seasickness and anxiety, 21
Scientific concepts, evolution of, 2
Scientific system in medicine, 38
Scirrhous tubercle, 14
Secondary gain of organic disease, 54
Selye, H., stress syndrome, 100, 103
Semmelweis, I. P., 39
Sensibility as a physiological phenomenon, 9
Sexual difficulties, 198
  doubts of potency, 237
  excitation without outlet, 15
  in presence of organic symptom, 51
  underdevelopment, 276
Sexuality, 243
  active repudiation of, 272
  and eating, 245, 250, 346
  problems of (Lorand case), 313, 314
  taboos, 256
Shatzky, J., 80
Sheldon, J. H., 204, 219, 220, 221, 226, 231, 232, 244, 276, 297, 372
Shorr, E., 274, 279, 297
Sibling rivalry
  Lorand case, 312
  Masserman case, 337
Sieburg Asylum, 8 n.
Simmonds' cachexia, 239, 252
Simmonds' disease, 131, 165, 198, 204, 276
  differential diagnosis, 221-223
  Nicolle's case of Miss M., 231, 232
Skin disease
  and the sympathetic nervous system, 27
  change in texture, 253
  cutaneous lesions by hypnotic suggestion, 27
  edema, 24
  manifestations of the narcissistic personality, 49
  psychosomatic aspects of, 26, 27
  systemic lupus erythematosus, 45
Skoda, J., 39
Smallpox, 117
Smith, C. H., 343 n.
Smith, T., 26
Social behavior, pregenital determinants in, 322
Social environment, patient's relation to, 77; *see also* family environment
Social service work with parents, 295
Société de Biologie, 16
Socioeconomic factors, role in personality development, 251
Soemmering, S. T., 39
Soma and psyche, unity of, 1
Somatization and libidization, 94, 95
Somatopsychic medicine, nineteenth century, 8, 13, 17
Somnambulism, 129
  and other automatic behavior, 10
Soskin, S., 296
Spastic disorders, 54
Species specificity and the psychic system, 98
Speech, expression of ideas, 70
Spencer, H., 14
Spinoza, B., parallelistic position on mind and body, 7
Stainbrook, E., *6-35,* 129, 130
Starvation
  an extreme case of (Gull's case of K. R.), 139
  Farquharson and Hyland cases, 219
  self-imposed, 275

Starvation *(cont.)*
  somatic results of, 128
State of mind, role in disease causation, 8
Stengel, E., 343 n., 351
Stephens, L. E. W., 254, 273
Sticker, G., 16
Stiller, B., 21
Stokes, W., 20, 35
Stomach
  cramp, 146
  emotionally conditioned disturbances of, 71
  neuroses of, 21
  secretions and nervous excitation, 17
Structural alteration, 44
  methods of perceiving, 45
Structure, pathological, and pathological function, 74
Strümpell, E. A., 31
Sugar tolerance, 204
Suggestion therapy, 8
  for hypochondria, 54
Suicide
  impulses (Lorand case), 313
  prevention of, 31
Superego
  conflict, 90
  reducing severity of (Lorand case), 316
Sweeney, J. S., 220, 226, 297
Sydenham, T., 8, 119
Symbolic equation, 93
Sympathetic nervous system and skin disease, 27
Symptoms, variability in anorexia, 157
Symptomatology in Lasègue's diagrammatic sketch, 145-155
Syphilitic cachexia, 122

Talion fear (Masserman case), 342
Tarchanoff, I. R., 16

Tension
  premenstrual (Moulton cases), 294
  relation of psychological and vascular, 23
Therapeutics, 124, 125, 126
Therapy
  analytic, 300
  first psychoanalytic approach, 165
  goals, 353
  hormone (Grote and Meng cases), 172
  insulin, 168
  occupational, 225
  ovarian, 239
  psychoanalytically oriented (Grote and Meng cases), 174
  separation from parents (Charcot's case of the Angoulême girl), 163
  suggestion, 8, 54
  variety of approaches, 199
Thermodynamics
  and psychosomatic medicine, 15
  influence on Freud, 15 n.
Thinking, feeling, and doing, 8
Thomas, E. J., 103
Thomas, W. A., 297
Thrombosis, 120
  experiments on, 40
Thyroid deficiency, Nicolle's case of Miss M., 232
Timelessness, 3
Tooth decay and mental strain, 27
Transactionalism, 102
Transference, positive, 52
Transference relationship, difficulty in developing (Lorand case), 315
Trauma
  cranial posttraumatic symptoms, 31
  early, 248
  in infancy, 90

INDEX

Treatment, 142
  choice of psychotherapy or analysis, 51
  eating at frequent intervals, 224
  goal of, 223
  nonsomatic, of somatic illness (Grote and Meng cases), 176
  psychoanalytic (Lorand case), 315
  removal from environmental figures, 224, 228
  suggestive therapy, 54
  surgical, 126
  two fundamentals of (Nicolle's case of Miss M.), 229
Trousseau, A., 29, 35, 114, 115, 122, 154
Tubercular phthisis, 116
Tuke, D. H., 10, 12, 15, 18, 35, 129
Tumescence of the eye, 94
Tumor
  and headache, 122
  of the brain, 111
Tupper, W. R., 297

Ulcer, 59
  and amenorrhea, 19
Ulcer, duodenal, 20, 346
Ulcer, gastric
  nineteenth-century etiological theories of, 20
Ulcer, peptic, 20
  character structure for, 91
  etiology of, 73
  psychosomatic determinants of, 18, 19
  revised views of, 75
Ulcerative colitis, 94
  and diarrhea, 100
Ultracentrifugation for identifying cell constituents, 40
Unconscious
  concept of, 3
  emotional logic of (Masserman case), 342
  relationship to other components of the mind, 3
  repressed, 48
  role of, 354
Unconscious anxiety and patient's defensive attitude, 51
Unconscious behavior, concept of, 15 n.
  theories of, 10
Unconscious conflict
  and organic need to be sick, 52
  Lorand case, 312
  physical expression of, 53
Unconscious memory, 48
Unconscious mental functioning, 352
Unwanted child, feelings of being an (Lorand case), 314
Uric acid deposits, in childhood and old age, 114
Urinalysis, importance in diagnosis, 124
Urinary urgency and masculine aggressivity, 347
Uterus, influence of emotion on, 26

Vaginal smears, 274, 277
Van der Heide, C., 334 n., 351
Van der Kolk, S., 8 n.
Vascular diseases, 54
Vascular system, influence of mind on, 11
Vasoconstriction, 17
Vasomotor disturbance, 24
Vasomotor neurosis
  dysmenorrhea, 25
  migraine, 28
Vasomotor nerves and nutrition, 11
Vector concepts, 97
Venebles, J. F., 244
Vesalius, A., 38
Vidart, L., 244
Vienna School of Medicine, 39
Vieussens, R., 11

Villeneuve, 35
Visual disturbances, psychogenic, 83
Virchow, R., 20, 42, 44, 46, 56, 75, 120
   cellular pathology, 36, 37
   definition of disease, 41
   particularist concept, 62, 63
   regulation principle, 40
Vital force, 9
Vomiting, 143
   acid, 21
   and ego-syntonic obsession, 332 n.
   and psychotherapy, 178
   chronic (Masserman case), 344
   masochistic gratification in (Masserman case), 341
   Masserman case, 322-326
   of blood, 144
   of pregnancy, 21
   rejection of incorporated phallus (Moulton cases), 286
Von Bergmann, G., 75, 77, 165, 198
Von Feuchtersleben, E., 9, 33

Waller, J. S., *245-273*, 276, 286, 297, 298-300, *pass.* 312, 319, 352, 375
Waller, Kaufman, Deutsch cases
   case of P. D., 260-264
   case of E. G., 264-271
Ware, J., 35
Washburn, R. N., 343 n., 351
Weber, E., 16, 68
Weizsäcker, V., 165, 176, *181-197*, 198, 200, 201
Weizsäcker's cases
   case of Mrs. H. Q., 183-186
   case of Mrs. V. Q., 186-191
Wertheimer, M., 57, 68
White, W. A., 67, 77
Wilbur, D. L., 343 n. 351
Wilson, G., 346, 347, 351
Wood, A., 35
Wood, H. C., 23
Wundt, W., 16

Young, F., 221

Zilboorg, G., 8 n., 35
Zweig, S., 63
   synthesizing grasp of the born physician, 77
Zodiacus Medico-Gallicus, 9
Zondek, B., 170, 171
Zuckerman, S., 296

DO NOT DISCARD

THE LIBRARY
OF THE
WASHINGTON SCHOOL OF
PSYCHIATRY

REFERENCE ONLY
DO NOT REMOVE
FROM LIBRARY